SPRING

# 2013

# HOLLYWOOD
# SCREENWRITING
# DIRECTORY

*fw*
*media*

BURBANK, CALIFORNIA

Printed and bound in the United States of America.

Published by F+W Media, Inc.
3510 West Magnolia Boulevard
Burbank, California 91505
www.fwmedia.com

**Disclaimer**

Every reasonable effort has been made to ensure the accuracy of the information contained in the Hollywood Screenwriting Directory. F+W Media, Inc. cannot be held responsible for any inaccuracies, or the misrepresentation of those listed in the Hollywood Screenwriting Directory.

**Updates/Change Listing**

Please submit corrections and updates to corrections@screenwritingdirectory.com

Print ISBN 13: 978-1-59963-776-1
Print ISBN 10: 1-59963-776-6
ePub ISBN 13: 978-1-59963-782-2
ePub ISBN 10: 1-59963-782-0
PDF ISBN 13: 978-1-59963-779-2
PDF ISBN 10: 1-59963-779-0

# Contents

# How to Use the Hollywood Screenwriting Directory

Dear Fellow Screenwriter,

It's no secret that things in Hollywood move at a supersonic pace. New production companies are formed and execs move up the ladder or switch to new studios. And that's exactly why we put in overtime to produce this extensive spring 2013 edition of The Hollywood Screenwriting Directory, which brings you the most current contact information on more than 2,500 Industry insiders (up from the previous 1,500), along with updates on more than 40% of our listings.

What you hold in your hands is a very specialized directory created by The Writers Store based on our extensive experience serving the screenwriting community since 1982. It contains a range of people to contact regarding your script, from ambitious upstarts to established studio execs, along with management companies who package production deals and independent financiers/distributors with a production wing. For each listing, you'll find the kind of useable information you need: street and email addresses, whether or not they accept unsolicited material, and how they prefer to receive submissions.

While having access to this data is crucial, just as essential is an understanding of the right way to use it. These insiders are flooded with submissions daily. Any indication of incorrect format or other amateur flubs in the first few pages will quickly send your script to the trash.

We can't emphasize enough how important it is that your submission is polished and professional before you send it out for consideration. Screenwriting software makes producing an Industry-standard screenplay simple and straightforward. Programs like *Final Draft* and *Movie Magic Screenwriter* put your words into proper format as you type, letting you focus on a well-told story rather than the chore of margins and spacing. In these pages, we've also included a guide to proper screenplay format, along with sample title and first pages to help you send out a professional script.

Besides a properly packaged submission, it's also wise to know your audience before you send out any materials. If your script is an action thriller with a strong female lead, don't send it to Philip Seymour Hoffman's production company. Actors establish their own companies so that they're not reliant on studios for roles. Pad an actor's vanity (and his pipeline) by submitting materials catered specifically to him.

You may find that a good number of companies do not want unsolicited submissions. It's not that they're not open to new ideas; they're not open to liability. A script is property, and with it, come ramifications if not handled properly. If you choose to disregard "no unsolicited submissions," sending your script with a submission release form gives it a better chance of getting read. Consult with an entertainment attorney to draft an appropriate form, or consult a guide like *Clearance and Copyright by Michael C. Donaldson*, which has submission release form templates. It's also prudent to protect your work. We recommend registering your script with the *WGA (Writers Guild of America, West)* or the *ProtectRite registration service*.

A benefit of the digital age is that the same companies that are not open to receiving unsolicited submissions will gladly accept a query letter by email. Take advantage of this opportunity. Craft a well-written and dynamic query letter email that sells you and your script. We have included a sample query, and some tips and guidelines on how to write great query letters.

While Hollywood is a creative town it is, above all, professional. Do a service to yourself and the potential buyer by being courteous. If you choose to follow up by phone, don't be demanding and frustrated. These people are overworked and do not owe you anything. It's okay to follow up, but be sure to do so with respect. And if you pique a buyer's interest and she asks for a treatment, you must be ready to send off this vital selling tool at once! That's why we've also included a handy guide to writing treatments in this volume.

While it may oftentimes feel like the opposite, The Entertainment Industry is looking for new writers and fresh material. BUT (and this is important) they're also looking for those aspiring scribes to take the time to workshop their scripts with an experienced professional and get them to a marketable level. The Writers Store can help you get ready for the big leagues through our slate of *screenwriting courses*, *personalized coaching* and *Development Notes service*, which works in a format that mirrors the same process occurring in the studio ranks.

Hollywood is the pinnacle of competition and ambition. But that's not to say that dreams can't happen—they can, and they do. By keeping to these professional guidelines and working on your craft daily, you can find the kind of screenwriting success you seek.

Wishing you the best of luck,

Jesse Douma
Editor

# What is a Screenplay?

In the most basic terms, a screenplay is a 90-120 page document written in Courier 12pt font on 8 ½" x 11" bright white three-hole punched paper. Wondering why Courier font is used? It's a timing issue. One formatted script page in Courier font equals roughly one minute of screen time. That's why the average page count of a screenplay should come in between 90 and 120 pages. Comedies tend to be on the shorter side (90 pages, or 1 ½ hours) while Dramas run longer (120 pages, or 2 hours).

A screenplay can be an original piece, or based on a true story or previously written piece, like a novel, stage play or newspaper article. At its heart, a screenplay is a blueprint for the film it will one day become. Professionals on the set including the producer, director, set designer and actors all translate the screenwriter's vision using their individual talents. Since the creation of a film is ultimately a collaborative art, the screenwriter must be aware of each person's role and as such, the script should reflect the writer's knowledge.

For example, it's crucial to remember that film is primarily a visual medium. As a screenwriter, you must show what's happening in a story, rather than tell. A 2-page inner monologue may work well for a novel, but is the kiss of death in a script. The very nature of screenwriting is based on how to show a story on a screen, and pivotal moments can be conveyed through something as simple as a look on an actor's face. Let's take a look at what a screenplay's structure looks like.

## The First Page of a Screenplay

Screenwriting soft ware makes producing an Industry-standard script simple and straightforward. While screenplay formatting soft ware such as *Final Draft*, *Movie Magic Screenwriter*, *Movie Outline*, *Montage* and *Scriptly* for the iPad frees you from having to learn the nitty-gritty of margins and indents, it's good to have a grasp of the general spacing standards.

The top, bottom and right margins of a screenplay are 1". The left margin is 1.5". The extra half-inch of white space to the left of a script page allows for binding with brads, yet still imparts a feeling of vertical balance of the text on the page. The entire document should be single-spaced.

# Screenplay Elements

Following is a list of items that make up the screenplay format, along with indenting information. Again, screenplay software will automatically format all these elements, but a screenwriter must have a working knowledge of the definitions to know when to use each one.

## Ⓐ Fade In

The very first item on the first page should be the words FADE IN:.

## Ⓑ Page Numbers

The first page is never numbered. Subsequent page numbers appear in the upper right hand corner, 0.5" from the top of the page, flush right to the margin.

## Ⓒ Mores and Continueds

Use mores and continueds between pages to indicate the same character is still speaking.

## Ⓓ Scene Heading

**Indent: Left: 0.0" Right: 0.0" Width: 6.0"**

A scene heading is a one-line description of the location and time of day of a scene, also known as a "slugline." It should always be in CAPS. Example: EXT. WRITERS STORE – DAY reveals that the action takes place outside The Writers Store during the daytime.

## Ⓔ Subheader

**Indent: Left: 0.0" Right: 0.0" Width: 6.0"**

When a new scene heading is not necessary, but some distinction needs to be made in the action, you can use a subheader. But be sure to use these sparingly, as a script full of subheaders is generally frowned upon. A good example is when there are a series of quick cuts between two locations, you would use the term INTERCUT and the scene locations.

## Ⓕ Action

**Indent: Left: 0.0" Right: 0.0" Width: 6.0"**

The narrative description of the events of a scene, written in the present tense. Also less commonly known as direction, visual exposition, blackstuff, description or scene direction. Remember—only things that can be seen and heard should be included in the action.

## Sample Screenplay Page

(A) FADE IN:

(D) EXT. WRITERS STORE - DAY

(F) In the heart of West Los Angeles, a boutique shop's large
OPEN sign glows like a beacon.

(M) DISSOLVE TO:

INT. WRITERS STORE - SALES FLOOR - DAY

Writers browse the many scripts in the screenplay section.

(G) ANTHONY, Canadian-Italian Story Specialist extraordinaire,
30s and not getting any younger, ambles over.

(H) ANTHONY
(I) Hey, how's everyone doin' here?

A WRITING ENTHUSIAST, 45, reads the first page of "The
Aviator" by John Logan.

                    ENTHUSIAST
          Can John Logan write a killer first
          page or what?

                    ANTHONY
          You, sir, are a gentleman of
          refined taste.  John Logan is my
          non-Canadian idol.

The phone RINGS.  Anthony goes to--

(E) THE SALES COUNTER

And answers the phone.

                    ANTHONY (CONT'D)
          Writers Store, Anthony speaking.

                    VOICE
(J)          (over phone)
          Do you have Chinatown in stock?

I/E LUXURIOUS MALIBU MANSION - DAY

A FIGURE roams his estate, cell phone pressed to his ear.

                    ANTHONY (O.S.)
          'Course we have Chinatown!
          Robert Towne's masterpeice is
          arguably the Great American
          Screenplay...
                    (MORE) (C)

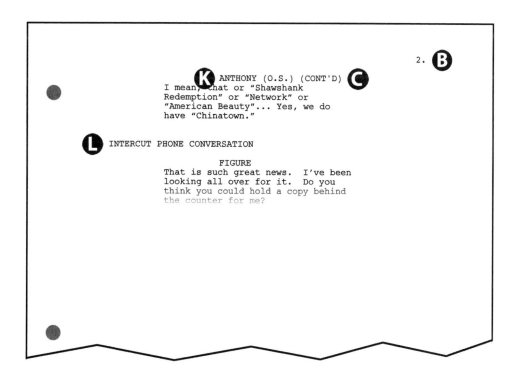

## Character

**Indent: Left: 2.0" Right: 0.0" Width: 4.0"**

**G** When a character is introduced, his name should be capitalized within the action. For example: The door opens and in walks LIAM, a thirty-something hipster with attitude to spare.

**H** A character's name is CAPPED and always listed above his lines of dialogue. Minor characters may be listed without names, for example TAXI DRIVER or CUSTOMER.

## **I** Dialogue

**Indent: Left: 1.0" Right: 1.5" Width: 3.5"**

Lines of speech for each character. Dialogue format is used anytime a character is heard speaking, even for off-screen and voice-overs.

## **J** Parenthetical

**Indent: Left: 1.5" Right: 2.0" Width: 2.5"**

A parenthetical is direction for the character, that is either attitude or action-oriented. Parentheticals are used very rarely, and only if absolutely necessary. Why? First, if you need to use a parenthetical to convey what's going on with your dialogue, then it probably needs a good re-write. Second, it's the director's job to instruct an actor, and everyone knows not to encroach on the director's turf!

## Ⓚ Extension

**Placed after the character's name, in parentheses**

An abbreviated technical note placed after the character's name to indicate how the voice will be heard onscreen, for example, if the character is speaking as a voice-over, it would appear as `LIAM (V.O.)`.

## Ⓛ Intercut

Intercuts are instructions for a series of quick cuts between two scene locations.

## Ⓜ Transition

**Indent: Left: 4.0" Right: 0.0" Width: 2.0"**

Transitions are film editing instructions, and generally only appear in a shooting script. Transition verbiage includes:

```
CUT TO:
DISSOLVE TO:
SMASH CUT:
QUICK CUT:
FADE TO:
```

As a spec script writer, you should avoid using a transition unless there is no other way to indicate a story element. For example, you might need to use `DISSOLVE TO:` to indicate that a large amount of time has passed.

## Shot

**Indent: Left: 0.0" Right: 0.0" Width: 6.0"**

A shot tells the reader the focal point within a scene has changed. Like a transition, there's rarely a time when a spec screenwriter should insert shot directions. Examples of Shots:

```
ANGLE ON --
EXTREME CLOSE UP --
LIAM'S POV --
```

## Spec Script vs. Shooting Script

A "spec script" literally means that you are writing a screenplay on speculation. That is, no one is paying you to write the script. You are penning it in hopes of selling the script to a buyer. Spec scripts should stick stringently to established screenwriting rules. Once a script is purchased, it becomes a shooting script, also called a production script. This is a version of the screenplay created for film production. It will include technical instructions, like film editing notes, shots, cuts and the like. All the scenes are numbered, and revisions are marked with a color-coded system. This is done so that the production assistants and director can then arrange the order in which the scenes will be shot for the most efficient use of stage, cast, and location resources.

A spec script should never contain the elements of shooting script. The biggest mistake any new screenwriter can make is to submit a script full of production language, including camera angles and editing transitions.

It can be very difficult to resist putting this type of language in your script. After all, it's your story and you see it in a very specific way. However, facts are facts. If you want to direct your script, then try to go the independent filmmaker route. But if you want to sell your script, then stick to the accepted spec screenplay format.

## Script Presentaction and Binding

Just like the format of a script, there are very specific rules for binding and presenting your script. The first page is the title page, which should also be written in Courier 12pt font. No graphics, no fancy pictures, only the title of your script, with "written by" and your name in the center of the page. In the lower left-hand or right-hand corner, enter your contact information.

In the lower left-hand or right-hand corner you can put Registered, WGA or a copyright notification, though this is generally not a requirement.

## Sample Screenplay Title Page

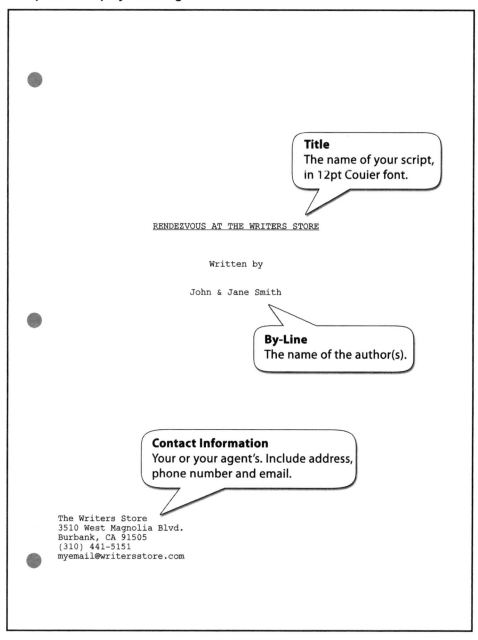

RENDEZVOUS AT THE WRITERS STORE

Written by

John & Jane Smith

The Writers Store
3510 West Magnolia Blvd.
Burbank, CA 91505
(310) 441-5151
myemail@writersstore.com

**Title**
The name of your script, in 12pt Couier font.

**By-Line**
The name of the author(s).

**Contact Information**
Your or your agent's. Include address, phone number and email.

# Query Letters

A query is a one-page, single-spaced letter that quickly tells who you are, what the work is, and why the work is appropriate for the market in question. Just as queries are used as the first means of contact for pitching magazine articles and novels, they work just the same for scripts.

A well-written query is broken down into three parts.

## Part I: Your Reason for Contacting/Script Details

Before even looking at the few sentences describing your story, a producer wants to see two other things:

1.  **What is it?** State the title, genre, and whether it's a full-length script or a shorter one.
2.  **Why are you contacting this market/person in particular?** There are thousands of individuals who receive scripts. Why have you chosen this person to review the material? Is it because you met them in person and they requested to see your work? Have they represented writers similar to yourself? Did you read that they were actively looking for zombie comedies? Spelling out your reason upfront shows that you've done your research, and that you're a professional.

## Part II: The Elevator Pitch

If you wrote the first paragraph correctly, you've got their attention, so pitch away. Explain what your story is in about 3-6 sentences. The point here is to intrigue and pique only. Don't get into nitty-gritty details of any kind. Hesitate using a whole lot of character names or backstory. Don't say how it ends or who dies during the climax or that the hero's father betrays him in Act II. Introduce us to the main character and his situation, then get to the key part of the pitch: the conflict.

Try to include tidbits here and there that make your story unique. If it's about a cop nearing retirement, that's nothing new. But if the story is about a retiring cop considering a sex change operation in his bid to completely start over, while the police union is threatening to take away his pension should he do this, then you've got something different that readers may want to see.

## Sample Query Letter

 **John. Q. Writer**
123 Main St.
Writerville, USA
(212) 555-1234
johnqwriter@email.com

Agent
JQA & Associates
678 Hollywood St.
Hollywood, CA 90210

**B** Dear Mr./Ms (Last Name):

**C** My name is John Q. Writer and we crossed paths at the Screenwriters World Conference in Los Angeles in October 2012. After hearing the pitch for my feature-length thriller, October Surprise, you requested that I submit a query, synopsis and the first 10 pages of the script. All requested materials are enclosed. This is an exclusive submission, as you requested.

**D** U.S. Senator Michael Hargrove is breaking ranks with his own political party to endorse another candidate for President of the United States. At the National Convention, he's treated like a rock star V.I.P. -- that is, until, he's abducted by a fringe political group and given a grim ultimatum: Use your speech on live TV to sabotage and derail the presidential campaign you're now supporting, or your family back home will not live though the night.

**E** The script was co-written with my scriptwriting partner, Joe Aloysius. I am a produced playwright and award-winning journalist. Thank you for considering October Surprise. I will be happy to sign any release forms that you request. May I send the rest of the screenplay?

Best,
John Q. Writer

# Part III: The Wrap Up

Your pitch is complete. The last paragraph is where you get to talk about yourself and your accomplishments. If the script has won any awards or been a finalist in a prominent competition, this is the place to say so. Mention your writing credentials and experience. Obviously, any paid screenwriting experience is most valuable, but feel free to include other tidbits such as if you're a magazine freelancer or a published novelist.

Sometimes, there won't be much to say at the end of a query letter because the writer has no credits, no contacts and nothing to brag about. As your mother would tell you: If you don't have anything nice to say, don't say anything at all. Keep the last section brief if you must, rather than going on and on about being an "active blogger" or having one poem published in your college literary magazine.

Following some information about yourself, it's time to wrap up the query and propose sending more material. A simple way to do this is by saying "The script is complete. May I send you the treatment and full screenplay?"

Here are the elements of a query letter in the example on the facing page:

**A** Include all of your contact information—including phone and e-mail—as centered information at the top.

**B** Use proper greetings and last names.

**C** Include a reason for contacting the reader.

**D** Try and keep the pitch to one paragraph.

**E** Regarding your credentials, be concise and honest.

# Treatments and Log Lines

## Introduction to the Treatment

Nobody reads a full script in Hollywood anymore. Execs don't want to put in the time to read a 90-page comedy script, much less a 180-page epic. They want to know if the goods are there before they invest their precious time, and this is where the treatment comes in. Think of it as reading the back cover of a book before you invest in buying it. You'd never just pay for a book without knowing what type of story to expect. So it is with the movie industry. The treatment is the essential selling tool that can make or break your script.

## What is a Treatment

A treatment is a short document written in prose form and in the present tense that emphasizes, with vivid description, the major elements of a screenplay.

That's a very broad definition, to be sure. And while the main purpose of a treatment is as a selling tool, there are variations of the definition to consider.

1.  A treatment could be your first attempt toward selling your screenplay to a producer, your first try at getting someone to pay you to write the script.
2.  A treatment could be a sales tool for a script that you've already written—a shorter, prose version of the screenplay's story for producers to read, to pique their interest in your project and entice them to read your screenplay.
3.  A treatment could describe how you intend to attack a rewrite, either of your own script or of another writer's script. Often when a producer hires a writer to do a rewrite, they'll ask for a treatment first.
4.  A treatment could be the first step toward writing your screenplay—it could be one of the first steps toward getting your story down on paper. Maybe you don't have time to write the screenplay yet—a treatment can help cement the story in your mind (and on paper) so that you can work on it later.

### Why Write a Treatment?

Ultimately, the best reason to write a treatment is that the process of writing your treatment can help you write a better script. It can be easier to find and solve structural challenges, plot incongruities, lapses in logic, etc. in the prose treatment format than it is to find and solve those challenges in the screenplay format.

Writing a screenplay is a step-by-step process, and some steps are more involved than others. Writing a treatment is a very achievable step in the screenwriting process, and taking that step from beginning to end can be a rewarding boost for your writing ego.

Writing a treatment helps give tangible shape to your story, and makes sharing your story with others simpler and more precise. If you can share your story with others, you can get feedback, which may open up more channels in your brain and help your story to grow. The treatment format is much easier to read and comprehend for people who aren't familiar with the screenplay format.

You might not be ready to write your complete screenplay yet—you might not have time, you might not be fully committed to the idea. Writing a treatment is a good stopgap measure, so that an idea doesn't just exist as an idea—it may exist as something you can sell, share with a collaborator, or simply file away for a rainy day.

### When is a Treatment Used

A treatment is usually used when you begin the process of selling your script. When you pitch your script to a producer and he shows interest in your script, he will most likely ask you to send over the treatment. This way, he can review the story and see if he is interested in reading the full script.

Think of the treatment as your business card—the thing you leave behind after you've pitched your story.

You may have heard of writers who sell a script based only a treatment. Yes, this happens, but this happens only for established writers with a track record of produced scripts. They have proven to Hollywood that they can write a blockbuster script, so buyers know that if they like the treatment, they will most likely love the script.

The treatment can also be used as an outline for the writer before he begins his script. It's smart to either outline or summarize a script before you begin writing. If you can complete the story in a smaller form, you know that you'll be able to sustain it in the longer script format. Architects don't erect a building without first designing a blueprint and then creating a model of the structure. The outline is your blueprint and the treatment is your model.

## Treatment vs. Synopsis, Coverage, Beat Sheet and Outline

The term treatment is thrown around loosely in Hollywood, and you can be sure that you'll hear a different definition each time you ask. Some buyers will request a treatment when they really want a synopsis, an outline or a beat sheet. So what are the definitions of the other items?

## Synopsis

A Synopsis is a brief description of a story's plot or a straightforward presentation of the scenes and events in a story. It is not a selling tool, but rather a summation of the story, and is typically no more than 2 pages long. It's generally used by professional script readers when writing coverage on a script.

## Coverage

Coverage is the name of the document generated by the buyer's in house script readers. The main purpose of this document is to assess the commercial viability of the script. The reader supplies the buyer with the basic identifying information of the script, a synopsis, their comments on the script and a rating chart on all of the elements of the script, including characters, dialogue, action, setting, and commercial appeal. The reader then rates the script "pass" (no, thanks. Don't call us, cause we're certainly not gonna call you) "consider" (maybe someone we know can rewrite this puppy into something marketable) or "recommend" (this is the script that will move me from script reader hell to producing heaven!).

## Beat Sheet

A Beat Sheet lists the sequence of major events that takes place in a script. It shows what will happen to the main character, and the order in which the events will occur. It can be anywhere from a short paragraph to three pages. Each beat is described in only 1-2 sentences.

Here is an extremely short example from "Die Hard."

1. New York Detective John McClane flies to Los Angeles to reconcile with his wife Holly at her company Christmas party.
2. When he arrives at Holly's high-rise office building, they argue and Holly leaves McClane alone in her executive bathroom.
3. From the bathroom, McClane hears terrorists, lead by Hans Gruber, break in and take over the building.
4. McClane witnesses the murder of Takagi, the CEO of the company, by Gruber and decides to take action.
5. McClane kills the brother of the lead henchman, Karl, and many other terrorists. He greatly angers Hans and Karl in the process.
6. McClane battles the terrorists with the help of a lone police officer.
7. The other police are against McClane and he feels alone in his fight. The police approach fails, so McClane is totally alone.
8. McClane fights Karl, kills him and prepares to go save Holly from Gruber.
9. Seemingly outnumbered, McClane appears to give up.
10. Using his New York wits, McClane kills Gruber and saves Holly.

## Outline

An outline is a list of the scenes that make up a screenplay, from FADE IN to FADE OUT. Every writer has a different method of outlining—some are very detailed, while some list only a sentence or even just a word for each scene.

A good way to start a screenplay is to write a beat sheet, an outline and then a treatment. If you work out the story problems with these three tools, you will find that writing the actual script is a breeze.

## Why Do I Need a Treatment

Besides being an important selling tool, a treatment allows you to see if your idea can sustain a feature-length film. Many writers take an idea straight to screenplay form, and then find 30 pages in that there is not enough story to continue the script. In this short summary form, you will also be able to identify any weaknesses in your plot, theme and characters.

It is much easier to find and solve these challenges in the prose treatment form than it is to locate them in the screenplay format.

## How Long Should It Be?

Sadly, there is no cut and dry length for a treatment. Generally, treatments vary in length from 1-25 pages.

A general rule—the more power the executive holds, the shorter the treatment you should send them. It is recommended to have a few different versions of your treatment. Besides a lengthy summary of the story, have a quick one pager on hand.

## What Is the Format?

Your treatment should be written in prose form, and in 12 point Courier font. In essence, the treatment looks like a short story. There should be one line of space between each paragraph, and no indenting.

**DON'T** insert dialogue, slug lines, or anything else in screenplay format.

**DO** use standard punctuation for dialogue.

However, be careful not to rely on much dialogue in your treatment in order to effectively tell the story in 10 pages or less. A few carefully chosen thematic lines will suffice. For instance, the treatment for "Forrest Gump" would likely use the line, "Life is like a box of chocolates. You never know what you're gonna get," because it is used throughout the script as a thematic tag line.

## What Should I Aspire to Do with the Treatment?

The treatment should not look, sound or read like an outline, a beat sheet or a screenplay. The essence of the story and the characters should be evoked through exhilarating language and imagery. It should sound like an excited moviegoer recanting the details of a film he just saw that was thought provoking, exhilarating and made him feel like he just had to share all the details with his friends. The prose you use in a treatment should be different than the narrative lines of a screenplay.

The beginning of the treatment has to grab the reader and not let go until the very end. Your reader should be able to see the script play out on the silver screen in front of his or her very eyes. After reading the treatment, the reader should be on fire to get this script to her boss, pronto!

# The Log Line

A Log Line is a one sentence description of your film. It's really that simple. You've seen log lines, even if you're not aware of it. In essence, TV Guide descriptions of films are log lines. A log line may describe the following elements:

- Genre—comedy, drama, thriller, love story, etc.
- Setting—time and place, locale, other pertinent information
- Plot—the main narrative thrust of the story
- Character—the lead character or group of characters
- Theme—the main subject of the movie

A log line need not contain the following elements:

- Character names (unless the characters are historical figures)
- Back story
- Qualitative judgments—"A hilarious story..." "A fascinating tale..."
- Comparisons to other films—"It's "Jaws' meets 'Mary Poppins'..."

Here are a few examples of log lines for well-known films. See if you can guess the film being described (the answers are right below, so don't cheat!):

1. A throwback to the serial adventure films of the 1930s, this film is the story of a heroic archeologist who races against the Nazis to find a powerful artifact that can change the course of history.
2. Set at a small American college in the early 1960s, this broad comedy follows a fraternity full of misfits through a year of parties, mishaps and food fights.
3. An illiterate boy looks to become a contestant on the Hindi version of "Who Wants to be A Millionaire" in order to re-establish contact with the girl he loves, who is an ardent fan of the show.

4. A man decides to change his life by saying 'yes' to everything that comes his way. On his journey, he wins $45,000, meets a hypnotic dog, obtains a nursing degree, travels the globe, and finds romance.

5. A behind-the-scenes view of the 2000 presidential election and the scandal that ensued in the weeks following.

Get the idea? The log line is designed to describe and to tease, like a line of advertising copy for your film. It has to be accurate, it can't be misleading. It's the first sentence a producer or executive is going to read, and you've got to make sure it isn't the last. Make it count.

By the way, the log lines above are for:

1. "Raiders of the Lost Ark"
2. "Animal House"
3. "Slumdog Millionaire"
4. "Yes Man"
5. "Recount"

## Why Is the Log Line Important in a Treatment?

The log line is the first sentence an executive will ever read from your hand. It's also the shorthand that executives will use to discuss your project with each other. If a junior executive reads your treatment and likes it, she'll need to tell her boss about the project in order to move it to the next step (probably a meeting between you and the boss).

The boss will ask the junior executive "What's it about?" The junior executive will respond with your log line, if you've written it well and accurately. You are helping to provide the junior executive with the tools she needs to help move your project forward. If you don't provide a log line at the beginning of your treatment, you rely on the junior executive's ability to digest your treatment and come up with a good log line of her own. Even in a collaborative art form like filmmaking, it's never a good idea to leave a job undone for someone else to do if you are more capable of doing it yourself. And who knows your story better than you do? Write a great log line for your treatment, and you'll know that your treatment is being discussed in your own words.

## Who Is the Log Line For

The log line is for the buyer: the executive, the producer, the agent. By writing a log line for your treatment, you are helping them to process your material more efficiently. Getting a movie made is a sales process, a constant, revolving door sales process. You sell your work to an agent, who then sells your work to a producer, who then sells it to a director, who then sells it to actors and key crew members.

Once the movie is made, the sales process starts all over again, as the producer has to sell the movie to distributors and marketing executives, who have to sell the film to theater owners who have to sell the film to audiences. A good log line can ride the film all the way from start to finish, helping to sell it at each step.

## Should the Log Line Refer to Other Movies?

No. It used to be popular to write log lines that were entirely film references. This practice became so prevalent that it became a cliché, and should be avoided if at all possible. Nothing says "schlock" as quickly as a "Die Hard" reference—the classic action movie reference that every movie strived for in the early 1990s. "Speed" was called "Die Hard" on a bus. "Passenger 57" was called "Die Hard" on a plane. Descriptive as these log lines may be, they read as lazy writing, and if your writing isn't even original in the log line, who will be interested in reading your treatment or your script? Avoid hucksterism, overselling and hype. It's a turnoff.

## How Long Should the Log Line Be

Your log line should be one sentence long. Pare it down to its essence, and don't let your sentence become a run-on. Try it out loud, see if it works. You don't have to follow every twist and turn of the plot in your log line, you only have to convey the flavor of the script. One sentence will do it.

## What Is the Difference Between the Log Line and the Theme?

Your log line is a sales tool that is a teaser and an invitation to read your script. The theme may be contained in the log line, but not necessarily. Theme is the real answer to "What is your script about?" and Theme need not be confined to a one sentence answer. Theme is often related to the discovery that your main character makes during the course of the film. For instance, in "Raiders of the Lost Ark," Indiana Jones discovers that people are actually more important to him than historical artifacts. In "Animal House," the Deltas discover that the camaraderie that they've discovered in their fraternity is the real lasting value of their college experience, not their class work or their social status on campus.

# In Closing

You've spent months or years (or even decades) on your script, and so it may be frustrating to jump through the hoops of the submission process—but it's important. Don't give readers an excuse to ignore your work. You must craft a killer query, treatment and log line before the script gets its big shot. Compose them well, and you're on your way to selling that screenplay.

# The Directory

## 100% ENTERTAINMENT

201 North Irving Boulevard
Los Angeles, CA 90004

**Phone:** 323-461-6360
**Fax:** 323-871-8203
**Email:** 100percent@iname.com
**Website:** www.100percent.com
**IMDB:** www.imdb.com/company/co0077804

**Submission Policy:** Accepts query letter from
unproduced, unrepresented writers via email
**Genre:** Memoir & True Stories, Science Fiction, TV
Drama
**Year Established:** 1998

### Stanley Isaacs
**Title:** President
**Phone:** 323-461-6360
**Email:** sisaacs100@mac.com
**IMDB:** www.imdb.com/name/nm0410570

## 100% TERRYCLOTH

421 Waterview Street
Los Angeles, CA 90293

**Phone:** 310-823-3432
**Fax:** 310-861-9093
**Email:** tm@terencemichael.com
**Website:** www.terencemichael.com
**IMDB:** www.imdb.com/company/co0194989

**Submission Policy:** Accepts query letter from
unproduced, unrepresented writers via email

### Terence Michael
**Title:** Producer
**Phone:** 310-823-3432
**Email:** tm@terencemichael.com

## 1019 ENTERTAINMENT

1680 North Vine Street, Suite 600
Hollywood, CA 90028

**Phone:** 323-645-6840
**Fax:** 323-645-6841
**Email:** info@1019ent.com
**Website:** www.1019ent.com
**IMDB:** www.imdb.com/company/co0263748

**Submission Policy:** Accepts query letter from
unproduced, unrepresented writers via email

**Genre:** Memoir & True Stories, TV Drama, TV
Sitcom

### Terry Botwick
**Title:** Principal
**Phone:** 323-645-6840
**Email:** terry@1019ent.com
**IMDB:** www.imdb.com/company/co0263748

### Ralph Winter
**Title:** Principal
**Phone:** 323-645-6840
**Email:** ralph@1019ent.com
**IMDB:** http://www.imdb.com/name/nm0003515

## 10X10 ENTERTAINMENT

1640 South Sepulveda Boulevard, Suite 450
Los Angeles, CA 90025

**Phone:** 310-575-1235
**Fax:** 310-575-1237
**IMDB:** www.imdb.com/company/co0112253

**Submission Policy:** Accepts query letter from
unproduced, unrepresented writers
**Genre:** Memoir & True Stories, TV Drama, TV
Sitcom
**Focus:** TV

### Brad Austin
**Title:** Director of Development
**Phone:** 310-575-1235
**IMDB:** www.imdb.com/name/nm4114614

### Ken Mok
**Title:** Producer/Founder
**Phone:** 310-575-1235
**IMDB:** www.imdb.com/name/nm0596298

## 1821 PICTURES

10900 Wilshire Boulevard, Suite 1400
Los Angeles, CA 90024

**Phone:** 310-860-1121
**Fax:** 310-860-1123
**Email:** asst@1821pictures.com
**Website:** www.1821pictures.com
**IMDB:** www.imdb.com/company/co0237259

**Submission Policy:** Accepts query letter from
unproduced, unrepresented writers via email
**Genre:** Animation, Memoir & True Stories, TV
Drama, TV Sitcom
**Year Established:** 2005

**Terry Douglas**
Title: Principal
Phone: 310-860-1121
Email: asst@1821pictures.com
IMDB: www.imdb.com/name/nm0234806

**Paris Kasidokostas-Latsis**
Title: Principal
Phone: 310-860-1121
Email: asst@1821pictures.com
IMDB: www.imdb.com/company/co0237259

**Billy Piché**
Title: Director of Development
Phone: 310-860-1121
Email: asst@1821pictures.com
IMDB: www.imdb.com/name/nm5046038/

## 19 ENTERTAINMENT, LTD

8560 West Sunset Boulevard, 9th Floor
West Hollywood, CA 90069

Phone: 310-777-1940
Fax: 310-777-1949
Email: contact@19.co.uk
Website: http://www.19.co.uk/
IMDB: www.imdb.com/company/co0085773

Submission Policy: Does not accept any unsolicited material
Genre: Animation, TV Drama, TV Sitcom

**Iain Pirie**
Title: President US
Phone: 310-777-1940
IMDB: www.imdb.com/name/nm2227040/

## 21 LAPS ENTERTAINMENT

c/o Twentieth Century Fox
10201 West Pico Boulevard
Building 41, Suite 400
Los Angeles, CA 90064

Phone: 310-369-7170
Fax: 310-969-0443
IMDB: www.imdb.com/company/co0158853

Submission Policy: Does not accept any unsolicited material
Genre: Action, Comedy, Drama
Focus: Feature Films, TV

**Dan Levine**
Title: President of Production
IMDB: www.imdb.com/name/nm0505782

**Shawn Levy**
Title: Principal
Phone: 310-369-4466
IMDB: www.imdb.com/name/nm0506613

**Billy Rosenberg**
Title: Senior Vice President Development
Phone: 310-369-7170
IMDB: www.imdb.com/name/nm1192785

## 25/7 PRODUCTIONS

10999 Riverside Drive, Suite 100
North Hollywood, CA 91602

Phone: 818-432-2800
Fax: 818-432-2810
Email: nfo@257productions.com
Website: http://257productions.com
IMDB: www.imdb.com/company/co0200336

Submission Policy: Accepts query letter from unproduced, unrepresented writers
Genre: Animation, Memoir & True Stories, TV Drama, TV Sitcom
Year Established: 2003

**David Broome**
Title: President
Phone: 818-432-2800
IMDB: www.imdb.com/company/co0200336

## 26 FILMS

8748 Holloway Drive
Los Angeles, CA, 90069

Phone: 310-205-9922
Fax: 310-206-9926
Email: asst@26films.com
Website: www.26films.com

Submission Policy: Accepts query letter from unproduced, unrepresented writers via email

**Elena Brooks**
Title: Director of Development
Phone: 310-205-9922
Email: asst@26films.com
IMDB: www.imdb.com/name/nm4542983/

**Nathalie Marciano**
Title: Principal
Phone: 310-205-9922
Email: asst@26films.com
IMDB: www.imdb.com/name/nm0545695

## 2929 PRODUCTIONS

1437 Seventh Street, Suite 250
Santa Monica, CA 90401

Phone: 310-309-5200
Fax: 310-309-5716
Website: www.2929entertainment.com

Submission Policy: Accepts query letter from
unproduced, unrepresented writers
Genre: Action, Drama, Memoir & True Stories

**Todd Wagner**
Title: Principal
Phone: 310-309-5200
IMDB: www.imdb.com/company/co0005596

**Shay Weiner**
Title: Creative Executive
Phone: 310-309-5200
IMDB: www.imdb.com/name/nm1674317/

## 2S FILMS

1437 Seventh Street, Suite 250
Los Angeles, CA 90025

Phone: 310-789-5450
Fax: 310-789-3060
Email: info@2sfilms.com
Website: www.2sfilms.com
IMDB: www.imdb.com/company/co0238996/

Submission Policy: Does not accept any unsolicited
material
Genre: Comedy, Feature Films, Romance
Focus: Feature Films
Year Established: 2007

**Allison Rayne**
Title: Vice President of Development
Phone: 310-789-5450
Email: info@2sfilms.com
IMDB: www.imdb.com/name/nm2588349/

**Molly Smith**
Title: Partner/Producer
Phone: 310-789-5450

Email: info@2sfilms.com
IMDB: www.imdb.com/company/co0238996

## 2WAYTRAFFIC - A SONY PICTURES ENTERTAINMENT COMPANY

Middenweg 1
PO Box 297
Hilversum 1217 HS
The Netherlands

Phone: +31(0)357508000
Fax: +31(0)357508020
Email: info@2waytraffic.com
Website: www.2waytraffic.com
IMDB: www.imdb.com/company/co0211160

Submission Policy: Accepts query letter from
unproduced, unrepresented writers
Focus: Feature Films, TV
Year Established: 2004

## 3311 PRODUCTIONS

8938 Keith
West Hollywood, CA 90069

Phone: 323-319-5060
Fax: 323-306-5534
Email: info@3311productions.com
Website: www.3311productions.com

Submission Policy: Accepts query letter from
produced or represented writers
Genre: Comedy, Drama, Feature Films
Focus: Feature Films

**Ross Jacobson**
Title: Executive/Producer
IMDB: www.imdb.com/name/nm2278951

**Mark Roberts**
Title: Executive
IMDB: www.imdb.com/name/nm4224736

**Eddie Vaisman**
Title: Executive/Producer
IMDB: www.imdb.com/name/nm4224744

## 34TH STREET FILMS

8200 Wilshire Boulevard, Suite 300
Beverly Hills, CA 90211

Phone: 323-315-7963
Fax: 323-315-7117

**Submission Policy:** Accepts query letter from unproduced, unrepresented writers
**Genre:** Action, Comedy, Family, Feature Films, Romance
**Focus:** Feature Films

### Poppy Hanks

**Title:** Senior Vice President (Production & Development)
**Phone:** 323-315-7963

### Matt Moore

**Title:** Executive Vice President
**Phone:** 323-315-7963
**IMDB:** www.imdb.com/name/nm0601597

### Amber Rasberry

**Title:** Director of Development
**Phone:** 323-315-7963
**IMDB:** www.imdb.com/name/nm2248393

## 360 PICTURES

301 North Canon Drive, Suite 207
Beverly Hills, CA 90210

**Phone:** 310-205-9900
**Fax:** 310-205-9909
**IMDB:** www.imdb.com/company/co0157610

**Submission Policy:** Does not accept any unsolicited material
**Genre:** Comedy, Science Fiction, Thriller

### Frank Mancuso

**Title:** President
**Phone:** 310-205-9900
**IMDB:** www.imdb.com/name/nm0541548

### Jennifer Nieves

**Title:** Vice President (Development)
**Phone:** 310-205-9900
**IMDB:** www.imdb.com/name/nm2707034

## 3 ARTS ENTERTAINMENT, INC.

9460 Wilshire Boulevard 7th Floor
Beverly Hills, CA 90212

**Phone:** 310-888-3200
**Fax:** 310-888-3210
**Website:** www.3arts.com
**IMDB:** www.imdb.com/company/co0070636/

**Submission Policy:** Accepts query letter from unproduced, unrepresented writers

**Genre:** Drama, TV Drama, TV Sitcom
**Focus:** Feature Films
**Year Established:** 1992

### Howard Klein

**Title:** Partner/Talent Manager
**Phone:** 310-888-3200
**Email:** hklein@3arts.com
**IMDB:** www.imdb.com/name/nm2232433

### Erwin Stoff

**Title:** Partner/Talent Manager
**Phone:** 310-888-3200
**IMDB:** www.imdb.com/name/nm0831098

## 3 BALL PRODUCTIONS

3650 Redondo Beach Avenue
Redondo Beach, CA 90278

**Phone:** 424-236-7500
**Fax:** 424-236-7501
**Email:** 3ball.reception@eyeworks.tv
**Website:** www.3ballproductions.com
**IMDB:** www.imdb.com/company/co0100000

**Submission Policy:** Accepts query letter from unproduced, unrepresented writers via email
**Genre:** TV, TV Drama
**Focus:** TV

### Brandt Pinvidic

**Title:** Executive Vice President Development
**Phone:** 424-236-7500
**IMDB:** www.imdb.com/name/nm1803480

### J.D. Roth

**Title:** CEO
**Phone:** 424-236-7500
**IMDB:** www.imdb.com/name/nm0744870

## 40 ACRES & A MULE FILMWORKS, INC.

75 South Elliot Place
Brooklyn, NY 11217

**Phone:** 718-624-3703
**Fax:** 718-624-2008
**Website:** www.40acres.com
**IMDB:** www.imdb.com/company/co0029134

**Submission Policy:** Does not accept any unsolicited material
**Genre:** Action, Comedy, Drama, Memoir & True Stories, TV Drama

**Spike Lee**
Title: Chairman
Phone: 718-624-3703
IMDB: www.imdb.com/name/nm0000490

## 44 BLUE PRODUCTIONS, INC.

4040 Vineland Avenue, Suite 105
Studio City, CA 11217

Phone: 818-760-4442
Fax: 818-760-1509
Email: reception@44blue.com
Website: www.44blue.com
IMDB: www.imdb.com/company/co0012712

Submission Policy: Does not accept any unsolicited material
Genre: Memoir & True Stories, TV Drama, TV Sitcom

**Rasha Drachkovitch**
Title: Co-Founder
Phone: 818-760-4442
Email: reception@44blue.com
IMDB: www.imdb.com/name/nm0236624

**Stephanie Drachkovitch**
Title: Co-Founder
Phone: 818-760-4442
Email: reception@44blue.com
IMDB: www.imdb.com/name/nm1729517

## 495 PRODUCTIONS

4222 Burbank Boulevard, 2nd Floor
Burbank, CA 91505

Phone: 818-840-2750
Fax: 818-840-7083
Email: info@495productions.com
Website: www.495productions.com
IMDB: www.imdb.com/company/co0192481

Submission Policy: Does not accept any unsolicited material
Genre: Reality, TV Drama, TV Sitcom
Focus: TV, Reality Programming (Reality TV, Documentaries, Special Events, Sporting Events)

**Stephanie Lydecker**
Title: Head of Development
Phone: 818-840-2750
Email: info@495productions.com
IMDB: www.imdb.com/name/nm1738248

**SallyAnn Salsano**
Title: President
Phone: 818-840-2750
Email: info@495productions.com
IMDB: www.imdb.com/name/nm1133163

## 4TH ROW FILMS

27 West 20th Street, Suite 1006
New York, NY 10011

Phone: 212-974-0082
Fax: 212-627-3090
Email: info@4throwfilms.com
Website: www.4throwfilms.com
IMDB: www.imdb.com/company/co0117932

Submission Policy: Does not accept any unsolicited material
Genre: Memoir & True Stories, TV Drama, TV Sitcom

**Susan Bedusa**
Title: Vice President, Development
Phone: 212-974-0082
Email: info@4throwfilms.com
IMDB: www.imdb.com/name/nm1513256

**Douglas Tirola**
Title: President / Producer
Phone: 212-974-0082
Email: info@4throwfilms.com
IMDB: imdb.com/name/nm0864263

## 51 MINDS ENTERTAINMENT

6565 Sunset Boulevard, Suite 301
Los Angeles, CA 90028

Phone: 323-466-9200
Fax: 323-466-9202
Email: info@51minds.com
Website: www.51minds.com
IMDB: www.imdb.com/company/co0166565

Submission Policy: Accepts query letter from unproduced, unrepresented writers via email
Genre: Comedy, Drama, Reality, TV Drama

**David Caplan**
Title: Vice President, Development
Phone: 323-466-9200
Email: info@51minds.com
IMDB: www.imdb.com/name/nm4933376

**Mark Cronin**
Title: Executive Producer
Phone: 323-466-9200
Email: info@51minds.com
IMDB: imdb.com/name/nm0188782

**Nicole Elliott**
Title: Executive, Development
Phone: 323-466-9200
Email: info@51minds.com
IMDB: www.imdb.com/name/nm1627222

## 59TH STREET FILMS

101 Destiny Drive
Lafayette, LA 70506

Phone: 337-280-9370
Email: 59thstreetfilms@gmail.com

Submission Policy: Accepts scripts from unproduced, unrepresented writers
Genre: Comedy, TV, TV Drama, TV Sitcom
Focus: Television

**Sarah Agor**
Title: Producer
IMDB: www.imdb.com/name/nm2706070

**Jennifer Jarrett**
Title: Producer
IMDB: www.imdb.com/name/nm1838264

**Nicholas Scott**
Title: Producer & Writer
IMDB: www.imdb.com/name/nm4641966

**Steve Sirkis**
Title: Producer & Director
IMDB: www.imdb.com/name/nm2401659

**Alfred Rubin Thompson**
Title: Producer
IMDB: www.imdb.com/name/nm0867022

## 5IVE SMOOTH STONES PRODUCTIONS

8500 Wilshire Boulevard, Suite #527
Beverly Hills, CA 90211

Website: www.5ivesmoothstones.com

Submission Policy: Accepts query letter from unproduced, unrepresented writers via email
Genre: Comedy, Family
Focus: Feature Films

**Terry Crews**
Title: Actor/CEO
IMDB: www.imdb.com/name/nm0187719

**Robert Wise**
Title: President Scripted Development

## 72ND STREET PRODUCTIONS

1041 North Formosa Avenue
West Hollywood, CA 90046

Phone: 323-850-3139
Fax: 323-850-3179
Email: contact@72ndstreetproductions.com
Website: www.72ndstreetproductions.com
IMDB: www.imdb.com/company/co0180596

Submission Policy: Accepts query letter from unproduced, unrepresented writers via email
Genre: Drama, Feature Films
Focus: Feature Films, TV, Media (Commercials/Branding/Marketing)

**Tim Harms**
Title: Producer
Phone: 323-850-3139
Email: tharms@72ndstreetproductions.com
IMDB: www.imdb.com/name/nm0363608

**Steven Krieger**
Title: President - Executive
Phone: 323-850-3139
Email: skrieger@72ndstreetproductions.com
IMDB: www.imdb.com/name/nm2544844

**Lee Krieger**
Title: President - Executive
Phone: 323-850-3139
Email: lkrieger@72ndstreetproductions.com
IMDB: www.imdb.com/name/nm1767218

## 72 PRODUCTIONS

8332 Melrose Avenue, 2nd Floor
West Hollywood, CA 90069

Phone: 310-278-1221
Fax: 310-278-1224
Website: www.72productions.com
IMDB: www.imdb.com/company/co0196483

Submission Policy: Accepts query letter from unproduced, unrepresented writers
Genre: Science Fiction, Thriller

**Jennifer Chaiken**
Title: Producer
Phone: 310-278-1221
IMDB: www.imdb.com/name/nm0149671

**Sebastian Dungan**
Title: Producer
Phone: 310-278-1221
IMDB: www.imdb.com/name/nm0242253

## 777 GROUP

1015 Gayley Avenue, Suite 1128
Los Angeles, CA 90024

Phone: 312-834-7770
Email: info@the777group.com
Website: www.the777group.com
IMDB: www.imdb.com/company/co0133127

Submission Policy: Accepts query letter from unproduced, unrepresented writers via email
Genre: Animation, Memoir & True Stories, TV Drama, TV Sitcom

**Marcello Robinson**
Title: CEO/President
Phone: 312-834-7770
Email: info@the777group.com
IMDB: www.imdb.com/name/nm0732883

## 7ATE9 ENTERTAINMENT

740 N. La Brea Avenue
Los Angeles, CA 90038

Phone: 323-936-6789
Fax: 323-937-6713
Email: info@7ate9.com
Website: www.7ate9.com/
IMDB: www.imdb.com/company/co0171281

Submission Policy: Does not accept any unsolicited material
Genre: TV
Focus: TV Mini-Series

**Artur Spigel**
Title: Creative Director
IMDB: www.imdb.com/name/nm1742493

## 8:38 PRODUCTIONS

10390 Santa Monica Boulevard, Suite 200
Los Angeles, CA 90064

Phone: 310-789-3056
Fax: 310-789-3077
IMDB: www.imdb.com/company/co0252672

Submission Policy: Does not accept any unsolicited material
Genre: Family, Romance

**Kira Davis**
Title: Producer
Phone: 310-789-3056
IMDB: www.imdb.com/name/nm0204987

## 8790 PICTURES, INC.

11400 West Olympic Boulevard, Suite 590
Los Angeles, CA 90064

Phone: 310-471-9983
Fax: 310-471-6366
Email: 8790pictures@gmail.com
IMDB: www.imdb.com/company/co0159892

Submission Policy: Accepts query letter from unproduced, unrepresented writers via email
Genre: Action, Animation, Comedy, Romance, TV Drama
Focus: Feature Films, TV

**Ralph Singleton**
Title: Writer/Producer
Phone: 310-471-9983
Email: 8790pictures@gmail.com
IMDB: www.imdb.com/name/nm0802326

**Joan Singleton**
Title: Writer/Producer
Phone: 310-471-9983
Email: 8790pictures@gmail.com
IMDB: www.imdb.com/name/nm0802306

## 8TH WONDER ENTERTAINMENT

7961 West 3rd Street
Los Angeles, CA 90048

Phone: 323-549-3456
Fax: 323-549-9475
Email: info@8thwonderent.com
Website: www.8thwonderent.com
IMDB: www. imdb.com/company/co0226729

Submission Policy: Accepts query letter from unproduced, unrepresented writers via email

**David Luong**
Title: Director of Development
Phone: 323-860-0319
Email: info@8thwonderent.com

**Michael McQuarn**
Title: CEO/President
Phone: 323-860-0319
Email: mcq@8thwonderent.com

## 900 FILMS

1611A South Melrose Drive, #362
Vista, CA 92081

Phone: 760-477-2470
Fax: 760-477-2478
Email: asst@900films.com
Website: www.900films.com
IMDB: www.imdb.com/company/co0086829

Submission Policy: Accepts query letter from
unproduced, unrepresented writers via email
Genre: Reality
Focus: Feature Films, TV, Post- Production
(Editing, Special Effects), Reality Programming
(Reality TV, Documentaries, Special Events,
Sporting Events), Media (Commercials/Branding/
Marketing)

**Krista Parkinson**
Title: VP of Development
Phone: 760-477-2470
Email: irene@900films.com
IMDB: www.imdb.com/name/nm2221276

## 9.14 PICTURES

1804 Chestnut Street, Suite 2
Philadelphia, PA 19103

Phone: 215-238-0707
Fax: 215-238-0663
Email: info@914pictures.com
Website: www.914pictures.com
IMDB: www.imdb.com/company/co0145535

Submission Policy: Accepts query letter from
unproduced, unrepresented writers via email
Year Established: 2002

**Don Argott**
Title: Owner/Producer
Phone: 215-238-0707 ext. 12#

Email: info@914pictures.com
IMDB: www.imdb.com/name/nm0034531

**Sheena Joyce**
Title: Owner
Phone: 215-238-0707 ext. 11#
Email: info@914pictures.com
IMDB: www.imdb.com/name/nm1852224

## AARDMAN ANIMATIONS

Gas Ferry Road
Bristol BS1 6UN
United Kingdom

Phone: +44 117-984-8485
Fax: +44 117-984-8486
Email: mail@aardman.com
Website: www.aardman.com
IMDB: www.imdb.com/company/co0103531

Submission Policy: Does not accept any unsolicited
material
Genre: Animation

**Alicia Gold**
Title: Head of Development, Features
Phone: +44 117-984-8485
Email: mail@aardman.com
IMDB: www.imdb.com/name/
nm1664759imdb.com/name/nm4211100

## ABANDON PICTURES, INC.

711 Route 302
Pine Bush, NY 12566

Phone: 845-361-9317
Fax: 845-361-9150
Email: info@abandoninteractive.com
Website: http://www.abandoninteractive.com
IMDB: www.imdb.com/company/co0025591

Submission Policy: Does not accept any unsolicited
material

**Karen Lauder**
Title: President & CEO
Phone: 845-361-9317
Email: info@abandoninteractive.com
IMDB: www.imdb.com/name/nm0490746

## ABBY LOU ENTERTAINMENT

1411 Edgehill Pl.
Pasadena, CA 91103

**Phone:** 626-795-7334
**Fax:** 626-795-4013
**Email:** ale@full-moon.com

**Submission Policy:** Accepts query letter from produced or represented writers
**Genre:** Feature Films
**Focus:** Feature Films

**George Le Fave**
**Title:** President
**IMDB:** www.imdb.com/name/nm2247957

**Cheryl Pestor**
**Title:** Executive VP
**IMDB:** www.imdb.com/name/nm2453743

## ABC STUDIOS

500 S Buena Vista St
Burbank, CA 91505

**Phone:** 818-460-7777

**Submission Policy:** Does not accept any unsolicited material
**Genre:** Media (Commercials/Branding/Marketing), TV, TV Drama, TV Sitcom
**Focus:** TV

**Gary French**
**Title:** Senior Vice President of Production
**IMDB:** www.imdb.com/name/nm2380686

**Brenda Kyle**
**Title:** Vice President of Production
**IMDB:** www.imdb.com/name/nm0477368

**Patrick Moran**
**Title:** Head of Creative Development
**IMDB:** www.imdb.com/name/nm3988896

**Robert Sertner**
**Title:** Executive Producer
**Email:** bobsertner@gmail.com
**IMDB:** www.imdb.com/name/nm0785750

## ABERRATION FILMS

1425 North Crescent Heights Boulevard, #203
West Hollywood, CA 90046

**Phone:** 323-656-1830
**Email:** aberrationfilms@yahoo.com
**Website:** http://www.aberrationfilms.com
**IMDB:** www.imdb.com/company/co0164476

**Submission Policy:** Accepts query letter from unproduced, unrepresented writers
**Genre:** Drama
**Focus:** Feature Films

**Susan Dynner**
**Title:** Director / Producer
**Phone:** 323-656-1830
**Email:** aberrationfilms@yahoo.com
**IMDB:** www.imdb.com/name/nm1309839

## ACAPPELLA PICTURES

8271 Melrose Avenue, Suite 101
Los Angeles, CA 90046

**Phone:** 323-782-8200
**Fax:** 323-782-8210
**Email:** charmaine@acappellapictures.com
**Website:** http://acappellapictures.com
**IMDB:** www.imdb.com/company/co0055414

**Submission Policy:** Accepts query letter from unproduced, unrepresented writers via email

**Charles Evans**
**Title:** President
**Phone:** 323-782-8200
**Email:** charmaine@acappellapictures.com
**IMDB:** www.imdb.com/name/nm0262509

**Charmaine Parcero**
**Title:** Executive Development / Production
**Phone:** 323-782-8200
**Email:** charmaine@acappellapictures.com
**IMDB:** www.imdb.com/name/nm0661019

## ACCELERATED ENTERTAINMENT LLC

10201 West Pico Boulevard, Building 6
Los Angeles, CA 90064

**Email:** cleestorm@acceleratedent.com
**Website:** www.acceleratedent.com
**IMDB:** www.imdb.com/company/co0208920

**Submission Policy:** Accepts query letter from unproduced, unrepresented writers via email
**Genre:** Drama, Memoir & True Stories
**Focus:** Feature Films

**Allison Calleri**
**Title:** Partner/Producer
**Email:** acalleri@acceleratedent.com
**IMDB:** www.imdb.com/name/nm1819857

**Jason Perr**
Title: Partner/Executive Producer
Email: jperr@acceleratedent.com
IMDB: www.imdb.com/name/nm1280790

**Christina Storm**
Title: Partner/Producer
Email: cleestorm@acceleratedent.com
IMDB: www.imdb.com/name/nm0497028

## A.C. LYLES PRODUCTIONS, INC.

5555 Melrose Avenue, Hart Building 409
Hollywood, CA 90038-3197

Phone: 323-956-5819
IMDB: www.imdb.com/company/co0074718

Submission Policy: Accepts query letter from
unproduced, unrepresented writers via email

**A.C. Lyles**
Title: Producer
Phone: 323-956-5819
Email: ac_lyles@paramount.com
IMDB: www.imdb.com/name/nm0528121

## ACT III PRODUCTIONS

100 North Crescent Dr, Suite 250
Beverly Hills, CA 90210

Phone: 310-385-4111
Fax: 310-385-4148
Website: http://www.normanlear.com/act_iii.html
IMDB: www.imdb.com/company/co0030401

Submission Policy: Accepts query letter from
unproduced, unrepresented writers

**Norman Lear**
Title: Chairman/CEO
Phone: 310-385-4111
Email: normanl@actiii.com
IMDB: www.imdb.com/name/nm0005131

**Brent Miller**
Title: VP of Development
Phone: 310-385-4111
IMDB: www.imdb.com/name/nm1226252

## ACTUAL REALITY PICTURES

Phone: 310-202-1272
Fax: 310-202-1502
Email: questions@arp.tv

Website: http://www.actualreality.tv
IMDB: www.imdb.com/company/co0004087

Submission Policy: Does not accept any unsolicited
material

**R.J. Cutler**
Title: President
Phone: 310-202-1272
IMDB: www.imdb.com/name/nm0191712

## ADAM FIELDS PRODUCTIONS

8899 Beverly Boulevard, Suite 821
West Hollywood, CA 90048

Phone: 310-859-9300
Fax: 310-859-4795
IMDB: www.imdb.com/company/co0064962

Submission Policy: Accepts query letter from
unproduced, unrepresented writers

**Adam Fields**
Title: President
Phone: 310-859-9300
IMDB: www.imdb.com/name/nm0276178

## ADELSTEIN PRODUCTIONS

144 South Beverly Dr, Suite 500
Beverly Hills, CA 90212

Phone: 310-860-5502

Submission Policy: Does not accept any unsolicited
material

**Marty Adelstein**
Title: Producer
Phone: 310-270-4570
IMDB: www.imdb.com/name/nm1374351

## AD HOMINEM ENTERPRISES

506 Santa Monica Boulevard, Suite 400
Santa Monica, CA 90401

Phone: 310-394-1444
Fax: 310-394-5401
IMDB: www.imdb.com/company/co0171502

Submission Policy: Does not accept any unsolicited
material
Focus: Feature Films

**Jim Burke**
Title: Partner
Phone: 310-394-1444
Email: jwb@adhominem.us
IMDB: www.imdb.com/name/nm0121724
Assistant: Adam Wagner

**Evan Endicott**
Title: Director of Development
Phone: 310-394-1444
IMDB: www.imdb.com/name/nm1529002

**Alexander Payne**
Title: Partner
Phone: 310-394-1444
IMDB: www.imdb.com/name/nm0668247
Assistant: Anna Musso

## ADULT SWIM

1065 Williams St NW
Atlanta, GA 30309

Phone: 404-827-1500
Website: www.adultswim.com
IMDB: www.imdb.com/company/co0153115

Submission Policy: Does not accept any unsolicited material

**Keith Crofford**
Title: Vice-President Production
IMDB: www.imdb.com/name/nm0188443

## AEGIS FILM GROUP

7510 Sunset Blvd
Ste 275
Los Angeles, CA 90046

Phone: 323-848-7977
Fax: 323-650-9954
Email: info@aegisfilmgroup.com
Website: www.aegisfilmgroup.com

Genre: Documentary, Feature Films
Focus: Feature Films

**Arianna Eisenberg**
Title: Owner
Phone: 323-848-7977
IMDB: www.imdb.com/name/nm1985255

**Steve Shultz**
Title: Executive Producer
Phone: 323-848-7977
IMDB: www.imdb.com/name/nm0795789

## AEI - ATCHITY ENTERTAINMENT INTERNATIONAL, INC.

9601 Wilshire Boulevard, #1202
Beverly Hills, CA 90210

Phone: 323-932-0407
Fax: 323-932-0321
Email: submissions@aeionline.com
Website: www.aeionline.com
IMDB: wwwimdb.com/company/co0010944

Submission Policy: Accepts query letter from unproduced, unrepresented writers

**Jennifer Pope**
Title: Submissions Coordinator
Phone: 323-932-0407
Email: jp@aeionline.com
IMDB: www.imdb.com/name/nm1026413

## A&E NETWORK

235 East 45th Street
New York, NY 10017

Phone: 212-210-1400
Fax: 212-210-9755
Email: feedback@aetv.com
Website: www.aetv.com
IMDB: www.imdb.com/company/co0056790

Submission Policy: Does not accept any unsolicited material

**Thomas Moody**
Title: Senior Vice-President Programming, Planning & Acquisitions
Phone: 212-210-1400
Email: feedback@aetv.com
IMDB: www.imdb.com/name/nm1664759

## AFTER DARK FILMS

8967 Sunset Boulevard
West Hollywood, CA 90069

Phone: 310-270-4260
Fax: 310-270-4262
Email: info@afterdarkfilms.com

**Website:** www.afterdarkfilms.com
**IMDB:** www.imdb.com/company/co0166161

**Submission Policy:** Does not accept any unsolicited material
**Genre:** Horror

**Stephanie Caleb**
**Title:** Executive Vice-President Acquisitions & Creative Affairs
**Phone:** 310-270-4260
**Email:** info@afterdarkfilms.com
**IMDB:** www.imdb.com/name/nm2554487

## AGAMEMNON FILMS, INC.

650 North Bronson Avenue, Suite B225
Los Angeles, CA 90004

**Phone:** 323-960-4066
**Fax:** 323-960-4067
**Website:** http://www.agamemnon.com
**IMDB:** www.imdb.com/company/co0004137

**Submission Policy:** Accepts query letter from unproduced, unrepresented writers via email
**Genre:** Action, Drama, Family, Reality, Thriller, TV Drama
**Focus:** TV, Reality Programming (Reality TV, Documentaries, Special Events, Sporting Events)

**Alex Butler**
**Title:** Senior Partner and Producer
**Phone:** 323-960-4066
**IMDB:** www.imdb.com/name/nm0124808

**Fraser Heston**
**Title:** President, CEO and Co-Founder
**IMDB:** www.imdb.com/name/nm0381699
**Assistant:** Heather Thomas

## AGGREGATE FILMS

100 Universal City Plaza
Bungalow 414
Universal City, CA 91608

**Phone:** 818-777-8180

**Submission Policy:** Does not accept any unsolicited material
**Genre:** Comedy, Family, Feature Films
**Focus:** Feature Films

**Jason Bateman**
**Title:** Principal
**IMDB:** www.imdb.com/name/nm0000867

**Jim Garavente**
**Title:** President
**IMDB:** www.imdb.com/name/nm4814574

## AGILITY STUDIOS

11928 1/2 Ventura Boulevard
Studio City, CA 91604

**Phone:** 310-314-1440
**Fax:** 310-496-3292
**Email:** info@agilitystudios.com
**Website:** www.agilitystudios.com
**IMDB:** www.imdb.com/company/co0293230

**Submission Policy:** Accepts query letter from unproduced, unrepresented writers via email
**Year Established:** 2008

**Scott Ehrlich**
**Title:** CEO
**Phone:** 310-314-1440
**Email:** info@agilitystudios.com
**IMDB:** www.imdb.com/name/nm3796990

## AHIMSA FILMS

6671 Sunset Boulevard, Suite 1593
Los Angeles, CA 90028

**Phone:** 323-464-8500
**Fax:** 323-464-8535
**IMDB:** www.imdb.com/company/co0202538

**Submission Policy:** Accepts query letter from unproduced, unrepresented writers

**Rebecca Yeldham**
**Title:** President
**Phone:** 323-464-8500
**IMDB:** www.imdb.com/name/nm0947344

## AHIMSA MEDIA

8060 Colonial Drive, Suite 204
Richmond, BC V7C 4V1
Canada

**Phone:** 604-785-3602
**Email:** info@ahimsamedia.com
**Website:** www.ahimsamedia.com
**IMDB:** www.imdb.com/company/co0222513

**Submission Policy:** Accepts query letter from unproduced, unrepresented writers via email
**Focus:** Media

**Erica Hargreave**
**Title:** President/Head of Creative and Interactive
**Phone:** 604-785-3602
**Email:** info@ahimsamedia.com
**IMDB:** www.imdb.com/name/nm2988128

## AIRMONT PICTURES

344 Mesa Road
Santa Monica, CA 90402

**Phone:** 310-985-3896
**IMDB:** www.imdb.com/company/co0176167

**Submission Policy:** Accepts query letter from unproduced, unrepresented writers

**Matthew Gannon**
**Title:** Producer
**Phone:** 310-985-3896
**IMDB:** www.imdb.com/name/nm0304478

## AKIL PRODUCTIONS

**Phone:** 212-608-2000
**Email:** info@akilproductions.com
**Website:** www.akilproductions.com

**Genre:** Drama, TV, TV Drama
**Focus:** TV

**Mara Akil**
**Title:** Executive Producer
**IMDB:** www.imdb.com/name/nm0015327

**Salim Akil**
**Title:** Principal
**IMDB:** www.imdb.com/name/nm0015328

## ALAN BARNETTE PRODUCTIONS

100 Universal City Plaza
Building 2352, Suite 101
Universal City, CA 91608

**Phone:** 818-733-0993
**Fax:** 818-733-3172
**Email:** dabarnette@aol.com
**IMDB:** www.imdb.com/company/co0056462

**Submission Policy:** Does not accept any unsolicited material

**Alan Barnette**
**Title:** Executive Producer
**Phone:** 818-733-0993
**Email:** dabarnette@aol.com
**IMDB:** www.imdb.com/name/nm0056002

## ALAN DAVID MANAGEMENT

8840 Wilshire Boulevard,
Suite 200
Beverly Hills, CA 90211

**Phone:** 310-358-3155
**Fax:** 310-358-3256
**Email:** ad@adgmp.com
**IMDB:** www.imdb.com/company/co0097077

**Submission Policy:** Does not accept any unsolicited material

**Alan David**
**Title:** President
**Phone:** 310-358-3155
**Email:** ad@adgmp.com
**IMDB:** www.imdb.com/name/nm2220960

## ALAN SACKS PRODUCTIONS

11684 Ventura Boulevard, Suite 809
Studio City, CA 91604

**Phone:** 818-752-6999
**Fax:** 818-752-6985
**Email:** asacks@pacbell.net
**IMDB:** www.imdb.com/company/co0013945

**Submission Policy:** Does not accept any unsolicited material

**Alan Sacks**
**Title:** Executive Producer
**Phone:** 818-752-6999
**Email:** asacks@pacbell.net
**IMDB:** www.imdb.com/name/nm0755286

## ALCHEMY ENTERTAINMENT

7024 Melrose Ave, Suite 420
Los Angeles, CA 90038

**Phone:** 323-937-6100
**Fax:** 323-937-6102
**IMDB:** www.imdb.com/company/co0094892

**Submission Policy:** Does not accept any unsolicited material

**Jason Barrett**
Title: Manager/Producer
Phone: 323-937-6100
IMDB: www.imdb.com/name/nm2249074

## ALCON ENTERTAINMENT, LLC

10390 Santa Monica Boulevard, Suite 250
Los Angeles, CA 90025

Phone: 310-789-3040
Fax: 310-789-3060
Email: info@alconent.com
Website: www.alconent.com
IMDB: www.imdb.com/company/co0054452

Submission Policy: Does not accept any unsolicited material
Genre: Feature Films

**Broderick Johnson**
Title: Co-Founder/Co-CEO
Phone: 310-789-3040
Email: info@alconent.com
IMDB: www.imdb.com/name/nm0424663

**Carl Rogers**
Title: Director, Development
Phone: 310-789-3040
Email: info@alconent.com
IMDB: www.imdb.com/name/nm0736770

**Steven Wegner**
Title: Executive Vice President, Development
Phone: 310-789-3040
Email: info@alconent.com
IMDB: www.imdb.com/name/nm1176853

## ALDAMISA ENTERTAINMENT

15760 Ventura Blvd.
Suite 1450
Encino, CA 91436

Phone: 818-753-2442
Fax: 818-753-2310
Email: sales@aldamisa.com
Website: www.aldamisa.com

Submission Policy: Accepts query letter from produced or represented writers
Genre: Action, Comedy, Crime, Drama, Fantasy, Feature Films, Horror, Romance, Thriller
Focus: Feature Films

**Sergei Bespalov**
Title: Co-Chairman
IMDB: www.imdb.com/name/nm3703488
Assistant: Michelle Faraji

**Marina Bespalov**
Title: Co-Chairman
IMDB: www.imdb.com/name/nm4208519
Assistant: Kirby Lodin

**James D. Brubaker**
Title: President
IMDB: www.imdb.com/name/nm0115384

**Russell Gray**
Title: Producer
IMDB: www.imdb.com/name/nm0336925

**Jere Hausfater**
Title: COO

**Michael Kupisk**
Title: Head of Development
IMDB: www.imdb.com/name/nm3161790
Assistant: Josh Baker

## ALEXANDER/ENRIGHT & ASSOCIATES

201 Wilshire, Boulevard, 3rd Floor
Santa Monica, CA 90401

Phone: 310-458-3003
Fax: 310-393-7238
IMDB: www.imdb.com/company/co0048897

Submission Policy: Accepts query letter from unproduced, unrepresented writers

**Les Alexander**
Title: Executive Producer
Phone: 310-458-3003
IMDB: www.imdb.com/name/nm0018573

## ALEXANDER/MITCHELL PRODUCTIONS

201 Wilshire Boulevard Third Floor
Santa Monica, CA 90401

Phone: 310-458-3003
Fax: 310-393-7238
IMDB: www.imdb.com/company/co0241249

Submission Policy: Accepts query letter from unproduced, unrepresented writers via email
Genre: Drama, Feature Films, TV
Focus: TV Movies

**Les Alexander**
Title: Principal (Executive Producer)
IMDB: www.imdb.com/name/nm0018573

**Jonathan Mitchell**
Title: Principal
IMDB: www.imdb.com/name/nm2927057

## ALEX ROSE PRODUCTIONS, INC.

8291 Presson Place
Los Angeles, CA 90069

Phone: 323-654-8662
Fax: 323-654-0196
IMDB: www.imdb.com/company/co0177705

Submission Policy: Accepts query letter from
unproduced, unrepresented writers

**Alexandra Rose**
Title: President/Writer/Producer
Phone: 323-654-8662
IMDB: www.imdb.com/name/nm0741228

## ALIANZA FILMS INTERNATIONAL LTD.

11941 Weddington Street, Suite #106
Studio City, CA 91607

Phone: 310-933-6250
Fax: 310-388-0874
Email: shari@alianzafilms.com
Website: http://www.alianzafilms.com
IMDB: www.imdb.com/company/co0022267

Submission Policy: Accepts query letter from
unproduced, unrepresented writers
Year Established: 1984

**Shari Hamrick**
Title: Executive
Phone: 310-933-6250
Email: shari@alianzafilms.com
IMDB: www.imdb.com/name/nm0359089

## A-LINE PICTURES

2231 Broadway #19
New York, NY 10024

Phone: 212-496-9496
Fax: 212-496-9497
Email: info@a-linepictures.com
Website: www.a-linepictures.com
IMDB: www.imdb.com/company/co0156447

Submission Policy: Does not accept any unsolicited
material
Year Established: 2005

**Caroline Baron**
Title: Producer
Phone: 212-496-9496
Email: info@a-linepictures.com
IMDB: www.imdb.com/name/nm0056205

## ALLAN MCKEOWN PRESENTS

1534 17th Street, #102
Santa Monica, CA 90404

Phone: 310-264-2474
Fax: 310-264-4663
Email: info@ampresents.tv
Website: www.ampresents.tv
IMDB: www.imdb.com/company/co0206885

Submission Policy: Accepts query letter from
unproduced, unrepresented writers via email
Year Established: 2007

**Allan McKeown**
Title: CEO/Producer
Phone: 310-264-2474
Email: info@ampresents.tv
IMDB: www.imdb.com/name/nm0571647

## ALLENTOWN PRODUCTIONS

100 Universal City Plaza
Building 2372B, Suite 114
Universal City, CA 91608

Phone: 818-733-1002
Fax: 818-866-4181
Email: writetous@allentownproductions.com
Website: www.allentownproductions.com
IMDB: www.imdb.com/company/co0122945

Submission Policy: Does not accept any unsolicited
material
Genre: Memoir & True Stories
Year Established: 1994

**Chris W. King**
Title: Director of Development
Phone: 818-733-1002
Email: writetous@allentownproductions.com
IMDB: www. imdb.com/name/nm1648242/

**James Moll**
Title: Founder/Producer/Director
Phone: 818-733-1002
Email: writetous@allentownproductions.com
IMDB: www.imdb.com/name/nm0002224

## ALLIANCE FILMS

45 Kings Street East Suite 300
Toronto, ON, Canada, M5C2Y7

Phone: 416-309-4200
Fax: 416-309-4290
Email: info@alliancefilms.com
Website: www.alliancefilms.com

Submission Policy: Does not accept any unsolicited material
Genre: Action, Comedy, Crime, Drama, Fantasy, Feature Films, Horror, Romance, Science Fiction, Thriller
Focus: Feature Films

**Xavier Marchand**
Title: President
IMDB: www.imdb.com/name/nm0545421

**Laurie May**
Title: Executive Vice President

**Mark Slone**
Title: Executive Vice President
IMDB: www.imdb.com/name/nm1093545

## ALLOY ENTERTAINMENT

6300 Wilshire Boulevard, Suite 2150
Los Angeles, CA 90048

Phone: 323-801-1373
Fax: 323-801-1355
Email: LAassistant@alloyentertainment.com
Website: www.alloyentertainment.com
IMDB: www.imdb.com/company/co0142434

Submission Policy: Accepts query letter from unproduced, unrepresented writers via email

**Bob Levy**
Title: Executive Vice-President of Film
Phone: 323-801-1373
Email: LAassistant@alloyentertainment.com
IMDB: www.imdb.com/name/nm2145920

## ALOE ENTERTAINMENT

433 North Camden Dr, Suite 600
Beverly Hills, CA 90210

Phone: 310-288-1886
Fax: 310-288-1801
Email: info@aloeentertainment.com
Website: www.aloeentertainment.com
IMDB: www.imdb.com/company/co0261920

Submission Policy: Does not accept any unsolicited material
Year Established: 1999

**Mary Aloe**
Title: Producer/President
Phone: 310-288-1886
Email: info@aloeentertainment.com
IMDB: www.imdb.com/name/nm0022053

## AL ROKER PRODUCTIONS

250 West 57th Street, Suite 1525
New York, NY 10019

Phone: 212-757-8500
Fax: 212-757-8513
Email: info@alroker.com
Website: www.alrokerproductions.com
IMDB: www.imdb.com/company/co0095131

Submission Policy: Does not accept any unsolicited material
Focus: Post-Production (Editing, Special Effects)
Year Established: 1994

**Tracie Brennan**
Title: VP Operations
Phone: 212-757-8500
Email: info@alroker.com
IMDB: www.imdb.com/name/nm2200420

**Al Roker**
Title: CEO
Phone: 212-757-8500
Email: info@alroker.com
IMDB: www.imdb.com/name/nm0737963

## ALTA LOMA ENTERTAINMENT

2706 Media Center Drive
Los Angeles, CA 90065-1733

Phone: 323-276-4211
Fax: 323-276-4500

**Website:** http://www.alta-loma.com
**IMDB:** www.imdb.com/company/co0008514

**Submission Policy:** Does not accept any unsolicited material

**Jason Burns**
**Title:** SVP of Development
**Phone:** 323-276-4211
**IMDB:** www.imdb.com/name/nm2135146

**Richard Rosenzweig**
**Title:** Executive Producer
**Phone:** 323-276-4211
**IMDB:** www.imdb.com/name/nm0742866

**J.W. Starrett**
**Title:** Director of Development
**Phone:** 323-276-4211
**IMDB:** www.imdb.com/name/nm2852786

## ALTURAS FILMS

2403 Main Street
Santa Monica, CA 90405

**Phone:** 310-401-6200
**Fax:** 310-401-6129
**Email:** info@alturasfilms.com
**Website:** www.alturasfilms.com
**IMDB:** www.imdb.com/company/co0169508

**Submission Policy:** Does not accept any unsolicited material
**Year Established:** 2004

**Marshall Rawlings**
**Title:** Owner/Producer
**Phone:** 310-401-6200
**Email:** reception@alturasfilms.com
**IMDB:** www.imdb.com/name/nm1987844

## A-MARK ENTERTAINMENT

233 Wilshire Boulevard, Suite 200
Santa Monica, CA 90401

**Phone:** 310-255-0900
**Email:** info@amarkentertainment.com
**Website:** www.amarkentertainment.com
**IMDB:** www.imdb.com/company/co0135086

**Submission Policy:** Does not accept any unsolicited material
**Year Established:** 2004

**Bruce McNall**
**Title:** Co-Chair
**Phone:** 310-255-0900
**Email:** info@amarkentertainment.com
**IMDB:** www.imdb.com/name/nm1557652

## AMBASSADOR ENTERTAINMENT

P. O. Box 1522
Pacific Palisades, CA 90272

**Phone:** 310-862-5200
**Fax:** 310-496-3140
**Email:** aspeval@ambassadortv.com
**Website:** www.ambassadortv.com
**IMDB:** www. imdb.com/company/co0175998

**Submission Policy:** Does not accept any unsolicited material
**Year Established:** 1999

**Albert Spevak**
**Title:** President
**Phone:** 310-862-5200
**Email:** aspeval@ambassadortv.com
**IMDB:** www.imdb.com/name/nm0818411

## AMBER ENTERTAINMENT

21 Ganton Street, 4th Floor
London
United Kingdom
W1F 98N

6030 Wilshire Blvd
Suite 300
Los Angeles, CA 90036

**Phone:** +44 207-292-7170/ 310-242-6445
**Email:** info@amberentertainment.com
**Website:** www.amberentertainment.com
**IMDB:** www.imdb.com/company/co0266476

**Submission Policy:** Does not accept any unsolicited material
**Genre:** Crime, Drama, Fantasy, Feature Films, Horror, Thriller
**Focus:** Feature Films
**Year Established:** 2010

**Lawrence Elman**
**Title:** Executive Producer
**IMDB:** www.imdb.com/name/nm3793846

**Ileen Maisel**
Title: Executive (London office)
Phone: +44 207-292-7170
Email: info@amberentertainment.com
IMDB: www.imdb.com/name/nm0537884

## AMBLIN ENTERTAINMENT

100 Universal Plaza
Bldg 477
Universal City, CA 91608

Phone: 818-733-7000
Fax: 818-509-1433

Submission Policy: Does not accept any unsolicited material
Genre: Action, Comedy, Drama, Fantasy, Feature Films, Science Fiction
Focus: Feature Film

**Steven Spielberg**
Title: Owner
Phone: 818-733-7000
IMDB: www.imdb.com/name/nm0000229

## AMBUSH ENTERTAINMENT

7364-1/2 Melrose Avenue
Los Angeles, CA 90046

Phone: 323-951-9197
Fax: 323-951-9998
Email: info@ambushentertainment.com
Website: www.ambushentertainment.com
IMDB: www.imdb.com/company/co0091524

Submission Policy: Accepts scripts from produced or represented writers
Year Established: 2000

**Miranda Bailey**
Title: Partner/Producer
Phone: 323-951-9197
Email: 323-951-9998
IMDB: www.imdb.com/name/nm0047419

## AMERICAN MOVING PICTURES

108 W 2nd St.
Suite 1012
Los Angeles, CA 90012

Website: www.americanmovingpictures.com

Submission Policy: Accepts query letter from unproduced, unrepresented writers via email
Genre: Comedy, Drama, Feature Films
Focus: Feature Films

**Matt D'Elia**
Title: Co-Founder
Email: matt@americanmovingpictures.com
IMDB: www.imdb.com/name/nm2532035

**Julian King**
Title: Co-Founder
Email: julian@americanmovingpictures.com
IMDB: www.imdb.com/name/nm2398047

## AMERICAN WORK INC.

7030 Delongpre
Los Angeles, CA 90028

Phone: 323-668-1100
Fax: 323-668-1133
IMDB: www. imdb.com/company/co0167015/

Submission Policy: Accepts query letter from unproduced, unrepresented writers
Genre: Comedy

**Scot Armstrong**
Title: Writer/Director/Producer
IMDB: www.imdb.com/name/nm0035905

## AMERICAN WORLD PICTURES

21700 Oxnard Street, Suite 1770
Woodland Hills, CA 91367

Phone: 818-340-9004
Fax: 818-340-9011
Email: info@americanworldpictures.com
Website: www.americanworldpictures.com
IMDB: www.imdb.com/company/co0054536

Submission Policy: Accepts scripts from unproduced, unrepresented writers
Genre: Action, Comedy, Drama, Family, Horror, Romance, Thriller
Focus: Feature Films

**Dee Camp**
Title: Vice-President of Acquisitions
Phone: 818-340-9004
Email: dee@americanworldpictures.com
IMDB: www.imdb.com/name/nm3036636

**Dana Dubovsky**
Title: President of Production
Phone: 818-340-9004
Email: dana@americanworldpictures.com
IMDB: www.imdb.com/name/nm0239541

**Mark Lester**
Title: President/CEO
Phone: 818-340-9004
Email: mark@americanworldpictures.com
IMDB: www.imdb.com/name/nm0504495

## AMERICAN ZOETROPE

916 Kearny Street Sentinel Building
San Francisco, CA 94133

1641 North Ivar Avenue
Los Angeles, CA 90028

Phone: 415-788-7500
Fax: 415-989-7910
Email: contests@zoetrope.com
Website: www.zoetrope.com
IMDB: www.imdb.com/company/co0020958

Submission Policy: Accepts scripts from
unproduced, unrepresented writers
Genre: Action, Crime, Memoir & True Stories,
Thriller
Year Established: 1972

**Francis Coppola**
Title: Emeritus
Phone: 415-788-7500
IMDB: www.imdb.com/name/nm0000338

**Michael Zakin**
Title: VP, Production & Acquisitions
Phone: 323-460-4420
IMDB: www.imdb.com/name/nm2943902

## AMY ROBINSON PRODUCTIONS

101 Broadway, Suite 405
Brooklyn, NY 11211

Phone: 718-599-2202
Fax: 718-408-9553
Email: arobinsonprod@aol.com
IMDB: www.imdb.com/company/co0055694

Submission Policy: Accepts query letter from
unproduced, unrepresented writers via email

**Gabrielle Cran**
Title: Director of Development
Phone: 718-599-2202
Email: arobinsonprod@aol.com
IMDB: www.imdb.com/name/nm1660887

**Amy Robinson**
Title: Producer
Phone: 718-599-2202
Email: arobinsonprod@aol.com
IMDB: www.imdb.com/name/nm0732364

## ANCHOR BAY FILMS

9242 Beverly Boulevard Suite 201
Beverly Hills, CA 90210

Phone: 424-204-4166
Email: questions@anchorbayent.com
Website: www.anchorbayent.com

Submission Policy: Accepts query letter from
unproduced, unrepresented writers
Genre: Crime, Horror, Thriller
Year Established: 1997

**Bill Clark**
Title: President
Phone: 424-204-4166
IMDB: www.imdb.com/name/nm0163694

## ANDREA SIMON ENTERTAINMENT

4230 Woodman Ave.
Sherman Oaks, CA 91423

Phone: 818-380-1901
Fax: 818-380-1932
Email: asimon@andreasimonent.com
IMDB: www.imdb.com/company/co0102747

Submission Policy: Accepts query letter from
unproduced, unrepresented writers
Genre: Comedy, Drama, Feature Films, TV

**Anna Henry**
Title: Director of Development
IMDB: www.imdb.com/name/nm1326063

**Andrea Simon**
Title: Principal / Producer
Email: asimon@andreasimonent.com
IMDB: www.imdb.com/name/nm2231084

## ANDREW LAUREN PRODUCTIONS

36 East 23rd Street, Suite 6F
New York, NY 10010

**Phone:** 212-475-1600
**Fax:** 212-529-1095
**Email:** asst@andrewlaurenproductions.com
**Website:** www.andrewlaurenproductions.com
**IMDB:** www. imdb.com/company/co0032488/

**Submission Policy:** Accepts scripts from
unproduced, unrepresented writers
**Genre:** Drama
**Focus:** Feature Films, TV

### Andrew Lauren
**Title:** Chairman & CEO
**Phone:** 212-475-1600
**Email:** asst@andrewlaurenproductions.com
**IMDB:** www.imdb.com/name/nm0491054

### Dave Platt
**Title:** Creative Executive
**Phone:** 212-475-1600
**Email:** asst@andrewlaurenproductions.com
**IMDB:** www.imdb.com/name/nm5255879

## ANGELWORLD ENTERTAINMENT LTD.

New Bridge House
30-34 New Bridge Street
London
EC4 V6BJ

6 Triq Ta Fuq Il Widien
Mellieha
Malta

**Email:** asst@angelworldentertainment.com
**Website:** www.angelworldentertainment.com

**Submission Policy:** Accepts query letter from
unproduced, unrepresented writers via email
**Focus:** Feature Films
**Year Established:** 2007

### Darby Angel
**Title:** CEO/Producer
**Email:** chris@angelworldentertainment.com
**IMDB:** www.imdb.com/name/nm3786007
**Assistant:** Christopher Tisa

### Max Mai
**Title:** Development Associate
**Email:** max@angelworldentertainment.com
**IMDB:** www.imdb.com/name/nm4221777

### John Michaels
**Title:** Head Production/Executive Producer

## ANIMUS FILMS

914 Hauser Boulevard
Los Angeles, CA 90036

**Phone:** 323-988-5557
**Fax:** 323-571-3361
**Email:** info@animusfilms.com
**Website:** www.animusfilms.com
**IMDB:** www.imdb.com/company/co0092860

**Submission Policy:** Accepts query letter from
unproduced, unrepresented writers
**Genre:** Memoir & True Stories, Thriller
**Year Established:** 2003

### Jim Young
**Title:** Producer
**Phone:** 323-988-5557
**Email:** info@animusfilms.com
**IMDB:** www.imdb.com/name/nm1209063

## ANNAPURNA PICTURES

**Phone:** 310-724-5678
**Fax:** 310-724-8111
**Website:** www.annapurnapics.com
**IMDB:** www.imdb.com/company/co0323215

**Submission Policy:** Does not accept any unsolicited
material
**Genre:** Action, Comedy, Crime, Drama, Feature
Films, Memoir & True Stories, Thriller, TV Drama
**Focus:** Feature Films

### David Distenfeld
**Title:** Development Executive
**IMDB:** www.imdb.com/name/nm3367048

### Megan Ellison
**Title:** Producer
**IMDB:** www.imdb.com/name/nm2691892

## ANNE CARLUCCI PRODUCTIONS

9200 Sunset Boulevard
Penthouse 20
Los Angeles, CA 90069

**Phone:** 310-550-9545
**Fax:** 310-550-8471
**Email:** acprod@sbcglobal.net
**IMDB:** www.imdb.com/company/co0094863

**Submission Policy:** Accepts query letter from unproduced, unrepresented writers
**Genre:** Memoir & True Stories

**Anne Carlucci**
**Title:** Executive Producer
**Phone:** 310-913-5626
**Email:** acprod@sbcglobal.net
**IMDB:** www.imdb.com/name/nm0138243

## AN OLIVE BRANCH PRODUCTIONS, INC.

12400 Wilshire Boulevard, Suite 1275
Los Angeles, CA 90025

**Phone:** 310-860-6088
**Fax:** 310-362-8922
**Email:** info@anolivebranchmedia.com
**Website:** www.anolivebranchmedia.com
**IMDB:** www.imdb.com/company/
co0055694imdb.com/company/co0308344

**Submission Policy:** Accepts scripts from produced or represented writers
**Genre:** Drama
**Focus:** Feature Films

**Cybill Lui**
**Title:** Principal/Producer
**Phone:** 310-860-6088
**Email:** cybill@anolivebranchmedia.com
**IMDB:** www.imdb.com/name/nm3359236

**George Zakk**
**Title:** Principal/Producer
**Phone:** 310-860-6088
**Email:** george@anolivebranchmedia.com
**IMDB:** www.imdb.com/name/nm0952327

## ANOMALY ENTERTAINMENT

10990 Wilshire Boulevard
Eighth Floor
Los Angeles, CA 90024

**Genre:** Documentary, Drama, Feature Films, Memoir & True Stories, Period, TV
**Focus:** Feature Films, Television

**Stephen J. Rivele**
**Title:** President & CEO
**IMDB:** www.imdb.com/name/nm0729151

**Christopher Wilkinson**
**Title:** Principal
**IMDB:** www.imdb.com/name/nm0929349

## ANONYMOUS CONTENT

3532 Hayden Avenue
Culver City, CA 90232

**Phone:** 310-558-3667
**Fax:** 310-558-4212
**Email:** filmtv@anonymouscontent.com
**Website:** www.anonymouscontent.com

**Submission Policy:** Accepts query letter from unproduced, unrepresented writers via email
**Genre:** Action, Comedy, Crime, Drama, Family, Memoir & True Stories, Thriller, TV Drama, TV Sitcom
**Focus:** Feature Films, TV, Media (Commercials/Branding/Marketing)
**Year Established:** 1999

**Matt DeRoss**
**Title:** Vice-President, Features
**Phone:** 310-558-3667
**Email:** mattd@anonymouscontent.com
**IMDB:** www.imdb.com/name/nm2249185

**Steve Golin**
**Title:** CEO

**Emmeline Yang**
**Title:** Director of Development
**Phone:** 310-558-3667
**IMDB:** www.imdb.com/name/nm2534779

## ANTIDOTE FILMS

PO Box 150566
Brooklyn, NY 11215-0566

**Phone:** 646-486-4344
**Email:** info@antidotefilms.com
**Website:** www.antidotefilms.com

**Submission Policy:** Does not accept any unsolicited material
**Genre:** Documentary, Feature Films
**Focus:** Feature Films
**Year Established:** 2000

**James Debbs**
Title: Supervisor
Phone: 646-486-4344 x305
IMDB: www.imdb.com/name/nm0999455

**Takeo Hori**
Title: Vice President
Phone: 646-486-4344 x300
IMDB: www.imdb.com/name/nm0394659

**Gerry Kim**
Title: Director of Operation

**Jeffrey Levy-Hinte**
Title: President
Phone: 646-486-4344 x301
Email: jeff@antidotefilms.com
IMDB: www.imdb.com/name/nm0506664

## APATOW PRODUCTIONS

11788 W Pico Blvd
Los Angeles, CA 90064

Phone: 310-943-4400
Fax: 310-479-0750
IMDB: http://www.imdb.com/company/
co0073081/?ref_=fn_al_co_1

Submission Policy: Does not accept any unsolicited material
Genre: Action, Comedy, Documentary, Drama, Feature Films, Romance, TV, TV Drama
Focus: Feature Films, Television
Year Established: 2000

**Judd Apatow**
Title: Writer, Director, Producer, President
IMDB: http://www.imdb.com/name/
nm0031976/?ref_=fn_al_nm_1
Assistant: Amanda Glaze, Rob Turbovsky, Michael Lewen

## APERTURE ENTERTAINMENT

7620 Lexington Avenue
West Hollywood, CA 90046

Phone: 323-848-4069
Email: agasst@aperture-ent.com
IMDB: www.imdb.com/company/co0265611

Submission Policy: Accepts scripts from unproduced, unrepresented writers
Genre: Action, Fantasy, Horror, Science Fiction, Thriller

Focus: Feature Films, TV
Year Established: 2009

**Adam Goldworm**
Title: Manager/Producer
Phone: 323-848-4069
Email: adam@aperture-ent.com
IMDB: www.imdb.com/name/nm0326411
Assistant: David Okubo

## APPIAN WAY

9255 Sunset Boulevard
West Hollywood, CA 90069

Phone: 310-300-1390
Fax: 310-300-1388

Submission Policy: Does not accept any unsolicited material
Genre: Crime, Detective, Drama, Feature Films, Memoir & True Stories, Thriller
Focus: Feature Films

**Madison Ainley**
Title: Assistant

**Aaron Criswell**
Title: Development
IMDB: www.imdb.com/name/nm2082839

**Jennifer Davisson Killoran**
Title: Head of Production
IMDB: www.imdb.com/name/nm2248832

**Leonardo DiCaprio**
Title: CEO
IMDB: www.imdb.com/name/nm0000138

**Alex Mace**
Title: Executive
IMDB: www.imdb.com/name/nm2858852

**Nathaniel Posey**
Title: Executive

**John Ridley**
Title: Vice President of Production
IMDB: www.imdb.com/name/nm4244643

## APPLE AND HONEY FILM CORP

9190 West Olympic Boulevard, Suite 363
Beverly Hills, CA 90212

Phone: 310-556-5639
Fax: 310-556-1295

**Email:** quarrel@pacbell.net
**IMDB:** www.imdb.com/company/co0069050

**Submission Policy:** Accepts query letter from unproduced, unrepresented writers via email

**David Brandes**
**Title:** Writer, Producer, Director
**Phone:** 310-556-5639
**Email:** quarrel@pacbell.net
**IMDB:** www.imdb.com/name/nm0104617

## APPLESEED ENTERTAINMENT

7715 Sunset Blvd
Ste 101
Hollywood, CA 90046

**Phone:** 818-718-6000
**Fax:** 818-556-5610
**Email:** queries@appleseedent.com
**Website:** www.appleseedent.com/
**IMDB:** www.imdb.com/company/co0176039

**Submission Policy:** Accepts query letter from unproduced, unrepresented writers via email
**Genre:** Comedy, Drama, Family, Feature Films

**Lynne Moses**
**Title:** Executive
**Email:** lynne@appleseedent.com
**IMDB:** www.imdb.com/name/nm1030988

**Ben Moses**
**Title:** Executive
**Email:** ben@appleseedent.com
**IMDB:** www.imdb.com/name/nm0608558

## ARC LIGHT FILMS

8447 Wilshire Boulevard, Suite 101
Beverly Hills, CA 90211

**Phone:** 310-777-8855
**Fax:** 310-777-8882
**Email:** info@arclightfilms.com
**Website:** www.arclightfilms.com

**Submission Policy:** Accepts query letter from unproduced, unrepresented writers via email
**Focus:** Feature Films

**Mike Gabrawy**
**Title:** Vice-President Creative
**Phone:** 310-475-2330

**Email:** info@arclightfilms.com
**IMDB:** www.imdb.com/name/nm0300166

**Gary Hamilton**
**Title:** Managing Director
**Phone:** 310-528-5888
**Email:** gary@arclightfilms.com
**IMDB:** www.imdb.com/name/nm0357861

## ARENAS ENTERTAINMENT

3375 Barham Boulevard
Los Angeles, CA 90068

**Phone:** 323-785-5555
**Fax:** 323-785-5560
**Email:** general@arenasgroup.com
**Website:** www.arenasgroup.com
**IMDB:** www.imdb.com/company/co0051527

**Submission Policy:** Accepts query letter from unproduced, unrepresented writers via email
**Focus:** Feature Films
**Year Established:** 1988

**Santiago Pozo**
**Title:** CEO
**IMDB:** www.imdb.com/name/nm0694815

## ARGONAUT PICTURES

**Phone:** 310-359-8481
**Website:** www.argonautpictures.com

**Submission Policy:** Accepts query letter from unproduced, unrepresented writers
**Genre:** Drama, Feature Films
**Focus:** Feature Films

**Giovanni Agnelli**
**Title:** Owner
**IMDB:** www.imdb.com/name/nm1278301

**Scott Bloom**
**Title:** Owner
**IMDB:** www.imdb.com/name/nm0089231

**Carter Hall**
**Title:** Executive Assistant
**Email:** carter@argonautpictures.com
**IMDB:** www.imdb.com/name/nm3050292

**Paul Marashlian**
**Title:** Senior VP Development
**Email:** Paul@argonautpictures.com
**IMDB:** www.imdb.com/name/nm2281671

**Karim Mashouf**
Title: Owner
IMDB: www.imdb.com/name/nm3196690

**Manny Mashouf**
Title: Owner
IMDB: www.imdb.com/name/nm3196705

## ARIESCOPE PICTURES

10750 Cumpston St
North Hollywood, CA 91601

Email: info@ariescope.com
Website: www.ariescope.com

Submission Policy: Accepts query letter from
unproduced, unrepresented writers
Genre: Comedy, Crime, Fantasy, Horror, Romance,
Thriller, TV, TV Drama
Focus: Feature Films, Television

**Will Barratt**
Title: Principal
IMDB: www..imdb.com/name/nm1701139

**Adam Green**
Title: Principal
IMDB: www.imdb.com/name/nm1697112

**Cory Neal**
Title: Principal
IMDB: www.imdb.com/name/nm1425628

## ARS NOVA

511 West 54th Street
New York, NY 10019

Phone: 212-586-4200
Fax: 212-489-1908
Email: info@arsnovaent.com
Website: www.arsnovaent.com
IMDB: www.imdb.com/company/co0176042

Submission Policy: Accepts scripts from
unproduced, unrepresented writers
Genre: Action, Comedy, Fantasy, Myth, Science
Fiction

**Jillian Apfelbaum**
Title: Producer
Phone: 212-586-4200
Email: japfelbaum@arsnovaent.com
IMDB: www.imdb.com/name/nm2249752

**Jon Steingart**
Title: Producer
Phone: 212-586-4200
Email: japfelbaum@arsnovaent.com
IMDB: www.imdb.com/name/nm0826050

## ARTFIRE FILMS

740 N. La Brea Ave.
Hollywood, CA 90038

Phone: 323-937-7188
Fax: 323-937-6713
Email: contact@artfirefilms.com
Website: http://artfirefilms.com/
IMDB: http://www.imdb.com/company/
co0188290/?ref_=fn_al_co_1

Submission Policy: Does not accept any unsolicited
material
Genre: Action, Comedy, Crime, Documentary,
Drama, Feature Films, Horror, Period, Romance,
Science Fiction
Focus: Feature Films
Year Established: 2007

**Jennah Dirksen**
Title: Creative Executive
IMDB: http://www.imdb.com/name/
nm3302694/?ref_=fn_al_nm_1

**Dan Fireman**
Title: Principal
IMDB: http://www.imdb.com/name/
nm2379207/?ref_=fn_al_nm_1

**Ara Katz**
Title: Producer
IMDB: http://www.imdb.com/name/
nm1433420/?ref_=fn_al_nm_1

**Andy Spellman**
Title: Executive Producer

**Arthur Spigel**
Title: Principal
IMDB: http://www.imdb.com/name/
nm1742493/?ref_=fn_al_nm_1

## ARTICLE 19 FILMS

247 Centre Street, Suite 7W
New York, NY 10013

Phone: 212-777-1987
Fax: 212-777-2585

**Email:** article19films@gmail.com
**Website:** http://article19films.com
**IMDB:** www.imdb.com/company/co0164965

**Submission Policy:** Accepts query letter from unproduced, unrepresented writers
**Genre:** Memoir & True Stories

**Filippo Bozotti**
**Title:** Producer-Executive
**Phone:** 212-777-1987
**Email:** article19films@gmail.com
**IMDB:** www.imdb.com/name/nm1828075

## ARTISTS PRODUCTION GROUP (APG)

9348 Civic Center Drive, 2nd Floor
Beverly Hills, CA 90210

**Phone:** 310-300-2400
**Fax:** 310-300-2424
**IMDB:** www.imdb.com/company/co0024601

**Submission Policy:** Accepts scripts from produced or represented writers

**Chris George**
**Title:** Creative Executive
**Phone:** 310-300-2400
**IMDB:** www.imdb.com/name/nm0313383

## ARTISTS PUBLIC DOMAIN

225 West 13th Street
New York, NY 10011

**Email:** info@artistspublicdomain.com
**Website:** www.artistspublicdomain.com

**Submission Policy:** Accepts query letter from unproduced, unrepresented writers
**Genre:** Comedy, Drama, Family, Feature Films, Memoir & True Stories, Romance, Sociocultural, Thriller
**Focus:** Feature Films

**Andrew Adair**
**Title:** Head of Production
**IMDB:** www.imdb.com/name/nm4253715

**Hunter Gray**
**Title:** Producer
**IMDB:** www.imdb.com/name/nm0336683

**Alex Orlovsky**
**Title:** Producer
**IMDB:** www.imdb.com/name/nm0650164

## A. SMITH & COMPANY PRODUCTIONS

9911 West Pico Boulevard, Suite 250
Los Angeles, CA 90035

**Phone:** 310-432-4800
**Fax:** 310-551-3085
**Email:** info@asmithco.com
**Website:** www.asmithco.com
**IMDB:** www.imdb.com/company/co0095150

**Submission Policy:** Accepts query letter from unproduced, unrepresented writers via email

**Christmas Rini**
**Title:** VP, Development
**Phone:** 310-432-4800
**Email:** info@asmithco.com
**IMDB:** www.imdb.com/name/nm2859471

**Arthur Smith**
**Title:** CEO
**Phone:** 310-432-4800
**Email:** info@asmithco.com
**IMDB:** wwwimdb.com/name/nm0807368

## ASYLUM ENTERTAINMENT

15301 Ventura Blvd
Suite 400 Building B
Sherman Oaks, CA 91403

**Phone:** 310-696-4401
**Fax:** 310-696-4891
**Email:** info@asylument.com
**Website:** www.asylument.com

**Submission Policy:** Accepts scripts from unproduced, unrepresented writers
**Genre:** Action, Crime, Fantasy, Horror, Memoir & True Stories, Science Fiction, Thriller, TV Drama

**Marielle Skouras**
**Title:** Director of Development
**Phone:** 310-696-4401
**Email:** info@asylument.com
**IMDB:** www.imdb.com/name/nm4413245

## ATLAS ENTERTAINMENT (PRODUCTION BRANCH OF MOSAIC)

9200 Sunset Boulevard, 10th Floor
Los Angeles, CA 90069

Phone: 310-786-8900
Fax: 310-777-2185
IMDB: www.imdb.com/company/co0028338

**Submission Policy:** Does not accept any unsolicited material
**Focus:** Feature Films, TV

**Alex Gartner**
Title: Producer
Phone: 310-786-8105
IMDB: www.imdb.com/name/nm0308672

**Andy Horwitz**
Title: Vice President (Motion Pictures & Television)
Phone: 310-786-4948
IMDB: www.imdb.com/name/nm2191045

**Jake Kurily**
Title: Vice President (Motion Pictures & Television)
Phone: 310-786-8974
IMDB: www.imdb.com/name/nm2464228

## ATLAS MEDIA CORPORATION

242 West 36th Street, 11th Floor
New York, NY, 10018

Phone: 212-714-0222
Fax: 212-714-0240
Email: info@atlasmediacorp.com
Website: www.atlasmediacorp.com
IMDB: www.imdb.com/company/co0280783

**Submission Policy:** Accepts query letter from produced or represented writers
**Genre:** Memoir & True Stories

**Glen Freyer**
Title: Sr. Vice-President Development
Phone: 212-714-0222
Email: info@atlasmediacorp.com
IMDB: www.imdb.com/name/nm0294662

**Andrew Jacobs**
Title: Director Of Development
Phone: 212-714-0222
Email: info@atlasmediacorp.com

## ATMOSPHERE ENTERTAINMENT MM, LLC

4751 Wilshire, Boulevard, 3rd Floor
Los Angeles, CA, 90010

Phone: 323-549-4350
Fax: 323-549-9832
IMDB: www.imdb.com/company/co0014103

**Submission Policy:** Accepts scripts from produced or represented writers
**Genre:** Fantasy, Horror, Thriller

**David Hopwood**
Title: SVP, Film & TV Development
Phone: 323-549-4350
IMDB: www.imdb.com/name/nm2055027

## AUTOMATIC PICTURES

5225 Wilshire Blvd
Suite 525
Los Angeles, CA 90036

Phone: 323-935-1800
Fax: 323-935-8040
Email: automaticstudio@mail.com
Website: www.automaticpictures.net

**Submission Policy:** Accepts query letter from unproduced, unrepresented writers via email
**Genre:** Fantasy
**Focus:** Video Games

**Nate Barlow**
Title: VP of New Media
Email: nate@automaticpictures.net
IMDB: www.imdb.com/name/nm0055269

**Frank Beddor**
Title: Principal
IMDB: www.imdb.com/name/nm0065980
Assistant: Bo Liebman

**Liz Cavalier**
Title: Creative Executive
IMDB: www.imdb.com/name/nm2248983

## AUTOMATIK ENTERTAINMENT

8322 Beverly Boulevard, Suite 303C
Los Angeles, CA 90048

Phone: 323-677-2486
Fax: 323-657-5354
Email: info@imglobalfilm.com
Website: www.imglobalfilm.com
IMDB: www.imdb.com/company/co0323227

**Submission Policy:** Does not accept any unsolicited material

Genre: Action, Comedy, Fantasy, Thriller
Focus: Feature Films, TV

**Bailey Conway**
Title: Vice President, Production and Development
Phone: 323-677-2486
Email: office@automatikent.com
IMDB: www.imdb.com/name/nm2811848

**Brian Kavanaugh-Jones**
Title: President-Producer
Phone: 323-677-2486
Email: office@automatikent.com
IMDB: www.imdb.com/name/nm2271939
Assistant: Alex Saks

## BAD HAT HARRY

10201 West Pico Boulevard
Building 50
Los Angeles, CA 90064

Phone: 310-369-2080
Email: reception@badhatharry.com
Website: www.badhatharry.com
IMDB: www.imdb.com/company/co0057712

Submission Policy: Accepts scripts from produced or represented writers
Genre: Action, Fantasy, Myth, Science Fiction, Thriller, TV Drama

**Mark Berliner**
Title: Vice President (Development)
Phone: 310-369-2080
IMDB: www.imdb.com/name/nm2249392

**Bryan Singer**
Title: Chief Executive Officer
Phone: 310-369-2080
IMDB: www.imdb.com/name/nm0001741

## BAD ROBOT

1221 Olympic Boulevard
Santa Monica, CA 90404

Phone: 310-664-3456
Fax: 310-664-3457
Website: http://www.badrobot.com
IMDB: wwwimdb.com/company/co0021593

Submission Policy: Does not accept any unsolicited material
Genre: Action, Drama, Fantasy, Science Fiction, TV

Drama
Focus: Feature Films, TV

**J.J. Abrams**
Title: Chairman (Chief Executive Officer)
Phone: 310-664-3456
IMDB: www.imdb.com/name/nm0009190
Assistant: Morgan Dameron

**David Baronoff**
Title: Executive (New Media, Film & Television
IMDB: www.imdb.com/name/nm2343623

**Bryan Burk**
Title: Partner, Executive Vice President
IMDB: www.imdb.com/name/nm1333357
Assistant: Max Taylor

**Jonathan Cohen**
Title: Executive
Assistant: Veronica Baker

**Kevin Jarzynski**
Title: Executive
IMDB: www.imdb.com/name/nm1704653
Assistant: Veronica Baker

**Kathy Lingg**
Title: Head of Television
IMDB: www.imdb.com/name/nm2489727
Assistant: Matthew Owens

**Lindsey Paulson Weber**
Title: Head of Film
IMDB: www.imdb.com/name/nm1439829
Assistant: Corrine Aquino

**Athena Wickham**
Title: Executive of Television
IMDB: www.imdb.com/name/nm2204043
Assistant: Casey Haver

## BALDWIN ENTERTAINMENT GROUP, LTD.

3000 West Olympic Boulevard Suite 2510
Santa Monica, CA

Phone: 310-243-6634
Email: info@baldwinent.com
Website: www.baldwinent.com
IMDB: www.imdb.com/company/co0057712mdb.com/company/co0145519

Submission Policy: Does not accept any unsolicited material
Genre: Action, Comedy, Drama, Memoir & True

Stories, Romance
**Focus:** Feature Films
**Year Established:** 2009

**Karen Baldwin**
**Title:** Senior Vice-President
**Phone:** 310-243-6634
**IMDB:** www.imdb.com/name/nm0049945

**Howard Baldwin**
**Title:** Producer/President
**Phone:** 310-243-6634
**IMDB:** www.imdb.com/name/nm0049920

**Ryan Wuerfel**
**Title:** Creative Executive
**Phone:** 310-243-6634
**Email:** ryan@baldwinent.com
**IMDB:** www.imdb.com/name/nm3601274

## BALLYHOO, INC.

6738 Wedgewood Place
Los Angeles, CA 90068

**Phone:** 323-874-3396

**Submission Policy:** Accepts scripts from unproduced, unrepresented writers
**Genre:** Action, Comedy, Feature Films
**Focus:** Feature Films

**Michael Besman**
**Title:** Producer
**Phone:** 323-874-3396
**IMDB:** www.imdb.com/name/nm0078698

## BALTIMORE PICTURES

8306 Wilshire Blvd
PMB 1012
Beverly Hills, CA 90211

**Phone:** 310-234-8988
**Website:** www.levinson.com/index_bsc.htm
**IMDB:** www.imdb.com/company/co0038108

**Submission Policy:** Does not accept any unsolicited material
**Genre:** Comedy, Crime, Drama, Feature Films, Romance, Science Fiction, Thriller
**Focus:** Feature Films

**Barry Levinson**
**Title:** Principal (Director/Producer/Writer)
**IMDB:** www.imdb.com/name/nm0001469

**Jason Sosnoff**
**Title:** Director Of Development
**IMDB:** www.imdb.com/name/nm0815369

## BANDITO BROTHERS

3115 South La Cienega Blvd.
Los Angeles, CA 90016

**Phone:** 310-559-5404
**Fax:** 310-559-5230
**Email:** info@banditobrothers.com
**Website:** www.banditiobrothers.com

**Genre:** Action, Comedy, Drama, Fantasy, Feature Films, Science Fiction, Thriller
**Focus:** Feature Films

**Suzanne Hargrove**
**Title:** Managing Director
**IMDB:** www.imdb.com/name/nm2597628

**Max Leitman**
**Title:** COO
**IMDB:** www.imdb.com/name/nm2649648

**Mike McCoy**
**Title:** CEO & Creative Director
**IMDB:** www.imdb.com/name/nm0566788

**Jay Pollak**
**Title:** Managing Director & Executive Producer

**Jacob Rosenberg**
**Title:** Chief Technology Officer
**IMDB:** www.imdb.com/name/nm0742230

**Scott Waugh**
**Title:** Founder
**IMDB:** www.imdb.com/name/nm0915304

## BARNSTORM FILMS

73 Market Street
Venice, CA 90291

**Phone:** 310-396-5937
**Fax:** 310-450-4988
**Email:** tbtb@comcast.net
**IMDB:** www.imdb.com/company/co0044065

**Submission Policy:** Accepts query letter from unproduced, unrepresented writers

**Tony Bill**
**Title:** Producer/Director
**Phone:** 310-396-5937

**Email:** tbtb@comcast.net
**IMDB:** www.imdb.com/name/nm0082300

## BARNSTORM PICTURES LLC

8524 Fontana Street
Downey, CA 90241

**IMDB:** www.imdb.com/company/co0221137

**Submission Policy:** Does not accept any unsolicited material
**Genre:** Feature Films
**Focus:** Feature Films

**Elaine Chin**
**Title:** Producer
**IMDB:** www.imdb.com/name/nm1227183

**Justin Lin**
**Title:** Producer/Director
**IMDB:** www.imdb.com/name/nm0510912

## BARRY FILMS

4081 Redwood Avenue
Los Angeles, CA 90066

**Phone:** 310-871-3392
**Email:** mail@barryfilms.com
**Website:** www.barryfilms.com
**IMDB:** www.imdb.com/company/co0075789

**Submission Policy:** Accepts query letter from unproduced, unrepresented writers via email
**Genre:** Action, Animation, Detective, Fantasy, Romance
**Focus:** Feature Films

**Benito Mueller**
**Title:** Producer
**Phone:** 310-871-3392
**Email:** benito@barryfilms.com
**IMDB:** www.imdb.com/name/nm1762339

## BASRA ENTERTAINMENT

68-444 Perez Road, Suite O
Cathedral City, CA 92234

**Phone:** 760-324-9855
**Fax:** 760-324-9035
**Email:** info@basraentertainment.com
**Website:** www.basraentertainment.com
**IMDB:** www.imdb.com/company/co0092056

**Submission Policy:** Accepts query letter from unproduced, unrepresented writers
**Year Established:** 2002

**Daniela Ryan**
**Title:** Producer
**Phone:** 760-324-9855
**Email:** daniela@basraentertainment.com
**IMDB:** www.imdb.com/name/nm0752491

## BAUER MARTINEZ STUDIOS

601 Cleveland Street, Suite 501
Clearwater, FL 33755

**Phone:** 727-210-1408
**Fax:** 727-210-1470
**Email:** cindy@bauermartinez.com
**Website:** http://www.bauermartinez.com/
**IMDB:** www.imdb.com/company/co0025891

**Submission Policy:** Accepts query letter from unproduced, unrepresented writers

**Phillipe Martinez**
**Title:** Producer/CEO
**Phone:** 727-210-1408
**Email:** cindy@cinepropictures.com
**IMDB:** www.imdb.com/name/nm0553662

## BAY FILMS

631 Colorado Avenue
Santa Monica, CA 90401

**Phone:** 310-319-6565
**Fax:** 310-319-6570

**Submission Policy:** Does not accept any unsolicited material
**Genre:** Action, Comedy, Drama, Fantasy, Feature Films, Science Fiction, Thriller
**Focus:** Feature Films

**Michael Bay**
**Title:** CEO
**IMDB:** www.imdb.com/name/nm0000881
**Assistant:** Talley Singer

**Matthew Cohan**
**Title:** Vice President of Development
**IMDB:** www,imdb.com/name/nm0169134

**Michael Kase**
**Title:** VP of Production
**IMDB:** www.imdb.com/name/nm0440476

## BAYONNE ENTERTAINMENT

6560 West Sunset Boulevard Ninth Floor
West Hollywood, CA 90069

**Phone:** 310-777-1940
**Fax:** 310-889-9323
**Email:** assistant@bayonne-ent.com

**Submission Policy:** Accepts query letter from
produced or represented writers
**Genre:** Comedy, Drama, Fantasy, Science Fiction,
TV, TV Drama, TV Sitcom
**Focus:** Television

### Rob Lee
**Title:** President
**IMDB:** www.imdb.com/name/nm0498098

## BAZELEVS PRODUCTION

Pudovkina St
6/1
Moscow 119285
Russia

**Phone:** +7 495-223-04-00
**Email:** film@bazelevs.ru
**Website:** www.bazelevs.ru
**IMDB:** www.imdb.com/company/co0042742

**Submission Policy:** Does not accept any unsolicited
material
**Genre:** Feature Films

### Timur Bekmambetov
**Title:** CEO/Director/Producer
**Phone:** +7 495-223-04-00
**Email:** film@bazelevs.ru
**IMDB:** www.imdb.com/name/nm0067457

## BBC FILMS

Room 6023
BBC Television Centre
Wood Lane, London W12 7RJ
UK

**Phone:** +44 20-8576-7265
**Fax:** +44 20-8576-7268
**Website:** www.bbc.co.uk/bbcfilms/
**IMDB:** www.imdb.com/company/co0103694

**Submission Policy:** Accepts scripts from
unproduced, unrepresented writers
**Genre:** Action, Comedy, Crime, Detective, Fantasy,
Horror, Memoir & True Stories, Myth, Romance,
Science Fiction, Thriller, TV Drama, TV Sitcom
**Focus:** Feature Films, TV

### Jamie Laurenson
**Title:** Development
**Phone:** +44 20-8576-7265
**IMDB:** www.imdb.com/name/nm0491191

### Joe Oppenheimer
**Title:** Development
**Phone:** +44 20-8576-7265
**IMDB:** www.imdb.com/name/nm0649189

## BCDF PICTURES

P.O. Box 849
Kerhonkson, NY 12446

**Phone:** 212.945-8618
**Fax:** 917-591-7589
**Email:** submissions@bcdfpictures.com/
info@bcdfpictures.com
**Website:** www.bcdfpictures.com

**Submission Policy:** Accepts query letter from
unproduced, unrepresented writers via email
**Genre:** Comedy, Crime, Drama, Family, Feature
Films, Romance, Thriller
**Focus:** Feature Films

### Claude Dal Farra
**Title:** Principal
**IMDB:** www.imdb.com/name/nm3894387

### Brice Dal Farra
**Title:** Principal
**IMDB:** www.imdb.com/name/nm3894454/

### Lauren Munsch
**Title:** Producer
**IMDB:** www.imdb.com/name/nm3907323

### Paul Prokop
**Title:** Executive Producer
**IMDB:** www.imdb.com/name/nm2373782

## BEACON PICTURES

2900 Olympic Blvd
2nd Floor
Santa Monica, CA 90404

**Phone:** 310-260-7000
**Fax:** 310-260-7096

**Email:** contactus@beaconpictures.com
**Website:** www.beaconpictures.com

**Submission Policy:** Does not accept any unsolicited material
**Genre:** Action, Comedy, Crime, Detective, Drama, Family, Fantasy, Feature Films, Romance, Science Fiction, Thriller, TV, TV Drama
**Focus:** Feature Films, Television
**Year Established:** 1990

**Peter Almond**
Title: Producer

**Armyan Berstein**
Title: Chairman
IMDB: www.imdb.com/name/nm0077000

**Jeffrey Crooks**
Title: Director of Special Projects
IMDB: www.imdb.com/name/nm3715349

**Suzann Ellis**
Title: President
Email: sellis@beaconpictures.com
IMDB: www.imdb.com/name/nm0255104

**Glenn Klekowski**
Title: Beacon TV
IMDB: www.imdb.com/name/nm0459192

**Rudy Langlais**
Title: Producer

**Mark Pennell**
Title: Producer
Email: mpennell@beaconpictures.com
IMDB: www.imdb.com/name/nm0672075

**Joeanna Sayler**
Title: Beacon TV

## BEE HOLDER PRODUCTIONS

**Phone:** 310-860-1005
**Fax:** 310-860-1007
**Email:** asst@beeholder.com

**Submission Policy:** Accepts query letter from unproduced, unrepresented writers
**Genre:** Comedy, Crime, Detective, Documentary, Drama, Feature Films, Thriller
**Focus:** Feature Films

**Dan Fugardi**
Title: Director of Development
Email: dan@beeholder.com
IMDB: www.imdb.com/name/nm2809882

**John Hill**
Title: Assistant
IMDB: www.imdb.com/name/nm4787026

**Chad Hively**
Title: Assistant
Email: chad@beeholder.com
IMDB: www.imdb.com/name/nm3510973

**Steven Lee Jones**
Title: President
IMDB: www.imdb.com/name/nm2831867

**Michelle Jones**
Title: Executive
IMDB: www.imdb.com/name/nm4786947

## BEFORE THE DOOR PICTURES

1138 Hyperion Ave
Los Angeles, CA 90029

**Phone:** 323-644-5525
**Fax:** 323-644-5528
**Email:** staff@beforethedoor.com
**Website:** www.beforethedoor.com/
**IMDB:** www.imdb.com/company/co0271126

**Submission Policy:** Does not accept any unsolicited material
**Genre:** Action, Crime, Drama, Feature Films, Science Fiction, Thriller, TV, TV Sitcom
**Focus:** Feature Films, TV, New Media

**Sean Akers**
Title: Development / Web
IMDB: www.imdb.com/name/nm3577109

**Neal Dodson**
Title: Partner / Producer
IMDB: www.imdb.com/name/nm0230306

**Corey Moosa**
Title: Partner / Producer
IMDB: www.imdb.com/name/nm0602161

**Zachary Quinto**
Title: Partner / Producer
IMDB: www.imdb.com/name/nm0704270

## BELISARIUS PRODUCTIONS

1901 Avenue of the Stars Second Floor
Los Angeles, CA 90067

**Phone:** 310-461-1361
**Fax:** 310-461-1362

**Submission Policy:** Does not accept any unsolicited
material
**Genre:** Crime, Detective, Drama, Thriller, TV, TV
Drama
**Focus:** Television

**David Bellisario**
**Title:** Producer
**IMDB:** www.imdb.com/name/nm0069072

**Donald Bellisario**
**Title:** Executive Producer
**IMDB:** www.imdb.com/name/nm0069074

**Shane Brennan**
**Title:** Producer
**IMDB:** www.imdb.com/name/nm0107402

**Chas Floyd Johnson**
**Title:** Co-Executive Producer
**IMDB:** www.imdb.com/name/nm0424759

**Mark Horowitz**
**Title:** Co-Executive Producer
**IMDB:** www.imdb.com/name/nm0395317

**John C. Kelley**
**Title:** Co-Executive Producer
**IMDB:** www.imdb.com/name/nm0445931

## BELLADONNA PRODUCTIONS

164 West 25th Street 9th Floor
New York, NY 10001

**Phone:** 212-807-0108
**Fax:** 212-807-6263
**Email:** mail@belladonna.bz
**Website:** www.belladonna.bz
**IMDB:** www.imdb.com/company/co0003224

**Submission Policy:** Accepts query letter from
unproduced, unrepresented writers
**Genre:** Comedy, Memoir & True Stories, Thriller
**Year Established:** 1994

**René Bastian**
**Title:** Owner/Producer
**Phone:** 212-807-0108

**Email:** mail@belladonna.bz
**IMDB:** www.imdb.com/name/nm0060459

## BELLWETHER PICTURES

**Submission Policy:** Accepts query letter from
unproduced, unrepresented writers via email
**Genre:** Action, Comedy, Drama, Science Fiction
**Focus:** Feature Films, Media
**Year Established:** 2011

**Kai Cole**
**Title:** Producer/Co-Founder
**IMDB:** www.imdb.com/name/nm474)874

**Joss Whedon**
**Title:** Writer/Producer/Co-Founder
**IMDB:** www.imdb.com/name/nm0923736

## BENAROYA PICTURES

8383 Wilshire Blvd
Suite 310
Beverly Hills, CA 90212
USA

**Phone:** 323-883-0056
**Fax:** 866-220-5520
**Email:** general@benaroyapics.com
**Website:** www.benaroyapics.com
**IMDB:** www.imdb.com/company/co0232586

**Submission Policy:** Accepts query let er from
unproduced, unrepresented writers via email
**Genre:** Drama
**Focus:** Feature Films
**Year Established:** 2006

**Michael Benaroya**
**Title:** Founder-CEO
**Phone:** 323-883-0056
**IMDB:** www.imdb.com/name/nm2918260

**Joe Jenckes**
**Title:** Head of Production
**Phone:** 323-883-0056
**Email:** joel@benaroyapics.com
**IMDB:** www.imdb.com/name/nm3765270

**Clayton Young**
**Title:** Business Development
**Phone:** 323-883-0056
**Email:** clay@benaroyapics.com
**IMDB:** www.imdb.com/name/nm4464240

## BENDERSPINK

5870 West Jefferson Boulevard, Studio E
Los Angeles, CA 90016

**Phone:** 323-904-1800
**Fax:** 323-297-2442
**Email:** info@benderspink.com
**Website:** www.benderspink.com
**IMDB:** www.imdb.com/company/co0044439

**Submission Policy:** Does not accept any unsolicited material
**Genre:** Action, Comedy, Crime, Detective, Fantasy, Horror, Memoir & True Stories, Myth, Romance, Science Fiction, Thriller, TV Drama, TV Sitcom

### Chris Bender
**Title:** Founder
**Phone:** 323-904-1800
**Email:** info@benderspink.com
**IMDB:** www.imdb.com/name/nm0818940

### J.C. Spink
**Title:** Founder
**Phone:** 323-904-1800
**Email:** info@benderspink.com
**IMDB:** www.imdb.com/name/nm0818940

## BERK LANE ENTERTAINMENT

9595 Wilshire Boulevard, Suitee 900
Beverly Hills, CA 90212

**Phone:** 310-300-8410
**Email:** info@berklane.com
**IMDB:** wwwimdb.com/company/co0183891

**Submission Policy:** Does not accept any unsolicited material
**Genre:** Action, Comedy, Crime

### Jason Berk
**Title:** Co-Chairman
**Phone:** 310-300-8410
**Email:** info@berklane.com
**IMDB:** www.imdb.com/name/nm1357809

### Matt Lane
**Title:** Co-Chairman
**Phone:** 310-300-8410
**Email:** info@berklane.com
**IMDB:** www.imdb.com/name/nm2325262

## BERLANTI TELEVISION

500 South Buena Vista Street
Old Animation Building, 2B-5
Burbank, CA 91521

**Phone:** 818-560-4536
**Fax:** 818-560-3931
**IMDB:** www.imdb.com/company/co0192672

**Submission Policy:** Accepts query letter from unproduced, unrepresented writers
**Genre:** TV Drama

### Greg Berlanti
**Title:** Writer-Producer-Director
**IMDB:** www.imdb.com/name/nm0075528

## BERMANBRAUN

2900 West Olympic Boulevard, 3rd Floor
Sanata Monica, CA, 90404

**Phone:** 310-255-7272
**Fax:** 310-255-7058
**Email:** info@bermanbraun.com
**Website:** www.bermanbraun.com
**IMDB:** www.imdb.com/company/co0199425

**Submission Policy:** Does not accept any unsolicited material

### Chris Cowan
**Title:** Executive, Head of Unscripted Television
**Phone:** 310-255-7272
**Email:** info@bermanbraun.com
**IMDB:** www.imdb.com/name/nm0184544

### Andrew Mittman
**Title:** Executive, Head of Feature Film
**Phone:** 310-255-7272
**Email:** info@bermanbraun.com
**IMDB:** www.imdb.com/name/nm3879410

## BERNERO PRODUCTIONS

500 S. Buena Vista Street, Suite 2D-4
Burbank, CA 91521

**Phone:** 818-560-1442
**Email:** info@berneroproductions.com
**Website:** www.berneroproductions.com
**IMDB:** www.imdb.com/company/co0281008

**Submission Policy:** Accepts query letter from unproduced, unrepresented writers via email

**Bob Kim**
Title: Producer
IMDB: www.imdb.com/name/nm2344755

## BETH GROSSBARD PRODUCTIONS

5168 Otis Avenue
Tarzana, CA 91356

Phone: 818-758-2500
Fax: 818-705-7366
Email: bgpix@sbcglobal.net
IMDB: www.imdb.com/company/co0037144

Submission Policy: Accepts query letter from
produced or represented writers
Genre: TV Drama, TV Sitcom

**Beth Grossbard**
Title: Executive Producer
Email: bgpix@sbcglobal.net
IMDB: www.imdb.com/name/nm0343526

## BET NETWORKS

One BET Plaza
1235 W St NE
Washington, DC 20018-1211

Phone: 202-608-2000
Fax: 206-608-2631
Website: www.bet.com
IMDB: www.imdb.com/company/co0176390

Submission Policy: Does not accept any unsolicited
material
Genre: Comedy, Documentary, Drama, Feature
Films, TV, TV Drama, TV Sitcom
Focus: Feature Films, TV

**Rickey Austyn Biggers**
Title: Director of Development
Phone: 310-481-3741
Email: austyn.biggers@bet.net
IMDB: www.imdb.com/name/nm2056137

**Robyn Lattaker-Johnson**
Title: Sr. VP - Development, Original Programming
IMDB: www.imdb.com/name/nm0426464

## BIG FOOT ENTERTAINMENT INC.

1214 Abbot Kinney Boulevard
Los Angeles, CA 90291

Phone: 310-593-4646
Email: info@bigfoot.com
Website: www.bigfoot.com
IMDB: www.imdb.com/company/co0261687

Submission Policy: Accepts query letter from
unproduced, unrepresented writers via email
Genre: Action, Animation, Drama, Fantasy, Myth,
Science Fiction, Thriller
Focus: Feature Films, TV
Year Established: 2004

**Ashley Jordan**
Title: CEO
Email: ashley@bigfootcorp.com
IMDB: www.imdb.com/name/nm1248442

## BIG TALK PRODUCTIONS

26 Nassau Street
London
W1W 7AQ

Phone: +44 (0) 20-7255-1131
Fax: +44 (0) 20-7255-1132
Email: info@bigtalkproductions.com
Website: www.bigtalkproductions.com

Submission Policy: Does not accept any unsolicited
material
Genre: Action, Comedy, Crime, Science Fiction,
TV Drama, TV Sitcom

**Rachael Prior**
Title: Head of Development - Fim
Phone: +44 (0) 20-7255-1131
Email: info@bigtalkproductions.com
IMDB: www.imdb.com/name/nm0975099

## BIRCH TREE ENTERTAINMENT INC.

10620 Southern Highlands Parkway
Suite 110-418
Las Vegas, NV 89141

Phone: 702-858-2782
Fax: 702-583-7928
Email: sales@birchtreefilms.com
Website: http://www.birchtreeentertainment.com/
IMDB: www.imdb.com/company/co0114722

Submission Policy: Accepts scripts from produced
or represented writers
Genre: Action
Focus: Feature Films

**Art Birzneck**
Title: President/CEO
Phone: 702-858-2782
Email: sales@birchtreefilms.com
IMDB: www.imdb.com/name/nm1010723

## BISCAYNE PICTURES

500 South Buena Vista Street
Animation Building
Burbank, CA 91521-1802

Phone: 310-777-2007
Email: info@biscaynepictures.com
Website: www.biscaynepictures.com
IMDB: www.imdb.com/company/co0152645

Submission Policy: Accepts query letter from unproduced, unrepresented writers via email

**Jeff Silver**
Title: President-Producer
Phone: 310-777-2007
Email: info@biscaynepictures.com
IMDB: www.imdb.com/name/nm0798711

## BIX PIX ENTERTAINMENT

3511 West Burbank Boulevard
Burbank, CA 91505

Phone: 818-953-7474
Fax: 818-953-9948
Email: info@bixpix.com
Website: www.bixpix.com
IMDB: www.imdb.com/company/co0187260

Submission Policy: Accepts query letter from unproduced, unrepresented writers
Genre: Fantasy
Year Established: 1998

**Kelli Bixler**
Title: Founder/President/Executive Producer
Phone: 818-953-7474
Email: info@bixpix.com
IMDB: www.imdb.com/name/nm1064778

## BLACK BEAR PICTURES

185 Franklin St
4th Floor
New York, NY 10013

Phone: 212-931-5714
Fax: 212-966-3311

Email: info@blackbearpictures.com
Website: www.blackbearpictures.com

Submission Policy: Accepts query letter from unproduced, unrepresented writers
Genre: Comedy, Drama, Feature Films, Romance
Focus: Feature Films
Year Established: 2011

**Amanda Greenblatt**
Title: Executive Assistant
IMDB: www.imdb.com/name/nm1716375

**Teddy Schwarzman**
Title: Co-Founder/Principal
IMDB: www.imdb.com/name/nm3267061

**Ben Stillman**
Title: Creative Executive
IMDB: www.imdb.com/name/nm4212466

## BLACKLIGHT TRANSMEDIA

9465 Wilshire Boulevard
Beverly Hills, CA 90212

Phone: 310-858-2196
Email: info@blacklighttransmedia.com
Website: www.blacklighttransmedia.com
IMDB: www.imdb.com/company/co0333337

Submission Policy: Accepts scripts from produced or represented writers
Focus: Feature Films

**Justin Catron**
Title: Creative Executive
Phone: 310-858-2196
Email: info@blacklighttransmedia.com
IMDB: www.imdb.com/name/nm2031037

**Zak Kadison**
Title: Founder/CEO
Phone: 310-858-2196
Email: info@blacklighttransmedia.com
IMDB: www.imdb.com/name/nm1780162

## BLACK SHEEP ENTERTAINMENT

11271 Ventura Boulevard, #447
Studio City, CA 91604

Phone: 310-424-5085
Fax: 310-424-7117
Email: info@blacksheept.com
IMDB: www.imdb.com/company/co0029807

**Submission Policy:** Accepts query letter from unproduced, unrepresented writers
**Year Established:** 2009

**Steven Feder**
**Title:** Owner/Writer/Producer/Director
**Phone:** 310-424-5085
**Email:** steven@blacksheepent.com
**IMDB:** www.imdb.com/name/nm027009

## BLEIBERG ENTERTAINMENT

225 South Clark Drive
Beverly Hills, CA 90211

**Phone:** 310-273-0003
**Fax:** 310-273-0007
**Email:** info@bleibergent.com
**Website:** www.bleibergent.com
**IMDB:** www.imdb.com/company/co0165151

**Submission Policy:** Accepts query letter from unproduced, unrepresented writers via email
**Focus:** Feature Films, TV

**Ehud Bleiberg**
**Title:** CEO/Founder
**Phone:** 310-273-0003
**Email:** ehud@bleibergent.com
**IMDB:** www.imdb.com/name/nm0088173

**Nicholas Donnermeyer**
**Title:** Vice-President Acquisitions & Development
**Phone:** 310-273-0003
**Email:** nick@bleibergent.com
**IMDB:** www.imdb.com/name/nm2223730

## BLIND WINK PRODUCTIONS

8 Mills Place 2nd Floor
Pasadena, CA 91105

**Phone:** 626-600-4100
**Email:** info@blindwink.com
**Website:** www.blindwink.com

**Submission Policy:** Does not accept any unsolicited material
**Genre:** Action, Comedy, Crime, Drama, Family, Fantasy, Feature Films, Science Fiction, Thriller
**Focus:** Feature Films

**James Ward Byrkit**
**Title:** Creative & Story
**IMDB:** www.imdb.com/name/nm0126096

**Jonathan Krauss**
**Title:** Head of Film Production & Development
**IMDB:** www.imdb.com/name/nm0470310

**Nils Peyron**
**Title:** Executive Vice President
**IMDB:** www.imdb.com/name/nm3741163

**Josh Pincus**
**Title:** Director of Development

**Will Stahl**
**Title:** Senior Vice President of Gaming Development

**Gore Verbinski**
**Title:** Principal
**IMDB:** www.imdb.com/name/nm0893659

## BLONDIE GIRL PRODUCTIONS

1040 North Las Palmas
Building 40
Los Angeles, CA 90038

**Phone:** 323-860-8610
**Fax:** 323-860-8601
**Email:** jessica@blondiegirlprod.com
**Website:** www.blondiegirlproductions.com/
**IMDB:** www.imdb.com/company/co0261290

**Submission Policy:** Does not accept any unsolicited material
**Genre:** TV
**Focus:** TV

**Jessica Rhodes**
**Title:** Producing Partner
**IMDB:** www.imdb.com/name/nm1224043

**Ashley Tisdale**
**Title:** Principal
**IMDB:** www.imdb.com/name/nm0864308

**Jennifer Tisdale**
**Title:** Coordinator (Development & Production)
**IMDB:** www.imdb.com/name/nm1056279

## BLUEGRASS FILMS

100 Universal City Plaza
Bungalow 4171
Universal City, CA 91608

**Phone:** 818-777-3200
**Fax:** 818-777-0020
**IMDB:** www.imdb.com/company/co0376117

**Submission Policy:** Does not accept any unsolicited
material
**Genre:** Action, Crime, Drama, Fantasy, Romance,
Science Fiction, Thriller
**Focus:** Feature Films, TV

**Michael Clear**
Title: Creative Executive
IMDB: www.imdb.com/name/nm2752795

**Nicholas Nesbitt**
Title: Creative Executive
IMDB: www.imdb.com/name/nm1704779

**Scott Stuber**
Title: Producer
IMDB: www.imdb.com/name/nm0835959

## BLUEPRINT PICTURES

43-45 Charlotte Street
London W1T 1RS
United Kingdom

**Phone:** +44 0207-580-6915
**Fax:** +44 0207-580-6934
**Email:** asst@blueprintpictures.com

**Submission Policy:** Does not accept any unsolicited
material
**Year Established:** 2004

**Graham Broadbent**
Title: Producer
Phone: +44 0207-580-6915
Email: asst@blueprintpictures.com
IMDB: www.imdb.com/name/nm0110357

## BLUE SKY STUDIOS

One American Lane
Greenwich, CT 06831

**Phone:** 203-992-6000
**Fax:** 203-992-6001
**Email:** info@blueskystudios.com
**Website:** www.blueskystudios.com
**IMDB:** www.imdb.com/company/co0047265

**Submission Policy:** Does not accept any unsolicited
material
**Focus:** Feature Films
**Year Established:** 1997

**Lisa Fragner**
Title: Head (Feature Development)
IMDB: www.imdb.com/name/nm0289591

**Chris Wedge**
Title: Vice-President
IMDB: www.imdb.com/name/nm0917188

## BLUMHOUSE PRODUCTIONS

5555 Melrose Avenue
Lucy Bungalow 103
Los Angeles, CA 90038

**Phone:** 323-956-4480
**IMDB:** www.imdb.com/company/co0098315

**Submission Policy:** Accepts query letter from
unproduced, unrepresented writers
**Genre:** Action, Horror, Thriller
**Year Established:** 2000

**Jason Blum**
Title: Producer
IMDB: www.imdb.com/name/nm0089658

**Jessica Hall**
Title: Director Of Development
IMDB: www.imdb.com/name/nm4148859

## BOBKER/KRUGAR FILMS

1416 North La Brea Avenue
Hollywood, CA 90028

**Phone:** 323-469-1440
**Fax:** 323-802-1597
**IMDB:** www.imdb.com/company/co0163148

**Submission Policy:** Accepts query letter from
unproduced, unrepresented writers

**Daniel Bobker**
Title: Producer
IMDB: www.imdb.com/name/nm0090394

**Ehren Kruger**
Title: Writer / Producer
IMDB: www.imdb.com/name/nm0472567

## BOGNER ENTERTAINMENT

269 South Beverly Drive, Suite 8
Beverly Hills, CA 90212

**Phone:** 310-553-0300
**Email:** info.beitv@gmail.com

**Website:** www.bognerentertainment.com
**IMDB:** www.imdb.com/company/co0068550

**Submission Policy:** Accepts scripts from
unproduced, unrepresented writers
**Genre:** Horror, Thriller
**Year Established:** 2000

**Oliver Bogner**
**Title:** Vice-President Development & Casting
**Email:** oliverbogner@gmail.com
**IMDB:** www.imdb.com/name/nm3331124

**Jonathan Bogner**
**Title:** President
**Email:** jsbogner@aol.com
**IMDB:** www.imdb.com/name/nm0091845

## BOKU FILMS

1438 North Gower Street
Box 87
Hollywood, CA 90028

**Phone:** 323-860-7710
**Fax:** 323-860-7706
**IMDB:** www.imdb.com/company/co0047458

**Submission Policy:** Does not accept any unsolicited
material
**Genre:** Thriller, TV Drama

**Alan Poul**
**Title:** Producer/Director
**IMDB:** www.imdb.com/name/nm0693561

## BOLD FILMS

6464 Sunset Boulevard, Suite 800
Los Angeles, CA 90028

**Phone:** 323-769-8900
**Fax:** 323-769-8954
**Email:** info@boldfilms.com
**Website:** www.boldfilms.com
**IMDB:** www.imdb.com/company/co0135575

**Submission Policy:** Does not accept any unsolicited
material
**Genre:** Action, Fantasy, Horror, Thriller
**Focus:** Feature Films, TV

**Garrick Dion**
**Title:** Senior Vice-President of Development
**IMDB:** www.imdb.com/name/nm1887182

**Jon Oakes**
**Title:** Vice-President of Development
**IMDB:** www.imdb.com/name/nm1198333

**Stephanie Wilcox**
**Title:** Creative Executive
**IMDB:** www.imdb.com/name/nm3432545

## BONA FIDE PRODUCTIONS

8899 Beverly Boulevard, Suite 804
Los Angeles, CA 90048

**Phone:** 310-273-6782
**Fax:** 310-273-7821
**IMDB:** www.imdb.com/company/co0063938

**Submission Policy:** Accepts query letter from
unproduced, unrepresented writers
**Focus:** Feature Films
**Year Established:** 1993

**Albert Berger**
**Title:** Producer
**IMDB:** www.imdb.com/name/nm0074100

**Ken Furer**
**Title:** Director of Development
**IMDB:** www.imdb.com/name/nm1738727

## BORDERLINE FILMS

545 8th Ave
11th Floor
New York, NY 10018

**Email:** contact@blfilm.com
**Website:** www.blfilm.com

**Submission Policy:** Does not accept any unsolicited
material
**Genre:** Crime, Detective, Drama, Feature Films,
Thriller
**Focus:** Feature Films

**Antonio Campos**
**Title:** Principal
**IMDB:** www.imdb.com/name/nm1290515

**Sean Durkin**
**Title:** Principal
**IMDB:** www.imdb.com/name/nm1699934

**Josh Mond**
**Title:** Principal
**IMDB:** www.imdb.com/name/nm1317614

## BOSS MEDIA

9440 Santa Monica Boulevard, Suite 400
Beverly Hills, CA 90210

**Phone:** 310-205-9900
**Fax:** 310-205-9909
**IMDB:** www.imdb.com/company/co0341936

**Submission Policy:** Does not accept any unsolicited
material

### Frank Mancuso
**Title:** President
**IMDB:** www.imdb.com/name/nm0541548

### Jennifer Nleves Gordon
**Title:** Vice President (Development)
**IMDB:** www.imdb.com/name/nm2707034

## BOXING CAT PRODUCTIONS

11500 Hart Street
North Hollywood, CA 91605

**Phone:** 818-765-4870
**Fax:** 818-765-4975
**IMDB:** www.imdb.com/company/co0080834

**Submission Policy:** Accepts query letter from
unproduced, unrepresented writers via email
**Genre:** Comedy, Family
**Focus:** Feature Films, TV

### Tim Allen
**Title:** Actor/Producer
**IMDB:** www.imdb.com/name/nm0000741

## BOY WONDER PRODUCTIONS

68 Jay Street, Suite 423
Brooklyn, NY 11201

**Phone:** 347-632-2961
**Fax:** 347-332-6953
**Email:** info@boywonderproductions.net
**Website:** www.boywonderproductions.net
**IMDB:** www.imdb.com/company/co0255525

**Submission Policy:** Accepts query letter from
unproduced, unrepresented writers via email
**Genre:** Memoir & True Stories, TV Drama, TV
Sitcom
**Year Established:** 2006

### Michael Morrisesy
**Title:** President/Producer
**IMDB:** www.imdb.com/name/nm3155184

## BOZ PRODUCTIONS

429 Santa Monica Boulevard, Suite 710
Santa Monica, CA 90401

**Phone:** 323-876-3232
**Email:** bozenga@sbcglobal.net
**Website:** www.bozproductions.com/
**IMDB:** www.imdb.com/company/co0068487

**Submission Policy:** Accepts query letter from
unproduced, unrepresented writers

### Bo Zenga
**Title:** Writer/Director/Producer
**Email:** bozenga@sbcglobal.net
**IMDB:** www.imdb.com/name/nm0954848

## BRANDED FILMS

4000 Warner Boulevard
Building 139, Suite 107
Burbank, CA 91522

**Phone:** 818-954-7969
**Email:** info@branded-films.com
**Website:** www.branded-films.com
**IMDB:** www.imdb.com/company/co0347637

**Submission Policy:** Does not accept any unsolicited
material
**Genre:** Comedy
**Focus:** Feature Films, TV
**Year Established:** 2011

### Beau Bauman
**Title:** President
**Email:** beau@branded-films.com
**IMDB:** www.imdb.com/name/nm0062149

### Russell Brand
**Title:** Founder/Actor/Producer
**IMDB:** www.imdb.com/name/nm1258970
**Assistant:** Lee Sacks

### Nik Linnen
**Title:** Partner-Producer
**IMDB:** www.imdb.com/name/nm3800556

## BRANDMAN PRODUCTIONS

2062 North Vine Street, Suite 5
Los Angeles, CA 90068

**Phone:** 323-463-3224
**Fax:** 323-463-0852
**IMDB:** www.imdb.com/company/co0082006

**Submission Policy:** Accepts query letter from
unproduced, unrepresented writers

**Michael Bradman**
**Title:** President/Producer
**IMDB:** www.imdb.com/name/nm0104701

## BRIGHTLIGHT PICTURES

The Bridge Studios
2400 Boundary Road
Burnaby, BC V5M 3Z3
Canada

**Phone:** 604-628-3000
**Fax:** 604-628-3001
**Email:** info@brightlightpictures.com
**Website:** www.brightlightpictures.com
**IMDB:** www.imdb.com/company/co0065717

**Submission Policy:** Does not accept any unsolicited
material
**Genre:** Comedy, Drama
**Focus:** Feature Films, TV
**Year Established:** 2001

**Stephen Hegyes**
**Title:** Co-Chairman/Producer
**IMDB:** www.imdb.com/name/nm0373812

**Kyle McCachen**
**Title:** Creative Executive
**IMDB:** www.imdb.com/name/nm5131630

**Rebecca Nield**
**Title:** Creative Executive
**IMDB:** www.imdb.com/name/nm2422059

**Shawn Williamson**
**Title:** Co-Chairman/Producer
**IMDB:** www.imdb.com/name/nm0932144

## BROKEN CAMERA PRODUCTIONS

San Antonio, TX

**Phone:** 210-454-8103
**Email:** info@brokencameraproductions.com
**Website:** www.brokencameraproductions.com

**Submission Policy:** Accepts query letter from
unproduced, unrepresented writers via email
**Genre:** Comedy, Drama, Feature Films, Thriller
**Focus:** Feature Films

**Lynette C. Aleman**
**Title:** Producer
**Phone:** 210-317-4647
**Email:** lynette@brokencameraproductions.com
**IMDB:** www.imdb.com/name/nm4074593

**David Y. Duncan**
**Title:** Producer
**Phone:** 210-884-5234
**Email:** dave@brokencameraproductions.com
**IMDB:** www.imdb.com/name/nm2839229

**Matthew Garth**
**Title:** Producer
**Phone:** 210-454-8103
**Email:** matthew@brokencameraproductions.com
**IMDB:** www.imdb.com/name/nm2123288

## BROOKLYN FILMS

3815 Hughes Ave.
Culver City, CA 90232

**Phone:** 310-841-4300
**Fax:** 310-204-3464
**IMDB:** www.imdb.com/company/co0088618

**Submission Policy:** Accepts query letter from
unproduced, unrepresented writers
**Genre:** Crime, Drama, Feature Films, TV
**Focus:** Feature Films

**Jon Avnet**
**Title:** Director / Producer
**IMDB:** www.imdb.com/name/nm0000816

**Marsha Oglesby**
**Title:** Producer
**IMDB:** www.mdb.com/name/nm0644749

## BRUCE COHEN PRODUCTIONS

8292 Hollywood Blvd
Los Angeles, CA 90069

**Phone:** 323-650-4567
**Fax:** 323-843-9534

**Submission Policy:** Does not accept any unsolicited material
**Genre:** TV, TV Drama
**Focus:** Television

**Bruce Cohen**
Title: Principal
IMDB: www.imdb.com/name/nm0169260

**Jessica Leventhal**
Title: Creative Executive
IMDB: www.imdb.com/name/nm4202199

## BUCKAROO ENTERTAINMENT

10202 W Washington Blvd
David Lean Bldg, Suite 100
Culver City, CA 90232

**Phone:** 310-244-4646

**Submission Policy:** Does not accept any unsolicited material
**Genre:** Crime, Detective, Fantasy, Feature Films, Horror, Thriller
**Focus:** Feature Films

**Ryan Carroll**
Title: Executive
IMDB: www.imdb.com/name/nm1498070

**Joshua Donen**
Title: Partner
IMDB: www.imdb.com/name/nm0232433

**Sam Raimi**
Title: Partner
IMDB: www.imdb.com/name/nm0000600

## BUENA VISTA HOME ENTERTAINMENT

500 S. Buena Vista St.
Burbank, CA 91521-6369
USA

**Phone:** 818-560-1000
**Website:** http://www.bvhe.com/
**IMDB:** http://www.imdb.com/company/co0049546/?ref_=fn_al_co_1

**Submission Policy:** Does not accept any unsolicited material
**Genre:** Action, Animation, Comedy, Crime, Documentary, Drama, Family, Fantasy, Feature Films, Horror, Memoir & True Stories, Romance, Science Fiction, Thriller, TV, TV Sitcom

**Focus:** Feature Films, Television, Shorts
**Year Established:** 1952

## BUENA VISTA PICTURES

500 S Buena Vista St
Burbank, CA 91521

**Phone:** 818-560-1000
**Website:** http://www.disney.com/
**IMDB:** http://www.imdb.com/company/co0044279/?ref_=fn_al_co_1

**Submission Policy:** Does not accept any unsolicited material
**Genre:** Action, Animation, Comedy, Crime, Documentary, Drama, Family, Fantasy, Feature Films, Horror, Memoir & True Stories, Romance, Science Fiction, Thriller, TV, TV Drama, TV Sitcom
**Focus:** Feature Films, Television, Shorts
**Year Established:** 1932

**Nadia Aleyd**
Title: Casting
IMDB: http://www.imdb.com/name/nm0019022/?ref_=fn_al_nm_1

**Louanne Brickhouse**
IMDB: http://www.imdb.com/name/nm1749168/?ref_=fn_al_nm_1

**Kristin Burr**
Title: Executive Vice President
IMDB: http://www.imdb.com/name/nm0123013/?ref_=fn_al_nm_1

**Jeanne Hobson**
Title: Senior Vice President of Domestic Sale and Distribution
IMDB: http://www.imdb.com/name/nm2653496/?ref_=fn_al_nm_1

**John Lasseter**
Title: Chief Creative Officer, Disney Animation
IMDB: http://www.imdb.com/name/nm0005124/?ref_=fn_al_nm_1

**Cherise McVicar**
Title: Senior Vice President of National Promotions and Mobile Marketing
IMDB: http://www.imdb.com/name/nm2660270/?ref_=fn_al_nm_1

**Todd Murata**
Title: Executive
IMDB: http://www.imdb.com/name/
nm0613611/?ref_=fn_al_nm_1

## BUENA VISTA TELEVISION

500 S Buena Vista St
Burbank, CA 91521

Phone: 818-460-6552
Fax: 818-460-5296
Email: bvtv.webmaster@disney.com
Website: http://www.disneyabc.tv/
IMDB: http://www.imdb.com/company/
co0078478/?ref_=fn_al_co_1

Submission Policy: Does not accept any unsolicited
material
Genre: Action, Animation, Comedy, Crime,
Documentary, Drama, Family, Fantasy, Feature
Films, Memoir & True Stories, Romance, Science
Fiction, Thriller, TV Drama, TV Sitcom
Focus: Feature Films, Television
Year Established: 1957

## BUNIM-MURRAY PRODUCTIONS

6007 Sepulveda Boulevard
Van Nuys, CA 91411

Phone: 818-756-5100
Fax: 818-756-5140
Email: bmp@bunim-murray.com
Website: www.bunim-murray.com

Submission Policy: Does not accept any unsolicited
material
Genre: Documentary, TV
Focus: Television, Reality TV Programming

**Erin Cristall**
Title: SVP of Development
IMDB: www.imdb.com/name/nm0188058

**Scott Freeman**
Title: EVP of Current Programming & Development
IMDB: www.imdb.com/name/nm1321720

**Cara Goldberg**
Title: Production Executive

**Gil Goldschein**
Title: President
IMDB: www.imdb.com/name/nm2251455

**John Greco**
Title: Vice President of Production

**Jeff Jenkins**
Title: EVP of Entertainment & Programming
IMDB: www.imdb.com/name/nm0420870

**Jonathan Murray**
Title: Chairman
IMDB: www.imdb.com/name/nm0615086

## BURLEIGH FILMWORKS

22287 Mulholland Highway, Suite 129
Calabasas, CA 91302

Phone: 818-224-4686
Fax: 818-223-9089
IMDB: www.imdb.com/company/co0176271

Submission Policy: Accepts query letter from
unproduced, unrepresented writers

**Steve Burleigh**
Title: Producer
Email: steve.burleigh@burleighfilmworks.com
IMDB: www.imdb.com/name/nm0122114

## BURNSIDE ENTERTAINMENT INC.

2424 North Ontario Street
Burbank, CA 91504

Phone: 818-565-5986
Email: mail@burnsideentertainment.com
Website: www.burnsideentertainment.com
IMDB: www.imdb.com/company/co0180518

Submission Policy: Accepts query letter from
unproduced, unrepresented writers

**Glen Trotiner**
Title: Producer/Partner
IMDB: www.imdb.com/name/nm0873641

## CALIBER MEDIA COMPANY

5670 Wilshire Blvd.
Ste 1600
Los Angeles, CA 90036

Phone: 310-786-9210
Website: http://www.calibermediaco.com/
IMDB: http://www.imdb.com/company/
co0228420/?ref_=fn_al_co_1

**Submission Policy:** Accepts query letter from unproduced, unrepresented writers
**Genre:** Action, Crime, Drama, Family, Feature Films, Horror, Sociocultural, Thriller
**Focus:** Feature Films
**Year Established:** 2008

### Jack Heller
**Title:** Principal
**IMDB:** http://www.imdb.com/name/nm2597331/?ref_=fn_al_nm_1

### Dallas Sonnier
**Title:** Principal
**IMDB:** http://www.imdb.com/name/nm2447772/?ref_=fn_al_nm_1

### Morgan White
**Title:** Director of Production and Development
**IMDB:** http://www.imdb.com/name/nm4765803/?ref_=fn_al_nm_2

## CALLAHAN FILMWORKS

3800 Barham Boulevard
Suite 500
Los Angeles, CA 90068

**Phone:** 323-878-0645
**Fax:** 323-878-0649

**Submission Policy:** Does not accept any unsolicited material
**Genre:** Action, Comedy, Crime, Drama, Family, Fantasy, Feature Films, Romance, TV, TV Sitcom
**Focus:** Feature Films, Television

### Omar El-Hajoui
**Title:** Executive Assistant
**IMDB:** www.imdb.com/name/nm5389420

### Michael Ewing
**Title:** Partner
**IMDB:** www.imdb.com/name/nm0263989

### Chris Osbrink
**Title:** Creative Executive
**IMDB:** www.imdb.com/name/nm1644713

### Peter Segal
**Title:** Partner
**IMDB:** www.imdb.com/name/nm0781842

## CAMELOT ENTERTAINMENT GROUP

10 Universal City Plaza NBC/Universal Building
Floor 20
Universal City, CA 91608

**Phone:** 818-308-8858
**Fax:** 818-308-8848
**Email:** submissions@camelotfilms.com
**Website:** www.camelotent.com/index.php
**IMDB:** www.imdb.com/company/co0006731/?ref_=fn_al_co_1

**Submission Policy:** Accepts scripts from unproduced, unrepresented writers
**Genre:** Action, Animation, Comedy, Drama, Family, Horror, Memoir & True Stories, Romance, Science Fiction, Thriller, TV Drama
**Focus:** Feature Films, Television

### Robert Atwell
**Title:** Chairman
**IMDB:** www.imdb.com/name/nm0041164/?ref_=fn_al_nm_2

### Steven Istock
**Title:** Partner
**IMDB:** www.imdb.com/name/nm1916408/?ref_=fn_al_nm_1

### Jessica Kelly
**Title:** President of Distribution

## CAMELOT PICTURES

9255 Sunset Boulevard, Suite 711
Los Angeles, CA 90069

**Phone:** 310-288-3000
**Fax:** 310-288-3054
**Email:** info@camelot-pictures.com
**Website:** www.camelot-pictures.com
**IMDB:** www.imdb.com/company/co0084122/

**Submission Policy:** Accepts query letter from unproduced, unrepresented writers via email
**Genre:** Comedy, Drama, Family
**Focus:** Feature Films

### Gary Gilbert
**Title:** President
**IMDB:** www.imdb.com/name/nm1344784

### Jordan Horowitz
**Title:** Vice-President, Production and Development
**IMDB:** www.imdb.com/name/nm0395302

## CANADIAN BROADCASTING COMPANY

181 Queen Street
Ottawa, ON, Canada, K1P 1K9

**Phone:** 613-288-6000
**Email:** liaison@cbc.ca
**Website:** http://www.cbc.ca/
**IMDB:** http://www.imdb.com/company/
co0045850/?ref_=fn_al_co_1

**Submission Policy:** Does not accept any unsolicited
material
**Genre:** Action, Animation, Comedy, Crime,
Documentary, Drama, Family, Feature Films,
Memoir & True Stories, Period, TV, TV Sitcom
**Focus:** Feature Films, Television
**Year Established:** 2007

### Suzanne Colvin-Goulding
**Title:** Head of Physical Production for TV Arts &
Entertainment, CBC English Television
**IMDB:** http://www.imdb.com/name/
nm0003681/?ref_=fn_al_nm_1

### Jenny Hacker
**Title:** Executive of Creative/Comedy
**IMDB:** http://www.imdb.com/name/
nm4236429/?ref_=fn_al_nm_1

### Hebert Lacroix
**Title:** President
**IMDB:** http://www.imdb.com/name/
nm4522750/?ref_=fn_al_nm_1

### Anton Leo
**Title:** Head of Comedy
**IMDB:** http://www.imdb.com/name/
nm2502480/?ref_=fn_al_nm_2

### Scott McEwen
**Title:** Head of Drama Development
**IMDB:** http://www.imdb.com/name/
nm1469582/?ref_=fn_al_nm_2

### David Ridgen
**Title:** Producer
**IMDB:** http://www.imdb.com/name/
nm3236527/?ref_=fn_al_nm_1

### Jennifer Stewart
**Title:** Director of Acquisitions and Development
**IMDB:** http://www.imdb.com/name/
nm4219237/?ref_=fn_al_nm_1

### Trevor Walton
**Title:** Head (Co-Productions)
**IMDB:** http://www.imdb.com/name/
nm4280633/?ref_=fn_al_nm_1

### Kim Wilson
**Title:** Head of Creative CBC Children's
Programming

## CAPACITY PICTURES

PO Box 96143
Las Vegas, NV 89193

**Phone:** 310-247-8534
**Email:** capacitypictures@gmail.com
**IMDB:** http://www.imdb.com/company/
co0192878/?ref_=fn_al_co_1

**Submission Policy:** Does not accept any unsolicited
material
**Genre:** Comedy, Crime, Drama, Horror, Thriller
**Focus:** Feature Films
**Year Established:** 2008

### Wayne Allen Rice
**Title:** Executive
**IMDB:** http://www.imdb.com/name/
nm0723573/?ref_=fn_al_nm_1

### Rich Heller
**Title:** Executive
**IMDB:** http://www.imdb.com/name/
nm0375378/?ref_=fn_al_nm_1

## CAPITAL ARTS ENTERTAINMENT

23315 Clift on Plaza
Valencia, CA 91354

**Phone:** 818-343-8950
**Fax:** 818-343-8962
**Email:** info@capitalarts.com
**Website:** www.capitalarts.com
**IMDB:** www.imdb.com/company/co0009722

**Submission Policy:** Accepts query letter from
unproduced, unrepresented writers via email
**Genre:** Action, Comedy, Horror, Thriller
**Year Established:** 1995

### Mike Elliot
**Title:** Partner/Producer
**IMDB:** www.imdb.com/name/nm0254291

## CAPTIVATE ENTERTAINMENT

100 Universal City Plaza
Bungalow 4111
Universal City, CA 91608

**Phone:** 818-777-6711
**Fax:** 818-733-4303
**IMDB:** www.imdb.com/company/co0263292

**Submission Policy:** Does not accept any unsolicited material
**Genre:** Action, Comedy, Drama, Fantasy, Myth, Romance, Science Fiction, Thriller
**Focus:** Feature Films, TV

**Tony Shaw**
**Title:** Creative Executive
**Email:** tony.shaw@univfilms.com
**IMDB:** www.imdb.com/name/nm4130192

**Ben Smith**
**Title:** Producer
**IMDB:** www.imdb.com/name/nm3328356

**Jeffrey Weiner**
**Title:** Chairman/CEO
**IMDB:** www.imdb.com/name/nm1788648

## CARNIVAL FILMS

3rd Fl
55 New Oxford Street
London WC1A 1BS

**Phone:** +44 0203 618 6600
**Fax:** +44 023 618 8900
**Email:** info@carnivalfilms.co.uk
**Website:** www.carnivalfilms.co.uk

**Submission Policy:** Does not accept any unsolicited material
**Genre:** Documentary, Drama, Thriller, TV, TV Drama
**Focus:** TV

**Henrietta Colvin**
**Title:** Head of Development
**IMDB:** www.imdb.com/name/nm2188710

**Kimberly Hikaka**
**Title:** Production Executive
**IMDB:** www.imdb.com/name/nm2529465

**Sam Symons**
**Title:** Development Executive
**IMDB:** www.imdb.com/name/nm1599585

**Steven Williams**
**Title:** Development Executive
**IMDB:** www.imdb.com/name/nm1034831

## CASEY SILVER PRODUCTIONS

506 Santa Monica Boulevard, Suite 322
Santa Monica, CA 90401

**Phone:** 310-566-3750
**Fax:** 310-566-3751
**IMDB:** www.imdb.com/company/co0058884

**Submission Policy:** Does not accept any unsolicited material
**Genre:** Action, Comedy, Drama, Family, Thriller
**Focus:** Feature Films

**Matthew Reynolds**
**Title:** Creative Executive
**Email:** matthew@caseysilver.com
**IMDB:** www.imdb.com/name/nm2303863

**Casey Silver**
**Title:** Chairman
**Email:** casey@caseysilver.com
**IMDB:** www.imdb.com/name/nm0798661

## CASTLE ROCK ENTERTAINMENT

335 North Maple Drive, Suite 350
Beverly Hills, CA 90210-3867

**Phone:** 310-285-2300
**Fax:** 310-285-2345
**IMDB:** www.imdb.com/company/co0040620

**Submission Policy:** Accepts scripts from produced or represented writers

**Rob Reiner**
**Title:** Director/Producer/Writer
**Email:** rob.reiner@castle-rock.com
**IMDB:** www.imdb.com/name/nm0001661

**Andrew Scheinman**
**Title:** Producer/Director
**Email:** andres.scheinman@castle-rock.com
**IMDB:** www.imdb.com/name/nm0770650

## CATAPULT FILMS

832 Third Street, Suite 303
Santa Monica, CA 90403-1155

**Phone:** 310-395-1470
**Fax:** 310-401-0122
**IMDB:** www.imdb.com/company/co0100754

**Submission Policy:** Accepts scripts from produced or represented writers

**Lisa Josefsberg**
**Title:** Producer
**IMDB:** www.imdb.com/name/nm2248853

## CBS FILMS

11800 Wilshire Blvd
Los Angeles, CA 90025

**Phone:** 310-575-7700
**Website:** www.cbsfilms.com

**Submission Policy:** Does not accept any unsolicited material
**Genre:** Action, Drama, Fantasy, Romance, Science Fiction
**Focus:** Feature Film

**Maria Faillace**
**Title:** Senior Vice President of Production
**IMDB:** www.imdb.com/name/nm1299267

**Wolfgang Hammer**
**Title:** Co-President
**IMDB:** www.imdb.com/name/nm1424985

**Terry Press**
**Title:** Co-President
**IMDB:** www.imdb.com/name/nm1437110

**Mark Ross**
**Title:** Vice President of Production
**IMDB:** www.imdb.com/name/nm0743653

## CECCHI GORI PICTURES

5555 Melrose Avenue
Bob Hope 203
Los Angeles, CA 90038

**Phone:** 323-956-5954
**Fax:** 323-862-2254
**Email:** info@cgglobalmedia.com
**Website:** www.cecchigoripictures.com

**Genre:** Drama, Family, Feature Films, Horror, Romance, Thriller
**Focus:** Feature Films

**Dana Galinsky**
**Title:** Development Coordinator
**IMDB:** www.imdb.com/name/nm1919300

**Niels Juul**
**Title:** CEO
**IMDB:** www.imdb.com/name/nm3887220

**Jennifer Parker**
**Title:** Development
**IMDB:** www.imdb.com/name/nm4487725

**Andy Scott**
**Title:** Art Director
**IMDB:** www.imdb.com/name/nm4866101

**Alex Shub**
**Title:** VP of Business & Legal Affairs

## CELADOR FILMS

39 Long Acre
London, WC2E 9LG
United Kingdom

**Phone:** +44 20-7845-6800
**Fax:** +44 20-7845-6801
**Website:** www.celador.co.uk
**IMDB:** www.imdb.com/company/co0152921

**Submission Policy:** Accepts scripts from produced or represented writers
**Year Established:** 1989

**Paul Smith**
**Title:** Chairman/Executive Producer
**Email:** psmith@celador.co.uk
**IMDB:** www.imdb.com/name/nm0809531

## CENTROPOLIS ENTERTAINMENT

1445 North Stanley
3rd Floor
Los Angeles, CA 90046

**Phone:** 323-850-1212
**Fax:** 323-850-1201
**Email:** info@centropolis.com
**Website:** www.centropolis.com
**IMDB:** www.imdb.com/company/co0050111

**Submission Policy:** Accepts scripts from produced or represented writers
**Genre:** Action, Fantasy, Memoir & True Stories, Myth, Romance
**Year Established:** 1985

**Roland Emmerich**
Title: Partner/Producer
IMDB: www.imdb.com/name/nm0000386

**Ute Emmerich**
Title: Partner/Producer
IMDB: www.imdb.com/name/nm0256498

## CHAIKEN FILMS

802 Potrero Avenue
San Francisco, CA 94110

Phone: 415-826-7880
Fax: 415-826-7882
Email: info@chaikenfilms.com
Website: www.chaikenfilms.com
IMDB: www.imdb.com/company/co0064208

Submission Policy: Accepts query letter from
unproduced, unrepresented writers
Genre: Memoir & True Stories
Year Established: 1998

**Jennifer Chaiken**
Title: Producer
Email: jen@chaikenfilms.com
IMDB: www.imdb.com/name/nm0149671

## CHARTOFF PRODUCTIONS

1250 Sixth Street, Suite 101
Santa Monica, CA 90401

Phone: 310-319-1960
Fax: 310-319-3469
Email: hendeechartoff@cs.com
IMDB: www.imdb.com/company/co0094865

Submission Policy: Accepts scripts from produced
or represented writers
Year Established: 1986

**Robert Chartoff**
Title: CEO/Producer
IMDB: www.imdb.com/name/nm0153590

## CHERNIN ENTERTAINMENT

1733 Ocean Avenue, Suite 300
Santa Monica, CA 90401

Phone: 310-899-1205
Website: www.cherninent.com
IMDB: www.imdb.com/company/co0286257

Submission Policy: Accepts scripts from produced
or represented writers
Genre: Action, Comedy, TV Drama, TV Sitcom
Focus: Feature Films
Year Established: 2009

**Peter Chernin**
Title: Principle
IMDB: www.imdb.com/name/nm1858656

**Dylan Dark**
Email: dc@cherninent.com
IMDB: www.imdb.com/name/nm1249995

**Jesse Henderson**
Title: Director of Development
Email: jh@cherninent.com

**Katherine Pope**
Title: President (Television)
Email: kp@cherninent.com
IMDB: www.imdb.com/name/nm0691142

**Ivana Schechter-Garcia**
Title: Creative Executive

**Pavun Shetty**
Title: Director of Television
Email: ps@cherninent.com

**Jenno Topping**
Title: Executive Vice-President
Email: jt@cherninent.com
IMDB: www.imdb.com/name/nm0867768

## CHERRY SKY FILMS

2100 Sawtelle Boulevard.,
Suite 101
Los Angeles, CA 90025

Phone: 310-479-8001
Fax: 310-479-8815
Email: contact@cherryskyfilms.com
Website: www.cherryskyfilms.com

Submission Policy: Does not accept any unsolicited
material
Genre: Comedy, Drama, Family, Feature Films,
Romance
Focus: Feature Films
Year Established: 2001

**Jeffrey Gou**
Title: Producer
IMDB: www.imdb.com/name/nm2370188

**Joan Huang**
Title: Producer
IMDB: www.imdb.com/name/nm0399009

## CHESTNUT RIDGE PRODUCTIONS

8899 Beverly Boulevard, Suite 800
Los Angeles, CA

Phone: 310-285-7011
IMDB: www.imdb.com/company/co0273538

Submission Policy: Does not accept any unsolicited material
Year Established: 2009

**Paula Wagner**
Title: Owner/Producer
IMDB: www.imdb.com/name/nm0906048

## CHEYENNE ENTERPRISES LLC

406 Wilshire Boulevard
Santa Monica, CA 90401

Phone: 310-455-5000
Fax: 310-688-8000
IMDB: www.imdb.com/company/co0041195

Submission Policy: Accepts scripts from produced or represented writers
Year Established: 2000

**Arnold Rifkin**
Title: President/Producer
IMDB: www.imdb.com/name/nm0726476

**Joshua Rowley**
Title: Director of Development
IMDB: www.imdb.com/name/nm2282373

## CHICAGOFILMS

253 W 72nd St
Suite 1108
New York, NY 10023
USA

Phone: 212-721-7700
Fax: 212-721-7701
IMDB: www.imdb.com/company/co0012485

Submission Policy: Accepts scripts from produced or represented writers

**Bob Balaban**
Title: Actor/Producer
IMDB: www.imdb.com/name/nm0000837

## CHICKFLICKS

8861 St Ives Drive
Los Angeles, CA 90069

Phone: 310-854-7210
Email: info@chickflicksinc.com
Website: www.chickflicksinc.com
IMDB: www.imdb.com/company/co0156986

Submission Policy: Accepts scripts from produced or represented writers
Genre: Comedy, Fantasy, Memoir & True Stories, Myth, Romance

**Stephanie Austin**
Title: Producer (Managing Partner)
Phone: 310-854-7210
Email: stephanie@chickflicksinc.com
IMDB: www.imdb.com/name/nm0042520

**Sara Risher**
Title: Producer (Managing Partner)
Phone: 310-854-7210
Email: sara@chickflicksinc.com
IMDB: www.imdb.com/name/nm0728260

## CHOTZEN/JENNER PRODUCTIONS

4178 Dixie Canyon Ave.
Sherman Oaks, CA 91423

Phone: 323-465-9877
Fax: 323-460-6451
IMDB: www.imdb.com/company/co0176334

Submission Policy: Accepts scripts from produced or represented writers
Genre: TV Drama, TV Sitcom
Year Established: 1990

**Yvonne Chotzen**
Title: Producer/Partner
IMDB: www.imdb.com/name/nm0159278

**William Jenner**
Title: Producer/Partner
IMDB: www.imdb.com/name/nm0421076

## CHRIS/ROSE PRODUCTIONS

3131 Torreyson Place
Los Angeles, CA 90046

**Phone:** 323-851-8772
**Fax:** 323-851-0662
**IMDB:** www.imdb.com/company/co0040069

**Submission Policy:** Accepts scripts from produced or represented writers
**Genre:** Memoir & True Stories, TV Drama, TV Sitcom

**Robert Christiansen**
**Title:** Executive Producer
**Phone:** 310-781-0833
**IMDB:** www.imdb.com/name/nm0160222

## CHUBBCO FILM CO.

373 North Kenter Avenue
Los Angeles, CA 90049

**Phone:** 310-729-5858
**Fax:** 310-933-1704
**Email:** chubbco@gmail.com
**IMDB:** www.imdb.com/company/co0026094

**Submission Policy:** Does not accept any unsolicited material
**Genre:** Action, Crime, Memoir & True Stories

**Caldecot Chubb**
**Title:** Producer
**Email:** chubbco@gmail.com
**IMDB:** www.imdb.com/name/nm0160941

## CHUCK FRIES PRODUCTIONS

9903 Santa Monica Boulevard, Suite 870
Beverly Hills, CA 90212

**Phone:** 310-203-9520
**Fax:** 310-203-9519
**IMDB:** www.imdb.com/company/co0040068

**Submission Policy:** Accepts scripts from produced or represented writers
**Genre:** Crime, Detective

**Charles Fries**
**Title:** Chairman/President/CEO
**IMDB:** www.imdb.com/name/nm0295594

## CINDY COWAN ENTERTAINMENT, INC.

8265 West Sunset Boulevard, Suite 205
Los Angeles, CA 90046

**Phone:** 323-822-1082
**Fax:** 323-822-1086
**Email:** info@cowanent.com
**Website:** http://cowanent.com/
**IMDB:** www.imdb.com/company/co0094925

**Submission Policy:** Accepts scripts from produced or represented writers
**Year Established:** 1999

**Cindy Cowan**
**Title:** President
**IMDB:** www.imdb.com/name/nm0184546

## CINEMA EPHOCH

10 Universal City Plaza, 20th Floor
Universal City, CA 91608

**Phone:** 818-753-2345
**Email:** acquisitions@cinemaepoch.com
**Website:** www.cinemaepoch.com
**IMDB:** www.imdb.com/company/co0028810

**Submission Policy:** Accepts query letter from unproduced, unrepresented writers
**Genre:** Action, Comedy, Crime, Detective, Horror, Memoir & True Stories, Myth, Thriller
**Year Established:** 2001

**Gregory Hatanaka**
**Title:** President/Distributor/Producer
**IMDB:** www.imdb.com/name/nm0368693

## CINEMAGIC ENTERTAINMENT

9229 Sunset Boulevard, Suite 610
West Hollywood, CA 90069

**Phone:** 310-385-9322
**Fax:** 310-385-9347
**Website:** www.cinemagicent.com
**IMDB:** www.imdb.com/company/co0183883

**Submission Policy:** Accepts query letter from unproduced, unrepresented writers
**Genre:** Action, Crime, Detective, Fantasy, Horror, Myth, Science Fiction, Thriller

**Lee Cohn**
**Title:** Vice-President, Development
**IMDB:** www.imdb.com/name/nm2325144

## CINEMA LIBRE STUDIO

8328 De Soto Avenue
Canoga Park, CA 91304

**Phone:** 818-349-8822
**Fax:** 818-349-9922
**Email:** project@CinemaLibreStudio.com
**Website:** www.CinemaLibreStudio.com
**IMDB:** www.imdb.com/company/co0132224

**Submission Policy:** Accepts query letter from unproduced, unrepresented writers
**Year Established:** 2003

### Philippe Diaz
**Title:** Producer/Owner
**IMDB:** www.imdb.com/name/nm0225034

## CINE MOSAIC

130 West 25th Street, 12th Floor
New York, NY 10001

**Phone:** 212-625-3797
**Fax:** 212-625-3571
**Email:** info@cinemosaic.net
**Website:** www.cinemosaic.net
**IMDB:** www.imdb.com/company/co0124029

**Submission Policy:** Accepts scripts from produced or represented writers
**Genre:** Action, Memoir & True Stories, TV Drama
**Year Established:** 2002

### Lydia Pilcher
**Title:** Independent Producer/Founder
**IMDB:** www.imdb.com/name/nm0212990

## CINESON ENTERTAINMENT

4519 Varna Ave.
Sherman Oaks, CA 91423

**Phone:** 818-501-8246
**Fax:** 818-501-3647
**Email:** cineson@cineson.com
**Website:** http://www.cineson.com
**IMDB:** http://www.imdb.com/company/co0127539/?ref_=fn_al_co_1

**Submission Policy:** Does not accept any unsolicited material
**Genre:** Comedy, Crime, Drama, Feature Films, Memoir & True Stories, Period, Romance, Thriller, TV

**Focus:** Feature Films, Television
**Year Established:** 1999

### Andy Garcia
**Title:** Producer / Director
**IMDB:** http://www.imdb.com/name/nm0000412/?ref_=fn_al_nm_1

## CINETELE FILMS

8255 Sunset Boulevard
Los Angeles, CA 90046

**Phone:** 323-654-4000
**Fax:** 323-650-6400
**Email:** info@cinetelfilms.com
**Website:** www.cinetelfilms.com
**IMDB:** www.imdb.com/company/co0017447

**Submission Policy:** Does not accept any unsolicited material
**Genre:** Crime, Horror, Thriller, TV Drama
**Year Established:** 1985

### Paul Hertzberg
**Title:** President/CEO
**IMDB:** www.imdb.com/name/nm0078473

## CINEVILLE

3400 Airport Avenue
Santa Monica, CA 90405

**Phone:** 310-397-7150
**Fax:** 310-397-7155
**Email:** info@cineville.com
**Website:** www.cineville.com
**IMDB:** www.imdb.com/company/co0063993

**Submission Policy:** Accepts query letter from unproduced, unrepresented writers
**Genre:** Comedy, Memoir & True Stories, Romance
**Year Established:** 1990

### Carl Colpaert
**Title:** President
**IMDB:** www.imdb.com/name/nm0173207

## CIRCLE OF CONFUSION

8931 Ellis Avenue
Los Angeles, CA 90034

**Phone:** 310-691-7000
**Fax:** 310-691-7099
**Email:** queries@circleofconfusion.com

**Website:** www.circleofconfusion.com
**IMDB:** www.imdb.com/company/co0090153

**Submission Policy:** Accepts query letter from unproduced, unrepresented writers
**Genre:** Action, Comedy, Crime, Detective, Fantasy, Horror, Memoir & True Stories, Myth, Romance, Science Fiction, Thriller, TV Drama, TV Sitcom

**Stephen Emery**
**Title:** Executive Vice-President Production and Development
**Email:** stephen@circleofconfusion.com
**IMDB:** www.imdb.com/name/nm1765323

## CITY ENTERTAINMENT

266 1/2 South Rexford Drive
Beverly Hills, CA 90212

**Phone:** 310-273-3101
**Fax:** 310-273-3676
**IMDB:** www.imdb.com/company/co0093881

**Submission Policy:** Does not accept any unsolicited material

**Joshua Maurer**
**Title:** President/Producer
**IMDB:** www.imdb.com/name/nm0561027

## CLARITY PICTURES LLC.

1107 Fair Oaks Ave
Ste 155
South Pasadena, CA 91030
USA

**Phone:** 310-226-7046
**Fax:** 310-388-5846
**Email:** info@claritypictures.net
**Website:** http://www.claritypictures.net/
**IMDB:** http://www.imdb.com/company/co0151012/?ref_=fn_al_co_1

**Submission Policy:** Does not accept any unsolicited material
**Genre:** Comedy, Documentary, Horror, TV Sitcom
**Focus:** Feature Films
**Year Established:** 2004

**David Basulto**
**Title:** President, Producer
**IMDB:** http://www.imdb.com/name/nm0060617/?ref_=fn_al_nm_1

**Loren Basulto**
**Title:** Vice President of Production
**IMDB:** http://www.imdb.com/name/nm1457923/?ref_=fn_al_nm_1

## CLASS 5 FILMS

200 Park Avenue South, 8th Floor
New York, NY 10003

**Phone:** 917-414-9404
**IMDB:** www.imdb.com/company/co0113781

**Submission Policy:** Accepts query letter from unproduced, unrepresented writers

**Edward Norton**
**Title:** Producer/Actor/Director/Writer
**IMDB:** www.imdb.com/name/nm0001570

## CLEAR PICTURES ENTERTAINMENT

12400 Ventura Boulevard, Suite 306
Studio City, CA 91604

**Phone:** 818-980-5460
**Fax:** 818-980-4716
**Email:** clearpicturesinc@aol.com
**IMDB:** www.imdb.com/company/co0171732

**Submission Policy:** Accepts query letter from unproduced, unrepresented writers via email
**Genre:** Drama, Memoir & True Stories, TV Drama
**Focus:** Feature Films, TV
**Year Established:** 2009

**Elizabeth Fowler**
**Title:** Principle
**IMDB:** www.imdb.com/name/nm2085583

## CLEARVIEW PRODUCTIONS

1180 South Beverly Drive, Suite 700
Los Angeles, CA 90035

**Phone:** 310-271-7698
**Fax:** 310-278-9978

**Submission Policy:** Does not accept any unsolicited material

**Albert Ruddy**
**Title:** Producer
**IMDB:** www.imdb.com/name/nm0748665

## CLIFFORD WERBER PRODUCTIONS

232 South Beverly Drive, Suite 224
Beverly Hills, CA 90212

**Phone:** 310-288-0900
**Fax:** 310-288-0600
**IMDB:** www.imdb.com/company/co0097249

**Submission Policy:** Accepts query letter from produced or represented writers

**Clifford Werber**
**Title:** Producer
**IMDB:** www.imdb.com/name/nm0921222

## CLOSED ON MONDAYS ENTERTAINMENT

3800 Barham Boulevard Suite 100
Los Angeles, CA 90068

**Phone:** 818-526-6707
**IMDB:** www.imdb.com/company/co0186526

**Submission Policy:** Does not accept any unsolicited material
**Year Established:** 2003

**Joe Nozemack**
**Title:** Prodocer/Co-founder
**IMDB:** www.imdb.com/name/nm1060496

## CLOUD EIGHT FILMS

39 Long Acre
London WC2E 9LG
United Kingdom

**Phone:** +44 20-7845-6877
**IMDB:** www.imdb.com/company/co0265704

**Submission Policy:** Accepts scripts from produced or represented writers
**Year Established:** 2009

**Christian Colson**
**Title:** Chairman/Producer
**Phone:** +44 20 7845 6988
**IMDB:** www.imdb.com/name/nm1384503

## CODEBLACK ENTERTAINMENT

111 Universal Hollywood Dr, Suite 2260
Universal City, CA 91608

**Phone:** 818-286-8600
**Fax:** 818-286-8649
**Email:** info@codeblackentertainment.com

**Website:** www.codeblackentertainment.com
**IMDB:** www.imdb.com/company/co0172361

**Submission Policy:** Does not accept any unsolicited material
**Year Established:** 2005

**Jeff Clanagan**
**Title:** CEO
**IMDB:** www.imdb.com/name/nm0163335

## CODE ENTERTAINMENT

9229 Sunset Boulevard, Suite 615
Los Angeles, CA 90069

**Phone:** 310-772-0008
**Fax:** 310-772-0006
**Email:** contact@codeentertainment.com
**Website:** www.codeentertainment.com
**IMDB:** www.imdb.com/company/co0143069

**Submission Policy:** Accepts scripts from produced or represented writers
**Year Established:** 2005

**Bart Rosenblatt**
**Title:** Producer
**Phone:** 310-772-0008 ext. 3
**IMDB:** www.imdb.com/name/nm0742386

## COLLEEN CAMP PRODUCTIONS

6464 Sunset Boulevard, Suite 800
Los Angeles, CA 90028

**Phone:** 323-463-1434
**Fax:** 323-463-4379
**Email:** asst@ccprods.com
**IMDB:** www. imdb.com/company/co0092983

**Submission Policy:** Accepts query letter from unproduced, unrepresented writers

**Colleen Camp**
**Title:** Producer
**IMDB:** www.imdb.com/name/nm0131974

## COLOR FORCE

1524 Cloverfield Boulevard, Suite C
Santa Monica, CA 90404

**Phone:** 310-828-0641
**Fax:** 310-828-0672
**IMDB:** www.imdb.com/company/co0212151

**Submission Policy:** Accepts query letter from unproduced, unrepresented writers
**Genre:** Action, Comedy
**Year Established:** 2007

### Nina Jacobson
**Title:** Producer
**Email:** nina.jacobson@colorforce.com
**IMDB:** www.imdb.com/name/nm1749221

## COLOSSAL ENTERTAINMENT

PO Box 461010
Los Angeles, CA 90046

**Phone:** 323-656-6647
**Email:** clsslent@aol.com
**IMDB:** www.imdb.com/company/co0176684

**Submission Policy:** Accepts query letter from unproduced, unrepresented writers

### Graham Ludlow
**Title:** Producer / Writer
**IMDB:** www.imdb.com/name/nm0524905

### Kelly Rowan
**Title:** Producer
**IMDB:** www.imdb.com/name/nm0746414

## COLUMBIA PICTURES

10202 West Washington Boulevard Thalberg Building
Culver City, CA 90232

**Phone:** 310-244-4000
**Fax:** 310-244-2626
**Website:** http://www.spe.sony.com/
**IMDB:** http://www.imdb.com/company/co0071509/?ref_=fn_al_co_1

**Submission Policy:** Does not accept any unsolicited material
**Genre:** Action, Animation, Comedy, Crime, Drama, Family, Fantasy, Feature Films, Horror, Memoir & True Stories, Period, Romance, Science Fiction, Thriller
**Focus:** Feature Films
**Year Established:** 1939

### Lauren Abrahams
**Title:** Vice President of Production
**IMDB:** http://www.imdb.com/name/nm1036268/?ref_=fn_al_nm_1

### Doug Belgrad
**Title:** President
**IMDB:** http://www.imdb.com/name/nm1000411/?ref_=fn_al_nm_1

### Debra Bergman
**Title:** Vice President of the Production Administration
**IMDB:** http://www.imdb.com/name/nm2984630/?ref_=fn_al_nm_1

### Elizabeth Cantillon
**Title:** Executive Vice President of Production
**IMDB:** http://www.imdb.com/name/nm0134578/?ref_=fn_al_nm_1
**Assistant:** Katherine Spada
katherine_spada@spe.sony.com

### Samuel C. Dickerman
**Title:** Executive Vice President of Production
**IMDB:** http://www.imdb.com/name/nm0225385/?ref_=fn_al_nm_1

### Pete Corral
**Title:** Senior Vice President of the Production Administration
**IMDB:** http://www.imdb.com/name/nm0180707/?ref_=fn_al_nm_1

### Foster Driver
**Title:** Creative Executive
**IMDB:** http://www.imdb.com/name/nm5372839/?ref_=fn_al_nm_1

### Eric Fineman
**Title:** Creative Executive
**IMDB:** http://www.imdb.com/name/nm2349857/?ref_=fn_al_nm_1

### DeVon Franklin
**Title:** Senior Vice President of Production
**IMDB:** http://www.imdb.com/name/nm2035952/?ref_=fn_al_nm_1

### Andrea Giannetti
**Title:** Executive Vice President of Production
**IMDB:** http://www.imdb.com/name/nm1602150/?ref_=fn_al_nm_1

### Andy Given
**Title:** Senior Vice President of the Production Administration
**IMDB:** http://www.imdb.com/name/nm0321429/?ref_=fn_al_nm_1

**Jonathan Kadin**
**Title:** Senior Vice President of Production
**IMDB:** http://www.imdb.com/name/
nm2142367/?ref_=fn_al_nm_1
**Assistant:** Ashley Johnson
ashley_johnson@spe.sony.com

**Hannah Minghella**
**Title:** President of Production
**IMDB:** http://www.imdb.com/name/
nm1098742/?ref_=fn_al_nm_1
**Assistant:** Mahsa Moayeri
mahsa_moayeri@spe.sony.com

**Adam Moos**
**Title:** Vice President of the Production
Administration
**IMDB:** http://www.imdb.com/name/
nm0602149/?ref_=fn_al_nm_1

**Rachel O'Connor**
**Title:** Senior Vice President of Production
**IMDB:** http://www.imdb.com/name/
nm1471418/?ref_=fn_al_nm_2

**Amy Pascal**
**Title:** Chairman
**IMDB:** http://www.imdb.com/name/
nm1166871/?ref_=fn_al_nm_1

## COMEDY ARTS STUDIOS

2500 Broadway
Santa Monica, CA 90404

**Phone:** 310-382-3677
**Fax:** 310-382-3170
**IMDB:** www.imdb.com/company/co0220109

**Submission Policy:** Accepts query letter from
unproduced, unrepresented writers
**Genre:** TV Drama, TV Sitcom

**Stu Smiley**
**Title:** Owner/Executive Producer
**IMDB:** www.imdb.com/name/nm0806979

## COMPLETION FILMS

60 East 42nd Street, Suite 4600
New York, NY 10165

**Phone:** 718-693-2057
**Fax:** 888-693-4133
**Email:** info@completionfilms.com

**Website:** www.completionfilms.com
**IMDB:** www.imdb.com/company/co0175660

**Submission Policy:** Accepts query letter from
unproduced, unrepresented writers
**Genre:** Memoir & True Stories

**Kisha Imani Cameron**
**Title:** President
**IMDB:** www.imdb.com/name/nm0131650

## CONCEPT ENTERTAINMENT

334 1/2 North Sierra Bonita Avenue
Los Angeles, CA 90036

**Phone:** 323-937-5700
**Fax:** 323-937-5720
**Email:** enquiries@conceptentertainment.biz
**Website:** www.conceptentertainment.biz
**IMDB:** www..imdb.com/company/co0096670

**Submission Policy:** Accepts query letter from
unproduced, unrepresented writers
**Genre:** Action, Comedy, Crime, Detective, Fantasy,
Horror, Memoir & True Stories, Myth, Romance,
Science Fiction, Thriller, TV Drama, TV Sitcom

**David Faigenblum**
**Title:** Producer/Manager
**IMDB:** www.imdb.com/name/nm1584960

## CONSTANTIN FILM

9200 West Sunset Boulevard, Suite 800
West Hollywood, CA 90069

Feilitzschstr. 6
Munich, Bavaria D-80802
Germany

**Phone:** 310-247-0300/ +49-89-44-44-60-0
**Fax:** 310-247-0305/ +49-89-44-44-60-666
**Email:** zentrale@constantin-film.de
**Website:** www.constantin-film.de
**IMDB:** www.imdb.com/company/co0002257

**Submission Policy:** Accepts query letter from
produced or represented writers
**Genre:** Action, Crime, Feature Films, Thriller, TV
**Focus:** Feature Films, Television
**Year Established:** 1950

**Fred Kogel**
**Title:** Germany - CEO
**Email:** elisabeth.kasch@constantin-film.de

**IMDB:** www.imdb.com/name/nm1827684
**Assistant:** Elisabeth Kasch

**Robert Kultzer**
**Title:** LA - Executive
**Phone:** 310-247-0300 ext. 3
**Email:** robert.kultzer@constantin-film.de
**IMDB:** www.imdb.com/name/nm0474709

**Herman Weigel**
**Title:** Germany - Executive Producer
**Email:** hermanweigel@constantin.film.de
**IMDB:** www.imdb.com/name/nm0917833

**Friedrich Wildfeuer**
**Title:** Germany - Head of TV Production
**Email:** zentrale@constantin-film.de
**IMDB:** www.imdb.com/name/nm0928662

**Stefan Wood**
**Title:** Germany - Development
**Email:** stefan.wood@constatin-film.de
**IMDB:** www.imdb.com/name/nm0940008

## CONTENT MEDIA CORPORATION PLC

225 Arizona Ave, Suite #250
Santa Monica, CA 90401

**Phone:** 310-576-1059
**Fax:** 310-576-1859
**Email:** jcassistant@contentmediacorp.com
**Website:** www.contentmediacorp.com
**IMDB:** www.imdb.com/company/co0366223

**Submission Policy:** Accepts query letter from unproduced, unrepresented writers

**Jamie Carmichael**
**Title:** President, Film Division
**Email:** jamie.carmichael@contentmediacorp.com
**IMDB:** www.imdb.com/name/nm0138430

## CONTRAFILM

1531 N Cahuenga Blvd
Los Angeles, CA 90028

**Phone:** 323-467-8787
**Fax:** 323-467-7730

**Submission Policy:** Accepts query letter from unproduced, unrepresented writers
**Genre:** Drama, Feature Films, Horror, Thriller
**Focus:** Feature Films

**Alexandra Church**
**Title:** Creative Executive
**IMDB:** www.imdb.com/name/nm0161344

**Tripp Vinson**
**Title:** Producer
**IMDB:** www.imdb.com/name/nm1246087
**Assistant:** Tara Farney

**Tucker Williams**
**Title:** Creative Executive
**IMDB:** www.imdb.com/name/nm2606099

## CONUNDRUM ENTERTAINMENT

325 Wilshire Boulevard, Suite 201
Santa Monica, CA 90401

**Phone:** 310-319-2800
**Fax:** 310-319-2808
**IMDB:** www.imdb.com/company/co0030016

**Submission Policy:** Accepts scripts from produced or represented writers
**Genre:** Comedy

**Bobby Farrelly**
**Title:** Executive
**IMDB:** www.imdb.com/name/nm0268370

**Peter Farrelly**
**Title:** Executive
**IMDB:** www.imdb.com/name/nm0268380

## COOPER'S TOWN PRODUCTIONS

302A West 12th Street, Suite 214
New York, NY 10014

**Phone:** 212-255-7566
**Fax:** 212-255-0211
**Email:** info@copperstownproductions.com
**Website:** www.copperstownproductions.com
**IMDB:** www.imdb.com/company/co0132168

**Submission Policy:** Accepts query letter from unproduced, unrepresented writers
**Genre:** Memoir & True Stories
**Focus:** Feature Films

**Phillip Hoffman**
**Title:** Partner
**IMDB:** www.imdb.com/name/nm0000450

**Sara Murphy**
**Title:** Head, Development (Executive)
**IMDB:** www.imdb.com/name/nm2072976

## COQUETTE PRODUCTIONS

8105 West Third Street
Los Angeles, CA 90048

**Phone:** 323-801-1000
**Fax:** 323-801-1001

**Submission Policy:** Does not accept any unsolicited material
**Genre:** Comedy, Crime, Drama, Romance, TV, TV Drama, TV Sitcom
**Focus:** Television

**David Arquette**
**Title:** Principal
**IMDB:** www.imdb.com/name/nm0000274

**Jeff Bowland**
**Title:** Executive
**IMDB:** www.imdb.com/name/nm0101188

**Courtney Cox**
**Title:** Principal
**IMDB:** www.imdb.com/name/nm0001073

**Thea Mann**
**Title:** Head of Development
**IMDB:** www.imdb.com/name/nm0542996

## CORNER STORE ENTERTAINMENT

9615 Brighton Way
Ste 201
Beverly Hills, CA 90210

**Phone:** 310-276-6400
**Fax:** 310-276-6410
**Website:** www.cornerstore-ent.com

**Submission Policy:** Does not accept any unsolicited material
**Genre:** Comedy, Drama, Feature Films, Romance
**Focus:** Feature Flms

**Scott Prisand**
**Title:** Principal
**IMDB:** www.imdb.com/name/nm1964055

**Matthew Weaver**
**Title:** Principal
**IMDB:** www.imdb.com/name/nm2822461

## CRAVE FILMS

3312 Sunset Boulevard
Los Angeles, CA 90026

**Phone:** 323-669-9000
**Fax:** 323-669-9002
**Website:** www.cravefilms.com
**IMDB:** www.imdb.com/company/co0146364

**Submission Policy:** Does not accept any unsolicited material
**Genre:** Drama
**Focus:** Feature Films

**David Ayer**
**Title:** Writer/Director/Producer
**Email:** david@cravefilms.com
**IMDB:** www.imdb.com/name/nm0043742

**Alex Ott**
**Title:** Vice-President, Productions
**Email:** alex@cravefilms.com
**IMDB:** www.imdb.com/name/nm1944773

## CREANSPEAK PRODUCTIONS LLC

120 South El Camino Drive
Beverly Hills, CA 90212

**Phone:** 310-273-8217
**Email:** info@creanspeak.com
**IMDB:** www.imdb.com/company/co0097231

**Submission Policy:** Accepts query letter from unproduced, unrepresented writers via email
**Genre:** Action, Comedy, Drama, Family, Memoir & True Stories
**Focus:** Feature Films, TV, Post-Production (Editing, Special Effects), Reality Programming (Reality TV, Documentaries, Special Events, Sporting Events), Media (Commercials/Branding/Marketing)

**Kelly Crean**
**Title:** Founder/Executive
**Phone:** 310-273-8217
**Email:** info@creanspeak.com
**IMDB:** www.imdb.com/name/nm1047631

**Jon Freis**
**Title:** Vice-President/Executive
**Phone:** 310-273-8217
**Email:** info@creanspeak.com
**IMDB:** www.imdb.com/name/nm2045371

## CRESCENDO PRODUCTIONS

252 North Larchmont Boulevard, Suite 200
Los Angeles, CA 90004

**Phone:** 323-465-2222
**Fax:** 323-464-3750
**IMDB:** ww.imdb.com/company/co0025116

**Submission Policy:** Accepts query letter from unproduced, unrepresented writers
**Focus:** Feature Films, TV, Reality Programming (Reality TV, Documentaries, Special Events, Sporting Events)

**Don Cheadle**
**Title:** Actor/Executive
**Phone:** 323-465-2222
**IMDB:** www.imdb.com/name/nm0000332

## CREST ANIMATION PRODUCTIONS

333 North Glenoaks Boulevard, Suite 300
Burbank, CA 91502

**Phone:** 818-846-0166
**Fax:** 818-846-6074
**Email:** info@crestcgi.com
**Website:** www.crestcgi.com
**IMDB:** www.imdb.com/company/co0218880

**Submission Policy:** Accepts query letter from unproduced, unrepresented writers via email
**Genre:** Animation
**Focus:** Feature Films

**Gregory Kasunich**
**Title:** Production Coordinator/Manager
**Phone:** 818-846-0166
**Email:** gkasunich@crestcgi.com
**IMDB:** www.imdb.com/name/nm3215310

**Richard Rich**
**Title:** President/Writer
**Phone:** 818-846-0166
**Email:** info@crestcgi.com
**IMDB:** www.imdb.com/name/nm0723704

## CRIME SCENE PICTURES

3450 Cahuenga Boulevard W, Suite 701
Los Angeles, CA 90068

**Phone:** 323-963-5136
**Fax:** 323-963-5137
**Email:** info@crimescenepictures.net
**Website:** www.crimescenepictures.net
**IMDB:** www.imdb.com/company/co0326645

**Submission Policy:** Does not accept any unsolicited material

**Focus:** Feature Films
**Year Established:** 2010

**Brett Hedblom**
**Title:** Director of Development
**IMDB:** www.imdb.com/name/nm3916261

**Jennifer Marmor**
**Title:** Creative Executive
**IMDB:** www.imdb.com/name/nm4420063

**Adam Ripp**
**Title:** Writer/Producer/Director
**IMDB:** www.imdb.com/name/nm0728063

## CRISPY FILMS

2812 Santa Monica Blvd
Ste 205
Santa Monica, CA 90404

**Phone:** 310-453-4545
**Email:** crispyfilms@gmail.com

**Submission Policy:** Does not accept any unsolicited material
**Genre:** Comedy, Drama, Romance
**Focus:** Feature Film

**Jonathan Schwartz**
**Title:** Producer
**Phone:** 310-453-4545
**IMDB:** www.imdb.com/name/nm2009933

**Andrea Sperling**
**Title:** Producer
**Phone:** 310-453-4545
**IMDB:** www.imdb.com/name/nm0818304

## CROSS CREEK PICTURES

9220 West Sunset Boulevard, Suite 100
West Hollywood, CA 90069

**Phone:** 310-248-4061
**Fax:** 310-248-4068
**Email:** info@crosscreekpictures.com
**Website:** www.crosscreekpictures.com
**IMDB:** www.imdb.com/company/co0285648

**Submission Policy:** Accepts query letter from unproduced, unrepresented writers via email
**Genre:** Drama
**Focus:** Feature Films, TV

**Stephanie Hall**
**Title:** Development
**Email:** stephanie@crosscreekpicture.com
**IMDB:** www.imdb.com/name/nm24206

**Brian Oliver**
**Title:** President
**Email:** brian@crosscreekpicture.com
**IMDB:** www.imdb.com/name/nm1003922

**John Shepherd**
**Title:** Creative Executive
**Phone:** 310-248-4061
**Email:** info@crosscreekpicture.com
**IMDB:** www.imdb.com/name/nm3005173

## CROSSROADS FILMS

1722 Whitley Avenue
Los Angeles, CA 90028

**Phone:** 310-659-6220
**Fax:** 310-659-3105
**Website:** www.crossroadsfilms.com/
**IMDB:** www.imdb.com/company/co0061179

**Submission Policy:** Accepts query letter from unproduced, unrepresented writers
**Genre:** Comedy, Crime, Drama, Romance, Thriller
**Focus:** Feature Films, TV, Media (Commercials/Branding/Marketing)

**Camille Taylor**
**Title:** Producer/Partner
**Phone:** 310-659-6220
**IMDB:** www.imdb.com/name/nm0852088

## CRUCIAL FILMS

2220 Colorado Avenue, 5th Floor
Santa Monica, CA 90404

**Phone:** 310-865-8249
**Fax:** 310-865-7068
**Email:** crucialfilms.asst@gmail.com
**IMDB:** www.imdb.com/company/co0049027

**Submission Policy:** Does not accept any unsolicited material
**Genre:** Action, Comedy, Crime, Drama, Fantasy, Horror, Romance, Thriller
**Focus:** Feature Films, TV

**Daniel Schnider**
**Title:** Head of Production & Development/Producer
**Phone:** 310-865-8249

**Email:** crucialfilms.asst@gmail.com
**IMDB:** www.imdb.com/name/nm3045845

## CRYSTAL LAKE ENTERTAINMENT, INC.

4420 Hayvenhurst Avenue
Encino, CA 91436

**Phone:** 818-995-1585
**Fax:** 818-995-1677
**Email:** sscfilms@earthlink.net
**IMDB:** www.imdb.com/company/co0067362

**Submission Policy:** Accepts query letter from unproduced, unrepresented writers via email
**Genre:** Horror, Science Fiction, Thriller
**Focus:** Feature Films, TV

**Sean Cunningham**
**Title:** Producer/Director/Writer
**Phone:** 818-995-1585
**Email:** sscfilms@earthlink.net
**IMDB:** www.imdb.com/name/nm0192446

**Geoff Garrett**
**Title:** Creative Executive/Producer/Production Manager/Cinematographer
**Phone:** 818-995-1585
**Email:** sscfilms@earthlink.net
**IMDB:** www.imdb.com/name/nm0308117

## CRYSTAL SKY PICTURES, LLC

10203 Santa Monica Boulevard, 5th Floor
Los Angeles, CA 90067

**Phone:** 310-843-0223
**Fax:** 310-553-9895
**Email:** info@crystalsky.com
**Website:** www.crystalsky.com
**IMDB:** www.imdb.com/company/co0004724

**Submission Policy:** Accepts query letter from unproduced, unrepresented writers via email
**Genre:** Action, Comedy, Crime, Drama, Family, Fantasy, Horror, Science Fiction, Thriller
**Focus:** Feature Films

**Eric Breiman**
**Title:** Executive/Producer/Production Manager/Actor
**Phone:** 310-843-0223
**Email:** info@crystalsky.com

**Florent Gaglio**
Title: Executive
Phone: 310-843-0223
Email: info@crystalsky.com
IMDB: www.imdb.com/name/nm2904382

**Steven Paul**
Title: Executive/CEO
Phone: 310-843-0223
Email: info@crystalsky.com
IMDB: www.imdb.com/name/nm0666999

## CUBE VISION

9000 West Sunset Boulevard
West Hollywood, CA 90069

Phone: 310-461-3490
Fax: 310-461-3491
Website: http://www.icecube.com/
IMDB: www.imdb.com/company/co0044714

Submission Policy: Accepts query letter from
unproduced, unrepresented writers
Genre: Action, Animation, Comedy, Crime, Drama,
Family, Romance, Thriller
Focus: Feature Films, TV, Reality Programming
(Reality TV, Documentaries, Special Events,
Sporting Events)

**Matt Alvarez**
Title: Partner
Phone: 310-461-3490
IMDB: www.imdb.com/name/nm0023297
Assistant: Lawtisha Fletcher

**Ice Cube**
Title: Owner/Partner
Phone: 310-461-3495
IMDB: www.imdb.com/name/nm0001084
Assistant: Nancy Leiviska

## CURB ENTERTAINMENT

3907 West Alameda Avenue
Burbank, CA 91505

Phone: 818-843-8580
Fax: 818-566-1719
Email: info@curbentertainment.com
Website: www.curbentertainment.com
IMDB: www.mdb.com/company/co0089886

Submission Policy: Accepts query letter from
unproduced, unrepresented writers via email

Genre: Animation, Comedy, Crime, Drama, Family,
Horror, Romance, Science Fiction, Thriller
Focus: Feature Films, TV
Year Established: 1984

**Mona Kirton**
Title: Director/Head, Distribution Services
Phone: 818-843-8580
Email: mkirton@curb.com
IMDB: www.imdb.com/name/nm1310398

**Carole Nemoy**
Title: President/Executive Producer
Phone: 818-843-8580
Email: ccurb@curb.com
IMDB: www.imdb.com/name/nm0626002

**Christy Peterson**
Title: Acquisitions
Phone: 818-843-8580
Email: cpeterson@curb.com

## CYAN PICTURES

410 Park Avenue, 15th Floor
New York, NY 10022

Phone: 212-274-1085
Email: info@cyanpictures.com
IMDB: www.imdb.com/company/co0080910

Submission Policy: Accepts query letter from
unproduced, unrepresented writers via email
Genre: Comedy, Crime, Drama, Horror, Memoir &
True Stories, Romance, Science Fiction, Thriller
Focus: Feature Films, Reality Programming (Reality
TV, Documentaries, Special Events, Sporting
Events)

**Alexander Burns**
Title: CFO
Phone: 212-274-1085
Email: info@cyanpictures.com

**Joshua Newman**
Title: CEO
Phone: 212-274-1085
Email: newman@cyanpictures.com
IMDB: www.imdb.com/name/nm1243333

**Wes Schrader**
Title: Vice-President of Distribution
Phone: 212-274-1085
Email: schrader@cyanpictures.com

## CYPRESS FILMS, INC.

630 Ninth Avenue, Suite 415
New York, NY 10036

**Phone:** 212-262-3900
**Fax:** 212-262-3925
**Website:** www.cypressfilms.com
**IMDB:** www.imdb.com/company/co0044830

**Submission Policy:** Accepts query letter from
unproduced, unrepresented writers via email
**Genre:** Comedy, Drama, Family, Romance, Science
Fiction
**Focus:** Feature Films

### Jessica Forsythe
**Title:** Submissions Director
**Email:** jforsythe@cypressfilms.com

### Jon Glascoe
**Title:** Co-Founder/Executive Producer/Writer
**Phone:** 212-262-3900
**Email:** jglascoe@cypressfilms.com
**IMDB:** www.imdb.com/name/nm0321797

### Joseph Pierson
**Title:** President/Director/Producer
**Phone:** 212-262-3900
**Email:** joseph@cypressfilms.com
**IMDB:** www.imdb.com/name/nm0682777

## CYPRESS POINT PRODUCTIONS

3000 Olympic Boulevard
Santa Monica, CA 90404

**Phone:** 310-315-4787
**Fax:** 310-315-4785
**Email:** cppfilms@earthlink.net
**IMDB:** www.imdb.com/company/co0038030

**Submission Policy:** Accepts query letter from
unproduced, unrepresented writers via email
**Genre:** Action, Comedy, Crime, Drama, Family,
Memoir & True Stories, Romance, Science Fiction,
Thriller
**Focus:** TV

### Gerald Abrams
**Title:** Chairman
**Phone:** 310-315-4787
**Email:** cppfilms@earthlink.net
**IMDB:** www.imdb.com/name/nm0009181

### Michael Waldron
**Title:** Director, Development
**Phone:** 310-315-4787
**Email:** cppfilms@earthlink.net
**IMDB:** www.imdb.com/name/nm1707236

## DAKOTA PICTURES

4133 Lankershim Boulevard
North Hollywood, CA 91602

**Phone:** 818-760-0099
**Fax:** 818-760-1070
**Email:** info@dakotafilms.com
**Website:** www.dakotafilms.com

**Submission Policy:** Does not accept any unsolicited
material
**Genre:** Action, Animation, Comedy, Crime, Drama,
Family, Fantasy, Memoir & True Stories, Thriller
**Focus:** Feature Films, TV, Reality Programming
(Reality TV, Documentaries, Special Events,
Sporting Events)

### A.J. DiAntonio
**Title:** Producer/Production Executive
**Phone:** 818-760-0099
**Email:** info@dakotafilms.com
**IMDB:** www.imdb.com/name/nm1472504

### Matt Magielnicki
**Title:** Producer/Development Executive
**Phone:** 818-760-0099
**Email:** info@dakotafilms.com
**IMDB:** www.imdb.com/name/nm2616148

### Troy Miller
**Title:** Founder/Director/Producer
**Phone:** 818-760-0099
**Email:** info@dakotafilms.com
**IMDB:** www.imdb.com/name/nm0003474

## DANIEL L. PAULSON PRODUCTIONS

9056 Santa Monica Boulevard, Suite 203A
West Hollywood, CA 90069

**Phone:** 310-278-9747
**Fax:** 310-278-3751
**Email:** dlpprods@sbcglobal.net

**Submission Policy:** Does not accept any unsolicited
material
**Genre:** Action, Comedy, Crime, Detective, Drama,
Family, Reality, Romance, Thriller, TV Sitcom

**Focus:** Feature Films, TV, Reality Programming (Reality TV, Documentaries, Special Events, Sporting Events)

**Steve Kennedy**
**Title:** Director/Adminstration
**Phone:** 310-278-9747
**Email:** dlpprods@sbcglobal.net
**IMDB:** www.imdb.com/name/nm0448346

**Daniel Paulson**
**Title:** President/Executive
**Phone:** 310-278-9747
**Email:** dlpprods@sbcglobal.net
**IMDB:** www.imdb.com/name/nm0667340

## DANIEL OSTROFF PRODUCTIONS

2046 North Hillhurst Ave. #120
Los Angeles, CA 90027

**Phone:** 323-284-8824
**Email:** oteamthe@gmail.com
**IMDB:** www.imdb.com/company/co0138101

**Submission Policy:** Accepts query letter from unproduced, unrepresented writers
**Genre:** Detective, TV Sitcom
**Focus:** Feature Films, TV, Reality Programming (Reality TV, Documentaries, Special Events, Sporting Events)

**Daniel Ostroff**
**Title:** Producer
**Phone:** 323-284-8824
**Email:** oteamthe@gmail.com
**IMDB:** www.imdb.com/name/nm0652491

## DANIEL PETRIE JR. & COMPANY

18034 Ventura Boulevard, Suite 445
Encino, CA 91316

**Phone:** 818-708-1602
**Fax:** 818-774-0345
**IMDB:** www.imdb.com/company/co0120842

**Submission Policy:** Accepts query letter from unproduced, unrepresented writers
**Genre:** Action, Comedy, Crime, Detective, Drama, Horror, Romance, Science Fiction, Thriller
**Focus:** Feature Films, TV

**Rick Dugdale**
**Title:** Vice-President/Executive/Producer/Production Manager

**Phone:** 818-708-1602
**IMDB:** www.imdb.com/name/nm1067987

**Daniel Petrie,**
**Title:** Director/Writer/Producer
**Phone:** 818-708-1602
**IMDB:** www.imdb.com/name/nm0677943

## DANIEL SLADEK ENTERTAINMENT CORPORATION

8306 Wilshire Boulevard, Suite 510
Beverly Hills, CA 90211

**Phone:** 323-934-9268
**Fax:** 323-934-7362
**Email:** danielsladek@mac.com
**Website:** www.danielsladek.com

**Submission Policy:** Does not accept any unsolicited material
**Genre:** Action, Comedy, Crime, Drama, Fantasy, Horror, Memoir & True Stories, Reality, Romance, Science Fiction, Thriller
**Focus:** Feature Films, TV, Reality Programming (Reality TV, Documentaries, Special Events, Sporting Events)
**Year Established:** 1998

**Daniel Sladek**
**Title:** President/Producer
**Phone:** 323-934-9268
**Email:** danielsladek@mac.com
**IMDB:** www.imdb.com/name/nm0805202

## DANJAQ

2400 Broadway
Ste 310
Santa Monica, CA 90404

**Phone:** 310-449-3185

**Submission Policy:** Does not accept any unsolicited material
**Genre:** Action
**Focus:** Feature Films

**Barbara Broccoli**
**Title:** Vice President of Development & Production
**IMDB:** www.imdb.com/name/nm0110483

**David Pope**
**Title:** CEO
**Phone:** 310-449-3185
**IMDB:** www.imdb.com/name/nm0691102

**Michael Wilson**
Title: President
Phone: 310-449-3185
IMDB: www.imdb.com/name/nm0933865

## DAN LUPOVITZ PRODUCTIONS

936 Alandele Avenue
Los Angeles, CA 90036

Phone: 323-930-0769
Fax: 310-385-0196
Email: dlupovitz@aol.com

Submission Policy: Accepts query letter from
unproduced, unrepresented writers via email
Genre: Comedy, Drama, Romance
Focus: Feature Films, TV

**Randy Albelda**
Title: Development
Phone: 323-930-0769

**Dan Lupovitz**
Title: Executive/Producer
Phone: 323-930-0769
Email: dlupovitz@aol.com
IMDB: www.imdb.com/name/nm0526991

## DAN WINGUTOW PRODUCTIONS

534 Laguardia Pl., Suite 3
New York, NY 10012

Phone: 212-477-1328
Fax: 212-254-6902

Submission Policy: Accepts query letter from
unproduced, unrepresented writers
Genre: Comedy, Crime, Drama, Fantasy, Horror,
Romance, Science Fiction, Thriller
Focus: Feature Films, TV

**Caroline Moore**
Title: Co-Producer
Phone: 212-477-1328
IMDB: www.imdb.com/name/nm0601006

**Dan Wigutow**
Title: Executive Producer
Phone: 212-477-1328
IMDB: www.imdb.com/name/nm0927887

## DARIUS FILMS INCORPORATED

1020 Cole Avenue, Suite 4363
Los Angeles, CA 90038

Phone: 310-728-1342
Fax: 310-494-0575
Email: info@dariusfilms.com
Website: www.dariusfilms.com
IMDB: www.imdb.com/company/co0133523

Submission Policy: Accepts query letter from
produced or represented writers
Genre: Comedy, Crime, Detective, Drama, Fantasy,
Memoir & True Stories, Romance, Science Fiction,
Thriller
Focus: Feature Films, TV

**Daniel Baruela**
Title: Development
Phone: 310-728-1342
Email: info@dariusfilms.com
IMDB: www.imdb.com/name/nm3758990

**Nicholas Tabarrok**
Title: President/Actor/Producer
Phone: 310-728-1342
Email: info@dariusfilms.com
IMDB: www.imdb.com/name/nm0002431

## DARK CASTLE ENTERTAINMENT

1601 Main Street
Venice, CA 90291

Phone: 310-566-6100
Fax: 310-566-6188

Submission Policy: Accepts query letter from
produced or represented writers
Genre: Action, Crime, Drama, Feature Films,
Horror, Thriller
Focus: Feature Films
Year Established: 1999

**Steve Richards**
Title: Co-President
IMDB: www.imdb.com/name/nm0724345

**Andrew Rona**
Title: Co-President
IMDB: www.imdb.com/name/nm0739868
Assistant: Dash Boam

**Joel Silver**
Title: Partner
IMDB: www.imdb.com/name/nm0005428

## DARK HORSE ENTERTAINMENT

8425 West 3rd Street, Suite 400
Los Angeles, CA 90048

Phone: 323-655-3600
Fax: 323-655-2430
Website: www.dhentertainment.com/
IMDB: www.imdb.com/company/co0020061

Submission Policy: Does not accept any unsolicited
material
Genre: Action, Animation, Comedy, Crime, Drama,
Family, Fantasy, Horror, Memoir & True Stories,
Romance, Science Fiction, Thriller
Focus: Feature Films

**Keith Goldberg**
Title: Senior Vice-President Production
Phone: 323-655-3600
Email: keithg@darkhorse.com
IMDB: www.imdb.com/name/nm1378991

**Mike Richardson**
Title: President/Producer
Phone: 323-655-3600
Email: miker@darkhorse.com
IMDB: www.imdb.com/name/nm0724700
Assistant: Pete Cacioppo

## DARKO ENTERTAINMENT

1041 North Formosa Avenue,
West Hollywood, CA 90046

Phone: 323-850-2480
Fax: 323-850-2481
Email: info@darko.com
Website: www.darko.com
IMDB: www.imdb.com/company/co0118694

Submission Policy: Does not accept any unsolicited
material
Genre: Fantasy, Horror, Thriller
Focus: Feature Films, TV

**Jeff Cullota**
Title: Vice President (Production and Development)
IMDB: www.imdb.com/name/nm2261214

## DARK SKY FILMS

16101 S 108th Ave
Orland Park, IL 60467

Phone: 800-323-0442
Email: info@darkskyfilms.com
Website: www.darkskyfilms.com

Submission Policy: Does not accept any unsolicited
material
Genre: Horror, Thriller
Focus: Feature Films

**Malik Ali**
Title: Executive
IMDB: www.imdb.com/name/nm0019446

**Greg Newman**
Title: Executive
IMDB: www.imdb.com/name/nm0628103

**Todd Wieneke**
Title: Producer
IMDB: www.imdb.com/name/nm2663562

## DARKWOODS PRODUCTIONS

301 East Colorado Boulevard, Suite 705
Pasadena, CA 91101

Phone: 323-454-4580
Fax: 323-454-4581
IMDB: www.imdb.com/company/co0029398

Submission Policy: Does not accept any unsolicited
material
Genre: Comedy, Crime, Drama, Fantasy, Horror,
Memoir & True Stories, Romance, Science Fiction,
Thriller
Focus: Feature Films

**Frank Darobont**
Title: Partner/Director/Writer/Producer
Phone: 323-454-4582
IMDB: www.imdb.com/name/nm0001104
Assistant: Alex Whit

**Denise Huth**
Title: Vice-President, Production
Phone: 323-454-4580
IMDB: www.imdb.com/name/nm1040337

## DARREN STAR PRODUCTIONS

9200 Sunset Boulevard, Suite 430
Los Angeles, CA 90069

**Phone:** 310-274-2145
**Fax:** 310-274-1455
**Email:** d.star.prodco@gmail.com
**IMDB:** www.imdb.com/company/co0020963

**Submission Policy:** Accepts query letter from unproduced, unrepresented writers
**Genre:** Crime, Drama, Memoir & True Stories, Romance, TV Drama, TV Sitcom
**Focus:** Feature Films, TV

### Charles Pugliese
**Title:** Vice-President Production and Development
**Phone:** 310-274-2145
**IMDB:** www.imdb.com/name/nm1551399

### Darren Star
**Title:** Creator/Executive Producer/Writer
**Phone:** 310-274-2145
**IMDB:** www.imdb.com/name/nm0823015

## DAVE BELL ASSOCIATES

3211 Cahuenga Boulevard West
Los Angeles, CA 90068

**Phone:** 323-851-7801
**Fax:** 323-851-9349
**Email:** dbamovies@aol.com
**IMDB:** www.imdb.com/company/co0033679

**Submission Policy:** Accepts query letter from unproduced, unrepresented writers via email
**Genre:** Drama, Family, Horror, Memoir & True Stories, Romance, Science Fiction
**Focus:** Feature Films, TV, Reality Programming (Reality TV, Documentaries, Special Events, Sporting Events)

### Dave Bell
**Title:** President
**Phone:** 323-851-7801
**Email:** dbamovies@aol.com
**IMDB:** www.imdb.com/name/nm1037012

### Fred Putman
**Title:** Director, TV
**Phone:** 323-851-7801
**IMDB:** www.imdb.com/name/nm1729656

### Ted Weiant
**Title:** Director, Motion Pictures
**Phone:** 323-851-7801
**Email:** dbamovies@aol.com
**IMDB:** www.imdb.com/name/nm1059707

## DAVID EICK PRODUCTIONS

100 Universal City Plaza
Universal City, CA 91608

**Phone:** 818-501-0146
**Fax:** 818-733-2522
**IMDB:** www.imdb.com/company/co0176813

**Submission Policy:** Accepts query letter from unproduced, unrepresented writers
**Genre:** Action, Drama, Science Fiction, Thriller
**Focus:** TV

### David Eick
**Title:** President
**Phone:** 818-501-0146
**IMDB:** www.imdb.com/name/nm0251594

## DAVIS ENTERTAINMENT

10201 W Pico Blvd
# 31-301
Los Angeles, CA 90064

**Phone:** 310-556-3550
**Fax:** 310-556-3688
**IMDB:** www.imdb.com/company/co0022730

**Submission Policy:** Accepts scripts from produced or represented writers

### John Davis
**Title:** Executive/Chairman/Founder
**IMDB:** www.imdb.com/name/nm0204862

### John Fox
**Title:** President of Production
**IMDB:** www.imdb.com/name/nm2470810

## DEED FILMS

**Phone:** 419-685-4842
**Email:** sdonely@deedfilms.com
**Website:** www.deedfilms.com
**IMDB:** www.imdb.com/company/co0323092

**Submission Policy:** Accepts query letter from unproduced, unrepresented writers via email
**Genre:** Comedy, Crime
**Focus:** Feature Films
**Year Established:** 2008

### Scott Donley
**Title:** President
**IMDB:** www.imdb.com/name/nm4238094

## DEERJEN FILMS

222 W 23rd St
New York, NY 10011

**Website:** www.deerjen.com

**Submission Policy:** Accepts query letter from produced or represented writers
**Genre:** Comedy, Drama, Feature Films, Period, Romance, Thriller
**Focus:** Feature Films

### Jen Gatien
**Title:** Producer
**Email:** jen@deerjen.com
**IMDB:** www.imdb.com/name/nm0309684

## DEFIANCE ENTERTAINMENT

6605 Hollywood Boulevard, Suite 100
Los Angeles, CA 91401

**Phone:** 323-393-0132
**Email:** info@defiance-ent.com
**Website:** www.defiance-ent.com
**IMDB:** www.imdb.com/company/co0236811

**Submission Policy:** Accepts query letter from unproduced, unrepresented writers via email
**Genre:** Action, Comedy, Crime, Drama, Fantasy, Horror, Myth, Science Fiction, Thriller
**Focus:** Feature Films, TV, Media (Commercials/Branding/Marketing)
**Year Established:** 2006

### Brian Keathley
**Title:** President/CEO
**Email:** brian@defiance-ent.com
**IMDB:** www.imdb.com/name/nm0444080

### Clare Kramer
**Title:** COO
**Email:** clare@defiance-ent.com
**IMDB:** www.imdb.com/name/nm0004456

## DE LINE PICTURES

4000 Warner Boulevard Building 66, Room 147
Burbank, CA 91522

**Phone:** 818-954-5200
**Fax:** 818-954-5430
**IMDB:** http://www.imdb.com/company/co0033149/?ref_=fn_al_co_1

**Submission Policy:** Does not accept any unsolicited material
**Genre:** Action, Animation, Comedy, Crime, Drama, Family, Fantasy, Period, Romance, Science Fiction, Thriller
**Focus:** Feature Films
**Year Established:** 2001

### Donald De Line
**Title:** President
**IMDB:** http://www.imdb.com/name/nm0209773/?ref_=fn_al_nm_1
**Assistant:** Matt Gamboa matt@delinepictures.com

### Ally Israelson
**Title:** Story Editor

### Jacob Robinson
**Title:** Vice President of Development
**IMDB:** http://www.imdb.com/name/nm1563784/?ref_=fn_al_nm_2

## DELVE FILMS

20727 High Desert Ct
Suite 4+5
Bend, OR 97701

**Phone:** 424-703-3583
**Email:** info@delvefilms.com
**Website:** www.delvefilms.com

**Submission Policy:** Accepts query letter from produced or represented writers
**Genre:** Comedy, Documentary, Drama, Fantasy, Feature Films, Romance, Thriller
**Focus:** Feature Films

### Nate Salciccioli
**Title:** Vice President
**Phone:** 541-788-6139
**Email:** nate@delvefilms.com
**IMDB:** www.imdb.com/name/nm4244606

### Isaac Testerman
**Title:** President
**Email:** isaac@delvefilms.com
**IMDB:** www.imdb.com/name/nm4107099

## DEMAREST FILMS

100 North Crescent Drive
Suite 350
Beverly Hills, CA 90210

**Phone:** 310-385-4310

**Submission Policy:** Does not accept any unsolicited material
**Genre:** Crime, Drama, Fantasy, Feature Films, Thriller, TV Sitcom
**Focus:** Feature Films

**Sam Englebardt**
Title: Principal
IMDB: www.mdb.com/name/nm1583132
Assistant: Linda Goetz

**Brian Flanagan**
Title: Vice President

**William D. Johnso**
Title: Principal
IMDB: www.imdb.com/name/nm4207924

**Michael Lambert**
Title: Principal
IMDB: www.imdb.com/name/nm2236003

## DEPTH OF FIELD

1724 Whitley Avenue
Los Angeles, CA 90028

Phone: 323-466-6500
Fax: 323-466-6501
IMDB: www.imdb.com/company/co0113177

**Submission Policy:** Accepts scripts from produced or represented writers
**Focus:** Feature Films

**Andrew Miano**
Title: Executive Producer
IMDB: www.imdb.com/name/nm0583948

**Chris Weitz**
Title: Ower
IMDB: www.imdb.com/name/nm0919363

## DESERT WIND FILMS

13603 Marina Pointe Dr
Ste D529
Marina Del Rey, CA 90292

Phone: 661-200-3509
Fax: 310-499-5254
Email: media@desertwindfilms.com
Website: www.desertwindfilms.com

**Submission Policy:** Accepts query letter from unproduced, unrepresented writers

**Genre:** Feature Films
**Focus:** Feature Films

**T.J. Amato**
Title: President
IMDB: www.imdb.com/name/nm2125600

**Danny Amato**
Title: Production Coordinator
IMDB: www.imdb.com/name/nm3824734

**Steven Camp**
Title: CFO
IMDB: www.imdb.com/name/nm3823972

**Josh Mills**
Title: CEO & Managing Director
IMDB: www.imdb.com/name/nm1836231

**Jeffrey James Ward**
Title: Associate Producer
IMDB: www.imdb.com/name/nm3823932

## DI BONAVENTURA PICTURES

5555 Melrose Avenue
DeMille Building, 2nd Floor
Los Angeles, CA 90038

Phone: 323-956-5454
Fax: 323-862-2288

**Submission Policy:** Does not accept any unsolicited material
**Genre:** Action, Fantasy, Science Fiction, Thriller
**Focus:** Feature Films

**Lorenzo di Bonaventura**
Title: President/Producer
IMDB: www.imdb.com/name/nm0225146

**Erik Howsam**
Title: Senior Vice-President Production
IMDB: www.imdb.com/name/nm1857184

**David Ready**
Title: VP (Executive)
IMDB: http://www.imdb.com/name/nm2819401/

**Mark Vahradian**
Title: President of Production
(Executive)http://www.imdb.com/name/nm1680607/
IMDB: http://www.imdb.com/name/nm1680607/

## DI BONAVENTURA PICTURES TELEVISION

500 South Buena Vista Street Animation Building,
Suite 3F-3
Burbank, CA 91521

IMDB: http://www.imdb.com/company/co0341152/

Submission Policy: Does not accept any unsolicited
material
Genre: Science Fiction, Thriller, TV Drama
Focus: Television
Year Established: 2011

### Lorenzo di Bonaventura
Title: Partner
IMDB: http://www.imdb.com/name/nm0225146/
Assistant: Elizabeth Kiernan

### Dan McDermott
Title: Partner
IMDB: http://www.imdb.com/name/nm1908145/

## DIFFERENT DUCK FILMS

18 Wardell Ave.,
Rumson, NJ 07760

Email: DifferentDuckFilms@hotmail.com

Submission Policy: Does not accept any unsolicited
material
Genre: Comedy, Drama, Family, Fantasy, Thriller
Focus: Feature Films

### Rob Margolies
Title: Principal
IMDB: www.imdb.com/name/nm1827689

## DIMENSION FILMS

345 Hudson St
13th Fl
New York, NY 10014

Phone: 646-862-3400
Website: www.weinsteinco.com

Submission Policy: Does not accept any unsolicited
material
Genre: Action Comedy, Horror, Science Fiction,
Thriller
Focus: Feature Films

### Andrew Kramer
Title: President
IMDB: www.imdb.com/name/nm2985328

### Jeff Maynard
Title: Post Production
IMDB: www.imdb.com/name/nm0963230

### Matthew Signer
Title: Production & Creative Affairs
IMDB: www.imdb.com/name/nm1529449

### Bob Weinstein
Title: Co-Chairman
IMDB: www.imdb.com/name/nm0918424

## DINO DE LAURENTIIS COMPANY

100 Universal City Plaza Bungalow 5195
Universal City, CA 91608

Phone: 818-777-2111
Fax: 818-886-5566
Email: ddlcoffice@ddlc.net
Website: www.ddlc.net

Submission Policy: Does not accept any unsolicited
material
Genre: Action, Crime, Detective, Drama, Feature
Films, Horror, Romance, Science Fiction, Thriller,
TV, TV Drama
Focus: Feature Films

### Stuart Boros
Title: Executive of Business Affairs
IMDB: www.imdb.com/name/nm0097214

### Martha De Laurentiis
Title: President
IMDB: www.imdb.com/name/nm0776646

### Lorenzo De Maio
Title: President of Production
IMDB: www.imdb.com/name/nm1298951

### Bobby Gonzales
Title: Assistant
IMDB: www.imdb.com/name/nm5260285

### Meryl Pestano
Title: Assistant
IMDB: www.imdb.com/name/nm2535378

## DINOVI PICTURES

720 Wilshire Boulevard, Suite 300
Santa Monica, CA 90401

Phone: 310-458-7200
Fax: 310-458-7211
IMDB: http://www.imdb.com/company/co0062957/

**Submission Policy:** Accepts scripts from produced or represented writers
**Genre:** Drama, Romance
**Focus:** Feature Films
**Year Established:** 1993

**Denise DiNovi**
**Title:** Chief Executive Officer
**IMDB:** www.imdb.com/name/nm0224145
**Assistant:** Maureen Poon Fear

**Alison Greenspan**
**Title:** President
**IMDB:** http://www.imdb.com/name/nm1327019/
**Assistant:** Rebecca Rajkowski

## DMG ENTERTAINMENT

644 North Cherokee Avenue
Melrose Gate
Los Angeles, CA 90004

**Phone:** 310-275-3750
**Fax:** 310-275-3770
**Email:** info@dmg-entertainment.com
**Website:** http://www.h2f-entertainment.com

**Submission Policy:** Accepts query letter from unproduced, unrepresented writers
**Genre:** Action, Comedy, Drama, Horror, Romance, Science Fiction, Thriller
**Focus:** Feature Films, TV

**Chris Cowles**
**Title:** Producer
**IMDB:** www.imdb.com/name/nm1038319

**Brian McCurly**
**Title:** Assistant

## DNA FILMS

10 Amwell Street
London EC1R 1UQ

**Phone:** +44 020-7843-4410
**Fax:** +44 020-7843-4411
**Email:** info@dnafilms.com
**Website:** www.dnafilms.com

**Submission Policy:** Does not accept any unsolicited material
**Genre:** Comedy, Crime, Drama, Horror, Romance, Thriller
**Focus:** Feature Films
**Year Established:** 1999

**Andrew Macdonald**
**Title:** Partner
**Phone:** +44 020 7843 4410
**IMDB:** www.imdb.com/name/nm0531602

**Allon Reich**
**Title:** Partner
**Phone:** +44 020 7843 4410
**IMDB:** www.imdb.com/name/nm0716924

## DOBRE FILMS

**Phone:** 310-926-6439
**Email:** dobrefilms@dobrefilms.com
**Website:** www.dobrefilms.com

**Submission Policy:** Accepts scripts from unproduced, unrepresented writers
**Genre:** Action, Comedy, Crime, Detective, Drama, Fantasy, Horror, Myth, Romance, Science Fiction, TV Drama, TV Sitcom
**Focus:** Feature Films, TV

**Christopher D'Elia**
**Title:** CEO Director/Producer
**Phone:** 310-926-6439
**Email:** cdelia@dobrefilms.com
**IMDB:** www.imdb.com/name/nm3179988

**Michael Klein**
**Title:** President - Producer/Manager
**Phone:** 323-510-0818
**Email:** mklein@dobrefilms.com
**IMDB:** www.imdb.com/name/nm3180840

## DOUBLE FEATURE FILMS

9320 Wilshire Boulevard #200
Beverly Hills, CA 90212

**Phone:** 310-887-1100
**Email:** dffproducerdesk@gmail.com

**Submission Policy:** Does not accept any unsolicited material
**Genre:** Action, Comedy, Drama, Fantasy, Myth, Thriller
**Focus:** Feature Films
**Year Established:** 2005

**Taylor Latham**
**Title:** VP Development
**IMDB:** http://www.imdb.com/name/nm2281897/

**Carla Santos Shamberg**
Title: EVP / Partner
IMDB: http://www.imdb.com/name/nm0534411/

**Michael Shamberg**
Title: Co-Chair/Partner
IMDB: www.imdb.com/name/nm0787834

**Stacey Sher**
Title: Co-Chari/Partner
IMDB: www.imdb.com/name/nm0792049

**Ameet Shukla**
Title: Creative Executive
IMDB: www.imdb.com/name/nm2627415

## DOUBLE NICKEL ENTERTAINMENT

234 West 138th Street
New York, NY 10030

Phone: 646-435-4390
Fax: 212-694-6205
Email: admin@doublenickelentertainment.com
Website: www.doublenickelentertainment.com

Submission Policy: Accepts query letter from
unproduced, unrepresented writers via email
Genre: Drama
Focus: Feature Films

**Adam Callan**
Title: Creative Executive
IMDB: http://www.imdb.com/name/nm2565555/

**Jenette Kahn**
Title: Partner/Producer
IMDB: www.imdb.com/name/nm1986495

**Adam Richman**
Title: Partner/Producer
IMDB: www.imdb.com/name/nm0725013

## D. PETRIE PRODUCTIONS, INC.

13201 Haney Place
Los Angeles, CA 90049

Phone: 310-394-2608
Fax: 310-395-8530
Email: dgpetrie@aol.com

Submission Policy: Accepts query letter from
unproduced, unrepresented writers via email
Genre: Drama
Focus: TV

**June Petrie**
Title: Producer/Co-Producer
Phone: 310-394-2608
IMDB: www.imdb.com/name/nm0677968

**Dorothea Petrie**
Title: Owner/Executive Producer
Phone: 310-394-2608
Email: dgpetrie@aol.com
IMDB: www.imdb.com/name/nm0677955
Assistant: John Cockrell

## DREAMBRIDGE FILMS

207 West 25th St
6th Floor
New York, NY 10001

Phone: 323-927-1907
Website: www.dreambridgefilms.com/
IMDB: www.imdb.com/company/co0248660

Submission Policy: Accepts query letter from
unproduced, unrepresented writers
Genre: Comedy, Drama, Family, Feature Films
Focus: Feature Films

**Todd J. Labarowski**
Title: President
Email: todd27@mac.com
IMDB: www.imdb.com/name/nm1132640

## DREAMWORKS

100 Universal City Plaza
Universal City, CA 91608

Phone: 818-733-7000
Email: info@dreamworksstudios.com
Website: www.dreamworksstudios.com/
IMDB: www.imdb.com/company/co0252576

Submission Policy: Does not accept any unsolicited
material
Genre: Action, Comedy, Crime, Drama, Fantasy,
Feature Films, Period, Romance, Science Fiction,
Thriller, TV, TV Drama
Focus: Feature Films, TV

**Holly Bario**
Title: President
Email: info@wif.org
IMDB: www.imdb.com/name/nm2302370/

**Chloe Dan**
**Title:** Vice President (Production)
**Email:** Chloe_Dan@DreamworksStudios.com
**IMDB:** www.imdb.com/name/nm2676603

**Mia Maniscalco**
**Title:** Creative Executive
**Email:** mia_maniscalco@dreamworksstudios.com
**IMDB:** www.imdb.com/name/nm4103271

**Andrea McCall**
**Title:** Senior Vice President (Story Development)
**Email:** andrea_mccall@dreamworksstudios.com
**IMDB:** www.imdb.com/name/nm2569503

**Andrea McCall**
**Title:** Senior Vice President (Story Department)
**Email:** andrea_mccall@dreamworksstudios.com

**Steven Spielberg**
**Title:** Chairman
**IMDB:** www.imdb.com/name/nm0000229

## DREAMWORKS ANIMATION

1000 Flower Street
Glendale, CA 91201

**Phone:** 818-695-5000
**Fax:** 818-695-3510
**Website:** http://www.dreamworksanimation.com/
**IMDB:** http://www.imdb.com/company/
co0129164/?ref_=fn_al_co_1

**Submission Policy:** Does not accept any unsolicited
material
**Genre:** Action, Animation, Comedy, Documentary,
Family, Fantasy, Feature Films, Horror, Science
Fiction, TV
**Focus:** Feature Films, Television Shorts, Video
Games
**Year Established:** 2004

**Kyle Arthur Jefferson**
**Title:** Director
**IMDB:** http://www.imdb.com/name/
nm2200868/?ref_=fn_al_nm_1

**Nancy Bernsein**
**Title:** Head of Global Production
**IMDB:** http://www.imdb.com/name/
nm0077110/?ref_=fn_al_nm_1

**Suzanne Buirgy**
**Title:** Production Executive
**IMDB:** http://www.imdb.com/name/
nm1330174/?ref_=fn_al_nm_1

**Ben Cawood**
**Title:** Creative Executive
**IMDB:** http://www.imdb.com/name/
nm1374730/?ref_=fn_al_nm_1

**Bill Damaschke**
**Title:** Chief Creative Officer
**IMDB:** http://www.imdb.com/name/
nm0198632/?ref_=fn_al_nm_1

**Karen Foster**
**Title:** Development Executive
**IMDB:** http://www.imdb.com/name/
nm2259946/?ref_=fn_al_nm_2

**Jane Hartwell**
**Title:** Executive of Production
**IMDB:** http://www.imdb.com/name/
nm0367286/?ref_=fn_al_nm_1

**Jill Hopper**
**Title:** Production Executive
**IMDB:** http://www.imdb.com/name/
nm0394411/?ref_=fn_al_nm_1

**Diane Ikermiyashiro**
**Title:** Creative Executive
**IMDB:** http://www.imdb.com/name/
nm2155308/?ref_=fn_al_nm_1

**Amie Karp**
**Title:** Creative Executive of Development
**IMDB:** http://www.imdb.com/name/
nm2047897/?ref_=fn_al_nm_1
**Assistant:** Peter Cacioppo
peter.cacioppo@dreamworks.com

**Jeffrey Katzenberg**
**Title:** Chief Executive Officer
**IMDB:** http://www.imdb.com/name/
nm0005076/?ref_=fn_al_nm_1

**Chris Kuser**
**Title:** Senior Executive of Development
**IMDB:** http://www.imdb.com/name/
nm1936914/?ref_=fn_al_nm_1
**Assistant:** Beth Cannon

**Tom McGrath**
Title: Director (Producer)
IMDB: http://www.imdb.com/name/
nm0569891/?ref_=fn_al_nm_1

**Damon Ross**
Title: Senior Executive of Development
IMDB: http://www.imdb.com/name/
nm1842613/?ref_=fn_al_nm_1

**Gregg Taylor**
Title: Head of Development
Assistant: Diana Theobald
Diana.Theobald@dreamworks.com

**Jeffrey Wike**
Title: Director of Research and Development
IMDB: http://www.imdb.com/name/
nm5204969/?ref_=fn_al_nm_1

## DUNE ENTERTAINMENT

2121 Avenue of the Stars
Suite 2570
Los Angeles, CA 90067

Phone: 310-432-2288

Submission Policy: Does not accept any unsolicited material
Genre: Action, Comedy, Drama, Fantasy, Feature Films, Horror, Romance, Science Fiction, Thriller
Focus: Feature Films

**Larry Bernstein**
Title: Chief Financial Officer
IMDB: www.imdb.com/name/nm2955628

**Greg Coote**
Title: Chief Creative Officer

**Wendy Weller**
Title: Senior Vice President
IMDB: www.imdb.com/name/nm2956152

## DUPLASS BROTHERS PRODUCTIONS

902 East Fifth Street
Austin, TX 78702

Email: info@duplassbrothers.com
Website: www.duplassbrothers.com

Submission Policy: Accepts query letter from unproduced, unrepresented writers via email
Genre: Comedy, Drama, Feature Films, Horror,

Thriller
Focus: Feature Films

**Mark Duplass**
Title: Producer
IMDB: www.imdb.com/name/nm0243233

**Jay Duplass**
Title: Producer
IMDB: www.imdb.com/name/nm0243231

**Stephanie Langhoff**
Title: Producer
IMDB: www.imdb.com/name/nm1293297

## EALING STUDIOS

Ealing Studios
Ealing Green
London, England W5 5EP

Phone: +44-0-20-8567-6655
Fax: +44-0-20-8758-8658
Email: info@ealingstudios.com
Website: www.ealingstudios.com

Submission Policy: Does not accept any unsolicited material
Genre: Comedy, Documentary, Drama, Family, Feature Films, Romance, Thriller, TV
Focus: Feature Films, Television

**Nic Martin**
Title: Development Executive

**Sophie Meyer**
Title: Head of Development
IMDB: www.mdb.com/name/nm1623306

**James Spring**
Title: Managing Director
IMDB: www.imdb.com/name/nm2020191

**Barnaby Thompson**
Title: Head of Studio
IMDB: www.imdb.com/name/nm0859877

## ECHO BRIDGE ENTERTAINMENT

8383 Wilshire Boulevard, Suite 530
Beverly Hills, CA 90211

Phone: 323-658-7900
Fax: 323-658-7922
Email: info@ebellc.com
Website:
https://www.echobridgeentertainment.com/

**Submission Policy:** Does not accept any unsolicited material
**Genre:** Action, Detective, Drama, Fantasy, Feature Films, Horror, Romance, Science Fiction, Thriller
**Focus:** Feature Films

**Bobby Rock**
**Title:** Head (Acquisitions)
**Email:** brock@echobridgehe.com
**IMDB:** http://www.imdb.com/name/nm0734148/?ref_=fn_al_nm_1

**Leonard Shapiro**
**Title:** Executive (Acquisitions)
**Email:** lshapiro@ebellc.com
**IMDB:** http://www.imdb.com/name/nm0788558/

## ECHO FILMS

c/o Allen Keshishian/Brillstein Entertainment Partners
9150 Wilshire Boulevard, Suite 350
Beverly Hills, CA 90212

**Phone:** 323-935-2909

**Submission Policy:** Does not accept any unsolicited material
**Genre:** Comedy, Drama, Romance
**Focus:** Feature Films

**Jennifer Aniston**
**Title:** Producer

**Kristin Hahn**
**Title:** Producer

## ECHO LAKE PRODUCTIONS

421 South Beverly Drive,
8th Floor
Beverly Hills, CA 90212

**Phone:** 310-789-4790
**Fax:** 310-789-4791
**Email:** contact@echolakeproductions.com
**Website:** www.echolakeproductions.com

**Submission Policy:** Does not accept any unsolicited material
**Genre:** Drama, Reality, Thriller
**Focus:** Feature Films, TV, Reality Programming (Reality TV, Documentaries, Special Events, Sporting Events)

**Ida Diffley**
**Title:** Director of Development
**IMDB:** www.imdb.com/name/nm3000066

**Douglas Mankoff**
**Title:** President
**IMDB:** www.imdb.com/name/nm0542551

**James Smith**
**Title:** Executive Assistant

**Andrew Spaulding**
**Title:** President of Production
**IMDB:** www.imdb.com/name/nm1051748

**Jessica Staman**
**Title:** VP of Development
**IMDB:** www.imdb.com/name/nm1698445

## ECLECTIC PICTURES

7119 Sunset Boulevard, Suite 375
Los Angeles, CA 90046

**Phone:** 323-656-7555
**Fax:** 323-848-7761
**Email:** info@eclecticpictures.com
**Website:** www.eclecticpictures.com

**Submission Policy:** Accepts query letter from unproduced, unrepresented writers via email
**Focus:** Feature Films

**Patrick Muldoon**
**Title:** Production/Development
**Phone:** 323 656 7555
**IMDB:** www.imdb.com/name/nm0005258

**Benjamin Scott**
**Title:** Head of Development and Production
**Email:** benjamin@eclecticpictures.com
**IMDB:** www.imdb.com/name/nm2623559

**John Yarincik**
**Title:** Development
**Email:** john@eclecticpictures.com
**IMDB:** www.imdb.com/name/nm2432490

## EDEN ROCK MEDIA, INC.

1416 North LaBrea Avenue
Hollywood, CA 90028

**Phone:** 323-802-1718
**Fax:** 323-802-1832
**Email:** taugsberger@edenrockmedia.com
**Website:** www.edenrockmedia.com

**Submission Policy:** Does not accept any unsolicited material
**Genre:** Crime, Drama, Family, Memoir & True Stories, Science Fiction, Thriller
**Focus:** Feature Films, TV, Media (Commercials/Branding/Marketing)

**Thomas Ausberger**
**Title:** Producer
**IMDB:** http://www.imdb.com/name/nm0041835/

## EDMONDS ENTERTAINMENT

1635 North Cahuenga Boulevard, 6th Floor
Los Angeles, CA 90028

**Phone:** 323-860-1550
**Fax:** 323-860-1537
**Website:** http://www.edmondsent.com/site/main.html

**Submission Policy:** Accepts scripts from produced or represented writers
**Genre:** Drama, Family, Romance
**Focus:** Feature Films, TV, Reality Programming (Reality TV, Documentaries, Special Events, Sporting Events)

**Sheila Ducksworth**
**Title:** Sr. Vice-President, TV & Film

**Kenneth Edmonds**
**IMDB:** http://www.imdb.com/name/nm0004892/

**Tracey Edmonds**
**Title:** President/CEO
**IMDB:** http://www.imdb.com/name/nm0249525/?ref_=fn_al_nm_1
**Assistant:** Amy Ficken

## EDWARD R. PRESSMAN FILM CORPORATION

1639 11th Street, Suite 251
Santa Monica, CA 90404

**Phone:** 310-450-9692
**Fax:** 310-450-9705
**Website:** http://www.pressman.com/default.asp.html

**Submission Policy:** Does not accept any unsolicited material
**Genre:** Action, Comedy, Drama, Fantasy, Myth, Thriller
**Focus:** Feature Films
**Year Established:** 1969

**Jon Katz**
**Title:** COO/Business & Legal Affairs
**IMDB:** http://www.imdb.com/name/nm1853997/?ref_=fn_al_nm_1

**Edward Pressman**
**Title:** CEO/Chairman
**IMDB:** http://www.imdb.com/name/nm0696299/
**Assistant:** Danielle Halagarda

**Sarah Ramey**
**Title:** Head, Development & Creative Affairs
**Phone:** 212-489-3333
**IMDB:** http://www.imdb.com/name/nm2269975/

## EDWARD SAXON PRODUCTIONS

1526 14th Street #105
Santa Monica, CA 90404

**Phone:** 310-893-0903
**Email:** esaxon@saxonproductions.net
**Website:** www.saxonproductions.net

**Submission Policy:** Accepts query letter from unproduced, unrepresented writers via email
**Genre:** Action, Drama, Family, Memoir & True Stories, Romance
**Focus:** Feature Films, TV

**Ed Saxon**
**Title:** Producer
**IMDB:** http://www.imdb.com/name/nm0768324/

## EFISH ENTERTAINMENT, INC.

4236 Arch Street, Suite 407
Studio City, CA 91604

**Phone:** 818-509-9377
**Email:** info@efishentertainment.com
**Website:** www.efishentertainment.com

**Submission Policy:** Accepts query letter from unproduced, unrepresented writers via email
**Genre:** Action, Crime, Horror, Science Fiction
**Focus:** Feature Films
**Year Established:** 2009

**Eric Fischer**
**Title:** CEO/Producer
**Email:** ericasst@efishentertainment.com
**IMDB:** www.imdb.com/name/nm2737789
**Assistant:** Tatjana Bluchel

**Brianna Johnson**
**Email:** briannaasst@efishentertainment.com
**IMDB:** www.imdb.com/name/nm3776636

**Tom Reilly**
**Title:** CFO
**IMDB:** http://www.imdb.com/name/nm3948044/

**Mike Williams**
**Title:** Development
**Email:** mikeasst@efishentertainment.com
**IMDB:** http://www.imdb.com/name/nm3552724/?ref_=fn_al_nm_1

## EGO FILM ARTS

80 Niagara St
Toronto, ON M5V 1C5

**Phone:** 416-703-2137
**Email:** questions@egofilmarts.com
**Website:** www.egofilmarts.com

**Submission Policy:** Does not accept any unsolicited material
**Genre:** Action, Comedy, Crime, Documentary, Drama, Feature Films, Horror, Romance, Thriller, TV
**Focus:** Feature Films, Television

**Atom Egoyan**
**Title:** Founder
**IMDB:** www.imdb.com/name/nm0000382

## EIGHTH SQUARE ENTERTAINMENT

606 North Larchmont Boulevard, Suite 307
Los Angeles, CA 90004

**Phone:** 323-469-1003
**Fax:** 323-469-1516

**Submission Policy:** Does not accept any unsolicited material
**Genre:** Comedy, Crime, Drama, Thriller
**Focus:** Feature Films, TV, Theater

**Janette Jensen**
**Title:** Producer
**Email:** jjnomiddlename@yahoo.com
**IMDB:** http://www.imdb.com/name/nm1130073/

**Jeff Melnick**
**Title:** Producer
**IMDB:** http://www.imdb.com/name/nm0578179/

## ELECTRIC CITY ENTERTAINMENT

8409 Santa Monica Boulevard
West Hollywood, CA 90069

**Phone:** 323-654-7800
**Fax:** 323-654-7808
**Website:** www.electriccityent.com

**Submission Policy:** Accepts query letter from unproduced, unrepresented writers via email
**Genre:** Comedy, Drama, Feature Films, Romance
**Focus:** Feature Films
**Year Established:** 2012

**Lynette Howell**
**Title:** Producer/Partner
**IMDB:** www.imdb.com/name/nm1987578
**Assistant:** Jess Engel

**Katie McNeill**
**Title:** Vice President of Production
**IMDB:** www.imdb.com/name/nm3336352

**Jamie Patricof**
**Title:** Producer/Partner
**IMDB:** www.imdb.com/name/nm1364232
**Assistant:** Jack Hart

**Crystal Powell**
**Title:** Vice President of Production
**IMDB:** www.imdb.com/name/nm2476235

## ELECTRIC DYNAMITE

1741 Ivar Avenue
Los Angeles, CA 90028

**Phone:** 323-790-8040
**Fax:** 818-733-2651
**Website:** http://www.electricdynamite.com/
**IMDB:** http://www.imdb.com/company/co0190357/

**Submission Policy:** Accepts query letter from unproduced, unrepresented writers
**Genre:** Comedy, Fantasy, Science Fiction, TV Sitcom
**Focus:** Feature Films, TV, Media (Commercials/Branding/Marketing)

**Jack Black**
**Title:** Principal
**Phone:** 323-790-8000
**IMDB:** http://www.imdb.com/name/nm0085312/?ref_=fn_al_nm_1

**Priyanka Mattoo**
Title: Development
IMDB: http://www.imdb.com/name/
nm3339192/?ref_=fn_al_nm_1

## ELECTRIC ENTERTAINMENT

940 North Highland Ave, Suite A
Los Angeles, CA 90038

Phone: 323-817-1300
Fax: 323-467-7155
Website: http://www.electric-entertainment.com/

Submission Policy: Does not accept any unsolicited
material
Genre: Action, Animation, Comedy, Drama,
Memoir & True Stories, Reality, Science Fiction,
Thriller
Focus: Feature Films, TV, Reality Programming
(Reality TV, Documentaries, Special Events,
Sporting Events), Media (Commercials/Branding/
Marketing)

**Dean Devlin**
Title: President
IMDB: http://www.imdb.com/name/nm0002041
Assistant: Chase Friedman

**Rachel Olschan**
Title: Partner/Producer
IMDB: http://www.imdb.com/name/
nm1272673/?ref_=fn_al_nm_1

**Marc Roskin**
Title: VP Development
IMDB: http://www.imdb.com/name/
nm0743059/?ref_=fn_al_nm_1

## ELECTRIC FARM ENTERTAINMENT

3000 Olympic Boulevard
Building 3, Suite 1366
Santa Monica, CA 90404

Phone: 310-264-4199
Fax: 310-264-4196
Email: contact@electricfarment.com
Website: http://ef-ent.com/

Submission Policy: Accepts query letter from
unproduced, unrepresented writers via email
Genre: Action, Drama, Fantasy, Science Fiction
Focus: Feature Films, TV, Media (Commercials/
Branding/Marketing)

**Brent Friedman**
Title: Principal/Executive Producer

**Stan Rogow**
Title: Principal/Executive Producer
Assistant: Allison Lurie

## ELECTRIC SHEPHERD PRODUCTIONS

8306 Wilshire Boulevard, #2016
Beverly Hills, CA 90211

Phone: 310-433-5282
Fax: 323-315-7170
Email: admin@electricshepherdproductions.com
Website: www.electricshepherdproductions.com

Submission Policy: Accepts query letter from
unproduced, unrepresented writers via email
Genre: Action, Drama, Fantasy, Myth, Science
Fiction, Thriller
Focus: Feature Films, TV, Media (Commercials/
Branding/Marketing)

**Isa Dick Hackett**
Title: CEO/President
IMDB: http://www.imdb.com/name/
nm2357313/?ref_=fn_al_nm_1

**Kalen Egan**
Title: Development Associate

**Laura Leslie**
Title: Co-Owner

## ELEMENT PICTURES

21 Mespil Rd
Dublin 4
Ireland

Phone: 353-1-618-5032
Fax: 353-1-664-3737
Email: info@elementpictures.ie
Website: www.elementpictures.ie

Submission Policy: Accepts query letter from
unproduced, unrepresented writers
Genre: Action, Comedy, Documentary, Drama,
Feature Films, Horror, Science Fiction, TV, TV
Drama
Focus: Feature Films, TV

**Gillian Clarke**
Title: Development Executive Television

**Ed Guiney**
Title: Company Director
IMDB: www.imdb.com/name/nm0347384

**Andrew Lowe**
Title: Company Director
IMDB: www.imdb.com/name/nm1103466

**Lee Magiday**
Title: Producer
IMDB: www.imdb.com/name/nm3717662

**Emma Norton**
Title: Head of Development
IMDB: www.imdb.com/name/nm4499999

**Danny Takhar**
Title: Development Executive

## ELEPHANT EYE FILMS

89 Fifth Ave
Ste 306
New York, NY 10003

Phone: 212-488-8877
Fax: 212-488-8878
Email: info@elephanteyefilms.com
Website: www.elephanteyefilms.com

Submission Policy: Does not accept any unsolicited material
Genre: Action, Comedy, Drama, Fantasy, Memoir & True Stories
Focus: Feature Films

**Toni Branson**
Title: Production/Development Executive
Email: Toni@elephanteyefilms.com

**Kim Jose**
Title: Principal
Email: Kim@elephanteyefilms.com

**Dave Robinson**
Title: Principal
Email: Dave@elephanteyefilms.com

## ELEVATE ENTERTAINMENT

1925 Century Park East, Suite 2320
Los Angeles, CA 90067

Phone: 310-788-3490
Fax: 323-848-9867
Email: info@elevate-ent.com
Website: www.elevate-ent.com

Submission Policy: Accepts query letter from unproduced, unrepresented writers via email
Genre: Action, Animation, Comedy, Crime, Drama, Family, Fantasy, Memoir & True Stories, Romance, Science Fiction
Focus: Feature Films, TV

**Alex Cole**
Title: President/Manager
Phone: 310-557-0100
Email: acole@elevate-ent.com
IMDB: www.imdb.com/name/nm2251162
Assistant: Stephen Hale

**Jenny M. Wood**
Title: Manager/Producer
Phone: 323-951-9310
Email: jwood@elevate-ent.com

## ELIXIR FILMS

8033 West Sunset Boulevard, Suite 867
West Hollywood, CA 90046

Phone: 323-848-9867
Fax: 323-848-5945
Email: info@elixirfilms.com
Website: www.elixirfilms.com

Submission Policy: Does not accept any unsolicited material
Genre: Drama, Family
Focus: Feature Films

**David Alexanian**
Title: Producer

**Alexis Alexanian**
Title: Producer
Assistant: Joe Brinkman

## ELKINS ENTERTAINMENT

8306 Wilshire Boulevard
PMB 3643
Beverly Hills, CA 90211

Phone: 323-932-0400
Fax: 323-932-6400
Email: info@elkinsent.com
Website: www.elkinsent.com

Submission Policy: Accepts query letter from unproduced, unrepresented writers via email
Genre: Comedy, Drama, Memoir & True Stories, Reality, Romance

**Focus:** Feature Films, TV, Reality Programming (Reality TV, Documentaries, Special Events, Sporting Events)

**Hillard Elkins**
Title: President/Producer/Manager

**Sandi Love**
Title: Vice-President/Manager

## EMBASSY ROW LLC

325 Hudson St
Ste 601
New York, NY 10013

**Phone:** 212 507 9700
**Fax:** 212 507 9701
**Email:** info@embassyrow.com
**Website:** www.embassyrow.com

**Submission Policy:** Does not accept any unsolicited material
**Genre:** Action, Comedy, Drama, Fantasy, Science Fiction, TV Sitcom
**Focus:** Feature Films, TV, Reality Programming (Reality TV, Documentaries, Special Events, Sporting Events), Media (Commercials/Branding/Marketing)

**Michael Davies**
Title: President, Production

**Tammy Johnson**
Title: Sr. Vice-President, Production/General Manager

## EMBER ENTERTAINMENT GROUP

11718 Barrington Court, Suite 116
Los Angeles, CA 90049

**Phone:** 310-230-9759
**Fax:** 310-589-4850
**Email:** eeg.bronson@verizon.net

**Submission Policy:** Accepts query letter from unproduced, unrepresented writers via email
**Genre:** Action, Comedy, Drama, Fantasy, Science Fiction
**Focus:** Feature Films, TV

**Lindsay Dunlap**
Title: Producer
IMDB: http://www.imdb.com/name/nm0242397/

**Randall Frakes**
Title: President
IMDB: http://www.imdb.com/name/nm0289696/?ref_=fn_al_nm_1

**T.S. Goldberg**
Title: President, Physical Production

**J.A. Keller**
Title: Finance

## EMERALD CITY PRODUCTIONS, INC.

c/o Stankevich-Gochman
9777 Wilshire Boulevard, Suite 550
Beverly Hills, CA 90212

**Phone:** 310-859-8825
**Fax:** 310-859-8830

**Submission Policy:** Does not accept any unsolicited material
**Genre:** Drama, Fantasy, Science Fiction
**Focus:** Feature Films

**Barrie M. Osborne**
Title: Producer
IMDB: http://www.imdb.com/name/nm0651614/

## EM MEDIA

Antenna Media Centre
Beck Street
Nottingham
NG1 1EQ

**Phone:** +44-115-993-23-33
**Email:** info@em-media.org.uk
**Website:** www.em-media.org.uk

**Submission Policy:** Accepts query letter from unproduced, unrepresented writers
**Genre:** Comedy, Drama, Feature Films, Romance
**Focus:** Feature Films
**Year Established:** 2002

**Suzanne Alizart**
Title: Head of Content Creation
Email: Suzanne.Alizart@em-media.org
IMDB: www.imdb.com/name/nm2355251

**Anna Seifert-Speck**
Title: Development Executive
IMDB: www.imdb.com/name/nm3527106

**John Tobin**
Title: Head of Market Development
IMDB: www.imdb.com/name/nm3527690

**Debbie Williams**
Title: CEO
Phone: 0115-993-2333
Email: Debbie.Williams@em-media.org.uk
IMDB: www.imdb.com/name/nm3527737

## ENDEMOL ENTERTAINMENT

9255 W Sunset Blvd
Suite 1100
Los Angeles, CA 90069

Phone: 310-860-9914
Fax: 310-860-0073
Website: www.endemolusa.tv

Submission Policy: Accepts query letter from
produced or represented writers
Genre: TV, TV Drama, TV Sitcom
Focus: Television, Reality TV Programming

**Caroline Baumgard**
Title: SVP of Development
IMDB: www.imdb.com/name/nm0062313

**Noah Beery**
Title: VP of Production

**Aaron Bilgrad**
Title: SVP of Development

**Rob Day**
Title: SVP of Production
IMDB: www.imdb.com/name/nm1691117

**Chris Dickie**
Title: Coordinator of Development

**Jeremy Gold**
Title: Head of Scripted Division
IMDB: www.imdb.com/name/nm0325005

**David Goldberg**
Title: Chairman
IMDB: www.imdb.com/name/nm2499880

**Dave Hamilton**
Title: VP of Development

**Sean Loughlin**
Title: Executive Development & Producer

**Michael Weinberg**
Title: VP of Development

## ENDGAME ENTERTAINMENT

9100 Wilshire Boulevard, Suite 100W
Beverly Hills, CA 90212

Phone: 310-432-7300
Fax: 310-432-7301
Email: reception@endgameent.com
Website: www.endgameent.com

Submission Policy: Does not accept any unsolicited
material
Genre: Action, Animation, Comedy, Crime,
Detective, Drama, Memoir & True Stories,
Romance, Science Fiction, Thriller
Focus: Feature Films, TV, Reality Programming
(Reality TV, Documentaries, Special Events,
Sporting Events), Theater

**Adam Del Deo**
Title: Sr. Vice-President, Production
IMDB: http://www.imdb.com/name/
nm0215534/?ref_=fn_al_nm_1

**Julie Goldstein**
Title: President (Production)
IMDB: http://www.imdb.com/name/
nm0326252/?ref_=fn_al_nm_3

**Lucas Smith**
Title: Sr. Vice-President, Development
IMDB: http://www.imdb.com/name/
nm0809156/?ref_=fn_al_nm_1

**James Stern**
Title: Chairmen & CEO
IMDB: http://www.imdb.com/name/nm0827726/

## ENERGY ENTERTAINMENT

9348 Civic Center Drive
Mezzanine Level
Beverly Hills, CA 90210

Phone: 310-746-4872
Email: info@energyentertainment.net
Website: www.energyentertainment.net

Submission Policy: Does not accept any unsolicited
material
Genre: Comedy, Drama, Fantasy, Horror, Memoir
& True Stories, Science Fiction, Thriller
Focus: Feature Films
Year Established: 2001

**Michelle Arenal**
Title: Assistant

**Angelina Chen**
Title: Manager

**Derrick Eppich**
Title: Producer

**Brooklyn Weaver**
Title: Owner/Manager
IMDB: http://www.imdb.com/name/nm0915819/?ref_=fn_al_nm_1
Assistant: David Binns

## ENTERTAINMENT ONE GROUP

9465 Wilshire Boulevard, Suite 500
Los Angeles, CA 90212

Phone: 310-407-0960
Email: eonetv@entonegroup.com
Website: www.entonegroup.com

Submission Policy: Does not accept any unsolicited material
Genre: Animation, Comedy, Drama, Family, Feature Films, Horror, Romance, Thriller, TV, TV Drama, TV Sitcom
Focus: TV, Reality Programming (Reality TV, Documentaries, Special Events, Sporting Events), Media (Commercials/Branding/Marketing)

**Adam Blumberg**
Title: Director of Development

**Swin Chang**
Title: Director of Development (Kids Television)

**Jeff Hevert**
Title: Vice President (Current Programming and Development, Reality)

**Armand Leo**
Title: Vice President (Production)

**Michael Rosenberg**
Title: Executive Vice President (U.S. Scripted Television)

## ENTITLED ENTERTAINMENT

2038 Redcliff Street
Los Angeles, CA 90039

Phone: 323-469-9000
Fax: 323-660-5292

Website: http://www.entitledentertainment.com/index.html

Submission Policy: Does not accept any unsolicited material
Genre: Comedy, Crime, Drama, Family, Feature Films, Memoir & True Stories, TV
Focus: Feature Films, Television, Theater

**James Burke**
Title: Partner
IMDB: http://www.imdb.com/name/nm0121711/

**Scott Disharoon**
Title: Partner
IMDB: http://www.imdb.com/name/nm0228318/?ref_=fn_al_nm_1

## ENVISION MEDIA ARTS

5555 Melrose Avenue
Building 221, Suite 110
Los Angeles, CA 90038

Phone: 323-956-9687
Fax: 323-862-2205
Email: info@envisionma.com
Website: www.envisionma.com

Submission Policy: Accepts query letter from unproduced, unrepresented writers via email
Genre: Action, Comedy, Drama, Family, Fantasy, Myth, Romance, TV Drama, TV Sitcom
Focus: Feature Films, TV
Year Established: 2002

**David Buelow**
Title: President of Film & TV
Email: dbuelow@envisionma.com
IMDB: www.imdb.com/name/nm2149164

**Lee Nelson**
Title: CEO
Email: lnelson@envisionma.com
IMDB: www.imdb.com/name/nm0625540

**David Tish**
Title: Director of Development
Email: dtish@envisionma.com
IMDB: www.imdb.com/name/nm2953843

## EPIC LEVEL ENTERTAINMENT, LTD.

7095 Hollywood Boulevard #688
Hollywood, CA 91604

**Phone:** 818-752-6800
**Fax:** 818-752-6814
**Email:** info@epiclevel.com
**Website:** www.epiclevel.com

**Submission Policy:** Accepts query letter from unproduced, unrepresented writers via email
**Genre:** Action, Animation, Fantasy, Horror, Myth, Science Fiction, Thriller
**Focus:** Feature Films, TV, Reality Programming (Reality TV, Documentaries, Special Events, Sporting Events), Media (Commercials/Branding/Marketing)

**Paige Barnett**
**Title:** Associate Producer

**Cindi Rice**
**Title:** Producer

**John Rosenblum**
**Title:** Producer
**Email:** jfr@jfr.com
**IMDB:** http://www.jfr.com

## EPIGRAM ENTERTAINMENT

3745 Longview Valley Road
Sherman Oaks, CA 91423

**Phone:** 818-461-8937
**Fax:** 818-461-8919
**Email:** epigrament@sbcglobal.net

**Submission Policy:** Accepts query letter from unproduced, unrepresented writers via email
**Genre:** Comedy, Drama, Romance
**Focus:** Feature Films, TV, Media (Commercials/Branding/Marketing)

**Ellen Baskin**
**Title:** Vice-President, Development

**Val McLeroy**
**Title:** Partner

## EPIPHANY PICTURES, INC.

10625 Esther Avenue
Los Angeles, CA 90064

**Phone:** 310-815-1266
**Fax:** 310-815-1269
**Email:** submissions@epiphanypictures.com
**Website:** http://www.epiphanypictures.com/

**Submission Policy:** Accepts query letter from unproduced, unrepresented writers via email
**Genre:** Action, Animation, Comedy, Drama, Family, Fantasy, Memoir & True Stories, Myth, Reality, Romance, Science Fiction, Sociocultural, Thriller, TV Drama, TV Sitcom
**Focus:** Feature Films, TV, Reality Programming (Reality TV, Documentaries, Special Events, Sporting Events), Media (Commercials/Branding/Marketing)

**Joey DePaolo**
**Title:** Director of Development

**Scott Frank**
**Title:** Producer/Director
**Email:** scott@epiphanypictures.com

**Dan Halperin**
**Title:** Producer/Director
**Phone:** 310-452-0242
**Email:** dan@epiphanypictures.com

## EQUILIBRIUM ENTERTAINMENT

1259 S. Orange Grove Ave.
Los Angeles, CA 90019

**Phone:** 323-939-3555
**Fax:** 323-939-7523
**Email:** info@eq-ent.com
**Website:** www.eq-ent.com
**IMDB:** www.imdb.com/company/co0232623

**Submission Policy:** Accepts query letter from unproduced, unrepresented writers
**Genre:** Action, Comedy, Feature Films
**Focus:** Feature Films

**Demian Lichtenstein**
**Title:** President & CEO
**IMDB:** www.imdb.com/company/co0232623

## ESCAPE ARTISTS

10202 West Washington Boulevard
Astaire Building, 3rd Floor
Culver City, CA 90232

**Phone:** 310-244-8833
**Fax:** 310-204-2151
**Email:** info@escapeartistsent.com
**Website:** www.escapeartistsent.com

**Submission Policy:** Does not accept any unsolicited material

**Genre:** Action, Comedy, Drama, Fantasy, Myth, Reality, Romance, Science Fiction
**Focus:** Feature Films, TV

**Todd Black**
Title: Partner/Producer
Email: todd_black@spe.sony.com
IMDB: www.imdb.com/name/nm0085542

**Jason Blumenthal**
Title: Partner/Producer
Email: jason_blumenthal@spe.sony.com
IMDB: www.imdb.com/name/nm0089820

**Steve Tisch**
Title: Partner/Producer
Email: steve_tisch@spe.sony.com

## E-SQUARED

531A North Hollywood Way
Suite 237
Burbank, CA 91505

**Phone:** 818-760-1901
**Email:** info@e2-esquared.com
**Website:** www.e2-esquared.com
**IMDB:** www.imdb.com/company/co0109424

**Submission Policy:** Accepts query letter from unproduced, unrepresented writers

**Chris Emerson**
Title: Producer / Manager
Email: esquaredasst@sbcglobal.net
IMDB: www.imdb.com/name/nm0256193

## EVENSTAR FILMS

**Phone:** 212-219-2020
**Fax:** 212-219-2323
**Email:** info@evenstarfilms.com
**Website:** www.evenstarfilms.com

**Submission Policy:** Does not accept any unsolicited material
**Genre:** Drama, Feature Films
**Focus:** Feature Films

**Jeremy Bloom**
Title: Artistic Executive

**Elizabeth Cuthrell**
Title: Producer
IMDB: www.imdb.com/name/nm0193876

**Steven Rinehart**
Title: Creative Consultant

**David Urrutia**
Title: Producer
IMDB: www.imdb.com/name/nm0882102

## EVERYMAN PICTURES

Santa Monica
1512 16th Street Suite 3
Santa Monica, CA 90404

**Phone:** 310-460-7080
**Fax:** 310-460-7081

**Submission Policy:** Does not accept any unsolicited material
**Genre:** Comedy, Drama, TV
**Focus:** Feature Films, Television

**Jennifer Perini**
Title: President (Development)
Assistant: Kristopher Fogel and Lauren Downey

**Jay Roach**
Title: Director/Chairman/CEO
Email: jay.roach@fox.com
IMDB: www.imdb.com/name/nm0005366

## EXCLUSIVE MEDIA

9100 Wilshire Boulevard,
Suite 401 East,
Beverly Hills,

**Phone:** 310-300-9000
**Fax:** 310-300-9001
**Email:** info@exclusivemedia.com
**Website:** www.exclusivemedia.com

**Submission Policy:** Accepts query letter from produced or represented writers
**Genre:** Action, Comedy, Crime, Documentary, Drama, Fantasy, Feature Films, Horror, Romance, Thriller
**Focus:** Feature Films

**Guy East**
Title: Co-Chairman
Email: geast@exclusivemedia.com
IMDB: www.imdb.com/name/nm0247524

**Kim Heinemann**
Title: Executive Assistant

**Shira Rockowitz**
Title: Director of Development & Production
IMDB: www.imdb.com/name/nm2798185

**Jennifer Ruper**
Title: Creative Executive
IMDB: www.imdb.com/name/nm1536288

**Nigel Sinclair**
Title: CEO/Co-Chairman
Email: nigelsinclair@spitfirepix.com
IMDB: www. imdb.com/name/nm0801691/
Assistant: Patricia Scott

**Glenn Zipper**
Title: Head of Documentary Features
Email: info@zipperbrothersfilms.com
IMDB: www.imdb.com/name/nm3581772

## EXILE ENTERTAINMENT

732 El Medio Ave.
Pacific Palisades, CA 90272

Phone: 310-573-1523
Fax: 310-573-0109
Email: exile_ent@yahoo.com
IMDB: www.imdb.com/company/co0063047

Submission Policy: Accepts query letter from
unproduced, unrepresented writers
Genre: Comedy, Drama, Feature Films, Horror
Focus: Feature Films

**Gary Ungar**
Title: Principal
IMDB: www.imdb.com/name/nm1316083

## EXODUS FILM GROUP

1211 Electric Ave
Venice, CA 90291

Phone: 310-684-3155
Email: info@exodusfilmgroup.com
Website: www.exodusfilmgroup.com
IMDB: www.imdb.com/company/co0080906/

Submission Policy: Does not accept any unsolicited
material
Genre: Animation, Comedy, Family, Feature Films
Focus: Animated Features

**Max Howard**
Title: Producer
Email: max@exodusfilmgroup.com
IMDB: www.imdb.com/name/nm0397492

## EYE ON THE BALL FILMS

PO Box 46877
Los Angeles, CA 90046

Phone: 323-935-0634
Fax: 323-935-4188
IMDB: www.imdb.com/company/co0102936

Submission Policy: Accepts query letter from
unproduced, unrepresented writers
Genre: Comedy, Feature Films
Focus: Feature Films

**Sergio Arau**
Title: Producer
Email: keepyoureye@aol.com
IMDB: www.imdb.com/name/nm0033190

**Yareli Arizmendi**
Title: Producer
Email: arauarizmendi@aol.com
IMDB: www.imdb.com/name/nm0034976

## FACE PRODUCTIONS

335 North Maple Drive, Suite 135
Beverly Hills, CA 90210

Phone: 310-205-2746
Fax: 310-285-2386

Submission Policy: Does not accept any unsolicited
material
Genre: Action, Comedy, Drama
Focus: Feature Films

**Billy Crystal**
Title: Actor/Writer/Producer
IMDB: www.imdb.com/name/nm0000345
Assistant: Kia Hellman

**Samantha Sprecher**
Title: Vice President (Development)
IMDB: http://www.imdb.com/name/nm0819616/
Assistant: Kia Hellman

## FAKE EMPIRE FEATURES

5555 Melrose Avenue
Marx Brothers Building #207
Hollywood, CA 90038

**Phone:** 323-956-8766

**Submission Policy:** Accepts scripts from produced
or represented writers
**Genre:** Comedy, Drama, Family, Feature Films
**Focus:** Feature Films

**Jay Marcus**
**Title:** Creative Executive
**IMDB:** www.imdb.com/name/nm1682408

**Lisbeth Rowinski**
**Title:** Vice President (Feature Film)
**IMDB:** www.imdb.com/name/nm2925164
**Assistant:** Ritu Moondra

## FAKE EMPIRE TELEVISION

400 Warner Boulevard
Building 138, Room 1101
Burbank, CA 91522

**Phone:** 818-954-2420
**Website:** http://fakeempire.com/about/

**Submission Policy:** Accepts scripts from produced
or represented writers
**Genre:** Comedy, Drama, Family, TV, TV Drama
**Focus:** TV

**Leonard Goldstein**
**Title:** Head, Television
**IMDB:** www.imdb.com/name/nm2325264
**Assistant:** Brittany Sever

**Stephanie Savage**
**Title:** Founder/Producer/Writer/Director
**IMDB:** http://www.imdb.com/name/
nm1335634/?ref_=fn_al_nm_l

**Stephanie Savage**
**Title:** Founder/Producer/Writer/Director
**IMDB:** http://www.imdb.com/name/
nm1335634/?ref_=fn_al_nm_l
**Assistant:** Kendall Sand

**Josh Schwatz**
**Title:** Founder/Producer/Writer/Director
**IMDB:** www.imdb.com/name/nm0777300

## FARRELL PAURA PRODUCTIONS

11150 Santa Monica Boulevard, Suite 450
Los Angeles, CA 90025

**Phone:** 310-477-7776
**Fax:** 310-477-7710

**Submission Policy:** Accepts query letter from
unproduced, unrepresented writers via email
**Genre:** Comedy, Crime, Drama, Feature Films,
Thriller
**Focus:** Feature Films

**Joseph Farrell**
**Title:** Executive

**Wayne Kline**
**Title:** Vice-President

**Catherine Paura**
**Title:** CEO

## FASTBACK PICTURES

**Phone:** 323-469-5719
**Email:** info@fastbackpictures.com
**Website:** www.fastbackpictures.com/
**IMDB:** www.imdb.com/company/co0151624

**Submission Policy:** Accepts query letter from
unproduced, unrepresented writers
**Genre:** Drama, Feature Films, Thriller
**Focus:** Feature Films

**Pascal Franchot**
**Title:** Producer
**Phone:** 323-717-5569
**Email:** pascal@fastbackpictures.com
**IMDB:** www.imdb.com/name/nm0289994

## FASTNET FILMS

1st Fl
75-76 Camden St Lower
Dublin 2
Ireland

**Phone:** +353 1 478 9566
**Fax:** +353 1 478 9567
**Email:** enquiries@fastnetfilms.com
**Website:** www.fastnetfilms.com

**Submission Policy:** Does not accept any unsolicited
material
**Genre:** Documentary, Drama, Reality
**Focus:** Documentary, Feature Films

**Megan Everett**
Title: Head of Development
IMDB: www.imdb.com/name/nm3210746

**Ian Jackson**
Title: Head of Development
IMDB: www.imdb.com/name/nm4127212

**Aoife McGonigal**
Title: Junior Producer
IMDB: www.imdb.com/name/nm3502464

## FEDORA ENTERTAINMENT

11846 Ventura Boulevard
Suite 140
Studio City, CA 91604

Phone: 818-508-5310
Email: peterca975@aol.com

Genre: Comedy, Drama, TV, TV Drama, TV Sitcom
Focus: Television

**Peter Tolan**
Title: Producer
IMDB: www.imdb.com/name/nm0865847

**Marla A. White**
Title: VP of Development
Email: marlaw825@me.com
IMDB: www.imdb.com/name/nm0925187

**Michael Wimer**
Title: Producer
IMDB: www.imdb.com/name/nm1057590

## FILM 360

9111 Wilshire Blvd
Beverly Hills, CA 90210

Phone: 310-272-7000
IMDB: http://www.imdb.com/company/co0192833/?ref_=fn_al_co_1

Submission Policy: Does not accept any unsolicited material
Genre: Action, Comedy, Crime, Drama, Family, Fantasy, Feature Films, Period, Science Fiction, Thriller
Focus: Feature Films
Year Established: 2009

**Ben Forkner**
Title: Producer
IMDB: http://www.imdb.com/name/nm2447927/?ref_=fn_al_nm_1

**Eric Kranzler**
Title: Producer
IMDB: http://www.imdb.com/name/nm1023394/?ref_=fn_al_nm_1

**Scott Lambert**
Title: Producer
IMDB: http://www.imdb.com/name/nm0483300/?ref_=fn_al_nm_1

**Daniel Rappaport**
Title: Producer
IMDB: http://www.imdb.com/name/nm0710883/?ref_=fn_al_nm_1

## FILM 44

1526 Cloverfield Blvd
Santa Monica, CA 90404

Phone: 310-586-4949
Fax: 310-586-4959
Email: info@film44.com
IMDB: www.imdb.com/company/co0152188

Submission Policy: Does not accept any unsolicited material
Genre: Action, Drama, Fantasy, Feature Films, Myth, Science Fiction, Thriller, TV, TV Drama
Focus: Feature Films, TV

**Braden Aftergood**
Title: SVP of Features
IMDB: www.imdb.com/name/nm2302240

**Peter Berg**
Title: Partner
IMDB: www.imdb.com/name/nm0000916

**Rebecca Hobbs**
Title: SVP of Television
IMDB: www.imdb.com/name/nm1778008

## FILMCOLONY

4751 Wilshire Boulevard Third Floor Los Angeles, CA 90010

Phone: 323-549-4343
Fax: 323-549-9824
Email: info@filmcolony.com

**Website:** http://www.filmcolony.com/
**IMDB:** http://www.imdb.com/company/
co0159642/?ref_=fn_al_co_1

**Submission Policy:** Does not accept any unsolicited
material
**Genre:** Comedy, Crime, Drama, Family, Fantasy,
Feature Films, Romance, Thriller, TV
**Focus:** Feature Films, Television
**Year Established:** 1998

**Melanie Donkers**
**Title:** Director of Development
**IMDB:** http://www.imdb.com/name/
nm1410650/?ref_=fn_al_nm_1

**Richard Gladstein**
**Title:** President
**IMDB:** http://www.imdb.com/name/
nm0321621/?ref_=fn_al_nm_1

**Anand Shah**
**Title:** Vice President
**IMDB:** http://www.imdb.com/name/
nm4337795/?ref_=fn_al_nm_1

## FILMDISTRICT

1540 2nd Street Suite 200
Santa Monica, CA 90401

**Phone:** 310-315-1722
**Fax:** 310-315-1723
**Email:** info@filmdistrict.com
**Website:** http://www.filmdistrict.com/
**IMDB:** http://www.imdb.com/company/
co0314851/?ref_=fn_al_co_1

**Submission Policy:** Does not accept any unsolicited
material
**Genre:** Action, Crime, Drama, Fantasy, Feature
Films, Horror, Romance, Thriller
**Focus:** Feature Films
**Year Established:** 2010

**Lia Buman**
**Title:** Executive Vice President of Acquisitions and
Operations
**IMDB:** http://www.imdb.com/name/
nm2513975/?ref_=fn_al_nm_1
**Assistant:** Patrick Reese

**Tim Headington**
**Title:** Partner
**IMDB:** http://www.imdb.com/name/
nm2593874/?ref_=fn_al_nm_1

**Graham King**
**Title:** Partner
**IMDB:** http://www.imdb.com/name/
nm0454752/?ref_=fn_al_nm_1

**Josie Liang**
**Title:** Coordinator of Acquisitions
**IMDB:** http://www.imdb.com/name/
nm4169347/?ref_=fn_al_nm_1

**Josh Peters**
**Title:** Coordinator of Acquisitions
**IMDB:** http://www.imdb.com/name/
nm5444016/?ref_=fn_al_nm_5

**Peter Schlessel**
**Title:** Chief Executive Officer
**IMDB:** http://www.imdb.com/name/
nm0772283/?ref_=fn_al_nm_1
**Assistant:** Jessica Freenborn

## FILM GARDEN ENTERTAINMENT

6727 Odessa Avenue
Van Nuys, CA 91406

**Phone:** 818-783-3456
**Fax:** 818-752-8186
**Website:** www.filmgarden.tv/
**IMDB:** www.imdb.com/company/co0011492

**Genre:** Memoir & True Stories, Period, TV
**Focus:** Reality TV, Documentary, TV Series

**Chris Deaux**
**Title:** VP of Development
**IMDB:** www.imdb.com/name/nm1614981

## FILM HARVEST

750 Lillian Way, Suite 6
LA, CA 90038

**Phone:** 310-926-4131
**Fax:** 323-481-8499
**Email:** info@filmharvest.com
**Website:** www.filmharvest.com

**Submission Policy:** Does not accept any unsolicited
material
**Genre:** Action, Documentary, Drama, Feature

Films, Horror, Memoir & True Stories, Science
Fiction, Thriller
**Focus:** Feature Films
**Year Established:** 2009

### Eben Kostbar
**Title:** Producer
**Email:** eben@filmharvest.com
**IMDB:** www.imdb.com/name/nm1670295

### Elana Kostbar
**Title:** Assistant
**Email:** info@filmharvest.com
**IMDB:** www.imdb.com/name/nm3657939

### Joseph McKelheer
**Title:** Executive Producer
**Email:** joe@filmharvest.com
**IMDB:** www.imdb.com/name/nm1559624/

## FILMNATION ENTERTAINMENT

345 North Maple Dr, Suite 202
Beverly Hills, CA 90210

**Phone:** 310-859-0088
**Fax:** 310-859-0089
**Website:** http://www.wearefilmnation.com/

**Submission Policy:** Accepts query letter from
unproduced, unrepresented writers
**Genre:** Action, Crime, Drama, Fantasy, Horror,
Thriller
**Focus:** Feature Films
**Year Established:** 2008

### Glen Basner
**Title:** Founder/CEO
**Email:** gbasner@wearefilmnation.com
**IMDB:** www.imdb.com/name/nm0059984

### Patrick Chu
**Title:** Director of Development
**Email:** pchu@wearefilmnation.com
**IMDB:** www.imdb.com/name/nm1776958

## FILM SCIENCE

201 Lavaca Street Suite 502
Austin, TX 78701

**Phone:** 917-501-5197
**Email:** info@filmscience.com
**Website:** www.filmscience.com

**Submission Policy:** Accepts query letter from
unproduced, unrepresented writers
**Genre:** Comedy, Drama, Family, Feature Films
**Focus:** Feature Films

### Anish Savjani
**Title:** Executive
**Email:** anish@filmscience.com
**IMDB:** www.imdb.com/name/nm1507013

## FILMSMITH PRODUCTIONS

3400 Airport Drive
Bldg D
Santa Monica, CA 90405

**Phone:** 310-260-8866
**Fax:** 310-397-7155
**Email:** filmsmith@mac.com
**IMDB:** www.imdb.com/company/co0017423

**Submission Policy:** Accepts query letter from
unproduced, unrepresented writers
**Genre:** Comedy, Crime, Drama, Feature Films,
Thriller, TV Sitcom
**Focus:** Feature Films

### Zachary Matz
**Title:** Producer
**IMDB:** www.imdb.com/name/nm0560693

## FIRST RUN FEATURES

The Film Center Building, 630 Ninth Avenue, Suite
1213
New York City, NY 10036

**Phone:** 212-243-0600
**Fax:** 212-989-7649
**Email:** info@firstrunfeatures.com
**Website:** http://www.firstrunfeatures.com/
**IMDB:** http://www.imdb.com/company/
co0002318/?ref_=fn_al_co_1

**Submission Policy:** Does not accept any unsolicited
material
**Genre:** Comedy, Drama, Fantasy, Romance, Thriller
**Focus:** Feature Films, Shorts
**Year Established:** 1979

### Marc Mauceri
**Title:** Vice President
**IMDB:** http://www.imdb.com/name/
nm1439609/?ref_=fn_al_nm_1

**Seymour Wishman**
Title: President
IMDB: http://www.imdb.com/name/
nm0936544/?ref_=fn_al_nm_1

## FIVE BY EIGHT PRODUCTIONS

4312 Clarissa Avenue
Los Angeles, CA 90027

Phone: 917-658-7545
Website: http://www.fivebyeight.com

Submission Policy: Accepts query letter from
unproduced, unrepresented writers via email
Genre: Drama
Focus: Feature Films, TV
Year Established: 2006

**Michael Connors**
Email: mike@fivebyeight.com
IMDB: www.imdb.com/name/nm2155421

**Sean Mullen**
Email: sean@fivebyeight.com
IMDB: www.imdb.com/name/nm2013693

## FIVE SMOOTH STONE PRODUCTIONS

106 Oakland Hills Court
Duluth, GA 30097

Phone: 770-476-7171
Website: http://www.5ivesmoothstones.com/

Submission Policy: Does not accept any unsolicited
material
Genre: Action, Drama, Memoir & True Stories
Focus: Feature Films

**Rick Middlemas**
Title: Partner

**Morgan Middlemas**
Title: Partner

## FLASHPOINT ENTERTAINMENT

9150 Wilshire Boulevard, Suite 247
Beverly Hills, CA 90212

Phone: 310-205-6300
Email: info@flashpointentertainment.com
Website: www.flashpointent.com

Submission Policy: Does not accept any unsolicited
material

Genre: Drama, Romance
Focus: Feature Films

**Tom Johnson**
Title: Director/Development
Phone: 310-205-6300
IMDB: www.imdb.com/name/nm1927361

**Laura Roman-Rockhold**
Title: Assistant
Phone: 310-205-6300
Email: info@flashpointent.com
IMDB: www.imdb.com/name/nm4099178

**Andrew Tennenbaum**
Title: Manager/Producer
IMDB: www.imdb.com/name/nm0990025

## FLAVOR UNIT ENTERTAINMENT

119 Washington Avenue, Suite 400
Miami Beach, FL 33139

Phone: 201-333-4883
Fax: 973-556-1770
Email: info@flavorunitentertainment.com
Website: www.flavorentertainment.com

Submission Policy: Accepts query letter from
unproduced, unrepresented writers via email
Genre: Comedy, Family, Romance, TV Drama
Focus: Feature Films, Television

**Otis Best**
Title: Producer/General Manager
Phone: 201-333-4883
IMDB: www.imdb.com/name/nm1454006

**Shakim Compere**
Title: CEO
Phone: 201-333-4883
IMDB: www.imdb.com/name/nm1406277
Assistant: Mark Jean

**Queen Latifah**
Title: CEO
Phone: 201-333-4883
IMDB: www.imdb.com/name/nm0001451

## FLOREN SHIEH PRODUCTIONS

20 W 22nd St
Ste 415
New York, NY 10010

**Phone:** 212-898-0890
**Email:** katherine@florenshieh.com
**IMDB:** www.imdb.com/company/co0287709

**Submission Policy:** Accepts query letter from unproduced, unrepresented writers
**Genre:** Drama, Feature Films
**Focus:** Feature Films

**Clay Floren**
**Title:** Producer
**IMDB:** www.imdb.com/name/nm2850202

**Aimee Shieh**
**Title:** Producer
**IMDB:** www.imdb.com/name/nm1848263

## FLOWER FILMS INC.

7360 Santa Monica Boulevard
West Hollywood, CA 90046

**Phone:** 323-876-7400
**Fax:** 323-876-7401

**Submission Policy:** Accepts scripts from produced or represented writers
**Genre:** Comedy, Drama, Family, Fantasy, Romance, Thriller, TV Drama
**Focus:** Feature Films, Television
**Year Established:** 1995

**Drew Barrymore**
**Title:** Partner
**IMDB:** www.imdb.com/name/nm0000106

**Chris Miller**
**Title:** Vice-President/Producer
**IMDB:** www.imdb.com/name/nm0588091
**Assistant:** Steven Acosta

**Ember Truesdell**
**Title:** Vice-President Development
**Email:** ember@flowerfilms.com
**IMDB:** www.imdb.com/name/nm1456092

## FOCUS FEATURES

100 Universal City Plaza Building 9128
Universal City, CA 91608

**Phone:** 818-777-7373
**Email:** press@filminfocus.com
**Website:** http://www.focusfeatures.com/
**IMDB:** http://www.imdb.com/company/co0042399/?ref_=fn_al_co_1

**Submission Policy:** Does not accept any unsolicited material
**Genre:** Action, Animation, Comedy, Crime, Documentary, Drama, Fantasy, Feature Films, Horror, Memoir & True Stories, Romance, Thriller, TV, TV Drama
**Focus:** Feature Films, Television
**Year Established:** 1975

**Jeb Brody**
**Title:** President of Production
**IMDB:** http://www.imdb.com/name/nm1330162/?ref_=fn_al_nm_1
**Assistant:** Rebecca Arzoian

**Andrew Karpen**
**Title:** President of Focus Features & Focus Features International
**IMDB:** http://www.imdb.com/name/nm2537917/?ref_=fn_al_nm_1

**Christopher Koop**
**Title:** Director of Production and Development
**IMDB:** http://www.imdb.com/name/nm3096137/?ref_=fn_al_nm_3

**Peter Kujawski**
**Title:** Executive Vice President of Film Acquisitions
**IMDB:** http://www.imdb.com/name/nm1081654/?ref_=fn_al_nm_1

**Josh McLaughlin**
**Title:** Senior Vice President of Production
**IMDB:** http://www.imdb.com/name/nm2249958/?ref_=fn_al_nm_1

**James Schamus**
**Title:** Chief Executive Officer
**IMDB:** http://www.imdb.com/name/nm0770005/?ref_=fn_al_nm_1

## FORENSIC FILMS

1 Worth Street, 2nd Floor
New York, NY 10013

**Phone:** 212-966-1110
**Fax:** (212) 966-1125
**Email:** forensicfilms@gmail.com

**Submission Policy:** Accepts query letter from unproduced, unrepresented writers via email
**Genre:** Comedy, Crime, Drama, Romance, Thriller
**Focus:** Feature Films

**Scott Macauley**
Title: Producer
IMDB: www.imdb.com/name/nm0531337

**Robin O'Hara**
Title: Producer
IMDB: www.imdb.com/name/nm0641327

## FORESIGHT UNLIMITED

2934 1/2 Beverly Glen Circle, Suite 900
Bel Air, CA 90077

Phone: 310-275-5222
Fax: 310-275-5202
Email: info@foresight-unltd.com
Website: www.foresight-unltd.com

Submission Policy: Accepts query letter from
unproduced, unrepresented writers via email
Genre: Action, Comedy, Crime, Drama, Romance,
Science Fiction, Thriller
Focus: Feature Films

**Tamara Birkemoe**
Title: President (Chief Operating Officer)
IMDB: www.imdb.com/name/nm1736077

**Scott Collette**
Title: Director (Development & Distribution)

**Mark Damon**
Title: CEO
IMDB: www.imdb.com/name/nm0198941

## FOREST PARK PICTURES

11210 Briarcliff Lane
Studio City, CA 91604-4277

Phone: 323-654-2735
Fax: 323-654-2735

Submission Policy: Accepts query letter from
unproduced, unrepresented writers
Genre: Drama, Feature Films, Horror, Thriller
Focus: Feature Films
Year Established: 2002

**Hayden Christensen**
Title: Partner
Phone: 323-848-2942 ext. 265
IMDB: www.imdb.com/name/nm0159789

**Tove Christensen**
Title: Partner
Phone: 323-848-2942 ext. 265
IMDB: www.imdb.com/name/nm0159922

## FORGET ME NOT PRODUCTIONS

New York

Email: info@4getmenotproductions.com
Website: www.4getmenotproductions.com

Submission Policy: Accepts query letter from
unproduced, unrepresented writers via email
Genre: Drama
Focus: Feature Films

**Harry Azano**
Title: Producer
Email: harryazano@gmail.com

**Jennifer Gargano**
Title: President/CEO/Producer
Email: jennifergargano@4getmenotproductions.com
IMDB: www.imdb.com/name/nm2470854

## FORTIS FILMS

8581 Santa Monica Boulevard, Suite 1
West Hollywood, CA 90069

Phone: 310-659-4533
Fax: 310-659-4373

Submission Policy: Accepts query letter from
unproduced, unrepresented writers
Genre: Comedy, Drama, Romance
Focus: Feature Films, TV

**Maggie Biggar**
Title: Partner
Phone: 310-659-4533
IMDB: www.imdb.com/name/nm0081772

**Sandra Bullock**
Title: Partner
Phone: 310-659-4533
IMDB: www.imdb.com/name/nm0000113

**Bryan Moore**
Title: Office Manager

## FORTRESS FEATURES

2727 Main Street Suite E
Santa Monica, CA 90405

Phone: 323-467-4700
Fax: (310) 275-2214
Website: http://www.fortressfeatures.com

**Submission Policy:** Does not accept any unsolicited material
**Genre:** Action, Comedy, Crime, Drama, Horror, Thriller
**Focus:** Feature Films
**Year Established:** 2004

### Bonnie Forbes
Title: Producer/Development
IMDB: www.imdb.com/name/nm1424832

### Brett Forbes
Title: Partner
IMDB: www.imdb.com/name/nm1771405

### Patrick Rizzotti
Title: Partner
IMDB: www.imdb.com/name/nm0729948

## FORWARD ENTERTAINMENT

9255 Sunset Boulevard, Suite 805
West Hollywood, CA 90069

Phone: 310-278-6700
Fax: 310-278-6770

**Submission Policy:** Accepts query letter from unproduced, unrepresented writers via email
**Genre:** Memoir & True Stories
**Focus:** Feature Films, TV

### Vera Mihailovich
Title: Partner
Email: vmihailovich@forward-ent.com
IMDB: www.imdb.com/name/nm2250568

### Adrienne Sandoval
Title: Executive Assistant
Email: asandoval@forward-ent.com
IMDB: www.imdb.com/name/nm2302898

### Connie Tavel
Title: Partner
Email: ctavel@forward-ent.com
IMDB: www.imdb.com/name/nm0851679

## FORWARD PASS

12233 W Olympic Blvd
Ste 340
Los Angeles, CA 90064

Phone: 310-207-7378
Fax: 310-207-3426
IMDB: www.imdb.com/company/co0035930

**Submission Policy:** Does not accept any unsolicited material
**Genre:** Crime, Detective, Drama, Feature Films, Memoir & True Stories, Period, Sociocultural, Thriller
**Focus:** Feature Films

### Michael Mann
Title: Writer / Producter / Director
IMDB: www.imdb.com/name/nm0000520

## FOURBOYS FILMS

4000 Warner Boulevard
Burbank, CA 91522

Phone: 818-954-4378
Fax: 818-954-5359
Email: info@fourboysfilms.com
Website: www.fourboysfilms.com

**Submission Policy:** Does not accept any unsolicited material
**Genre:** Animation, Comedy, TV Drama, TV Sitcom
**Focus:** Feature Films, TV

### Patricia Heaton
Title: Partner
IMDB: www.imdb.com/name/nm0005004

### David Hunt
Title: Partner
IMDB: www.imdb.com/name/nm0402408

### A.J. Morewitz
Title: President
Phone: 818-954-4378
IMDB: www.imdb.com/name/nm1031450

## FOX 2000 PICTURES

10201 West Pico Boulevard
Building 7B
Los Angeles, CA 90035

Phone: 310-369-2000
Fax: 310-369-4258
Website: http://www.fox.com/

**Submission Policy:** Does not accept any unsolicited material
**Genre:** Action, Animation, Comedy, Crime, Drama,

Family, Fantasy, Horror, Myth, Romance, Science
Fiction, Thriller
**Year Established:** 1996

**Elizabeth Gabler**
Title: President, Production
Email: elizabeth.gabler@fox.com
IMDB: www.imdb.com/name/nm1992894

**Riley Kathryn Ellis**
Title: Executive
Email: riley.ellis@fox.com

## FOX DIGITAL STUDIOS

10201 West Pico Boulevard
Los Angeles, CA 90035

Phone: 310-369-1000
Email: david.brooks@fox.com

**Submission Policy:** Accepts query letter from
produced or represented writers
**Genre:** Comedy, Crime, Drama, Feature Films,
Horror, Thriller, TV, TV Sitcom
**Focus:** Feature Films, Television

**David Worthen Brooks**
Title: Creative Director
IMDB: www.imdb.com/name/nm3652161

## FOX INTERNATIONAL PRODUCTIONS

10201 West Pico Boulevard
Los Angeles, CA 90035

Phone: 310-369-1000
Website: http://www.foxinternational.com/

**Submission Policy:** Does not accept any unsolicited
material
**Genre:** Action, Crime, Drama, Family, Romance,
Thriller
**Year Established:** 2008

**Anna Kokourina**
Title: Vice President (Production)
IMDB: http://www.imdb.com/name/
nm3916463/?ref_=fn_al_nm_1

**Marco Mehlitz**
Title: Head (Development)
IMDB: http://www.imdb.com/name/nm0576438/

**Sanford Panitch**
Title: President
Phone: 310-369-1000

Email: sanford.panitch@fox.com
IMDB: www.imdb.com/name/nm0659529

## FOX SEARCHLIGHT PICTURES

10201 West Pico Boulevard
Building 38
Los Angeles, CA 90035

Phone: 310-369-1000
Fax: 310-369-2359
Website: http://www.foxsearchlight.com/

**Submission Policy:** Does not accept any unsolicited
material
**Genre:** Action, Comedy, Crime, Drama, Family,
Fantasy, Horror, Romance, Thriller
**Year Established:** 1994

**Stephen Gilula**
Title: Co-President
Phone: 310-369-1000
Email: stephen.gilula@fox.com
IMDB: www.imdb.com/name/nm2322989

## FREDERATOR STUDIOS

2829 N. Glenoaks Blvd., Ste. 203 Burbank CA
91504

Phone: 818-848-3932
Email: hey@frederator.com
Website: www.frederator.com

**Submission Policy:** Accepts query letter from
unproduced, unrepresented writers via email
**Genre:** Animation, Comedy, Family, TV
**Focus:** Television, Shorts
**Year Established:** 1998

**Eric Homan**
Title: Vice-President, Development
Email: eric@frederator.com
IMDB: www.imdb.com/name/nm2302704

**Fred Selbert**
Title: President-Producer
Phone: 646-274-4601
Email: fred@frederator.com
IMDB: www.imdb.com/name/nm0782288
Assistant: Zoe Barton - zoe@frederator.com

## FREDERIC GOLCHAN PRODUCTIONS

c/o Radar Pictures
10900 Wilshire Boulevard, 14th Floor
Los Angeles, CA 90024

**Phone:** 310-208-8525
**Fax:** 310-208-1764
**Email:** fgfilm@aol.com

**Submission Policy:** Does not accept any unsolicited material
**Genre:** Action, Comedy, Crime, Drama, Thriller

**Frederic Golchan**
**Title:** President-Producer
**Email:** asstgolchan@gmail.com
**IMDB:** www.imdb.com/name/nm0324907
**Assistant:** Gaillaume Chiasoda

## FRED KUENERT PRODUCTIONS

1601 Hilts Ave. #2
Los Angeles, CA 90024

**Phone:** 310-470-3363
**Fax:** 310-470-0060

**Submission Policy:** Accepts query letter from unproduced, unrepresented writers via email
**Genre:** Action, Fantasy, Horror, Science Fiction, Thriller
**Focus:** Feature Films

**Sandra Chouinard**
**Title:** Partner

**Fred Kuenert**
**Email:** fkuehnert@earthlink.net
**IMDB:** www.imdb.com/name/nm0473896

## FREEDOM FILMS

15300 Ventura Blvd. #508
Sherman Oaks, CA 91403

**Phone:** 818-906-2339
**Fax:** 818-906-2342
**Email:** info@freedomfilmsllc.com
**Website:** www.freedomfilms.com

**Submission Policy:** Does not accept any unsolicited material
**Genre:** Action, Crime, Drama, Family, Feature Films, Horror, Thriller
**Focus:** Feature Films

**Carissa Buffel-Matusow**
**Title:** COO & Producer

**Warren Davis**
**Title:** Head of Development

**Alexandria Klipstein**
**Title:** Creative Executive
**IMDB:** www.imdb.com/name/nm2317077

**Kevin J Matusow**
**Title:** COO & Producer

**Brain Presley**
**Title:** CEO
**IMDB:** www.imdb.com/name/nm0696169

**Scott Robinson**
**Title:** Head of Production
**IMDB:** www.imdb.com/name/nm1558904

## FRELAINE

8383 Wilshire Blvd
5th Fl
Beverly Hills, CA 90211

**Phone:** 323-848-9729
**Fax:** 323-848-7219
**IMDB:** www.imdb.com/company/co0176000

**Submission Policy:** Accepts query letter from unproduced, unrepresented writers
**Genre:** Action, Fantasy, Feature Films, Period, Thriller
**Focus:** Feature Films

**James Jacks**
**Title:** Executive
**IMDB:** www.imdb.com/name/nm0413208

## FRESH & SMOKED

Studio City
10700 Ventura Blvd. Ste. 2D
Studio City, CA 91604

**Phone:** 818-505-1311
**Fax:** 818-301-2135
**Email:** bdtd@freshandsmoked.com
**Website:** www.freshandsmoked.com

**Submission Policy:** Accepts scripts from unproduced, unrepresented writers
**Genre:** Action, Animation, Comedy, Crime, Detective, Drama, Family, Fantasy, Horror, Memoir & True Stories, Myth, Romance, Science Fiction,

Thriller, TV Drama, TV Sitcom
**Focus:** Feature Films, TV, Post-Production (Editing, Special Effects), Reality Programming (Reality TV, Documentaries, Special Events, Sporting Events), Media (Commercials/Branding/Marketing)

**Monika Gosch**
**Title:** Producer
**Email:** monika@freshandsmoked.com
**IMDB:** www.imdb.com/name/nm2815838

**Jeremy Gosch**
**Title:** Director
**Email:** jeremy@freshandsmoked.com
**IMDB:** www.imdb.com/name/nm0331443

**Angela McIntyre**
**Title:** Internal Development
**Email:** angela@freshandsmoked.com

## FRIED FILMS

100 North Crescent Drive, Suite 350
Beverly Hills, CA 90210

**Phone:** 310-694-8150
**Fax:** 310-861-5454

**Submission Policy:** Accepts query letter from unproduced, unrepresented writers
**Genre:** Action, Comedy, Crime, Detective, Drama, Family, Romance, Thriller
**Focus:** Feature Films, TV
**Year Established:** 1990

**Robert Fried**
**Title:** Producer
**IMDB:** www.imdb.com/name/nm0294975

**Tyrrell Shaffner**
**Title:** Development Executive
**Phone:** 424-210-3607
**IMDB:** www.imdb.com/name/nm1656222

## FRIENDLY FILMS

100 North Crescent Drive, Suite 350
Beverly Hills, CA 90210

**Phone:** 310-432-1818
**Fax:** 310-432-1801
**Email:** info@friendly-films.com
**Website:** www.friendly-films.com

**Submission Policy:** Accepts query letter from unproduced, unrepresented writers

**Genre:** Comedy, Crime, Drama, Family, Science Fiction
**Focus:** Feature Films
**Year Established:** 2006

**David Friendly**
**Title:** Founder, Producer
**Phone:** 310-432-1800
**IMDB:** www.imdb.com/name/nm0295560

## FRONT STREET PICTURES

1950 Franklin St
Vancouver, BC V5L 1R2
Canada

**Phone:** 604-257-4720
**Fax:** 604-257-4739
**Email:** info@frontstreetpictures.com
**Website:** www.frontstreetpictures.com/
**IMDB:** www.imdb.com/company/co0149567

**Submission Policy:** Accepts query letter from unproduced, unrepresented writers
**Genre:** Action, Comedy, Crime, Drama, Fantasy, Feature Films, Thriller, TV, TV Drama
**Focus:** Feature Films, TV

**Harvey Kahn**
**Title:** Producer
**Email:** harvey@frontstreetpictures.com
**IMDB:** www.imdb.com/name/nm0434838

## FR PRODUCTIONS

2980 Beverly Glenn Cir., Suite 200
Los Angeles, CA 90077

**Phone:** 310-470-9212
**Fax:** 310-470-4905

**Submission Policy:** Accepts query letter from unproduced, unrepresented writers via email
**Genre:** Comedy, Crime, Drama, Family, Romance, Thriller
**Focus:** Feature Films

**Fred Roos**
**Title:** Producer/President
**Email:** frprod@earthlink.net
**IMDB:** www.imdb.com/name/nm0740407

## FULLER FILMS

P.O. BOX 976
Venice, CA 90294

**Phone:** 310-717-8842

**Submission Policy:** Does not accept any unsolicited material
**Genre:** Comedy, Crime, Drama
**Focus:** Feature Films

**Henry Beean**
**Title:** Writer/Director/Producer
**IMDB:** www.imdb.com/name/nm0063785

**Paul De Souza**
**Title:** Producer
**Email:** gopics@verizon.net
**IMDB:** www.imdb.com/name/nm0996278

## FUN LITTLE MOVIES

2227 W Olive Ave
Burbank, CA 91506

**Phone:** 323-467-6868
**Email:** Contact@funlittlemovies.com
**Website:** www.funlittlemovies.com/
**IMDB:** www.imdb.com/company/co0161105

**Submission Policy:** Accepts query letter from unproduced, unrepresented writers
**Genre:** Animation, Comedy, TV
**Focus:** TV

**Frank Chindamo**
**Title:** President
**Email:** frank@funlittlemovies.com
**IMDB:** www.imdb.com/name/nm0157828

## FURST FILMS

8954 West Pico Boulevard
2nd Floor
Los Angeles, CA 90035

**Phone:** 310-278-6468
**Fax:** 310-278-7401
**Email:** info@furstfilms.com
**Website:** www.furstfilms.com

**Submission Policy:** Accepts query letter from unproduced, unrepresented writers via email
**Genre:** Action, Crime, Detective, Drama, Horror, Thriller
**Focus:** Feature Films, TV, Reality Programming (Reality TV, Documentaries, Special Events, Sporting Events)

**Meredith Ditlow**
**Title:** Manager, Creative Affairs
**Email:** meredith@furstfilms.com
**IMDB:** www.imdb.com/name/nm1902828

**Bryan Furst**
**Title:** Principal/Producer
**IMDB:** www.imdb.com/name/nm1227576

**Jan-Willem van der Vaart**
**Title:** Creative Executive

## FURTHUR FILMS

100 Universal City Plaza
Building 5174
Universal City, CA 91608

**Phone:** 818-777-6700
**Fax:** 818-866-1278

**Submission Policy:** Accepts query letter from unproduced, unrepresented writers
**Genre:** Comedy, Crime, Drama, Romance, Thriller
**Focus:** Feature Films

**Michael Douglas**
**Title:** Producer
**IMDB:** www.imdb.com/name/nm0000140

**Andy Ziskin**
**Title:** Development

## FUSEFRAME

2332 Cotner Ave, Suite 200
Los Angeles, CA 90064

**Phone:** 424-208-1765

**Submission Policy:** Does not accept any unsolicited material
**Genre:** Horror, Thriller
**Focus:** Feature Films
**Year Established:** 2011

**Marcus Chait**
**Title:** Director of Film and New Media
**IMDB:** www.imdb.com/name/nm1483939

**Eva Konstantopoulos**
**Title:** Book to Screen Coordinator
**IMDB:** www.imdb.com/name/nm2192285

## FUSION FILMS

2355 Westwood Boulevard, Suite 117
Los Angeles, CA 90064

**Phone:** 310-441-1496
**Email:** info@fusionfilms.net
**Website:** http://www.fusionfilms.net/

**Submission Policy:** Accepts query letter from unproduced, unrepresented writers
**Genre:** Action, Animation, Comedy, Crime, Drama, Fantasy, Horror, Thriller
**Focus:** Feature Films, TV

### John Baldecchi
**Title:** Co-CEO, Producer
**IMDB:** www.imdb.com/name/nm0049689

### Jay Judah
**Title:** Creative Executive

## FUZZY DOOR PRODUCTIONS

5700 Wilshire Boulevard
Suite 325
Los Angeles, CA 90036

**Phone:** 323-857-8826
**Fax:** 323-857-8945

**Submission Policy:** Does not accept any unsolicited material
**Genre:** Animation, Comedy, Family, Feature Films, TV, TV Sitcom
**Focus:** Feature Films, Television

### Seth MacFarlane
**Title:** President
**IMDB:** www.imdb.com/name/nm0532235

## GAETA/ROSENZWEIG FILMS

150 Ocean Park Boulevard #322
Santa Monica, CA 90405-3572

**Phone:** 310-399-7101

**Submission Policy:** Accepts query letter from unproduced, unrepresented writers
**Genre:** Comedy, Crime, Drama, Horror, Thriller, TV Drama
**Focus:** Feature Films, TV

### Michael J. Gaeta
**Title:** Partner
**IMDB:** http://www.imdb.com/name/nm1357812/

### Alison R. Rosenzweig
**Title:** Partner
**IMDB:** www.imdb.com/name/nm0742851

## GALATEE FILMS

19 Avenue de Messine
Paris, France 75008

**Phone:** +33 1 44 29 21 40
**Fax:** +33 1 44 29 25 90
**Email:** mail@galateefilms.com
**Website:** www.galateefilms.com

**Submission Policy:** Accepts query letter from unproduced, unrepresented writers via email
**Genre:** Drama, Memoir & True Stories, Romance
**Focus:** Feature Films

### Christophe Barratier
**Title:** Producer
**IMDB:** www.imdb.com/name/nm0056725

### Nicolas Mauvernay
**Title:** Producer
**IMDB:** www.imdb.com/name/nm1241814

### Jacques Perrin
**Title:** Producer/CEO
**IMDB:** www.imdb.com/name/nm0674742

## GALLANT ENTERTAINMENT

16161 Ventura Boulevard, Suite 664
Encino, CA 91436

**Phone:** 818-905-9848
**Fax:** 818-906-9965
**Email:** mog@gallantentertainment.com
**Website:** www.gallantentertainment.com

**Submission Policy:** Accepts query letter from unproduced, unrepresented writers via email
**Genre:** Drama, Family, Romance, Thriller, TV Drama
**Focus:** Feature Films, TV, Reality Programming (Reality TV, Documentaries, Special Events, Sporting Events), Media (Commercials/Branding/Marketing)
**Year Established:** 1992

### K.R. Gallant
**Title:** Operations
**Email:** krg@gallantentertainment.com

**Michael Gallant**
Title: President/Producer
IMDB: www.imdb.com/name/nm0302572

## GARY HOFFMAN PRODUCTIONS

3931 Puerco Canyon Road
Malibu, CA 90265

Phone: 310-456-1830
Fax: 310-456-8866
Email: garyhofprods@charter.net

Submission Policy: Accepts query letter from unproduced, unrepresented writers via email
Genre: Action, Comedy, Crime, Drama, Romance, Thriller
Focus: Feature Films, TV

**Gary Hoffman**
Title: Producer/President
IMDB: www.imdb.com/name/nm0388888

**Ann Ryan**
Title: Development

## GARY SANCHEZ PRODUCTIONS

729 Seward St
2nd Fl
Los Angeles, CA 90038
USA

Phone: 323-465-4600
Fax: 323-465-0782
Email: gary@garysanchezprods.com
Website: www.garysanchezprods.com

Submission Policy: Does not accept any unsolicited material
Genre: Comedy
Focus: Feature Films, TV

**Will Ferrell**
Title: Founder/Executive Producer/Actor
IMDB: www.imdb.com/name/nm0002071

## GENEXT FILMS

5610 Soto Street
Huntington Park, CA 90255

Email: contact@genextfilms.com
Website: www.genextfilms.com

Submission Policy: Accepts query letter from unproduced, unrepresented writers via email

Genre: Comedy
Focus: Feature Films, TV

**Carlos Salas**
Title: CEO/Producer
IMDB: www.imdb.com/name/nm297?624
Assistant: Kathy Snyder

**Rossana Salas**
Title: CFO/Producer
IMDB: www.imdb.com/name/nm297)664

## GENREBEND PRODUCTIONS, INC.

233 Wilshire Boulevard, Suite 400
Santa Monica, CA 90401

Phone: 310-860-0878
Fax: 310-917-1065
Email: genrebend@elvis.com

Submission Policy: Accepts query letter from unproduced, unrepresented writers via email
Genre: TV Drama, TV Sitcom
Focus: Feature Films, TV

**Tom Lavagnino**
Title: Vice-President Creative Affairs, Writer
IMDB: www.imdb.com/name/nm049?706

**David Nutter**
Title: President/Director
IMDB: www.imdb.com/name/nm063?354

## GEORGE LITTO PRODUCTIONS, INC.

339 North Orange Drive
Los Angeles, CA 90036

Phone: 323-936-6350
Fax: 323-936-6762

Submission Policy: Accepts query letter from unproduced, unrepresented writers
Genre: Action, Comedy, Crime, Drama, Memoir & True Stories, Romance
Focus: Feature Films
Year Established: 1997

**Linda Lee**
Title: Executive Assistant

**George Litto**
Title: CEO/Owner
IMDB: www.imdb.com/name/nm0514788

## GERARD BUTLER ALAN SIEGEL ENTERTAINMENT/ EVIL TWINS

345 North Maple Drive
Beverly Hills, CA 90210

**Phone:** 310-278-8400

**Submission Policy:** Does not accept any unsolicited material
**Genre:** Comedy, Drama, Thriller
**Focus:** Feature Films

**Gerard Butler**
Title: Producer/Actor
IMDB: www.imdb.com/name/nm0124930

**Danielle Robinson**
Title: Director of Development

**Alan Siegel**
Title: Executive

## GERBER PICTURES

4000 Warner Boulevard
Building 138, Suite 1202
Burbank, CA 91522

**Phone:** 818-954-3046
**Fax:** 818-954-3706

**Submission Policy:** Does not accept any unsolicited material
**Genre:** Action, Animation, Comedy, Drama, Family, Romance, TV Drama, TV Sitcom
**Focus:** Feature Films, TV

**Bill Gerber**
Title: President
IMDB: http://www.imdb.com/name/nm0314088/
Assistant: James Leffler

**Carrie Gillogly**
Title: Creative Executive
IMDB: www.imdb.com/name/nm2235655

## GHOST HOUSE PICTURES

315 South Beverly Dr, Suite 216
Beverly Hills, CA 90212

**Phone:** 310-785-3900
**Fax:** 310-785-9176
**Email:** info@ghosthousepictures.com
**Website:** www.ghosthousepictures.com

**Submission Policy:** Does not accept any unsolicited material
**Genre:** Horror, Thriller, TV Drama, TV Sitcom
**Focus:** Feature Films, TV

**Aaron Lam**
Title: Executive
IMDB: www.imdb.com/name/nm1725478

**Sam Raimi**
Title: Director/Executive Producer
IMDB: www.imdb.com/name/nm0000600

## GIGANTIC PICTURES

New York
207 West 25th Street Suite 504
New York, NY 10001

**Phone:** (212) 925-5075
**Fax:** (212) 925-5061
**Email:** info@giganticpictures.com
**Website:** http://www.giganticpictures.com

**Submission Policy:** Accepts query letter from produced or represented writers
**Genre:** Comedy, Drama, Memoir & True Stories, Romance
**Focus:** Feature Films, TV

**Edward Bates**
Title: Producer
IMDB: www.imdb.com/name/nm0060901

**Brian Devine**
Title: Founder
IMDB: http://www.imdb.com/name/nm0222601/

## GIL ADLER PRODUCTIONS

c/o Peter Franciosa's office/United Talent Agency
9560 Wilshire Boulevard, Suite 500
Beverly Hills, CA 90212

**Submission Policy:** Does not accept any unsolicited material
**Genre:** Action, Horror, Thriller
**Focus:** Feature Films, TV, Reality Programming (Reality TV, Documentaries, Special Events, Sporting Events), Media (Commercials/Branding/ Marketing)

**Gil Adler**
Title: Producer
IMDB: www.imdb.com/name/nm0012155
Assistant: Ryan Lough

## GILBERT FILMS

8409 Santa Monica Boulevard
West Hollywood, CA 90069

Phone: 323-650-6800
Fax: 323-650-6810
Email: info@gilbertfilms.com
Website: www.gilbertfilms.com

Submission Policy: Does not accept any unsolicited
material
Genre: Comedy, Drama, Romance
Focus: Feature Films

**Shauna Bogetz**
Title: Director of Development
IMDB: www.imdb.com/name/nm2868191

**Gary Gilbert**
Title: CEO/President
IMDB: www.imdb.com/name/nm1344784

**Katie Slovon**
Title: Assistant
IMDB: www.imdb.com/name/nm4244578

## GIL NETTER PRODUCTIONS

1645 Abbot Kinney Boulevard, Suite 320
Venice, CA 90291

Phone: (310) 394-1644
Fax: (310) 899-6722

Submission Policy: Does not accept any unsolicited
material
Genre: Action, Comedy, Drama, Family, Romance
Focus: Feature Films

**Tom Carstens**
Title: Development Executive

**Gil Netter**
Title: Producer
IMDB: www.imdb.com/name/nm0626696
Assistant: Jennifer Ho

**Charles Thompson**

## GIRLS CLUB ENTERTAINMENT

30 Sir Francis Drake Blvd
PO Box 437
Ross, CA 94957

Phone: (415) 233-4060
Fax: (415) 233-4082
Email: info@girlsclubentertainment.com
Website: www.girlsclubentertainment.com

Submission Policy: Does not accept any unsolicited
material
Genre: Comedy, Crime, Drama, Memoir & True
Stories, Romance
Focus: Feature Films, TV, Reality Programming
(Reality TV, Documentaries, Special Events,
Sporting Events)

**Jennifer Siebel**
Title: Founder
IMDB: www.imdb.com/name/nm1308076

## GITLIN PRODUCTIONS

1310 Montana Avenue Second Floor
Santa Monica, CA 90403

Phone: (310) 209-8443
Fax: (310) 728-1749
Email: gitlinproduction@aol.com

Submission Policy: Accepts query letter from
unproduced, unrepresented writers via email
Genre: Action, Comedy, Drama
Focus: Feature Films, TV, Reality Programming
(Reality TV, Documentaries, Special Events,
Sporting Events)

**Richard Gitlin**

**Mimi Gitlin**
Title: President/Producer
IMDB: www.imdb.com/name/nm0689316

## GITTES, INC.

Los Angeles
16615 Park Lane Place
Los Angeles, CA 90049

Phone: (310) 472-2689

Submission Policy: Accepts query letter from
unproduced, unrepresented writers
Genre: Comedy, Drama
Focus: Feature Films

**Harry Gittes**
Title: Producer
Email: harry_gittes@spe.sony.com
IMDB: www.imdb.com/name/nm0321228

**Edward Wang**
Title: Director of Development
Phone: 310-244-4334
Email: edward_wang@spe.sony.com
IMDB: www.imdb.com/name/nm0910882

## GK FILMS

1540 2nd Street, Suite 200
Santa Monica, CA 90401

Phone: 310-315-1722
Fax: 310-315-1723
Email: contact@gk-films.com
Website: www.gk-films.com

Submission Policy: Does not accept any unsolicited material
Genre: Action, Animation, Comedy, Crime, Drama, Family, Fantasy, Memoir & True Stories, Romance, Science Fiction, Thriller, TV
Focus: Feature Films, TV
Year Established: 2007

**David Crocket**
Title: Creative Executive

**Graham King**
Title: CEO
IMDB: www.imdb.com/name/nm0454752
Assistant: Leah Williams, Michelle Reed

## GLASS EYE PIX

18 Bridge St.
#2G
Brooklyn, NY 11201

Phone: 718-643-6911
Email: feedback@glasseyepix.com
Website: www.glasseyepix.com

Submission Policy: Accepts query letter from unproduced, unrepresented writers via email
Genre: Crime, Drama, Horror, Science Fiction, Thriller
Focus: Horror Films

**Larry Fessenden**
Title: Executive
Email: larry@glasseyepix.com
IMDB: www.imdb.com/name/nm0275244

**Brent Kunkle**
Title: Executive
Email: brentkunkle@gmail.com
IMDB: www.imdb.com/name/nm2390962

**Peter Phok**
Title: Executive
Email: peter@peterphok.com
IMDB: www.imdb.com/name/nm1490961

## GLORY ROAD PRODUCTIONS

23638 Lyons Ave.
Suite #470
Newhall, CA 91321

Phone: 661-367-7545
Email: info@gloryroadproductions.com
Website: www.gloryroadproductions.com

Submission Policy: Does not accept any unsolicited material
Genre: Action, Comedy, Drama, Family, Fantasy, Feature Films, Horror
Focus: Feature Films

**Tara Bonacci**
Title: Producer
IMDB: www.imdb.com/name/nm1742721

**Erik Elseman**
Title: Executive Vice President
IMDB: www.imdb.com/name/nm4831920

**Val Mancini**
Title: Director of Development
IMDB: www.imdb.com/name/nm4441689

**Michael Reymann**
Title: President
IMDB: www.imdb.com/name/nm1478831

## GOFF-KELLAM PRODUCTIONS

8491 Sunset Boulevard, Suite 1000
West Hollywood, CA 90069

Phone: 310-666-9082
Fax: 323-656-1002
Email: info@goffproductions.com
Website: http://goffproductions.com

**Submission Policy:** Accepts query letter from unproduced, unrepresented writers via email
**Genre:** Comedy, Drama, Memoir & True Stories, Myth, Romance, Thriller
**Focus:** Feature Films
**Year Established:** 1998

### Gina Goff
**Title:** Producer
**IMDB:** www.imdb.com/name/nm0324574

### Laura Kellam
**Title:** Producer
**IMDB:** www.imdb.com/name/nm0445496

## GO GIRL MEDIA

3450 Cahuenga Boulevard West #802
Los Angeles, CA 90068

**Phone:** 310-472-8910
**Fax:** 818-924-9369
**Email:** info@gogirlmedia.com
**Website:** www.gogirlmedia.com

**Submission Policy:** Accepts query letter from unproduced, unrepresented writers via email
**Genre:** Animation, Comedy, Drama, Family, Memoir & True Stories, TV Drama, TV Sitcom
**Focus:** Feature Films, TV, Reality Programming (Reality TV, Documentaries, Special Events, Sporting Events)
**Year Established:** 2004

### Susie Carter
**Title:** Owner/Producer/Writer
**Email:** Susie@gogirlmedia.com
**IMDB:** www.imdb.com/name/nm0802053

### Don Priess
**Title:** Head of Production. Writer/Producer/Editor
**IMDB:** www.imdb.com/name/nm1043744

## GOLD CIRCLE FILMS

233 Wilshire Boulevard, Suite 650
Santa Monica, CA 90401

**Phone:** 310-278-4800
**Fax:** 310-278-0885
**Email:** info@goldcirclefilms.com
**Website:** www.goldcirclefilms.com

**Submission Policy:** Does not accept any unsolicited material
**Genre:** Action, Comedy, Drama, Family, Horror,
Romance, Science Fiction, Thriller
**Focus:** Feature Films
**Year Established:** 2000

### Paul Brooks
**Title:** President
**IMDB:** http://www.imdb.com/name/nm0112189/

### Brad Kessell
**IMDB:** http://www.imdb.com/name/nm1733186/?ref_=fn_al_nm_1

### Rayne Roberts
**Title:** Creative Executive
**IMDB:** http://www.imdb.com/name/nm2458963/?ref_=fn_al_nm_1

## GOLDCREST FILMS

65/66 Dean Street
London W1D 4PL
United Kingdom

**Phone:** +44 207-437-8696
**Fax:** +44 207-437-4448
**Email:** info@goldcrestfilms.com
**Website:** www.goldcrestfilms.com

**Submission Policy:** Does not accept any unsolicited material
**Genre:** Animation, Drama, Memoir & True Stories, Romance, TV Drama, TV Sitcom
**Focus:** Feature Films, TV, Post-Production (Editing, Special Effects), Reality Programming (Reality TV, Documentaries, Special Events, Sporting Events)
**Year Established:** 1977

### Stephen Johnston
**Title:** President
**IMDB:** www.imdb.com/name/nm1158125

## GOLDENRING PRODUCTIONS

4804 Laurel Canyon Boulevard
Room 570
Valley Village, CA 91607

**Phone:** 818-508-7425
**Email:** info@goldenringproductions.net
**Website:** www.goldenringproductions.net

**Submission Policy:** Accepts query letter from unproduced, unrepresented writers via email
**Genre:** Animation, Comedy, Family, Memoir & True Stories, TV Drama, TV Sitcom
**Focus:** Feature Films, TV

**Jane Goldenring**
Title: President/Producer
IMDB: www.imdb.com/name/nm0325553

**Jon King**
Title: Development
Email: jonnyfking@gmail.com

## GOLDSMITH-THOMAS PRODUCTIONS

239 Central Park West, Suite 6A
New York, NY 10024

Phone: 212-243-4147
Fax: 212-799-2545

Submission Policy: Accepts query letter from
unproduced, unrepresented writers
Genre: Comedy, Drama, Family, Memoir & True
Stories, Romance, TV Drama, TV Sitcom
Focus: Feature Films, TV

**Elaine Goldsmith-Thomas**
Title: President/Producer
IMDB: www.imdb.com/name/nm0326063
Assistant: Anabel Graff

## GOOD HUMOR TELEVISION

9255 West Sunset Boulevard #1040
West Hollywood, CA 90069

Phone: 310-205-7361
Fax: 310-550-7962

Submission Policy: Accepts query letter from
unproduced, unrepresented writers
Genre: Animation, Comedy, TV
Focus: TV

**Mike Clements**
Title: President/Executive Producer
IMDB: www.imdb.com/name/nm2540547

**Tom Werner**
Title: Owner/Executive Producer
IMDB: www.imdb.com/name/nm0921492

## GORILLA PICTURES

2000 West Olive Avenue
Burbank, CA 91506

Phone: 818-848-2198
Fax: 818-848-2232
Email: info@gorillapictures.net
Website: www.gorillapictures.net

Submission Policy: Does not accept any unsolicited
material
Genre: Action, Animation, Crime, Drama, Family,
Fantasy, Science Fiction, Thriller
Focus: Feature Films
Year Established: 1999

**Bill Gottlieb**
Title: CEO
Email: bill.gottlieb@gorillapictures.net
IMDB: www.imdb.com/name/nm1539281

**Don Wilson**
Title: Executive Vice-President of Development
Email: don.wilson@gorillapictures.net
IMDB: http://www.imdb.com/name/nm0933310/

## GOTHAM ENTERTAINMENT GROUP

85 John Street Penthouse 1
New York City, NY 10038

Phone: 814-253-5151
Fax: (801) 439-6998
Email: losangeles@gothamcity.com or
newyork@gothamcity.com
Website: www.gothamentertainmentgroup.com

Submission Policy: Accepts query letter from
unproduced, unrepresented writers via email
Genre: Action, Comedy, Crime, Drama, Romance,
Science Fiction, Thriller
Focus: Feature Films, TV, Reality Programming
(Reality TV, Documentaries, Special Events,
Sporting Events)

**Eric Kopeloff**
Title: Partner
IMDB: http://www.imdb.com/name/nm0465740/

**Joel Roodman**
Title: Partner
Email: joel@gothamentertainmentgroup.com
IMDB: www.imdb.com/name/nm0740211

## GRACIE FILMS

10201 W. Pico Blvd., Bldg. 41/42 Los Angeles, CA
90064

Phone: 310-369-7222
Email: graciefilms@aol.com
Website: http://www.graciefilms.com/

Submission Policy: Does not accept any unsolicited
material

**Genre:** Animation, Comedy, Drama, Family, Memoir & True Stories, Romance
**Focus:** Feature Films, TV

### Julie Ansell
**Title:** President (Motion Pictures)
**IMDB:** http://www.imdb.com/name/nm0030572/

### James Brooks
**Title:** Producer/Writer/Director
**IMDB:** www.imdb.com/name/nm0000985

### Richard Sakai
**Title:** President
**IMDB:** http://www.imdb.com/name/nm0757017/?ref_=fn_al_nm_1

## GRADE A ENTERTAINMENT

149 South Barrington Ave, Suite 719
Los Angeles, CA 90049

**Phone:** 310-358-8600
**Fax:** 310-919-2998
**Email:** development@gradeaent.com
**Website:** www.gradeaent.com

**Submission Policy:** Accepts query letter from unproduced, unrepresented writers via email
**Genre:** Fantasy
**Focus:** Feature Films, TV

### Andy Cohen
**Title:** Producer/Manager
**Email:** andy@gradeaent.com
**IMDB:** www.imdb.com/name/nm2221597

## GRAMMNET PRODUCTIONS

2461 Santa Monica Boulevard #521
Santa Monica, CA 90404

**Phone:** 310-317-4231
**Fax:** 310-317-4260

**Submission Policy:** Does not accept any unsolicited material
**Genre:** Comedy, Family, TV Drama, TV Sitcom
**Focus:** Feature Films, TV, Reality Programming (Reality TV, Documentaries, Special Events, Sporting Events), Theater

### Stella Bulochnikov
**Title:** Executive
**Phone:** 310-255-5089
**Assistant:** Melissa Panzer, mpanzer@lionsgate.com

### Kelsey Grammar
**Title:** Actor/Producer/CEO
**IMDB:** www.imdb.com/name/nm0001288
**Assistant:** Xochitl L. Olivas

## GRAND CANAL FILM WORKS

1187 Coast Village Road
Montecito, CA 93108

11135 Magnolia, SU 160
North Hollywood, CA 91601

**Phone:** 818-259-8237

**Submission Policy:** Does not accept any unsolicited material
**Focus:** Feature Films, TV, Reality Programming (Reality TV, Documentaries, Special Events, Sporting Events), Th eater

### Rick Brookwell
**Title:** Partner
**Email:** RBrookwell@GrandCanalFW.com
**IMDB:** http://www.imdb.com/name/nm2162558/

### Craig Haffner
**Title:** Partner
**Email:** CHaffner@GrandCanalFW.com
**IMDB:** http://www.imdb.com/name/nm0353121/?ref_=fn_al_nm_1

## GRAND PRODUCTIONS

16255 Venture Boulevard, Suite 400
Encino, CA 91436

**Phone:** 818-981-1497
**Fax:** (818) 380-3006
**Email:** grandproductions@mac.com

**Submission Policy:** Does not accept any unsolicited material
**Genre:** TV Drama, TV Sitcom
**Focus:** Feature Films, TV

### Gary Randall
**Title:** President/Owner/Executive Producer
**IMDB:** www.imdb.com/name/nm0709592

### Jennifer Stempel
**Title:** Development Executive
**IMDB:** www.imdb.com/name/nm4009105

## GRAN VIA PRODUCTIONS

1888 Century Park East
14th Floor
Los Angeles, CA 90067

**Phone:** 310-859-3060
**Fax:** 310-859-3066

**Submission Policy:** Does not accept any unsolicited material
**Genre:** Comedy, Drama, Fantasy, Science Fiction, TV Drama, TV Sitcom
**Focus:** Feature Films, TV

**Mark Ceryak**
**Title:** Creative Executive
**IMDB:** www.imdb.com/name/nm1641437

**Mark Johnson**
**Title:** President/Producer
**IMDB:** www.imdb.com/name/nm0425741
**Assistant:** Emily Eckert (Story Editor)

## GRAY ANGEL PRODUCTIONS

69 Windward Avenue
Venice, CA 90291

**Phone:** 310-581-0010
**Fax:** 310-396-0551

**Submission Policy:** Accepts query letter from unproduced, unrepresented writers
**Focus:** Feature Films

**Jaclyn Bashoff**
**Title:** President/Manager
**IMDB:** www.imdb.com/name/nm1902472

**Anjelica Huston**
**Title:** CEO/Producer
**IMDB:** www.imdb.com/name/nm0001378

## GRAZKA TAYLOR PRODUCTIONS

409 North Camden Drive, Suite 202
Beverly Hills, CA 90210

**Phone:** 310-246-1107
**Website:** www.grazkat.com

**Submission Policy:** Does not accept any unsolicited material
**Genre:** Drama, Memoir & True Stories, Romance
**Focus:** Feature Films, TV, Reality Programming

(Reality TV, Documentaries, Special Events, Sporting Events)

**Grazka Taylor**
**Title:** Producer
**Email:** grazka@grazkat.com
**IMDB:** www.imdb.com/name/nm0852429

## GREASY ENTERTAINMENT

6345 Balboa Boulevard
Building 4, Suite 375
Encino, CA 91316

**Phone:** 310-586-2300
**Email:** info@greasy.biz
**Website:** www.greasy.biz

**Submission Policy:** Accepts query letter from unproduced, unrepresented writers via email
**Genre:** Action, Comedy
**Focus:** Feature Films, TV

**Jon Heder**
**Title:** CFO/Actor/Executive
**IMDB:** www.imdb.com/name/nm1417647

**Dan Heder**
**Title:** Executive

**Doug Heder**
**Title:** CFO/Executive

## GREENESTREET FILMS

430 West Broadway 2nd Floor
New York City, NY 10012

**Phone:** 212-609-9000
**Fax:** 212-609-9099
**Email:** general@gstreet.com
**Website:** www.greenestreetfilms.com

**Submission Policy:** Accepts query letter from unproduced, unrepresented writers via email
**Genre:** Comedy, Drama, Horror, Romance, Thriller
**Focus:** Feature Films

**Matthew Honovic**
**Title:** Creative Executive
**Email:** http://www.imdb.com/name/nm2416270/?ref_=fn_al_nm_1

**John M Penotti**
**Title:** President
**IMDB:** http://www.imdb.com/name/nm0006597/

## GREEN HAT FILMS

4000 Warner Boulevard
Building 66
Burbank, CA 91522

**Phone:** (818) 954-3210
**Fax:** (818) 954-3214

**Submission Policy:** Does not accept any unsolicited material
**Genre:** Comedy, Drama, Memoir & True Stories, Thriller
**Focus:** Feature Films

**Diana Davis-Dyer**
**Title:** Executive Assistant

**Mark O'Connor**
**Title:** Director of Development

**Todd Phillips**
**Title:** President/Director
**IMDB:** www.imdb.com/name/nm0680846
**Assistant:** Joseph Garner

## GREENTREES FILMS

854-A 5th Street
Santa Monica, CA 90403

**Phone:** 310-899-1522
**Fax:** 310-496-2082
**Email:** info@greentreesfilms.com
**Website:** www.greentreesfilms.com

**Submission Policy:** Accepts query letter from unproduced, unrepresented writers via email
**Genre:** Comedy, Drama
**Focus:** Feature Films, TV, Reality Programming (Reality TV, Documentaries, Special Events, Sporting Events), Media (Commercials/Branding/Marketing)

**Jack Binder**
**Title:** Producer/President
**IMDB:** www.imdb.com/name/nm0082784

## GRINDSTONE ENTERTAINMENT GROUP

2700 Colorado Avenue
Suite 200
Santa Monica, CA 90404

**Phone:** 310-255-5761
**Fax:** 310-255-3766
**Website:** www.thegrindstone.net

**Submission Policy:** Accepts query letter from produced or represented writers
**Genre:** Action, Drama, Feature Films, Period, Thriller
**Focus:** Feature Films

**Ryan Black**
**Title:** Director of Development
**Email:** ryan@thegrindstone.net
**IMDB:** www.imdb.com/name/nm3337383

**Barry Brooker**
**Title:** President
**Email:** barry@thegrindstone.net
**IMDB:** www.imdb.com/name/nm1633269

**Teresa Sabatine**
**Title:** Executive Assistant
**Email:** teresa@thegrindstone.net
**IMDB:** www.imdb.com/name/nm3466608

**Stan Wertlieb**
**Title:** Partner & Head of Acquisitions
**Email:** stanwertlieb@gmail.com
**IMDB:** www.imdb.com/name/nm0921627

## GRIZZLY ADAMS PRODUCTIONS

201 Five Cities Drive SPC 172, Pismo Beach CA 93449

**Phone:** (877) 556-8536
**Fax:** (805) 556-0393
**Website:** http://www.grizzlyadams.com/

**Submission Policy:** Does not accept any unsolicited material
**Genre:** Drama, Family, Memoir & True Stories, TV
**Focus:** Feature Films, TV, Reality Programming (Documentaries)

**David W. Balsiger**
**Title:** Vice President
**IMDB:** http://www.imdb.com/name/nm1901322/

## GROSSO JACOBSON COMMUNICATIONS CORP.

1801 Avenue of the Stars, Suite 911
Los Angeles, CA 90067

767 Third Avenue
New York, NY 10017

373 Front Street East
Toronto, Ontario M5A 1G4
Canada

**Phone:** 310-788-8900
**Email:** grossojacobson@grossojacobson.com
**Website:** www.grossojacobson.com

**Submission Policy:** Accepts query letter from unproduced, unrepresented writers via email
**Genre:** Comedy, Crime, Drama, Horror, Thriller
**Focus:** Feature Films, TV, Reality Programming (Reality TV, Documentaries, Special Events, Sporting Events), Theater
**Year Established:** 1999

### Sonny Grosso
**Title:** Executive Producer
**Phone:** 212-644-6909
**IMDB:** http://www.imdb.com/name/nm0343780/?ref_=fn_al_nm_1

### Keith Johnson
**Title:** Sr. VP Development
**Phone:** 310-788-8900
**IMDB:** http://www.imdb.com/name/nm1702242/?ref_=fn_al_nm_8

## GROSS-WESTON PRODUCTIONS

10560 Wilshire Boulevard, Suite 801
Los Angeles, CA 90024

**Phone:** 310-777-0010
**Fax:** 310-777-0016
**Email:** gross-weston@sbcglobal.net

**Submission Policy:** Accepts scripts from produced or represented writers
**Genre:** Action, Comedy, Drama, Family, Romance, Science Fiction, Thriller
**Focus:** Feature Films, TV, Reality Programming (Reality TV, Documentaries, Special Events, Sporting Events), Theater

### Mary Gross
**Title:** Executive Producer
**IMDB:** http://www.imdb.com/name/nm0343437/

### Ann Weston
**Title:** Executive Producer
**IMDB:** http://www.imdb.com/name/nm0922912/?ref_=fn_al_nm_1

## GROUNDSWELL PRODUCTIONS

11925 Wilshire Boulevard, Suite 310
Los Angeles, CA 90025

**Phone:** 310-385-7540
**Fax:** 310-385-7541
**Email:** info@groundswellfilms.com
**Website:** www.groundswellfilms.com

**Submission Policy:** Does not accept any unsolicited material
**Genre:** Action, Comedy, Crime, Drama, Horror, Memoir & True Stories, Romance, Thriller
**Focus:** Feature Films, TV, Theater
**Year Established:** 2006

### Kelly Mullen
**Title:** Vice-President
**IMDB:** www.imdb.com/name/nm4133402

### Janice Williams
**Title:** Vice-President of Production
**IMDB:** www.imdb.com/name/nm1003921

## GUARDIAN ENTERTAINMENT, LTD.

71 5th Avenue
New York, NY 10003

**Phone:** 212-727-4729
**Fax:** 212-727-4713
**Email:** guardian@guardianltd.com
**Website:** http://www.guardianltd.com/

**Submission Policy:** Accepts query letter from unproduced, unrepresented writers via email
**Genre:** Drama, Horror, Science Fiction, Thriller
**Focus:** Feature Films, TV, Reality Programming (Reality TV, Documentaries, Special Events, Sporting Events), Media (Commercials/Branding/Marketing)

### Anita Agair
**Title:** Production Coordinator
**Email:** agair@guardianltd.com

**Richard Miller**
Title: CEO/Executive Producer
Email: rmiller@guardianltd.com

## GUNN FILMS

500 South Buena Vista Street
Old Animation Building, Suite 3-A7
Burbank, CA 91521

Phone: 818-560-6156
Fax: 818-842-8394

Submission Policy: Does not accept any unsolicited material
Genre: Action, Comedy, Drama, Family, Fantasy, Romance, Science Fiction, Thriller
Focus: Feature Films, TV
Year Established: 2001

**Andrew Gunn**
Title: Producer
Email: andrew.gunn@disney.com
IMDB: www.imdb.com/name/nm0348151

**Ann Marie Sanderlin**
Title: President
IMDB: http://www.imdb.com/name/nm1196285/
Assistant: Marc Brunswick
marc.brunswick@disney.com

## GUY WALKS INTO A BAR

236 West 27th Street #1000
New York, NY 10001

Phone: 212-941-1509
Email: info@guywalks.com
Website: www.guywalks.com

Submission Policy: Does not accept any unsolicited material
Genre: Animation, Comedy, Family, Fantasy, Romance, Science Fiction
Focus: Feature Films, TV, Media (Commercials/Branding/Marketing)

**Jonathan Coleman**
Title: Director of Development

**Todd Komarnicki**
Title: Partner/Producer
IMDB: www.imdb.com/name/nm0464548

## H2O MOTION PICTURES

8549 Hedges Place
Los Angeles, CA 90069, Suite 8

111 East 10th Street
New York, NY 10003

Phone: 323-654-5920
Fax: 323-654-5923
Email: h2o@h2omotionpictures.com
Website: www.h2omotionpictures.com

Submission Policy: Accepts query letter from unproduced, unrepresented writers via email
Focus: Feature Films

**Andras Hamori**
Title: Producer
IMDB: www.imdb.com/name/nm0358877

## HAMMER FILM PRODUCTIONS

52 Haymarket
London, United Kingdom,
SW1Y 4RP

Phone: +44 20 3002 9510
Email: info@hammerfilms.com
Website: www.hammerfilms.com

Submission Policy: Does not accept any unsolicited material
Genre: Action, Comedy, Documentary, Drama, Feature Films, Horror, Thriller, TV
Focus: Feature Films, Television
Year Established: 1934

**Simon Oakes**
Title: Co-Chairman & CEO
IMDB: www.imdb.com/name/nm2649227

**Marc Schipper**
Title: COO
IMDB: www.imdb.com/name/nm2649227

## HAND PICKED FILMS

2893 Sea Ridge Drive
Malibu, CA 90265

Phone: (310) 361-6832
Fax: (310) 456-1166
Email: info@handpickedfilms.net
Website: www.handpickedfilms.net

**Submission Policy:** Does not accept any unsolicited material
**Genre:** Animation, Comedy, Detective, Drama, Horror, Memoir & True Stories
**Focus:** Feature Films, TV, Reality Programming (Reality TV, Documentaries, Special Events, Sporting Events), Media (Commercials/Branding/Marketing)
**Year Established:** 2005

**Anthony Romano**
**Title:** Producer
**IMDB:** www.imdb.com/name/nm0738853

**Michel Shane**
**IMDB:** www.imdb.com/name/nm0788062

**Darren VanCleave**
**Title:** Executive
**IMDB:** http://www.imdb.com/name/nm2168166/

## HANDSOME CHARLIE FILMS

1720-1/2 Whitley Avenue
Los Angeles, CA 90028

**Phone:** 323-462-6013

**Submission Policy:** Does not accept any unsolicited material
**Genre:** Action, Comedy, Drama, Memoir & True Stories, Romance
**Focus:** Feature Films

**Kimberly Barton**
**Title:** Creative Executive

**Natalie Portman**
**Title:** President
**IMDB:** www.imdb.com/name/nm0000204

**Annette Savitch**
**Title:** VP Development

## HANNIBAL PICTURES

8265 Sunset Boulevard, Suite 107
West Hollywood, CA 90046

**Phone:** 323-848-2945
**Fax:** 323-848-2946
**Email:** contactus@hannibalpictures.com
**Website:** www.hannibalpictures.com

**Submission Policy:** Accepts query letter from unproduced, unrepresented writers via email
**Genre:** Action, Comedy, Crime, Drama, Memoir &

True Stories, Romance, Science Fiction, Thriller
**Focus:** Feature Films
**Year Established:** 1999

**Cam Canoon**
**Title:** Director of Development
**IMDB:** www.imdb.com/name/nm1359191

**Richard Del Castro**
**Title:** Chairman/CEO/Producer
**IMDB:** www.imdb.com/name/nm0215502

## HAPPY MADISON PRODUCTIONS

10202 West Washington Boulevard Judy Garland Building
Culver City, CA 90232

**Phone:** 310-244-3100
**Fax:** 310-244-3353
**Website:** http://www.adamsandler.com/happy-madison/
**IMDB:** http://www.imdb.com/company/co0059609/?ref_=fn_al_co_1

**Submission Policy:** Does not accept any unsolicited material
**Genre:** Action, Animation, Comedy, Drama, Fantasy, Romance, Thriller, TV, TV Sitcom
**Focus:** Feature Films, Television, Shorts
**Year Established:** 1999

**Jack Giarraputo**
**Title:** Partner
**IMDB:** http://www.imdb.com/name/nm0316406/?ref_=fn_al_nm_1
**Assistant:** Rachel Simmer

**Judit Maull**
**Title:** Executive
**IMDB:** http://www.imdb.com/name/nm1263796/?ref_=fn_al_nm_1

**Heather Parry**
**Title:** Head of Film
**IMDB:** http://www.imdb.com/name/nm1009782/?ref_=fn_al_nm_1

**Doug Robinson**
**Title:** Head of Television
**IMDB:** http://www.imdb.com/name/nm2120562/?ref_=fn_al_nm_1
**Assistant:** Brianna Riofrio

**Adam Sandler**
Title: Partner
IMDB: http://www.imdb.com/name/
nm0001191/?ref_=fn_al_nm_1

**Billy Wee**
Title: Vice President of Television

## HARPO FILMS, INC.

345 North Maple Dr, Suite 315
Beverly Hills, CA 90210

Phone: 310-278-5559

Submission Policy: Does not accept any unsolicited
material
Genre: Comedy, Drama, Fantasy, Horror, Memoir
& True Stories, Romance
Focus: Feature Films, TV

**Oprah Winfrey**
Title: Chairman/CEO/Producer
IMDB: www.imdb.com/name/nm0001856

## HARTSWOOD FILMS

3A Paradise Road
Richmond
Surrey
TW9 1RX

Nations and Regions Office
17 Cathedral Road
Cardiff
CF11 9HA

Phone: +44 (0) 20-3668-3060 +44 (0)29-2023-3333
Fax: +44 (0) 20-3668-3050 +44 (0)29-2022-5878
Email: films.tv@hartswoodfilms.co.uk
Website: http://www.hartswoodfilms.co.uk/
IMDB: http://www.imdb.com/company/
co0023675/?ref_=fn_al_co_1

Submission Policy: Does not accept any unsolicited
material
Genre: Comedy, Crime, Detective, Drama, Horror,
Thriller, TV, TV Drama, TV Sitcom
Focus: Television
Year Established: 1980

**Elaine Cameron**
Title: Head of Development
IMDB: http://www.imdb.com/name/
nm0131569/?ref_=fn_al_nm_1

**Beryl Vertue**
Title: Chairman
IMDB: http://www.imdb.com/name/
nm0895054/?ref_=fn_al_nm_1

**Debbie Vertue**
Title: General Manager
IMDB: http://www.imdb.com/name/
nm0895055/?ref_=fn_al_nm_1

**Sue Vertue**
Title: Producer
IMDB: http://www.imdb.com/name/
nm0895056/?ref_=fn_al_nm_1

## HASBRO, INC./HASBRO FILMS

Burbank
2950 North Hollywood Way Suite 100
Burbank, CA 91504

Phone: (818) 478-4320
Website: http://www.hasbro.com/?US

Submission Policy: Accepts query letter from
unproduced, unrepresented writers
Genre: Action, Animation, Comedy, Family,
Fantasy, Memoir & True Stories, Science Fiction
Focus: Feature Films

**Daniel Persitz**
Title: Creative Executive
IMDB: www.imdb.com/name/nm1974626

## HAXAN FILMS

PO Box 261370
Encino, CA 91426
USA

Fax: 310-888-4242
Website: http://www.haxan.com/
IMDB: http://www.imdb.com/company/
co0112898/?ref_=fn_al_co_1

Submission Policy: Accepts query letter from
unproduced, unrepresented writers
Genre: Comedy, Documentary, Drama, Horror,
Science Fiction, Thriller
Focus: Feature Films, Television
Year Established: 2004

**Robin Cowie**
Title: Producer
Email: rob@haxan.com

**IMDB:** http://www.imdb.com/name/
nm0184770/?ref_=fn_al_nm_1

**Gregg Hale**
**Title:** Executive
**IMDB:** http://www.imdb.com/name/
nm0354918/?ref_=fn_al_nm_1

**Andy Jenkins**
**IMDB:** http://www.imdb.com/name/
nm1075637/?ref_=fn_al_nm_2

**Eduardo Sánchez**
**IMDB:** http://www.imdb.com/name/
nm0844896/?ref_=fn_al_nm_1

**David Saunder**
**Title:** APA Talent and Literary Agency
**Phone:** 310-888-4200

## HAZY MILLS PRODUCTIONS

4024 Radford Avenue
Building 7 - 2nd Floor
Studio City, CA 91604

**Phone:** 818-840-7568
**Website:** http://www.hazymills.com/

**Submission Policy:** Does not accept any unsolicited
material
**Genre:** Comedy, Drama, Family, Horror
**Focus:** Feature Films, TV, Reality Programming
(Reality TV, Documentaries, Special Events,
Sporting Events)
**Year Established:** 2004

**Kiel Elliott**
**Title:** Development Executive

**Sean Hayes**
**IMDB:** www.imdb.com/name/nm0005003
**Assistant:** Jessie Kalick

## HBO FILMS & MINISERIES

2500 Broadway, Suite 400
Santa Monica, CA 90404

**Phone:** 310-382-3000
**Fax:** 310-382-3552

**Submission Policy:** Does not accept any unsolicited
material
**Genre:** Comedy, Drama, Family, Memoir & True
Stories, Romance, Thriller
**Focus:** TV

**Len Amato**
**Title:** President, Films
**IMDB:** www.imdb.com/name/nm0024163

**Kary Antholis**
**Title:** President, HBO Miniseries
**IMDB:** www.imdb.com/name/nm0030794

## HDNET FILMS

c/o Magnolia Pictures
49 W 27th St, 7th Fl
New York, NY 10001
USA

**Phone:** 212-924-6701
**Fax:** 212-924-6742
**IMDB:** http://www.imdb.com/company/
co0094788/?ref_=fn_al_co_1

**Submission Policy:** Accepts query letter from
unproduced, unrepresented writers
**Genre:** Comedy, Crime, Documentary, Drama,
Reality, Romance, Science Fiction, Thriller, TV
Drama
**Focus:** Feature Films, Television

## HEAVY DUTY ENTERTAINMENT

6121 Sunset Boulevard, Suite 103
Los Angeles, CA 90028

**Phone:** 323-209-3545
**Fax:** 323-653-1720
**Email:** info@heavydutyentertainment.com
**Website:** www.heavydutyentertainment.com

**Submission Policy:** Does not accept any unsolicited
material
**Genre:** Action, Comedy, Drama, Horror, Science
Fiction
**Focus:** Feature Films, TV

**Jeff Balis**
**Title:** Producer
**IMDB:** www.imdb.com/name/nm0050276

**Rhoades Rader**
**Title:** Producer
**IMDB:** www.imdb.com/name/nm0705476

## HEEL AND TOE FILMS

2058 Broadway
Santa Monica, CA 90404

**Phone:** 310-264-1866
**Fax:** 310-264-1865

**Submission Policy:** Does not accept any unsolicited material
**Genre:** Action, Drama, Romance, TV Drama
**Focus:** Feature Films, TV

**Paul Attanasio**
**Title:** Writer/Executive Producer
**Email:** paul.attanasio@fox.com
**IMDB:** www.imdb.com/name/nm0001921

**Katie Jacobs**
**Title:** Executive Producer
**Email:** katie.jacobs@fox.com
**IMDB:** www.imdb.com/name/nm0414498

## HEMISPHERE ENTERTAINMENT

20058 Ventura Blvd
#316
Woodland Hills, CA 91364

**Phone:** 818-888-2263
**Fax:** 818-888-3651
**Website:** www.hemisphereentertainment.com

**Submission Policy:** Accepts query letter from unproduced, unrepresented writers
**Genre:** Action, Crime, Drama, Family, Feature Films, Horror, Romance, Thriller
**Focus:** Feature Films

**Jamie Elliot**
**Title:** COO & EVP
**IMDB:** www.imdb.com/name/nm0254242

**Ralph E. Portillo**
**Title:** President & CEO
**IMDB:** www.imdb.com/name/nm1589685

**Brad Wilson**
**Title:** VP of Development
**IMDB:** www.imdb.com/name/nm0933085

## HENCEFORTH PICTURES

1411 Fifth Street, Suite 200
Santa Monica, CA 90401

**Phone:** 424-832-5517
**Fax:** 424-832-5564

**Submission Policy:** Does not accept any unsolicited material

**Genre:** Action, Crime, Drama, Thriller
**Focus:** Feature Films, TV

**Justine Jones**
**Title:** Vice-President of Development
**IMDB:** www.imdb.com/name/nm3540960

**William Monahan**
**Title:** Producer/Writer
**IMDB:** www.imdb.com/name/nm1184258

## HENDERSON PRODUCTIONS

4252 Riverside Drive
Burbank, CA 91505

**Phone:** 818-955-5702
**Fax:** (818) 955-7703

**Submission Policy:** Does not accept any unsolicited material
**Genre:** Comedy, Drama, Family, Romance
**Focus:** Feature Films, Theater

**Garry Marshall**
**Title:** Producer/Writer/Director
**IMDB:** www.imdb.com/name/nm0005190

## HEYDAY FILMS

4000 Warner Boulevard
Building 81, Room 207
Burbank, CA 91522

**Phone:** 818-954-3004
**Fax:** 818-954-3017
**Email:** office@heydayfilms.com

**Submission Policy:** Does not accept any unsolicited material
**Genre:** Action, Comedy, Crime, Drama, Fantasy
**Focus:** Feature Films, TV

**Jeffrey Clifford**
**Title:** President
**IMDB:** www.imdb.com/name/nm0166641
**Assistant:** Kate Phillips

**David Heyman**
**Title:** Partner
**IMDB:** http://www.imdb.com/name/nm0382268/
**Assistant:** Ollie Wiseman (011) 442078366333

## HGTV

9721 Sherrill Boulevard
Knoxville, TN 37932

**Phone:** 865-694-2700
**Fax:** 865-690-6595
**Website:** http://www.hgtv.com/
**IMDB:** http://www.imdb.com/company/
co0004908/?ref_=fn_al_co_2

**Submission Policy:** Does not accept any unsolicited
material
**Genre:** Documentary, Reality, TV
**Focus:** Feature Films, Television

**Burton Jablin**
**Title:** Executive Vice President

**Freddy James**
**Title:** Senior Vice President of Program
Development

**Steven Lerner**
**Title:** Vice President of Development

**Chris Moore**
**Title:** Vice President (Creative Director)

**Courtney White**
**Title:** Vice President of Development

## HIGH HORSE FILMS

100 Universal City Plaza
Building 2128, Suite E
Universal City, CA 91608

**Phone:** 323-939-8802
**Fax:** 323-939-8832

**Submission Policy:** Accepts query letter from
unproduced, unrepresented writers
**Genre:** Comedy, Romance, TV Drama, TV Sitcom
**Focus:** Feature Films, TV
**Year Established:** 1990

**Cynthia Chvatal**
**Title:** Producer
**IMDB:** www.imdb.com/name/nm0161558

**William Petersen**
**Title:** Actor/Producer
**IMDB:** www.imdb.com/name/nm0676973

## HIGH INTEGRITY PRODUCTIONS

11054 Ventura Blvd
Suite 324
Studio City, CA 91604 USA

**Phone:** 714 313 9606
**Website:** www.highintegrityproductions.com

**Submission Policy:** Accepts query letter from
unproduced, unrepresented writers
**Genre:** Animation, Feature Films, Horror, Romance,
Thriller
**Focus:** Feature Flms

**Dale Noble**
**Title:** President & CEO
**Phone:** 909-883-0417
**Email:** dale@highintegrityproductions.com
**IMDB:** www.imdb.com/name/nm2303672

## HOLLYWOOD GANG PRODUCTIONS

4000 Warner Boulevard
Building 139, Room 201
Burbank, CA 91522

**Phone:** 818-954-4999
**Fax:** 818-954-4448

**Submission Policy:** Does not accept any unsolicited
material
**Genre:** Action, Drama, Fantasy, Science Fiction,
Thriller
**Focus:** Feature Films

**Gianni Nunnari**
**Title:** President/Producer
**IMDB:** www.imdb.com/name/nm0638089

## HORIZON ENTERTAINMENT

1025 South Jefferson Parkway
New Orleans, LA 70125

**Phone:** 504-483-1177
**Fax:** 504-483-1173
**Email:** jsasst@horizonent.tv
**Website:** http://www.horizonent.tv/
**IMDB:** http://www.imdb.com/company/
co0225725/?ref_=fn_al_co_1

**Submission Policy:** Accepts query letter from
unproduced, unrepresented writers
**Genre:** Action, Comedy, Crime, Drama, Family,
Reality, Romance, Thriller, TV Drama
**Focus:** Feature Films, Television
**Year Established:** 2000

**Tom Benson**
**Title:** Executive Producer
**IMDB:** http://www.imdb.com/name/

nm3390271/?ref_=fn_al_nm_5
**Assistant:** Brittany Leigh Holtsclaw

**Melissa Dembrun Sciavicco**
**Title:** Coordinating Producer
**IMDB:** http://www.imdb.com/name/
nm2847926/?ref_=fn_al_nm_1

**Jason Sciavicco**
**Title:** Executive Producer
**IMDB:** http://www.imdb.com/name/
nm2217296/?ref_=fn_al_nm_1

**Dwayne Smalls**
**Title:** Production Manager
**IMDB:** http://www.imdb.com/name/
nm2979692/?ref_=fn_al_nm_1

## HUGHES CAPITAL ENTERTAINMENT

22817 Ventura Boulevard, Suite 471
Woodland Hills, CA 91364

**Phone:** 818-484-3205
**Email:** info@trihughes.com
**Website:** www.trihughes.com

**Submission Policy:** Accepts scripts from produced
or represented writers
**Genre:** Action, Comedy, Drama, Family, Romance
**Focus:** Feature Films

**Jacob Clymore**
**Title:** Executive Assistant
**Email:** jc@trihughes.com

**Patrick Hughes**
**Title:** President/Producer
**IMDB:** http://www.imdb.com/name/
nm1449018/?ref_=fn_al_nm_3

## HUTCH PARKER ENTERTAINMENT

Santa Monica
204 Santa Monica Boulevard Suite A
Santa Monica, CA 90401

**Email:** hutchparkerentertainment@gmail.com

**Submission Policy:** Accepts scripts from produced
or represented writers
**Genre:** Romance, Thriller
**Focus:** Feature Films
**Year Established:** 2012

**Aaron Ensweiler**
**Title:** Vice-President
**IMDB:** www.imdb.com/name/nm3943221

**Hutch Parker**
**Title:** Founder
**IMDB:** http://www.imdb.com/name/
nm0404446/?ref_=fn_al_nm_1

## HYDE PARK ENTERTAINMENT

14958 Ventura Boulevard Suite 100
Sherman Oaks, CA 91423

**Phone:** 818-783-6060
**Fax:** 818-783-6319
**Email:** contact@hydeparkentertainment.com
**Website:** www.hydeparkentertainment.com

**Submission Policy:** Accepts scripts from
unproduced, unrepresented writers via email
**Genre:** Action, Comedy, Crime, Drama, Fantasy,
Media (Commercials/Branding/Marketing),
Romance, Science Fiction, Thriller
**Focus:** Feature Films
**Year Established:** 1999

**Ashtok Amiraj**
**Title:** Chairman/CEO
**IMDB:** www.imdb.com/name/nm0002170

**Mike Dougherty**
**Title:** Creative Executive

**Marc Fiorentino**
**Title:** Development and Production Executive

## HYPNOTIC

12233 West Olympic Boulevard, Suite 255
Los Angeles, CA 90064

**Phone:** 310-806-6930
**Fax:** 310-806-6931

**Submission Policy:** Does not accept any unsolicited
material
**Genre:** Action, Comedy, Crime, Drama, Horror,
Thriller, TV Drama
**Focus:** Feature Films, TV

**Doug Liman**
**Title:** Vice Chairman/Producer
**IMDB:** www.imdb.com/name/nm0510731

**Lindsay Sloane**
**Title:** Development Executive

## ICON PRODUCTIONS

808 Wilshire Boulevard, Suite 400
Santa Monica, CA 90401

**Phone:** 310-434-7300
**Fax:** 310-434-7377
**Website:** http://www.iconmovies.com/

**Submission Policy:** Does not accept any unsolicited material
**Genre:** Action, Comedy, Crime, Drama, Feature Films, Horror, Memoir & True Stories, Science Fiction, Thriller, TV, TV Drama

### Mel Gibson
**Title:** Actor/Producer/Writer
**IMDB:** www.imdb.com/name/nm0000154

## ILLUMINATION ENTERTAINMENT

2230 Broadway Avenue
Santa Monica, CA 90404

**Phone:** 310-593-8800
**Fax:** 310-593-8850
**Email:** info@illuminationent.com
**Website:**
http://www.illuminationentertainment.com/
**IMDB:** http://www.imdb.com/company/
co0221986/?ref_=fn_al_co_1

**Submission Policy:** Does not accept any unsolicited material
**Genre:** Animation, Comedy, Drama, Family, Feature Films
**Focus:** Feature Films, Shorts
**Year Established:** 2010

### Brooke Breton
**Title:** Production Executive
**IMDB:** http://www.imdb.com/name/
nm0107868/?ref_=fn_al_nm_1
**Assistant:** Jenna Anderson

### Kit Giordano
**Title:** Vice President of Development
**IMDB:** http://www.imdb.com/name/
nm2109293/?ref_=fn_al_nm_1
**Assistant:** Colleen McAllister

### Dana Krupinski
**Title:** Director of Development
**IMDB:** http://www.imdb.com/name/
nm2145735/?ref_=fn_al_nm_1

### Christopher Meledandri
**Title:** Chief Executive Officer
**IMDB:** http://www.imdb.com/name/
nm0577560/?ref_=fn_al_nm_1
**Assistant:** Rachel Feinberg and Katie Kirnan

## IMAGE MOVERS

100 Universal City
Bungalow 5170
Los Angeles, CA 91608

**Phone:** 818-733-4000

**Submission Policy:** Does not accept any unsolicited material
**Genre:** Action, Animation, Comedy, Drama, Family, Fantasy, Feature Films, Period, Romance, Thriller, TV, TV Drama
**Focus:** Feature Films, Television

### Jackie Levine
**Title:** Executive Vice President

### Jack Rapke
**Title:** Partner
**IMDB:** www.imdb.com/name/nm0710759

### Jimmy Skodras
**Title:** Development Executive

### Steve Starkey
**Title:** Partner
**IMDB:** www.imdb.com/name/nm0823330

### Robert Zemeckis
**Title:** Partner
**IMDB:** www.imdb.com/name/nm0000709

## IMAGINE ENTERTAINMENT

9465 Wilshire Boulevard
7th Floor
Beverly Hills, CA 90212

**Phone:** 310-858-2000
**Fax:** 310-858-2020
**Website:** http://www.imagine-entertainment.com/

**Submission Policy:** Does not accept any unsolicited material
**Genre:** Action, Animation, Comedy, Crime, Drama, Family, Fantasy, Feature Films, Horror, Memoir & True Stories, Romance, Science Fiction, Thriller, TV Drama
**Focus:** Feature Films, Television

**Erin Fredman**
**Title:** Creative Executive

**Ron Howard**
**Title:** Chairman/Director
**IMDB:** www.imdb.com/name/nm0000165

## IMPACT PICTURES

9200 West Sunset Boulevard, Suite 800
West Hollywood, CA 90069

**Phone:** 310-247-1803

**Submission Policy:** Accepts query letter from
unproduced, unrepresented writers via email
**Genre:** Action, Comedy, Crime, Drama, Fantasy,
Horror, Romance, Science Fiction, Thriller
**Focus:** Feature Films

**Paul Anderson**
**Title:** Producer/Writer
**IMDB:** www.imdb.com/name/nm0027271
**Assistant:** Sarah Crompton

**Jeremy Bolt**
**Title:** Producer
**IMDB:** www.imdb.com/name/nm0093337

## IMPRINT ENTERTAINMENT

100 Universal City Plaza
Bungalow 7125
Universal City, CA 91608

**Phone:** 818-733-5410
**Fax:** (f) (818) 733-4307
**Email:** info@imprint-ent.com
**Website:** www.imprint-ent.com

**Submission Policy:** Does not accept any unsolicited
material
**Genre:** Action, Comedy, Crime, Drama, Fantasy,
Horror, Memoir & True Stories, Romance, Thriller
**Focus:** Feature Films, TV, Reality Programming
(Reality TV, Documentaries, Special Events,
Sporting Events), Media (Commercials/Branding/
Marketing)
**Year Established:** 2008

**Lee Arter**
**Title:** Creative Executive
**Email:** larter@imprint-ent.com

**Michael Becker**
**Title:** Executive

## IN CAHOOTS

4024 Radford Avenue
Editorial Building 2, Suite 7
Studio City, CA 91604

**Phone:** 818-655-6482
**Fax:** 818-655-8472

**Submission Policy:** Does not accept any unsolicited
material
**Genre:** Thriller, TV Drama, TV Sitcom
**Focus:** Feature Films, TV

**Reynolds Anderson**
**Title:** Creative Executive
**IMDB:** www.imdb.com/name/nm1568030

**Ken Kwapis**
**IMDB:** www.imdb.com/name/nm0477129

## INCOGNITO PICTURES

16027 Ventura Blvd
Suite 650
Encino, CA 91436

**Phone:** 818-724-4727
**Email:** info@incognitopictures.com
**Website:** www.incognitopictures.com

**Submission Policy:** Does not accept any unsolicited
material
**Genre:** Crime, Drama, Feature Films, Thriller
**Focus:** Feature Films

**Farnaz Fahid**
**Title:** VP of Production & Development
**IMDB:** www.imdb.com/name/nm1804747

**Drew Ruselowski**
**Title:** Assistant
**IMDB:** www.imdb.com/name/nm4866933

**Jack Selby**
**Title:** Chairman
**IMDB:** www.imdb.com/name/nm3095212

**Scott G. Stone**
**Title:** CEO
**IMDB:** www.imdb.com/name/nm1680597

## INDIAN PAINTBRUSH

1660 Euclid Street
Santa Monica, CA 90404

**Phone:** 310-566-0160
**Fax:** 310-566-0161
**Email:** info@indianpaintbrush.com
**Website:** www.indianpaintbrush.com

**Submission Policy:** Does not accept any unsolicited material
**Genre:** Action, Animation, Comedy, Drama, Family, Horror, Romance, Science Fiction, Thriller
**Focus:** Feature Films

**Mark Roybal**
Title: President, Production
IMDB: www.imdb.com/name/nm0747287
Assistant: Sam Roston

## INDICAN PRODUCTIONS

2565 Broadway, Suite 138
New York, NY 10025

**Phone:** 212-666-1500

**Submission Policy:** Does not accept any unsolicited material
**Genre:** Crime, Drama, Memoir & True Stories
**Focus:** Feature Films

**Julia Ormond**
Email: julia.ormond@fox.com
IMDB: www.imdb.com/name/nm0000566

## INDIE GENIUS PRODUCTIONS

361 Stryker Avenue
St. Paul, MN 55107

**Phone:** 646-596-0937
**IMDB:** http://www.imdb.com/company/co0097647/

**Submission Policy:** Accepts query letter from unproduced, unrepresented writers
**Genre:** Documentary
**Focus:** Feature Films
**Year Established:** 2007

**Curt Johnson**
Title: Principal
Email: curt_johnson@indiegeniusprod.com

## INDOMITABLE ENTERTAINMENT

1920 Main Street, Suite A
Santa Monica, CA 90405

225 Varick St
Ste 304
New York, NY 10014

**Phone:** 310-664-8700 212 352 1071
**Fax:** 310-664-8711 212 727 3860
**Email:** info@indomitable.com
**Website:** http://www.indomitableentertainment.com

**Submission Policy:** Accepts query letter from unproduced, unrepresented writers via email
**Genre:** Action, Comedy, Drama, Thriller, TV Sitcom
**Focus:** Feature Films

**Robert Deege**
Title: Vice President of Business & Creative Affairs
IMDB: www.imdb.com/name/nm1830098

**Dominic Ianno**
Title: Founder, CEO
IMDB: www.imdb.com/name/nm1746156

**Chris Mirosevic**
Title: Director of Film Services
IMDB: www.imdb.com/name/nm1746156

**Stuart Pollok**
Title: Executive Producer
IMDB: http://www.imdb.com/name/nm0689415/?ref_=fn_al_nm_1

## INDUSTRY ENTERTAINMENT

955 South Carrillo Drive, Suite 300
Los Angeles, CA 90048

**Phone:** 323-954-9000
**Fax:** 323-954-9009

**Submission Policy:** Accepts scripts from produced or represented writers
**Genre:** Comedy, Drama, Family, Fantasy, Horror, Romance, Thriller, TV Drama
**Focus:** Feature Films, TV

**Keith Addis**
Title: Chairman
IMDB: http://www.imdb.com/name/nm0011688/

## INFERNO ENTERTAINMENT

1888 Century Park East, Suite 1540
Los Angeles, CA 90067

**Phone:** 310-598-2550
**Fax:** 310-598-2551
**Website:** http://www.inferno-entertainment.com/

**Submission Policy:** Does not accept any unsolicited material
**Genre:** Action, Comedy, Crime, Drama, Family, Fantasy, Feature Films, Horror, Romance, Science Fiction, Thriller
**Focus:** Feature Films

### D.J. Gugenheim
**Title:** Vice President of Production
**IMDB:** www.imdb.com/name/nm1486759
**Assistant:** Aaron Himmel

### Campbell McInnes
**Title:** Production Development Executive
**IMDB:** www.imdb.com/name/nm0570577
**Assistant:** Roger Porter

## INFINITUM NIHIL

**Phone:** 323-651-2034
**Website:** www.infinitumnihil.com

**Submission Policy:** Does not accept any unsolicited material
**Genre:** Action, Comedy, Family, Fantasy, Feature Films, Myth, Romance
**Focus:** Feature Films

### Bobby DeLeon
**Title:** Development Associate
**IMDB:** www.imdb.com/name/nm3765677

### Christi Dembrowski
**Title:** President
**IMDB:** www.imdb.com/name/nm0218259
**Assistant:** Dawn Sierra & Erik Schmudde

### Johnny Depp
**Title:** Principal
**IMDB:** www.imdb.com/name/nm0000136

### Margaret French Isaac
**Title:** EVP of Production & Development
**IMDB:** www.imdb.com/name/nm0410504
**Assistant:** Brandon Zamel

### JJ Holiday
**Title:** Creative Research
**IMDB:** www.imdb.com/name/nm0006545

### Sam Sarkar
**Title:** Vice President of Development
**IMDB:** www.imdb.com/name/nm0765274

### Ben Tierney
**Title:** Creative Executive
**IMDB:** www.imdb.com/name/nm1599606

### Norman Todd
**Title:** Director of Development
**IMDB:** www.imdb.com/name/nm0865249

## INFORMANT MEDIA

10866 Wilshire Boulevard
4th Floor, Suite 422
Los Angeles, CA 90024

**Phone:** 310-470-9309
**Fax:** 310-347-4497
**Email:** development@informantmedia.com
**Website:** www.informantmedia.com

**Submission Policy:** Accepts query letter from unproduced, unrepresented writers via email
**Genre:** Action, Comedy, Drama, Fantasy, Romance, Thriller
**Focus:** Feature Films, TV

### Rick Bitzelberger
**Title:** Development
**Email:** development@informantmedia.com

## IN FRONT PRODUCTIONS

2000 Avenue Of The Stars
Century City, CA 90067

**Phone:** 424-288-2000
**Email:** aelkin@caa.com
**IMDB:** http://www.imdb.com/company/co0077065/

**Focus:** Television
**Year Established:** 1992

### Danny Jacobson
**Title:** Manager
**IMDB:** http://www.imdb.com/name/nm0414816/?ref_=fn_al_nm_1

## INK FACTORY

73 Wells Street
London W1T 3QG
UK

**Phone:** +44 20 7096 1698
**Email:** INFO@INKFACTORYFILMS.COM
**Website:** info@inkfactoryfilms.com

**Submission Policy:** Does not accept any unsolicited material
**Genre:** Action, Drama, Thriller
**Focus:** Feature Films
**Year Established:** 2010

### Stephen Cornwell
**Title:** Writer/Producer/Founder
**Phone:** 310-721-5409
**Email:** steven@inkonscreen.co.uk
**IMDB:** www.imdb.com/name/nm4051169

### Rhodri Thomas
**Email:** rhodri@inkonscreen.co.uk
**IMDB:** www.imdb.com/name/nm2905579

## INPHENATE

9701 Wilshire Boulevard
10th Floor
Beverly Hills, CA 90212

**Phone:** 310-601-7117
**Fax:** 310-601-7110

**Submission Policy:** Does not accept any unsolicited material
**Genre:** Comedy, Drama, Memoir & True Stories
**Focus:** Feature Films, TV, Reality Programming (Reality TV, Documentaries, Special Events, Sporting Events)

### Glenn Rigberg
**Title:** Producer
**IMDB:** www.imdb.com/name/nm0726572

## INTREPID PICTURES

1880 CENTURY PARK EAST, SUITE 900
LOS ANGELES, CA 90067

**Phone:** 310-566-5000
**Email:** info@intrepidpictures.com
**Website:** www.intrepidpictures.com

**Submission Policy:** Does not accept any unsolicited material
**Genre:** Action, Comedy, Feature Films, Horror, Thriller
**Focus:** Feature Films
**Year Established:** 2004

### Marc D. Evans
**Title:** Partner & Founder
**IMDB:** www.imdb.com/name/nm2162955

### Anil Kurian
**Title:** Vice President of Development
**IMDB:** www.imdb.com/name/nm1993005
**Assistant:** James Banks

### Trevor Macy
**Title:** Partner & Founder
**IMDB:** www.imdb.com/name/nm1006167

### Melinda Nishioka
**Title:** Coordinator
**Email:** melinda@intrepidpictures.com
**IMDB:** www.imdb.com/name/nm2325559

## IRISH DREAMTIME

3000 West Olympic Boulevard
Building 3, Suite 2332
Santa Monica, CA 90404

**Phone:** 310-449-4081
**Email:** info@irishdreamtime.com
**Website:** www.irishdreamtime.com

**Submission Policy:** Does not accept any unsolicited material
**Genre:** Action, Comedy, Crime, Drama, Memoir & True Stories, Romance, Thriller
**Focus:** Feature Films, TV
**Year Established:** 1996

### Keith Arnold
**Title:** Head of Development
**IMDB:** http://www.imdb.com/name/nm2993265/

### Pierce Brosnan
**Title:** Partner/Producer
**IMDB:** www.imdb.com/name/nm0000112

### Beau St. Clair
**Title:** Partner/Producer
**IMDB:** http://www.imdb.com/name/nm0820429/?ref_=fn_al_nm_1

## IRON OCEAN FILMS

1317 Luanne Ave
Fullerton, CA 92831

**Phone:** 323-957-9706

**Submission Policy:** Does not accept any unsolicited material
**Genre:** Crime, Drama, Feature Films, Thriller
**Focus:** Feature Films

**Jessica Biel**
Title: Principal
IMDB: www.imdb.com/name/nm0004754

**Michelle Purple**
Title: Principal
IMDB: www.imdb.com/name/nm0321977

## IRONWORKS PRODUCTION

517 W 35th St 2nd Floor
New York City, NY 10001

**Phone:** (212) 216-9780
**Fax:** (212) 239-9180
**Email:** ironworksproductions@pobox.com

**Submission Policy:** Accepts query letter from unproduced, unrepresented writers via email
**Genre:** Comedy, Drama, Romance, Thriller
**Focus:** Feature Films, TV, Reality Programming (Reality TV, Documentaries, Special Events, Sporting Events)

**Isa Freeling**
Title: Executive Vice President of Development
IMDB: http://www.imdb.com/name/nm2303742/

**Bruce Weiss**
Title: President/Producer
IMDB: www.imdb.com/name/nm0918933

## IRWIN ENTERTAINMENT

710 Seward Street
Los Angeles, CA 90038

**Phone:** 323-468-0700
**Fax:** 323-464-1001
**IMDB:** http://www.imdb.com/company/co0193199/?ref_=fn_al_co_1

**Submission Policy:** Does not accept any unsolicited material

**Genre:** Comedy, Reality
**Focus:** Feature Films, Television

**John Irwin**
Title: President
Email: john@irwinentertainment.com
IMDB: http://www.imdb.com/name/nm1685815/?ref_=fn_al_nm_2

## ISH ENTERTAINMENT

104 West 27th Street Second Floor
New York, NY 10001

**Phone:** 212-654-6445
**Email:** info@ish.tv
**Website:** http://www.ish.tv/
**IMDB:** http://www.imdb.com/name/nm4851905/?ref_=fn_al_nm_1

**Submission Policy:** Does not accept any unsolicited material
**Genre:** Documentary, Feature Films, Reality, TV
**Focus:** Feature Films, Television, Shorts
**Year Established:** 2008

**Chris Choun**
Title: Head of Production
IMDB: http://www.imdb.com/name/nm1780111/?ref_=fn_al_nm_1

**Melissa Cooper**
Title: Director of Development
IMDB: http://www.imdb.com/name/nm2435108/?ref_=fn_al_nm_5

**Michael Hirschorn**
Title: President
IMDB: http://www.imdb.com/name/nm1337695/?ref_=fn_al_nm_1

**Madison Merritt**
Title: Vice President of Development
IMDB: http://www.imdb.com/name/nm3117402/?ref_=fn_al_nm_1

**Larissa Neal**
Title: Coordinator of Production

**Wendy Roth**
Title: Executive Vice President of Production
IMDB: http://www.imdb.com/name/nm0745046/?ref_=fn_al_nm_1

**Michael Saffran**
Title: Executive
IMDB: http://www.imdb.com/name/
nm5249575/?ref_=fn_al_nm_3

## ITHACA PICTURES

8711 Bonner Drive
West Hollywood, CA 90048

Phone: 310-967-0112
Fax: 310-967-3053

Submission Policy: Does not accept any unsolicited
material
Genre: Drama, Memoir & True Stories
Focus: Feature Films

**Michael Fitzgerald**
Title: Executive
IMDB: www.imdb.com/name/nm028033

**Richard Romero**
Title: Producer
IMDB: www.imdb.com/name/nm2484143

## JACKHOLE INDUSTRIES

6834 Hollywood Blvd
Los Angeles, CA 90028

Phone: 323-860-5900

Submission Policy: Accepts query letter from
produced or represented writers
Genre: Comedy, TV, TV Sitcom
Focus: Television, Reality TV Programming

**Adam Carolla**
Title: Partner
IMDB: www.imdb.com/name/nm0004805

**Doug DeLuca**
Title: Producer
IMDB: www.imdb.com/name/nm0217891

**Daniel Kellison**
Title: Partner
IMDB: www.imdb.com/name/nm0446058

**Jimmy Kimmel**
Title: Partner
IMDB: www.imdb.com/name/nm0453994

## JAFFE/BRAUNSTEIN FILMS

12301 Wilshire Boulevard Suite 110 Los Angeles,
CA 90025

Phone: (310) 207-6600
Fax: (310) 207-6069

Submission Policy: Accepts scripts from produced
or represented writers
Genre: Comedy, Drama, Feature Films, Horror,
Romance, Science Fiction, Thriller, TV, TV Drama
Focus: Feature Films, Television

**Howard Braunstein**
Title: Owner/Executive Producer
IMDB: www.imdb.com/name/nm0105946

**Michael Jaffe**
Title: Partner
IMDB: http://www.imdb.com/name/
nm0415468/?ref_=fn_al_nm_1
Assistant: Lynn Delaney

## JANE STARTZ PRODUCTIONS

244 Fift h Avenue, 11th Floor
New York, NY 10001

Phone: 212-545-8910
Fax: 212-545-8909

Submission Policy: Accepts query letter from
unproduced, unrepresented writers
Genre: Animation, Comedy, Drama, Family,
Fantasy, Romance, Thriller
Focus: Feature Films, TV

**Kane Lee**
Title: VP Development and Production
IMDB: http://www.imdb.com/name/nm1634508/

**Carolyn Mao**
Title: Development Assistant
Email: cmao@janestartzproductions.com

**Jane Startz**
Title: President/Producer
IMDB: www.imdb.com/name/nm0823661

## JEAN DOUMANIAN PRODUCTIONS

595 Madison Avenue Suite 2200
New York City, NY 10022

Phone: 212-486-2626
Fax: 212-688-6236

**Submission Policy:** Accepts query letter from unproduced, unrepresented writers
**Genre:** Comedy, Drama, Feature Films, Horror, Memoir & True Stories, Period, Romance, Thriller, TV
**Focus:** Feature Films, Television

**Patrick Daily**
Title: Vice President of Production & Development
IMDB: www.imdb.com/name/nm4794210

**Jean Doumanian**
Title: Founder
IMDB: www.imdb.com/name/nm0235389

**Saul Nathan-Kazis**
Title: Executive Assistant
IMDB: www.imdb.com/name/nm2651163

**Kathryn Willingham**
Title: Assistant
IMDB: www.imdb.com/name/nm5187379

## JEFF MORTON PRODUCTIONS

10201 West Pico Boulevard Building 226
Los Angeles, CA 90035

Phone: 310-467-1123
Fax: 818-981-4152

**Submission Policy:** Does not accept any unsolicited material
**Focus:** Feature Films, TV

**Jeff Morton**
Title: Producer
Email: scoutspence@mindspring.com
IMDB: www.imdb.com/name/nm0608005

## JERRY BRUCKHEIMER FILMS & TELEVISION

1631 10th Street
Santa Monica, CA 90404

Phone: 310-664-6260
Fax: 310-664-6261
Website: http://www.jbfilms.com/
IMDB: www.imdb.com/company/co0217391

**Submission Policy:** Accepts query letter from unproduced, unrepresented writers
**Genre:** Action, Comedy, Crime, Detective, Drama, Family, Fantasy, Horror, Memoir & True Stories, Myth, Reality, Science Fiction, Thriller, TV Drama

**Focus:** Feature Films, TV, Reality Programming (Reality TV, Documentaries, Special Events, Sporting Events)

**Jerry Bruckheimer**
Title: President/Chairman/CEO
IMDB: www.imdb.com/name/nm0000988

**Jonathan Littman**
Title: President
IMDB: http://www.imdb.com/name/nm0514779/?ref_=fn_al_nm_l

**Ryan McKeithan**
Title: Manager, TV
IMDB: www.imdb.com/name/nm4915007

## JERRY WEINTRAUB PRODUCTIONS

190 North Canon Drive, Suite 204
Beverly Hills, CA 90210

Phone: 310-273-8800
Fax: 310-273-8502

**Submission Policy:** Does not accept any unsolicited material
**Genre:** Action, Comedy, Crime, Drama, Family, Memoir & True Stories, Science Fiction, Thriller
**Focus:** Feature Films

**Susan Ekins**
Title: Vice-President, Physical Production
Assistant: Betsy Dennis

**Jerry Weintraub**
Title: Producer
Assistant: Kimberly Pinkstaff

## JERSEY FILMS

PO Box 491246
Los Angeles, CA 90049

Phone: 310-550-3200
Fax: 310-550-3210
IMDB: www.imdb.com/company/co0010434

**Submission Policy:** Accepts query letter from unproduced, unrepresented writers
**Genre:** Action, Comedy, Drama, Memoir & True Stories, Romance, Thriller
**Focus:** Feature Films

**Danny DeVito**
Title: Executive
IMDB: www.imdb.com/name/nm0000362

**Nikki Grosso**
**Title:** Business Manager/Legal
**Phone:** 310-477-7704
**IMDB:** www.imdb.com/name/nm0343777

## JET TONE PRODUCTIONS

21/F Park Commercial Centre
No. 180 Tung Lo Wan Road
Hong Kong
China

**Phone:** 852-2336-1102
**Fax:** 852-2337-9849
**Email:** jettonc@nctvigator.com
**Website:** http://www.jettone.net/

**Submission Policy:** Accepts query letter from
unproduced, unrepresented writers via email
**Genre:** Action, Animation, Comedy, Crime, Drama,
Romance, Science Fiction, Thriller
**Focus:** Feature Films

**Wong Kar-wai**
**Title:** Producer/Director
**IMDB:** http://www.imdb.com/name/
nm0939182/?ref_=fn_al_nm_1

## JOEL SCHUMACHER PRODUCTIONS

10960 Wilshire Bvld. Suite 1900
Los Angeles, CA 90024

**Phone:** 310-472-7602
**Fax:** 310-270-4618
**IMDB:** http://www.imdb.com/company/
co0094915/?ref_=fn_al_co_1

**Submission Policy:** Does not accept any unsolicited
material
**Genre:** Action, Comedy, Crime, Drama, Fantasy,
Romance, Science Fiction, Thriller
**Focus:** Feature Films, TV, Media (Commercials/
Branding/Marketing)

**Aaron Cooley**
**Title:** Producer
**Phone:** 818-260-6065
**IMDB:** www.imdb.com/name/nm0177583

**Joel Schumacher**
**Title:** Executive/Owner
**Phone:** 310-472-7602
**IMDB:** www.imdb.com/name/nm0001708
**Assistant:** Jeff Feuerstein

## JOHN CALLEY PRODUCTIONS

10202 West Washington Boulevard
Crawford Building
Culver City, CA 90232

**Phone:** 310-244-7777
**Fax:** 310-244-4070
**IMDB:** http://www.imdb.com/company/
co0125552/?ref_=fn_al_co_1

**Submission Policy:** Does not accept any unsolicited
material
**Genre:** Action, Comedy, Detective, Drama,
Romance, Thriller
**Focus:** Feature Films, Television

**John Calley**
**Title:** Producer
**Phone:** 310-244-7777
**IMDB:** www.imdb.com/name/nm1886942

**Lisa Medwid**
**Title:** Executive Vice-President
**Phone:** 310-244-7777
**IMDB:** http://www.imdb.com/name/
nm1886942/?ref_=fn_al_nm_1

## JOHN GOLDWYN PRODUCTIONS

5555 Melrose Avenue, Dressing Room. 112
Los Angeles, CA 90038

**Phone:** 323-956-5054
**Fax:** 323-862-0055
**IMDB:** http://www.imdb.com/company/
co0177677/?ref_=fn_al_co_1

**Submission Policy:** Does not accept any unsolicited
material
**Genre:** Action, Comedy, Crime, Detective, Drama,
Memoir & True Stories, Thriller, TV Drama
**Focus:** Feature Films, Television
**Year Established:** 1991

**Erin David**
**Title:** Creative Executive
**IMDB:** www.imdb.com/name/nm1716252
**Assistant:** Rebecca Crow

**John Goldwyn**
**Title:** President
**IMDB:** www.imdb.com/name/nm0326415
**Assistant:** Jasen Laks

**Hilary Marx**
Title: Creative Executive
IMDB: www.imdb.com/name/nm1020576
Assistant: Rebecca Crow

## JOHN WELLS PRODUCTIONS

4000 Warner Boulevard
Building 1
Burbank, CA 91522-0001

Phone: 818-954-1687
Fax: 818-954-3657
Email: jwppa@warnerbros.com
IMDB: http://www.imdb.com/company/co0037310/

Submission Policy: Accepts query letter from unproduced, unrepresented writers
Genre: Action, Comedy, Drama, Family, Horror, Romance, Science Fiction, Thriller, TV Drama
Focus: Feature Films, Television

**Jinny Joung**
Title: Vice President (Television)
Assistant: Irene Lee irene.lee@jwprods.com

**Claire Polstein**
Title: President (Features)
IMDB: www.imdb.com/name/nm0689856
Assistant: Tessie Groff

**Andrew Stearn**
Title: President (Television)
IMDB: www.imdb.com/name/nm1048942
Assistant: Quinn Tivey quinn.tivey@jwprods.com

**John Wells**
Title: Principal
IMDB: www.imdb.com/name/nm2187561
Assistant: Kristin Martini

## JON SHESTACK PRODUCTIONS

409 N Larchmont Blvd
Los Angeles, CA 90004

Phone: 323-468-1113
Fax: 323-468-1114
IMDB: http://www.imdb.com/company/co0168855/?ref_=fn_al_co_1

Submission Policy: Does not accept any unsolicited material
Genre: Animation, Comedy, Crime, Drama, Family, Fantasy, Romance, Science Fiction, Thriller

Focus: Feature Films
Year Established: 2006

**Ginny Brewer**
Title: Producer, Vice President, Development
IMDB: http://www.imdb.com/name/nm2555285/?ref_=fn_al_nm_1

**Jonathan Shestack**
Title: Producer, President
IMDB: http://www.imdb.com/name/nm0792871/?ref_=fn_al_nm_1

**Jeremy Stein**
Title: Executive
IMDB: http://www.imdb.com/name/nm1867504/?ref_=fn_al_nm_6

## JOSEPHSON ENTERTAINMENT

1201 West 5th Street Suite M-170 Los Angeles, CA 90017

Phone: (213) 534-3995
IMDB: http://www.imdb.com/company/co0046572/

Submission Policy: Does not accept any unsolicited material
Genre: Action, Animation, Comedy, Crime, Drama, Family, Fantasy, Horror, Romance, Science Fiction, Sociocultural, Thriller, TV Drama
Focus: Feature Films, Television

**Barry Josephson**
Title: Producer/Founder
IMDB: http://www.imdb.com/name/nm0430742/?ref_=fn_al_nm_1
Assistant: Sean Bennett

**Tia Maggini**
Title: VP (Television)
Assistant: Mekita Faiye
mekita.faiye@josephsonent.com

## JUNCTION FILMS

9615 Brighton Way, Suite M110
Beverly Hills, CA 90210

Phone: 310-246-9799
Fax: 310-246-3824
IMDB: http://www.imdb.com/company/co0099841/

Submission Policy: Accepts query letter from unproduced, unrepresented writers
Genre: Action, Comedy, Crime, Drama, Horror,

Reality, Science Fiction, Thriller
**Year Established:** 2001

**Alwyn Kushner**
Title: Producer
IMDB: www.imdb.com/name/nm1672379

**Donald Kushner**
Title: Producer
IMDB: www.imdb.com/name/nm0476291

**Brad Wyman**
Title: Producer
Phone: 310-246-9799
IMDB: www.imdb.com/name/nm0943829

## JUNIPER PLACE PRODUCTIONS

4024 Radford Avenue, Bungalow 1
Studio City, CA 91604

Phone: 818-655-5043
Fax: 818-655-8402

**Submission Policy:** Accepts query letter from unproduced, unrepresented writers
**Genre:** TV Drama
**Focus:** Television
**Year Established:** -77

**Jeffrey Kramer**
Title: President/Executive Producer
IMDB: www.imdb.com/name/nm0469552

**John Tymus**
Title: Director of Development
IMDB: www.imdb.com/name/nm2002980

## KAPITAL ENTERTAINMENT

8687 Melrose Avenue
9th Floor
West Hollywood, CA 90069

Phone: 310-854-3221

**Submission Policy:** Does not accept any unsolicited material
**Genre:** TV, TV Drama, TV Sitcom
**Focus:** Television

**Cailey Buck**
Title: Director of Development

**Aaron Kaplan**
Title: Principal
Email: akaplan@kapital-ent.com
IMDB: www.imdb.com/name/nm3483168

## KAPLAN/PERRONE ENTERTAINMENT

280 South Beverly Drive, #513
Beverly Hills, CA 90212

Phone: 310-285-0116
Website: http://www.kaplanperrone.com/
IMDB: http://www.imdb.com/company/co0094257/

**Submission Policy:** Accepts scripts from produced or represented writers
**Genre:** Action, Comedy, Romance, Thriller, TV Drama
**Focus:** Feature Films, Television

**Tobin Babst**
Title: Manager and Partner

**Josh Goldenberg**
Title: Manager

**Aaron Kaplan**
Title: Executive and Partner

**Alex Lerner**
Title: Manager

**Sean Perrone**
Title: Executive and Partner

## KARZ ENTERTAINMENT

4000 Warner Boulevard Building 138, Suite 1205
Burbank, CA 91522

Phone: 818-954-1698
Fax: 818 954 1700
Email: karzent@aol.com
IMDB: http://www.imdb.com/company/co0033868/?ref_=fn_al_co_1

**Submission Policy:** Does not accept any unsolicited material
**Genre:** Action, Comedy, Crime, Documentary, Drama, Family, Fantasy, Feature Films, Horror, Romance, Thriller, TV, TV Sitcom
**Focus:** Feature Films, Television
**Year Established:** 1998

**Mike Karz**
**Title:** President
**IMDB:** http://www.imdb.com/name/
nm0440344/?ref_=fn_al_nm_1

**Josie Rosen**
**Title:** Executive Producer
**IMDB:** http://www.imdb.com/name/
nm0741998/?ref_=fn_al_nm_1

## KASSEN BROTHERS PRODUCTIONS

141 West 28th Street, Suite 301
New York, NY 10001

**Phone:** 212-244-2865
**Fax:** 212-244-2874
**IMDB:** www.imdb.com/company/co0183529

**Submission Policy:** Accepts query letter from
unproduced, unrepresented writers
**Genre:** Action, Drama, Memoir & True Stories, TV
Drama, TV Sitcom

**Adam Kassen**
**Title:** Partner/Writer/Director
**Phone:** 212-244-2865
**IMDB:** www.imdb.com/name/nm0440859

## KATALYST FILMS

6806 Lexington Avenue
Los Angeles, CA 90038

**Phone:** 323-785-2700
**Fax:** 323-785-2715
**Email:** info@katalystfilms.com
**Website:** www.katalystfilms.com
**IMDB:** http://www.imdb.com/company/
co0102320/?ref_=fn_al_co_1

**Submission Policy:** Accepts scripts from
unproduced, unrepresented writers
**Genre:** Action, Animation, Comedy, Crime, Drama,
Reality, Romance, Science Fiction, Thriller, TV, TV
Drama, TV Sitcom
**Focus:** Feature Films, Television

**Jason Goldberg**
**Title:** Producer
**IMDB:** www.imdb.com/name/nm0325229

**Ashton Kutcher**
**Title:** Actor/Executive Producer
**IMDB:** www.imdb.com/name/nm0005110

**Brinton Lukens**
**Title:** Director of Development
**IMDB:** http://www.imdb.com/name/
nm2483033/?ref_=fn_al_nm_1

## KENNEDY/MARSHALL COMPANY

619 Arizona Avenue
Second Floor
Santa Monica, CA 90401

**Phone:** 310-656-8400
**Fax:** 310-656-8430
**Website:** www.kennedymarshall.com

**Submission Policy:** Does not accept any unsolicited
material
**Genre:** Action, Comedy, Detective, Drama, Family,
Feature Films, Memoir & True Stories, Romance,
Science Fiction, Thriller, TV
**Focus:** Feature Films, Television

**James Erskine**
**Title:** Development Assistant

**Kiri Hart**
**Title:** VP of Development

**Frank Marshall**
**Title:** Principal
**IMDB:** www.imdb.com/name/nm0550881
**Assistant:** Mary T. Radford

**Grey Rembert**
**Title:** President of Production
**IMDB:** www.imdb.com/name/nm0718880

**Robert D. Zotnowski**
**Title:** Head of Television Development

## KERNER ENTERTAINMENT COMPANY

1888 Century Park East
Suite 1005
Los Angeles, CA 90067

**Phone:** 310-815-5100
**Fax:** 310-815-5110

**Submission Policy:** Does not accept any unsolicited
material
**Genre:** Action, Animation, Comedy, Drama,
Family, Fantasy, Feature Films
**Focus:** Feature Films

**Ben Haber**
Title: Vice President
IMDB: www.imdb.com/name/nm1852209

**Jordan Kerner**
Title: President
IMDB: www.imdb.com/name/nm0449549

**Lauren Waggoner**
Title: Executive Assistant
IMDB: www.imdb.com/name/nm3786942

## KGB FILMS

5555 Melrose Avenue, Lucy Bungalow 101
Los Angeles, CA 90038

Phone: 323-956-5000
Fax: 323-224-1876
Email: turbo@kgbfilms.com
Website: www.kgbfilms.com

Submission Policy: Accepts query letter from unproduced, unrepresented writers via email
Genre: Comedy, Crime, Drama, Feature Films, Memoir & True Stories, Romance, TV
Focus: Feature Films, Short, Television
Year Established: 1994

**Rosser Goodman**
Title: Producer/Director
IMDB: www.imdb.com/name/nm0329223

**Justin Hogan**
Title: Producer
IMDB: www.imdb.com/name/nm0389556

## KICKSTART PRODUCTIONS

3212 Nebraska Ave
Santa Monica, CA 90404

Phone: 310-264-1757
Website: www.kickstartent.com
IMDB: www.imdb.com/company/co0163548

Submission Policy: Does not accept any unsolicited material
Genre: Action, Animation, Comedy, Family, Feature Films, Science Fiction
Focus: Feature Films

**Loris Lunsford**
Title: Executive Producer
IMDB: www.imdb.com/name/nm0469603

**Jason Netter**
Title: President
IMDB: www.imdb.com/name/nm0626697

**Susan Norkin**
Title: Head of Production
IMDB: www.imdb.com/name/nm0635379

**Samantha Olsson**
Title: Vice President of Development
IMDB: www.imdb.com/name/nm2427387

## KILLER FILMS

18th East 16th Street, 4th Floor
New York, NY 10003

Phone: 212-473-3950
Fax: 212-807-1456
Website: http://www.killerfilms.com/
IMDB: http://www.imdb.com/company/co0030755/?ref_=fn_al_co_1

Submission Policy: Accepts query letter from unproduced, unrepresented writers
Genre: Comedy, Crime, Drama, Family, Horror, Romance, Thriller, TV Drama
Focus: Feature Films, Short, Television
Year Established: 1995

**David Hinojosa**
Title: Production and Development Executive
IMDB: www.imdb.com/name/nm3065267
Assistant: Gabrielle Nadig

**Pamela Koffler**
Title: Principal/Producer
IMDB: www.imdb.com/name/nm0463025
Assistant: Gabrielle Nadig

**Christine Vachon**
Title: Principal/Producer
IMDB: www.imdb.com/name/nm0882927
Assistant: Gabrielle Nadig

## KIM AND JIM PRODUCTIONS

787 N. Palm Canyon Drive
Palm Springs, CA 92262

Phone: 760-289-5464
Email: info@kimandjimproductions.com
Website: kimandjimproductions.com

Submission Policy: Accepts query letter from unproduced, unrepresented writers

**Genre:** Action, Comedy, Drama, Fantasy, Feature Films, Horror, Romance, Thriller

**Jim Casey**
Title: Vice Chairman
Email: jim@kimandjimproductions
IMDB: www.imdb.com/name/nm2816633

**Kim Waltrip**
Title: Vice Chairman
Email: assist@kimandjimproductions.com
IMDB: www.imdb.com/name/nm0910601

## KINETIC FILMWORKS

11018 Moorpark Street Suite 114
Toluca Lake, CA 91602

Phone: 818-505-3347
Email: kineticfilmworks@aol.com
Website: http://www.kineticfilmworks.com/
IMDB: http://www.imdb.com/company/co0224342/

Submission Policy: Accepts query letter from unproduced, unrepresented writers via email
Genre: Feature Films, Horror
Focus: Feature Films
Year Established: 2013

**Gary Jones**
Title: Partner
IMDB: http://www.imdb.com/name/nm0428109/?ref_=fn_al_nm_2

**Jeffrey Miller**
Title: Partner
IMDB: http://www.imdb.com/name/nm0588577/?ref_=fn_al_nm_1

## KINTOP PICTURES

7955 W Third St
Los Angeles, CA 90048

Phone: 323-634-1570
Fax: 323-634-1575
Email: kintopfilm@aol.com

Submission Policy: Accepts query letter from unproduced, unrepresented writers
Genre: Comedy, Documentary, Drama, Family, Feature Films, Horror, Romance, Thriller, TV
Focus: Feature Films, Television

**Deepak Nayar**
Title: Founder
IMDB: www.imdb.com/name/nm0623235

## KIPPSTER ENTERTAINMENT

420 West End Avenue, Suite 1G
New York, NY 10024

Phone: 212-496-1200
IMDB: http://www.imdb.com/company/co0310346/

Submission Policy: Does not accept any unsolicited material
Genre: Drama, Memoir & True Stories, TV Drama
Focus: Feature Films, Television

**Perri Kipperman**
Title: Producer, Partner
IMDB: www.imdb.com/name/nm1069530

**David Sterns**
Title: Producer, Partner
IMDB: www.imdb.com/name/nm3992907

## KOMUT ENTERTAINMENT

4000 Warner Boulevard Building 140, Suite 201
Burbank, CA 91522

Phone: 818-954-7631
IMDB: http://www.imdb.com/company/co0028360/

Submission Policy: Accepts query letter from unproduced, unrepresented writers
Genre: Thriller, TV Drama, TV Sitcom
Focus: Television

**Heather Hicks**
Title: Executive Assistant
IMDB: www.imdb.com/name/nm1337402

**David Kohan**
Title: Producer
IMDB: www.imdb.com/name/nm0463172
Assistant: Melissa Strauss
Melissa.Strauss@wbconsultant.com

**Max Mutchnick**
Title: Producer
IMDB: www.imdb.com/name/nm0616083

## K/O PAPER PRODUCTS (ALSO KNOWN AS: KURTZMAN ORCI PAPER PRODUCTS)

100 Universal City Plaza
Building 5125
Universal City, CA 91608

**Phone:** 818-733-9645
**Fax:** 818-733-6988
**IMDB:** http://www.imdb.com/company/co0315120/

**Submission Policy:** Does not accept any unsolicited material
**Genre:** Action, Animation, Drama, Fantasy, Science Fiction, TV, TV Drama
**Focus:** Feature Films, Television
**Year Established:** 1997

### Alex Kurtzman
**Title:** Producer/Writer
**IMDB:** www.imdb.com/name/nm0476064

### Roberto Orci
**Title:** Producer/Writer
**IMDB:** www.imdb.com/name/nm0649460

## KRANE MEDIA, LLC.

7932 Woodrow Wilson Drive
Los Angeles, CA 90046

**Phone:** 323-650-0942
**Fax:** 323-650-9132
**Email:** info@thekranecompany.com
**Website:** http://www.TheKraneCompany.com/
**IMDB:** http://www.imdb.com/company/co0323526/

**Submission Policy:** Does not accept any unsolicited material
**Genre:** Action, Comedy, Crime, Drama, Feature Films, Romance, Science Fiction, Thriller, TV, TV Drama
**Focus:** Feature Films, Television
**Year Established:** 1993

### Konni Corriere
**Title:** Associate Producer
**Email:** konni@thekranecompany.com
**IMDB:** http://pro.imdb.com/name/nm0180955/

### Jonathan Krane
**Title:** Chairman & CEO
**IMDB:** http://www.imdb.com/name/nm0006790/?ref_=fn_al_nm_1

## KRASNOFF FOSTER PRODUCTIONS

5555 Melrose Avenue Marx Brothers Building, Suite 110
Los Angeles, CA 90038

**Phone:** (323) 956-4668
**IMDB:** http://www.imdb.com/company/co0174525/

**Submission Policy:** Accepts query letter from unproduced, unrepresented writers
**Genre:** Action, Comedy, Drama, Memoir & True Stories, Romance, TV Drama, TV Sitcom
**Focus:** Feature Films, Television

### Gary Foster
**Title:** Partner
**IMDB:** http://www.imdb.com/name/nm0287811/?ref_=fn_al_nm_1
**Assistant:** Haley Totten

### Russ Krasnoff
**Title:** President/Partner
**Phone:** 310-244-3282
**IMDB:** www.imdb.com/name/nm0469929
**Assistant:** Beth Maurer

## LAKESHORE ENTERTAINMENT

9268 West Third Street
Beverly Hills, CA 90210

**Phone:** 310-867-8000
**Fax:** 310-300-3015
**Email:** info@lakeshoreentertainment.com
**Website:** www.lakeshoreentertainment.com
**IMDB:** http://www.imdb.com/company/co0005323/?ref_=fn_al_co_1

**Submission Policy:** Accepts query letter from produced or represented writers
**Genre:** Action, Comedy, Crime, Drama, Fantasy, Horror, Romance, Science Fiction, Thriller
**Focus:** Feature Films
**Year Established:** 1994

### Robert McMinn
**Title:** Senior Vice President of Development
**Phone:** 310-867-8000
**IMDB:** www.imdb.com/name/nm0573372

### Tom Rosenberg
**Title:** Chairman/CEO
**Phone:** 310-867-8000
**IMDB:** www.imdb.com/name/nm0742347
**Assistant:** Tiffany Shinn

**Richard Wright**
Title: Executive Vice President (Head, Development)
IMDB: http://www.imdb.com/name/nm0002999/?ref_=fn_al_nm_1

## LANDSCAPE ENTERTAINMENT

9465 Wilshire Boulevard Suite 500 Beverly Hills, CA 90212

Phone: 310-248-6200
Fax: 310-248-6300
IMDB: http://www.imdb.com/company/co0070807/

Submission Policy: Accepts query letter from unproduced, unrepresented writers
Genre: Action, Animation, Comedy, Crime, Drama, Family, Memoir & True Stories, Science Fiction, Thriller, TV Drama, TV Sitcom
Focus: Feature Films, Television
Year Established: 2007

**Bob Cooper**
Title: Chairman/CEO
IMDB: www.imdb.com/name/nm0178341
Assistant: Sandy Shenkman

**Tyler Mitchell**
Title: Head of Features
IMDB: www.imdb.com/name/nm1624685

## LANGLEY PARK PRODUCTIONS

4000 Warner Boulevard
Building 144
Burbank, CA 91522

Phone: 818-954-2930
Website: www.langleyparkpix.com
IMDB: http://www.imdb.com/company/co0297907/?ref_=fn_al_co_1

Submission Policy: Does not accept any unsolicited material
Genre: Action, Comedy, Crime, Drama, Romance, Thriller
Focus: Feature Films

**Rory Koslow**
Title: Vice President
Phone: 818-954-2930
IMDB: www.imdb.com/name/nm1739372
Assistant: Kari Cooper

**Kevin McCormick**
Title: Producer
Phone: 818-954-2930
IMDB: www.imdb.com/name/nm0565557
Assistant: Shamika Pryce

**Aaron Schmidt**
Title: Creative Executive
Phone: 818-954-2930
Email: aaron.schmidt@langleyparkpi ς.com
IMDB: www.imdb.com/name/nm2087164

## LARRIKIN ENTERTAINMENT

1801 Avenue Of The Stars, Suite 921
Los Angeles, CA 90067

Phone: 310-461-3030
Website: www.larrikin-ent.com
IMDB: http://www.imdb.com/company/co0369620/?ref_=fn_al_co_1

Submission Policy: Accepts scripts from produced or represented writers
Focus: Feature Films

**Greg Coote**
Email: linw@larrikin-ent.com
IMDB: http://www.imdb.com/name/nm0178505/?ref_=fn_al_nm_1
Assistant: Wayne Lin

**David Jones**
Title: Executive/Producer/Partner
IMDB: www.imdb.com/name/nm1963869

**Robert Lundberg**
Title: Head, Development & Production
Email: rll@larrikin-ent.com
IMDB: http://www.imdb.com/name/nm2302909/?ref_=fn_al_nm_1

## LAUNCHPAD PRODUCTIONS

4335 Van Nuys Boulevard Suite 339
Sherman Oaks, CA 91403

Phone: 818-788-4896
IMDB: http://www.imdb.com/company/co0164701/?ref_=fn_al_co_1

Submission Policy: Accepts query letter from unproduced, unrepresented writers via email
Genre: Comedy, Crime, Drama, Feature Films, Horror, Period, Science Fiction, Thriller

**Focus:** Feature Films
**Year Established:** 2005

**David Higgins**
Title: Partner
IMDB: http://www.imdb.com/name/
nm0383370/?ref_=fn_al_nm_2

**Angelique Higgins**
Title: President
Email: ahiggins@launchpadprods.com
IMDB: http://www.imdb.com/name/
nm1583157/?ref_=fn_al_nm_1

## LAURA ZISKIN PRODUCTIONS

10202 West Washington Boulevard
Astaire Building, Suite 1310
Culver City, CA 90232

Phone: 310-244-7373
Fax: 310-244-0073
IMDB: http://www.imdb.com/company/
co0095403/?ref_=fn_al_co_1

**Submission Policy:** Accepts query letter from
unproduced, unrepresented writers
**Genre:** Action, Drama, Fantasy, Romance, Science
Fiction, Thriller
**Focus:** Feature Films, TV
**Year Established:** 1995

**David Jacobson**
Title: Director of Development
IMDB: http://www.imdb.com/name/
nm5138376/?ref_=fn_al_nm_5

**Pamela Williams**
Title: President
IMDB: www.imdb.com/name/nm0931423

## LAURENCE MARK PRODUCTIONS

10202 West Washington Boulevard
Poitier Building
Culver City, CA 90232

Phone: 310-244-5239
Fax: 310-244-0055
IMDB: http://www.imdb.com/company/
co0027956/?ref_=fn_al_co_1

**Submission Policy:** Accepts query letter from
unproduced, unrepresented writers
**Genre:** Action, Comedy, Drama, Family, Fantasy,
Horror, Romance, Science Fiction, Thriller, TV

Drama
**Focus:** Feature Films, Television

**David Blackman**
Title: Senior Vice President
Phone: 310-244-5239
IMDB: www.imdb.com/name/nm1844320
Assistant: Peter Richman

**Tamara Chestna**
Title: Director of Development
Phone: 310-244-5239
IMDB: www.imdb.com/name/nm2309894

**Laurence Mark**
Title: President/Producer
Phone: 310-244-5239
IMDB: www.imdb.com/name/nm0548257

## LAVA BEAR FILMS

3201-B South La Cienega Boulevard
Los Angeles, CA 90016

Phone: 310-815-9600
Website: http://www.lavabear.com/
IMDB: http://www.imdb.com/company/co0296971/

**Submission Policy:** Does not accept any unsolicited
material
**Genre:** Action, Comedy, Crime, Drama, Family,
Fantasy, Romance, Science Fiction, Thriller
**Focus:** Feature Films
**Year Established:** 2011

**David Linde**
Title: Principle
Phone: 310-815-9603
Email: Dlinde@lavabear.com
IMDB: www.imdb.com/name/nm0511482
Assistant: Allison Warren

**Tory Metzger**
Title: President of Production
Email: Tmetzger@lavabear.com
IMDB: www.imdb.com/name/nm0582762
Assistant: Jon Frye

**Zachary Studin**
Title: Vice-President of Production
Email: Zstudin@lavabear.com
IMDB: www.imdb.com/name/nm1713122
Assistant: Jake Thomas

## LAWRENCE BENDER PRODUCTIONS

1015 Gayley Avenue Suite 1017
Los Angeles, CA 90024

**Phone:** 323-951-4600
**Fax:** 323-951-4601
**IMDB:** http://www.imdb.com/company/
co0093776/?ref_=fn_al_co_1

**Submission Policy:** Accepts query letter from
unproduced, unrepresented writers
**Genre:** Action, Comedy, Crime, Drama, Thriller
**Focus:** Feature Films

**Lawrence Bender**
**Title:** Partner
**IMDB:** www.imdb.com/name/nm0004744
**Assistant:** Vincent Gatewood

**Kevin Brown**
**Title:** Production
**IMDB:** www.imdb.com/name/nm0114019

**Janet Jeffries**
**Title:** Development
**IMDB:** www.imdb.com/name/nm0420377

## LD ENTERTAINMENT

9000 Sunset Blvd
Suite 600
West Hollywood, CA 90069

**Phone:** 310-275-9600
**Email:** info@identertainment.com
**Website:** www.identertainment.com

**Submission Policy:** Does not accept any unsolicited
material
**Genre:** Action, Comedy, Crime, Drama, Feature
Films, Horror, Thriller
**Focus:** Feature Films
**Year Established:** 2007

**Liz Berger**
**Title:** SVP of Publicity
**IMDB:** www.imdb.com/name/nm0074266

**David Dinerstein**
**Title:** President of Distribution
**IMDB:** www.imdb.com/name/nm2517209

**Jennifer Hilton Monroe**
**Title:** SVP of Production & Development
**IMDB:** www.imdb.com/name/nm0385268

**Mickey Liddell**
**Title:** President
**IMDB:** www.imdb.com/name/nm0509176

**Patrick Raymond**
**Title:** Director of Development
**IMDB:** www.imdb.com/name/nm4811895

## LEE DANIELS ENTERTAINMENT

315 West 36th Street Suite 1002
New York City, NY 10018

**Phone:** 212-334-8110
**Fax:** 212-334-8290
**Email:** info@leedanielsentertainment.com
**Website:** http://www.leedanielsentertainment.com/
**IMDB:** http://www.imdb.com/company/co0048235/

**Submission Policy:** Accepts query letter from
unproduced, unrepresented writers via email
**Genre:** Comedy, Crime, Drama, Feature Films,
Period, Romance, Thriller
**Focus:** Feature Films, Television
**Year Established:** 2001

**Lisa Cortes**
**Title:** Senior Vice President of Production
**IMDB:** http://www.imdb.com/name/
nm0181263/?ref_=fn_al_nm_1

**Lee Daniels**
**Title:** Chief Executive Officer
**IMDB:** http://www.imdb.com/name/nm0200005/
**Assistant:** Tito Crafts

**Doreen Oliver-Akinnuoye**
**Title:** Vice President of Development
**IMDB:** http://www.imdb.com/name/
nm1403094/?ref_=fn_al_nm_1

## LEGENDARY PICTURES

4000 Warner Boulevard
Building 76
Burbank, CA 91522

**Phone:** 818-954-3888
**Fax:** 818-954-3884
**Website:** http://www.legendarypictures.com
**IMDB:** http://www.imdb.com/company/co0159111/

**Submission Policy:** Does not accept any unsolicited
material
**Genre:** Action, Comedy, Crime, Drama, Family,
Fantasy, Memoir & True Stories, Romance, Science

Fiction, Thriller
**Focus:** Feature Films, TV
**Year Established:** 2005

**Alex Garcia**
**Title:** Senior Vice President of Creative Affairs
**IMDB:** www.imdb.com/name/nm1247503

**Alex Hedlund**
**Title:** Creative Executive
**Phone:** 818-954-3888
**IMDB:** www.imdb.com/name/nm2906163

**Jennifer Preston Bosari**
**Title:** Creative Executive
**Email:** jpreston@legendary.com

**Lauren Ruggiero**
**Title:** Director of Development
**Phone:** 818-954-3888
**IMDB:** www.imdb.com/name/nm4549739

**Jillan Share Zaks**
**Title:** Vice President (Creative Affairs)
**Email:** jillian.zaks@legendarypictures.com
**IMDB:** www.imdb.com/name/nm2949271

**Thomas Tull**
**Title:** Chairman/CEO
**Phone:** 818-954-3888
**IMDB:** www.imdb.com/name/nm2100078

## LESLIE IWERKS PRODUCTIONS

1322 2nd Street Suite 35
Santa Monica, 90401 CA

**Phone:** 310-458-0490
**Fax:** 310-458-7212
**Email:** info@leslieiwerks.com
**Website:** http://leslieiwerks.com/new/
**IMDB:** http://www.imdb.com/company/
co0188417/?ref_=fn_al_co_1

**Submission Policy:** Does not accept any unsolicited material
**Genre:** Documentary, Feature Films, TV
**Focus:** Feature Films, Television, Shorts
**Year Established:** 2006

**Leslie Iwerks**
**Title:** President
**Email:** leslie@leslieiwerks.com
**IMDB:** http://www.imdb.com/name/
nm0412649/?ref_=fn_al_nm_1

**Jane Kelly Kosek**
**Title:** Producer
**IMDB:** http://www.imdb.com/name/
nm1165704/?ref_=fn_al_nm_1

**Michael Tang**
**Title:** Co-Producer
**IMDB:** http://www.imdb.com/name/
nm4046664/?ref_=fn_al_nm_1

## LIAISON FILMS

44 Rue Des Acacias
Paris 75017
France

**Phone:** +33-1-55-37-28-28
**Fax:** +33-1-55-37-98-44
**Email:** contact@liasonfilms.com
**Website:** www.liasonfilms.com
**IMDB:** http://www.imdb.com/company/
co0120310/?ref_=fn_al_co_1

**Submission Policy:** Does not accept any unsolicited material
**Genre:** Action, Crime, Drama, Thriller
**Focus:** Feature Films

**Stephane Sperry**
**Title:** President
**Email:** stephane.sperry@liasonfilms.com
**IMDB:** www.imdb.com/name/nm0818373

## LIGHTSTORM ENTERTAINMENT

919 Santa Monica Boulevard
Santa Monica, CA 90401

**Phone:** 310-656-6100
**Fax:** 310-656-6102

**Submission Policy:** Does not accept any unsolicited material
**Genre:** Action, Crime, Drama, Family, Fantasy, Feature Films, Horror, Romance, Science Fiction, Thriller
**Focus:** Feature Films

**Geoff Burdick**
**Title:** Head of Post Production

**James Cameron**
**Title:** CEO
**IMDB:** www.imdb.com/name/nm0000116

**Jon Landau**
Title: COO
IMDB: www.imdb.com/name/nm0484457

**Rae Sanchini**
Title: Partner
IMDB: www.imdb.com/name/nm0761093

## LIKELY STORY

150 West 22nd Street, 9th Floor
New York, NY 10011

Phone: 917-484-8931
Email: info@likely-story.com
Website: www.likely-story.com
IMDB: www.imdb.com/company/co0190175

Submission Policy: Does not accept any unsolicited material
Focus: Feature Films

**Stefanie Azpiazu**
Title: VP, Production & Development
Phone: 917-484-8931
Email: info@likely-story.com
IMDB: www.imdb.com/name/nm1282412

**Anthony Bregman**
Title: Producer/Founder
Phone: 917-484-8931
Email: info@likely-story.com
IMDB: www.imdb.com/name/nm0106835

## LIN PICTURES

4000 Warner Blvd. Bldg 143
Burbank, CA 91522

Phone: 818-954-6759
Fax: 818-954-2329
Website: www.linpictures.com

Submission Policy: Does not accept any unsolicited material
Genre: Action, Comedy, Crime, Drama, Family, Fantasy, Feature Films, Romance, Science Fiction, Thriller, TV, TV Drama
Focus: Feature Films, Television

**Mark Bauch**
Title: Creative Executive
IMDB: www.imdb.com/name/nm3113076

**Jennifer Gwartz**
Title: Head of Television
IMDB: www.imdb.com/name/nm0350311
Assistant: Jeremy Katz

**Dan Lin**
Title: CEO
IMDB: www.imdb.com/name/nm1469853
Assistant: Ryan Halprin

**Jon Slll**
Title: SVP of Production
IMDB: www.imdb.com/name/nm1698314
Assistant: Ryan Halprin

**Seanne Winslow Wehrenfennig**
Title: Head of Development
IMDB: www.imdb.com/name/nm2253990

## LIONSGATE

2700 Colorado Avenue, Suite 200
Santa Monica, CA 90404

Phone: 310-449-9200
Fax: 310-255-3870
Email: general-inquiries@lgf.com
Website: http://www.lionsgate.com/

Submission Policy: Accepts query letter from unproduced, unrepresented writers via email
Genre: Action, Comedy, Crime, Drama, Family, Fantasy, Horror, Memoir & True Stories, Romance, Science Fiction, Thriller, TV
Focus: Feature Films, Television
Year Established: 1997

**Jon Feltheimer**
Title: Co-Chairman/CEO
Phone: 310-449-9200
Email: jfeltheimer@lionsgate.com
IMDB: www.imdb.com/name/nm1410838

**Matthew Janzen**
Title: Director of Development
Phone: 310-449-9200
IMDB: www.imdb.com/name/nm0418432

**Jina Jones**
Title: Director of Development
IMDB: http://www.imdb.com/name/nm1061205/

## LIQUID THEORY

6725 Sunset Blvd Ste 240
Los Angeles, CA 90028

Phone: 323-460-5658
Fax: 323-460-4814
Website: http://www.liquid-theory.com
IMDB: http://www.imdb.com/company/
co0113186/?ref_=fn_al_co_1

**Submission Policy:** Accepts query letter from
produced or represented writers
**Genre:** Animation, Comedy, Documentary, Drama,
Feature Films, Horror, Reality, Romance, Science
Fiction, Thriller, TV, TV Sitcom
**Focus:** Feature Films, Television
**Year Established:** 2001

### Matt Lambert
**Title:** Development Coordinator
**Email:** matt@liquid-theory.com
**IMDB:** http://www.imdb.com/name/
nm1479457/?ref_=fn_al_nm_2

### Austin Reading
**Title:** President
**IMDB:** http://www.imdb.com/name/
nm1474879/?ref_=fn_al_nm_1

### Julie Reading
**Title:** President
**IMDB:** http://www.imdb.com/name/
nm1474880/?ref_=fn_al_nm_1

## LITTLE ENGINE

500 South Buena Vista Street
Animation Building 3F-6
Burbank, CA 91521

Phone: 818-560-4670
Fax: 818-560-4014
Website: http://www.littleenginefilms.com/
IMDB: http://www.imdb.com/company/co0014340/

**Submission Policy:** Accepts query letter from
unproduced, unrepresented writers
**Genre:** Comedy, Crime, Drama, Romance, TV, TV
Drama
**Focus:** Feature Films, TV, Reality Programming
(Reality TV, Documentaries, Special Events,
Sporting Events)

### Mitchell Gutman
**Title:** Director of Development
**IMDB:** www.imdb.com/name/nm1393767

### Gina Matthews
**Title:** Partner/Producer
**IMDB:** www.imdb.com/name/nm0560033

### Grant Scharbo
**Title:** Partner/Producer
**IMDB:** www.imdb.com/name/nm0770090

## LLEJU PRODUCTIONS

3050 Post Oak Blvd.,
Suite 460
Houston, Texas 77056

Phone: 866-579-6444
Fax: 713-583-2214
Email: info@lleju.com
Website: http://www.lleju.com/index.html
IMDB: http://www.imdb.com/company/
co0250136/?ref_=fn_al_co_1

**Submission Policy:** Accepts query letter from
unproduced, unrepresented writers
**Genre:** Action, Comedy, Crime, Drama, Feature
Films, Horror, Thriller
**Focus:** Feature Films
**Year Established:** 2008

### Bill Perkins
**Title:** Executive
**IMDB:** http://www.imdb.com/name/
nm2645116/?ref_=fn_al_nm_1

### Keith Perkins
**IMDB:** http://www.imdb.com/name/
nm1344801/?ref_=fn_al_nm_1

### Cooper Richey
**IMDB:** http://www.imdb.com/name/
nm3295785/?ref_=fn_al_nm_1

## LONDINE PRODUCTIONS

1626 N. Wilcox Ave.
Ste. 480
Hollywood, CA 90028

Fax: 310-822-9025
IMDB: http://www.imdb.com/company/
co0183894/?ref_=fn_al_co_1

**Submission Policy:** Accepts query letter from
unproduced, unrepresented writers via email
**Genre:** Comedy, Drama, Feature Films, Thriller, TV
Drama

**Focus:** Feature Films
**Year Established:** 1988

**Cassius Weathersby**
Title: President
Email: cassiusii@aol.com
IMDB: http://www.imdb.com/name/
nm0915780/?ref_=fn_al_nm_1

**Nadine Weathersby**
Title: Vice President
IMDB: http://www.imdb.com/name/
nm2325321/?ref_=fn_al_nm_1

**Joshua Weathersby**
Title: Vice President
IMDB: http://www.imdb.com/name/
nm1500833/?ref_=fn_al_nm_1

## LUCASFILM LTD.

5858 Lucas Valley Rd
Nicasio, CA 94946

Phone: 415-662-1800
Website: www.lucasfilm.com
IMDB: www.imdb.com/company/co0071326

Submission Policy: Does not accept any unsolicited material
Genre: Action, Fantasy, Feature Films, Science Fiction
Focus: Feature Film

**David Anderman**
Title: General Councel
IMDB: www.imdb.com/name/nm2763931

**Kathleen Kennedy**
Title: Co-Chairman
IMDB: www.imdb.com/name/nm0005086

**George Lucas**
Title: Co-Chairman
IMDB: www.imdb.com/name/nm0000184

## LUCKY CROW FILMS

4335 Van Nuys Blvd.
Suite 355
Sherman Oaks, CA 91403

Phone: 818-783-7529
Fax: 818-783-7594
Email: info@indieproducer.net
Website: http://www.indieproducer.net/

IMDB: http://www.imdb.com/company/
co0102838/?ref_=fn_al_co_1

Submission Policy: Accepts query letter from unproduced, unrepresented writers via email
Genre: Documentary, Drama
Focus: Feature Films, Television
Year Established: 2004

**Kerry David**
Title: President
IMDB: http://www.imdb.com/name/
nm0202968/?ref_=fn_al_nm_1

**Jon Gunn**
Title: President
IMDB: http://www.imdb.com/name/
nm0348197/?ref_=fn_al_nm_1

## LYNDA OBST PRODUCTIONS

10202 West Washington Boulevard
Astaire Building, Suite 1000
Culver City, CA 90232

Phone: 310-244-6122
Fax: 310-244-0092
Website: http://www.lyndaobst.com/
IMDB: http://www.imdb.com/company/
co0071668/?ref_=fn_al_co_1

Submission Policy: Does not accept any unsolicited material
Genre: Action, Comedy, Crime, Drama, Family, Fantasy, Romance, Thriller
Focus: Feature Films, TV

**Rachel Abarbanell**
Title: Vice President of Production
IMDB: www.imdb.com/name/nm1561964

**Lynda Obst**
Title: Vice President of Production
IMDB: www.imdb.com/name/nm0643553

## MAD CHANCE PRODUCTIONS

4000 Warner Boulevard
Building 81, Room 208
Burbank, CA 91522

Phone: 818-954-3500
Fax: 818-954-3586
IMDB: http://www.imdb.com/company/
co0034487/?ref_=fn_al_co_1

**Submission Policy:** Does not accept any unsolicited material
**Genre:** Action, Comedy, Drama, Family, Fantasy, Romance, Science Fiction, Thriller
**Focus:** Feature Films

**Andrew Lazar**
Title: Producer
IMDB: www.imdb.com/name/nm0493662
Assistant: Wynn Wygal

**Miri Yoon**
Title: Executive
IMDB: www.imdb.com/name/nm1186661

## MAD HATTER ENTERTAINMENT

9229 Sunset Boulevard, Suite 225
West Hollywood, CA 90069

Phone: 310-860-0441
Website: http://www.madhatterentertainment.com
IMDB: http://www.imdb.com/company/co0266260/

**Submission Policy:** Accepts scripts from unproduced, unrepresented writers
**Genre:** Action, Animation, Comedy, Crime, Drama, Family, Fantasy, Horror, Myth, Science Fiction, Thriller, TV, TV Drama
**Focus:** Feature Films, Television

**Michael Connolly**
Title: Founder/Manager/Producer
Email: mike@madhatterentertainment.com
IMDB: www.imdb.com/name/nm0175326
Assistant: Kyle Smeehuyzen (Development Assistant)

## MADHOUSE ENTERTAINMENT

10390 Santa Monica Boulevard Suite 110
Los Angeles, CA 90025

Phone: 310-587-2200
Fax: 323-782-0491
Email: query@madhouseent.net
Website: http://www.madhouseent.net/
IMDB: http://www.imdb.com/company/co0202761/?ref_=fn_al_co_1

**Submission Policy:** Does not accept any unsolicited material
**Genre:** Action, Comedy, Crime, Drama, Romance, Science Fiction, Thriller

**Focus:** Feature Films, Television
**Year Established:** 2010

**Chris Cook**
Title: Manager
IMDB: http://www.imdb.com/name/nm2303601/?ref_=fn_al_nm_3

**Ryan Cunningham**
Title: Manager
IMDB: http://www.imdb.com/name/nm1400515/?ref_=fn_al_nm_1

**Adam Kolbrenner**
Title: Principal
IMDB: http://www.imdb.com/name/nm2221807/?ref_=fn_al_nm_1

**Robyn Meisinger**
Title: Principal
IMDB: http://www.imdb.com/name/nm1159733/?ref_=fn_al_nm_1

## MADRIK MULTIMEDIA

Los Angeles Center Studios
1201 West Fifth Street, Suite F222
Los Angeles, CA 90017

Phone: 213-596-5180
Email: info@madrik.com
Website: www.madrik.com

**Submission Policy:** Accepts query letter from unproduced, unrepresented writers
**Genre:** Feature Films, Media (Commercials/Branding/Marketing), Romance, TV Sitcom
**Focus:** Feature Films, Television, Media

**Chris Adams**
Title: Founder
Email: chris@madrik.com
IMDB: www.imdb.com/name/nm1886228

## MAGNET RELEASING

115 West 27th Street
Seventh Floor
New York City, NY 10001

Phone: 212-924-6701
Fax: 212-924-6742
Website: www.magnetreleasing.com

**Submission Policy:** Does not accept any unsolicited material

**Genre:** Action, Comedy, Crime, Family, Fantasy, Feature Films, Horror, Myth, Romance, Science Fiction, Thriller
**Focus:** Feature Films

**Mark Cuban**
Title: Executive
IMDB: www.imdb.com/name/nm1171860

**Todd Wagner**
Title: Executive
IMDB: www.imdb.com/name/nm0906136

## MALPASO PRODUCTIONS

4000 Warner Boulevard
Building 81
Burbank, CA 91522-0811

**Phone:** 818-954-3367
**Fax:** 818-954-4803
**IMDB:** http://www.imdb.com/company/co0010258/

**Submission Policy:** Does not accept any unsolicited material
**Genre:** Crime, Drama, Fantasy, Memoir & True Stories, Romance, Thriller
**Focus:** Feature Films
**Year Established:** 1967

**Clint Eastwood**
Title: Producer/Actor/Director
IMDB: www.imdb.com/name/nm0000142

**Robert Lorenz**
Title: Partner/Producer
IMDB: www.imdb.com/name/nm0520749
Assistant: Jessica Meier
jessica.meier@wbconsultant.com

## MANDALAY PICTURES

4751 Wilshire Boulevard, 3rd Floor
Los Angeles, CA 90010

**Phone:** 323-549-4300
**Fax:** 323-549-9832
**Email:** info@mandalay.com
**Website:** www.mandalay.com
**IMDB:** http://www.imdb.com/company/co0013922/?ref_=fn_al_co_1

**Submission Policy:** Accepts query letter from produced or represented writers
**Genre:** Action, Comedy, Drama, Family, Horror, Romance, Thriller

**Focus:** Feature Films
**Year Established:** 1995

**Joey De La Rosa**
Title: Creative Executive
Phone: 323-549-4300

**Peter Guber**
Title: Chairman/CEO
IMDB: www.imdb.com/name/nm0345542

**Adam Stone**
Title: Vice-President of Development
IMDB: www.imdb.com/name/nm2625826
Assistant: Jessica Smith

## MANDALAY TELEVISION

4751 Wilshire Boulevard, 3rd Floor
Los Angeles, CA 90010

**Phone:** 323-549-4300
**Fax:** 323-549-9832
**Email:** info@mandalay.com
**Website:** www.mandalay.com
**IMDB:** http://www.imdb.com/company/co0018094/?ref_=fn_al_co_1

**Submission Policy:** Does not accept any unsolicited material
**Genre:** Action, Comedy, Drama, Period, Romance, Thriller, TV Drama
**Focus:** Television

**Paul Schaeffer**
Title: Vice Chairman/COO
Phone: 323-549-4300
IMDB: www.imdb.com/name/nm2325215

## MANDATE PICTURES

2700 Colorado Avenue, Suite 501
Santa Monica, CA 90404

**Phone:** 310-360-1441
**Fax:** 310-360-1447
**Email:** info@mandatepictures.com
**Website:** www.mandatepictures.com
**IMDB:** http://www.imdb.com/company/co0142446/?ref_=fn_al_co_1

**Submission Policy:** Accepts query letter from unproduced, unrepresented writers via email
**Genre:** Comedy, Crime, Drama, Fantasy, Horror, Romance, Science Fiction, Thriller

**Focus:** Feature Films
**Year Established:** 2003

### Nicole Brown
**Title:** Executive Vice-President, Production
**Phone:** 310-255-5710
**Email:** nbrown@mandatepictures.com
**IMDB:** www.imdb.com/name/nm0114352

### Aaron Ensweiler
**Title:** Creative Executive
**Phone:** 310-255-5721
**Email:** aensweiler@mandatepictures.com
**IMDB:** www.imdb.com/name/nm3943221

### Nathan Kahane
**Title:** President
**Phone:** 310-255-5700
**IMDB:** www.imdb.com/name/nm1144042

## MANDEVILLE FILMS

500 South Buena Vista Street
Animation Building, 2G
Burbank, CA 91521-1783

**Phone:** (818) 560-7662
**Fax:** (818) 842-2937
**Website:** http://mandfilms.com/
**IMDB:** http://www.imdb.com/company/
co0064942/?ref_=fn_al_co_1

**Submission Policy:** Accepts query letter from
unproduced, unrepresented writers
**Genre:** Action, Drama, Family, Romance, TV
Drama
**Focus:** Feature Films, TV
**Year Established:** 1994

### Laura Cray
**Title:** Creative Executive
**Phone:** 818-560-4332
**IMDB:** www.imdb.com/name/nm1733050
**Assistant:** Liz Bassin

### David Hoberman
**Title:** Partner
**IMDB:** www.imdb.com/name/nm0387674
**Assistant:** Derek Steiner

### Todd Lieberman
**Title:** Partner
**IMDB:** http://www.imdb.com/name/nm0509414/
**Assistant:** Jacqueline Lesko

## MANDY FILMS

9201 Wilshire Boulevard, Suite 206
Beverly Hills, CA 90210

**Phone:** 310-246-0500
**Fax:** 310-246-0350
**IMDB:** http://www.imdb.com/company/
co0032786/?ref_=fn_al_co_1

**Submission Policy:** Accepts query letter from
unproduced, unrepresented writers
**Genre:** Action, Comedy, Fantasy, Science Fiction,
Thriller, TV, TV Drama
**Focus:** Feature Films, Television

### Leonard Goldberg
**Title:** President
**IMDB:** www.imdb.com/name/nm0325252

### Amanda Goldberg
**Title:** Vice-President of Development/Production
**IMDB:** www.imdb.com/name/nm0325144

## MANGUSTA PRODUCTIONS

145 6th Avenue
Suite #6E
New York, NY 10013

**Phone:** 212-463-9503
**Email:** info@mangustaproductions.com
**Website:** www.mangustaproductions.com

**Genre:** Comedy, Documentary, Drama, Feature
Films, Romance
**Focus:** Feature Films

### Blake Ashman
**Title:** Principal
**IMDB:** www.imdb.com/name/nm0039137

### Giancarlo Canavesio
**Title:** Founder & President
**IMDB:** www.imdb.com/name/nm2184875

### Shannon McCoy Cohn
**Title:** Producer
**IMDB:** www.imdb.com/name/nm3101571

### Sol Tryon
**Title:** Producer
**IMDB:** www.imdb.com/name/nm0874501

## MANIFEST FILM COMPANY

619 18th Street
Santa Monica, CA 90402

**Phone:** 310-899-5554
**Email:** info@manifestfilms.com
**Website:** http://janetyang.com
**IMDB:** http://www.imdb.com/company/
co0005048/?ref_=fn_al_co_1

**Submission Policy:** Accepts query letter from
unproduced, unrepresented writers
**Genre:** Comedy, Crime, Drama, Period, Thriller
**Focus:** Feature Films
**Year Established:** 1998

### Janet Yang
**Title:** President
**Email:** janetyang2013@gmail.com
**IMDB:** http://www.imdb.com/name/
nm0946003/?ref_=fn_al_nm_1

## MAPLE SHADE FILMS

4000 Warner Boulevard
Building 138, Room 1103
Burbank, CA 91522

**Phone:** 818-954-3137
**IMDB:** http://www.imdb.com/company/
co0100155/?ref_=fn_al_co_1

**Submission Policy:** Accepts query letter from
unproduced, unrepresented writers
**Genre:** Action, Drama, Fantasy, Thriller
**Focus:** Feature Films

### Ed McDonnell
**Title:** President
**IMDB:** www.imdb.com/name/nm0568093

## MARC PLATT PRODUCTIONS

100 Universal City Plaza, Bungalow 5163
Universal City, CA 91608

**Phone:** 818-777-8811
**Fax:** 818-866-6353
**IMDB:** http://www.imdb.com/company/
co0093810/?ref_=fn_al_co_1

**Submission Policy:** Accepts query letter from
unproduced, unrepresented writers
**Genre:** Action, Comedy, Crime, Drama, Family,

Fantasy, Horror, Romance, Thriller, TV Drama
**Focus:** Feature Films, Television

### Jared LeBoff
**Title:** Development
**Phone:** 818-777-9961
**IMDB:** www.imdb.com/name/nm1545176

### Marc Platt
**Title:** Producer
**Phone:** 818-777-1122
**Email:** platt@nbcuni.com
**IMDB:** www.imdb.com/name/nm0686887
**Assistant:** Joey Levy

### Adam Siegel
**Title:** President
**Phone:** 818-777-9544
**IMDB:** www.imdb.com/name/nm2132113

## MARK VICTOR PRODUCTIONS

2932 Wilshire Boulevard, Suite 201
Santa Monica, CA 90403

**Phone:** 310-828-3339
**Fax:** 310-828-9588
**Email:** info@markvictorproductions.com
**Website:** www.markvictorproductions.com

**Submission Policy:** Accepts query letter from
unproduced, unrepresented writers via email
**Genre:** Action, Animation, Horror, Thriller
**Focus:** Feature Films, TV, Reality Programming
(Reality TV, Documentaries, Special Events,
Sporting Events)

### Sarah Johnson
**Title:** Director of Development
**Phone:** 310-828-3339
**IMDB:** www.imdb.com/name/nm1154417

### Mark Victor
**Title:** Producer/Writer
**Phone:** 310-828-3339
**Email:** markvictorproductions@hotmail.com
**IMDB:** www.imdb.com/name/nm0896131

## MARK YELLEN PRODUCTION

183 South Orange Drive
Los Angeles, CA 90036

**Phone:** 323-935-5525
**Fax:** 323-935-5755

**Submission Policy:** Accepts query letter from
unproduced, unrepresented writers via email
**Genre:** Action, Family
**Focus:** Feature Films, TV, Media (Commercials/
Branding/Marketing)
**Year Established:** 2003

**Mark Yellen**
**Title:** Producer
**Phone:** 323-935-5525
**Email:** mark@myfilmconsult.com
**IMDB:** www.imdb.com/name/nm0947390

## MARTIN CHASE PRODUCTIONS

500 South Buena Vista Street
Burbank, CA 91521

**Phone:** 818-560-3952
**Fax:** 818-560-5113

**Submission Policy:** Does not accept any unsolicited
material
**Genre:** Family
**Focus:** Feature Films, TV
**Year Established:** 2000

**Debra Chase**
**Title:** President/Producer
**Phone:** 818-526-4252
**IMDB:** www.imdb.com/name/nm0153744

**Gaylyn Fraiche**
**Title:** Executive Vice-President
**Phone:** 818-526-4252
**IMDB:** www.imdb.com/name/nm2325210

**Josh Stewart**
**Title:** Executive Assistant
**Phone:** 818-526-4252

## MARTY KATZ PRODUCTIONS

22337 Pacific Coast Highway #327
Malibu, CA 90265

**Phone:** 310-589-1560
**Fax:** 310-589-1565
**Email:** martykatzproductions@earthlink.net

**Submission Policy:** Accepts query letter from
unproduced, unrepresented writers via email
**Genre:** Action, Comedy, Drama, Romance
**Focus:** Feature Films
**Year Established:** 1996

**Campbell Katz**
**Title:** Vice-President, Productions & Development
**Phone:** 310-589-1560
**Email:** martykatzproductions@earthlink.net
**IMDB:** www.imdb.com/name/nm0441645

**Marty Katz**
**Title:** Producer
**Phone:** 310-589-1560
**Email:** martykatzproductions@earthlink.net
**IMDB:** www.imdb.com/name/nm0441794

## MARVISTA ENTERTAINMENT

10277 W. Olympic Blvd
3rd Floor
Los Angeles, CA 90067
US

**Phone:** 310-737-0950
**Fax:** 310-737-9115
**Email:** info@marvista.net
**Website:** www.marvista.net

**Submission Policy:** Accepts query letter from
unproduced, unrepresented writers via email
**Focus:** Feature Films, TV

**Matt Freeman**
**Title:** Vice-President of Production & Development
**Phone:** 310-737-0950
**IMDB:** http://pro.imdb.com/name/nm0293513/

**Robyn Snyder**
**Title:** Executive Vice-President of Development &
Production
**Phone:** 310-737-0950
**Email:** rsnyder@marvista.net
**IMDB:** www.imdb.com/name/nm2237557

**Fernando Szew**
**Title:** CEO
**Phone:** 310-737-0950
**Email:** fszew@marvista.net
**IMDB:** www.imdb.com/name/nm2280496

## MASIMEDIA

11620 Oxnard Street
North Hollywood, California 91606

**Phone:** 818-358-4803
**Email:** submissions@masimedia.net
**Website:** http://www.masimedia.net/

**IMDB:** http://www.imdb.com/company/
co0155931/?ref_=fn_al_co_1

**Submission Policy:** Accepts scripts from
unproduced, unrepresented writers via email
**Genre:** Documentary, Horror
**Focus:** Feature Films, Television
**Year Established:** 2006

### Anthony Masi
**Title:** President
**IMDB:** http://www.imdb.com/name/
nm1502845/?ref_=fn_al_nm_1

## MASS HYSTERIA ENTERTAINMENT

8899 Beverly Boulevard, Suite 710
Los Angeles, CA 90048

**Phone:** 310-285-7800
**Fax:** 310-285-7801
**Email:** info@masshysteriafilms.com
**Website:** www.masshysteriafilms.com

**Submission Policy:** Accepts query letter from
unproduced, unrepresented writers via email
**Focus:** Feature Films, TV

### Daniel Grodnik
**Title:** President
**Phone:** 310-285-7800
**Email:** grodzilla@earthlink.net
**IMDB:** www.imdb.com/name/nm0342841

## MATADOR PICTURES

20 Gloucester Place
London W1U 8HA
United Kingdom

**Phone:** +44 (0) 20 7009-9640
**Fax:** +44 (0) 20 7009-9641
**Email:** admin@matadorpictures.com
**Website:** www.matadorpictures.com

**Submission Policy:** Accepts query letter from
unproduced, unrepresented writers via email
**Genre:** Action, Comedy, Drama, Romance
**Focus:** Feature Films
**Year Established:** 1999

### Orlando Cubit
**Title:** Development Executive
**Phone:** +44 (0) 20-7009-9640
**IMDB:** www.imdb.com/name/nm4919747

### Lucia Lopez
**Title:** Development Producer
**Phone:** +44 (0) 20-7009-9640
**IMDB:** www.imdb.com/name/nm2389416

### Nigel Thomas
**Title:** Producer
**Phone:** +44 (0) 20-7009-9640
**IMDB:** www.imdb.com/name/nm0859302

## MAVEN PICTURES

148 Spring Street
Fourth Floor
New York, NY 10012

**Phone:** 212-725-3550
**Fax:** 646-442-7500

**Submission Policy:** Does not accept any unsolicited
material
**Genre:** Action, Comedy, Drama, Feature Films,
Romance, Thriller
**Focus:** Feature Films

### Alex Francis
**Title:** SVP of Production & Development
**IMDB:** www.imdb.com/name/nm2123360

### Jenny Halper
**Title:** Development Executive
**IMDB:** www.imdb.com/name/nm3794516

### Hardy Justice
**Title:** SVP of Production & Development
**IMDB:** www.imdb.com/name/nm1155511

### Nic Marshall
**Title:** Director of Operations
**IMDB:** www.imdb.com/name/nm2090942

### Celine Rattray
**Title:** Principal
**IMDB:** www.imdb.com/name/nm1488027

### Trudie Styler
**Title:** Principal
**IMDB:** www.imdb.com/name/nm0836548

### Anita Sumner
**Title:** SVP of Creative Affairs
**IMDB:** www.imdb.com/name/nm0838856

## MAXIMUM FILMS & MANAGEMENT

33 West 17th Street, 11th Floor
New York, NY 10011

Phone: 212-414-4801
Fax: 212-414-4803
Email: lauren@maximumfilmsny.com
Website: www.maximumfilmsny.com

Submission Policy: Does not accept any unsolicited material
Focus: Feature Films, TV, Theater

**Marcy Drogin**
Title: Producer/Manager
Phone: 212-414-4801
IMDB: www.imdb.com/name/nm1216320

## MAYA ENTERTAINMENT GROUP

1201 West 5th Street, Suite T210
Los Angeles, CA 90017

Phone: 213-542-4420
Fax: 213-534-3846
Email: info@maya-entertainment.com
Website: www.maya-entertainment.com

Submission Policy: Accepts query letter from unproduced, unrepresented writers via email
Genre: Comedy, Drama, TV Drama
Focus: Feature Films, TV, Reality Programming (Reality TV, Documentaries, Special Events, Sporting Events)
Year Established: 2008

**Moctesuma Esparza**
Title: CEO/Chairman/Producer
Phone: 213-542-4420
IMDB: www.imdb.com/name/nm0260800

**Christina Hirigoyen**
Title: Development Executive
Phone: 213-542-4420
IMDB: www.imdb.com/name/nm3491113

## MAYHEM PICTURES

725 Arizona Avenue, Suite 402
Santa Monica, CA 90401

Phone: 310-393-5005
Fax: 310-393-5017

Submission Policy: Does not accept any unsolicited material
Genre: Comedy, Family, Memoir & True Stories
Focus: Feature Films, TV, Reality Programming (Reality TV, Documentaries, Special Events, Sporting Events)
Year Established: 2003

**Brad Butler**
Title: Creative Executive
Phone: 310-393-5005
Email: brad@mayhempictures.com
IMDB: www.imdb.com/name/nm2744089

**Mark Ciardi**
Title: Producer
Phone: 310-393-5005
Email: mark@mayhempictures.com
IMDB: www.imdb.com/name/nm0161891

**Victor Constantino**
Title: Sr. Vice-President of Production & Development
Phone: 310-393-5005
Email: victor@mayhempictures.com
IMDB: www.imdb.com/name/nm2028391

## MBST ENTERTAINMENT

345 North Maple Drive, Suite 200
Beverly Hills, CA 90210

Phone: 310-385-1820
Fax: 310-385-1834

Submission Policy: Accepts query letter from unproduced, unrepresented writers
Genre: Action, Comedy, Drama, Romance
Focus: Feature Films, TV, Theater
Year Established: 2005

**Jonathan Brandstein**
Title: Partner
Phone: 310-385-1820
IMDB: www.imdb.com/name/nm0104844

**Larry Brezner**
Title: Partner
Phone: 310-385-1820
IMDB: www.imdb.com/name/nm010836

## MEDIA 8 ENTERTAINMENT

15260 Ventura Boulevard, Suite 710
Sherman Oaks, CA 91403

Phone: 818-325-8000
Fax: 818-325-8020
Email: info@media8ent.com
Website: www.media8ent.com

**Submission Policy:** Does not accept any unsolicited material
**Genre:** Action, Comedy, Drama, Romance
**Focus:** Feature Films, TV
**Year Established:** 1993

### Stewart Hall
**Title:** President
**Phone:** 818-826-8000
**Email:** info@media8ent.com
**IMDB:** www.imdb.com/name/nm1279593

## MEDIA RIGHTS CAPITAL

1800 Century Park East/ 10th Floor
Los Angeles, CA 90067

**Phone:** 310-786-1600
**Fax:** 310-786-1601
**Email:** info@mrclp.com
**Website:** www.mrcstudios.com

**Submission Policy:** Does not accept any unsolicited material
**Genre:** Animation, Comedy, Drama, Feature Films, Romance, Thriller, TV, TV Drama, TV Sitcom
**Focus:** Feature Films, TV

### Brye Adler
**Title:** Vice President, Production

### Charlie Goldstein
**Title:** Vice President, Television Production
**IMDB:** www.imdb.com/name/nm0326177/

### Joe Hipps
**Title:** Vice President, Television Production & Creative Affairs

### Alex Jackson
**Title:** Creative Executive

### Asif Satchu
**Title:** Co-CEO
**Email:** www.imdb.com/name/nm2640007
**Assistant:** Maggie Settli

### Whitney Timmons
**Title:** Director, Television

### Modi Wiczyk
**Title:** Co-CEO
**IMDB:** www.imdb.com/name/nm1582943
**Assistant:** Maggie Settli

## MEDIA TALENT GROUP

9200 Sunset Boulevard, Suite 550
West Hollywood, CA 90069

**Phone:** 310-275-7900
**Fax:** 310-275-7910

**Submission Policy:** Accepts query letter from unproduced, unrepresented writers
**Focus:** Feature Films, TV
**Year Established:** 2009

### Chris Davey
**Title:** Producer/Manager
**Phone:** 310-275-7900
**IMDB:** www.imdb.com/name/nm1312702

### Geyer Kosinski
**Title:** Chairman/CEO
**Phone:** 310-275-7900
**IMDB:** www.imdb.com/name/nm0467083

## MEDUSA FILM

Via Aurelia Antica 422/424
Rome, Lazio 00165
Italy

**Phone:** +39-06-663-901
**Fax:** +39-06-66-39-04-50
**Email:** info.medusa@medusa.it
**Website:** http://www.medusa.it/
**IMDB:** http://www.imdb.com/company/co0117688/?ref_=fn_al_co_1

**Submission Policy:** Does not accept any unsolicited material
**Genre:** Comedy, Crime, Documentary, Drama, Family, Feature Films, Horror, Romance, Thriller
**Focus:** Feature Films
**Year Established:** 1916

### Faruk Alatan
**Title:** Head of Foreign Acquisitions
**IMDB:** http://www.imdb.com/name/nm0016092/?ref_=fn_al_nm_1

### Giampaolo Letta
**Title:** Vice Chairman and Managing Director
**IMDB:** http://www.imdb.com/name/nm2325586/?ref_=fn_al_nm_1

**Luciana Migliavacca**
Title: Head of Home Entertainment
IMDB: http://www.imdb.com/name/
nm3096618/?ref_=fn_al_nm_1

**Pier Paolo Zerilli**
Title: International Creative
IMDB: http://www.imdb.com/name/
nm1047259/?ref_=fn_al_nm_1

## MELEE ENTERTAINMENT

144 South Beverly Drive, Suite 402
Beverly Hills, CA 90212

Phone: 310-248-3931
Fax: 310-248-3921
Email: acquisitions@melee.com
Website: www.melee.com

Submission Policy: Does not accept any unsolicited
material
Focus: Feature Films
Year Established: 2003

**Scott Aronson**
Title: COO
Phone: 310-248-3931
IMDB: www.imdb.com/name/nm1529615

**Bryan Turner**
Title: CEO
Phone: 310-248-3931
IMDB: www.imdb.com/name/nm0877440

**Brittany Williams**
Title: Creative Executive
Phone: 310-248-3931
IMDB: www.imdb.com/name/nm2950356

## MEL STUART PRODUCTIONS, INC.

204 South Beverly Drive, Suite 109
Beverly Hills, CA 90210

Phone: 310-550-5872
Fax: 310-550-5895
Email: info@melstuartproductions.com
Website: www.melstuartproductions.com

Submission Policy: Accepts query letter from
unproduced, unrepresented writers via email
Focus: Feature Films, TV, Reality Programming
(Reality TV, Documentaries, Special Events,
Sporting Events)

**Mel Stuart**
Title: President
Phone: 310-550-5872
Email: info@melstuartproductions.com
IMDB: www.imdb.com/name/nm0835799

## MERCHANT IVORY PRODUCTIONS

PO Box 338
New York, NY 10276

372 Old Street, Office 150
London EC1V 9LT
United Kingdom

Phone: 212-582-8049
Fax: 212-706-8340/ +44-207-657-3988
Email: contact@merchantivory.com
Website: www.merchantivory.com

Submission Policy: Accepts query letter from
unproduced, unrepresented writers via email
Genre: Drama
Focus: Feature Films, Reality Programming (Reality
TV, Documentaries, Special Events, Sporting
Events)
Year Established: 1961

**Paul Bradley**
Title: London - Producer
Email: paul@merchantivory.co.uk
IMDB: www.imdb.com/name/nm0103364

**James Ivory**
Title: President/Director
Phone: 212-582-8049
Email: contact@merchantivory.com
IMDB: www.imdb.com/name/nm0412465

**Neil Jesuele**
Title: NY - Director of Development
Phone: 212-582-8049
Email: njesuele@merchantivory.com
IMDB: www.imdb.com/name/nm3134373

**Simon Oxley**
Title: London - Producer
Email: simon@merchantivory.co.uk
IMDB: www.imdb.com/name/nm1774746

## MERV GRIFFIN ENTERTAINMENT

130 South El Camino Drive
Beverly Hills, CA 90212

**Phone:** 310-385-2700
**Fax:** 310-385-2728
**Email:** firstname_lastname@griffgroup.com
**IMDB:** http://www.imdb.com/company/
co0093384/?ref_=fn_al_co_1

**Submission Policy:** Does not accept any unsolicited material
**Genre:** Action, Comedy, Crime, Documentary, Drama, Memoir & True Stories, Period, Reality, Romance, Thriller, TV, TV Drama, TV Sitcom
**Focus:** Feature Films, Television, Shorts
**Year Established:** 1964

**Mike Eyre**
**Title:** Executive Vice President

**Tony Griffin**
**Title:** Executive Film Development

**Robert Pritchard**
**Title:** President
**IMDB:** http://www.imdb.com/name/
nm2923017/?ref_=fn_al_nm_8

**Ron Ward**
**Title:** Vice Chairman
**IMDB:** http://www.imdb.com/name/
nm2302243/?ref_=fn_al_nm_4

## METRO-GOLDWYN-MEYER (MGM)

245 N Beverly Dr
Beverly Hills, CA 90210

**Phone:** 310-449-3000
**Website:** www.mgm.com

**Submission Policy:** Does not accept any unsolicited material
**Genre:** Action, Comedy, Crime, Drama, Family, Feature Films, Horror, Myth, Romance, Science Fiction, Thriller
**Focus:** Feature Films

**Gary Barber**
**Title:** Chairman & CEO
**Phone:** 310-449-3000
**IMDB:** www.imdb.com/name/nm0053388

**Cassidy Lange**
**Title:** Vice President of Production
**Phone:** 310-449-3000
**IMDB:** www.imdb.com/name/nm3719738

**Dene Stratton**
**Title:** CFO
**Phone:** 310-449-3000
**IMDB:** www.imdb.com/name/nm4682676

## MICHAEL DE LUCA PRODUCTIONS

10202 West Washington Boulevard
Astaire Building, Suite 3028
Culver City, CA 90232

**Phone:** 310-244-4990
**Fax:** 310-244-0449

**Submission Policy:** Does not accept any unsolicited material
**Genre:** Action, Comedy, Drama, Thriller
**Focus:** Feature Films

**Josh Bratman**
**Title:** Development Executive
**Phone:** 310-244-4916
**IMDB:** www.imdb.com/name/nm2302300
**Assistant:** Sandy Yep

**Michael De Luca**
**Title:** Producer
**Phone:** 310-244-4990
**IMDB:** www.imdb.com/name/nm0006894
**Assistant:** Kristen Detwiler

**Alissa Phillips**
**Title:** Development
**Phone:** 310-244-4918
**IMDB:** www.imdb.com/name/nm1913014
**Assistant:** Bill Karesh

## MICHAEL GRAIS PRODUCTIONS

321 South Beverly Drive, Suite M
Beverly Hills, CA 90210

**Phone:** 323-857-4510
**Fax:** 323-319-4002

**Submission Policy:** Accepts query letter from unproduced, unrepresented writers via email
**Genre:** Horror, Thriller
**Focus:** Feature Films, TV

**Michael Grais**
**Title:** Producer/Writer
**Phone:** 323-857-4510
**Email:** michaelgrais@yahoo.com
**IMDB:** www.imdb.com/name/nm0334457

## MICHAEL TAYLOR PRODUCTIONS

2370 Bowmont Drive
Beverly Hills, CA 90210

**Phone:** 213-821-3113
**Fax:** 213-740-3395
**Email:** taycoprod@aol.com

**Submission Policy:** Accepts query letter from unproduced, unrepresented writers via email
**Focus:** Feature Films, TV, Reality Programming (Reality TV, Documentaries, Special Events, Sporting Events)

**Michael Taylor**
**Title:** Producer
**Phone:** 213-821-3113
**IMDB:** www.imdb.com/name/nm0852888
**Assistant:** Yolanda Rodriguez

## MIDD KID PRODUCTIONS

10202 West Washington Boulevard
Fred Astaire Building, Suite 2010
Culver City, CA 90232

**Phone:** 310-244-2688
**Fax:** 310-244-2603

**Submission Policy:** Accepts query letter from unproduced, unrepresented writers
**Genre:** Crime, Detective, TV Drama
**Focus:** TV

**Marney Hochman**
**Title:** President of Development
**Phone:** 310-244-2688
**IMDB:** www.imdb.com/name/nm2701117
**Assistant:** Kent Rotherham

**Shawn Ryan**
**Title:** Principal
**Phone:** 310-244-2688
**IMDB:** www.imdb.com/name/nm0752841
**Assistant:** Kent Rotherham

## MIDNIGHT SUN PICTURES

10960 Wilshire Boulevard, Suite 700
Los Angeles, CA 90024

**Phone:** 310-902-0431
**Fax:** 310-450-4988

**Submission Policy:** Accepts query letter from produced or represented writers

**Genre:** Comedy, Drama, Horror, Romance
**Focus:** Feature Films, TV

**Renny Harlin**
**Title:** Producer/Director
**Phone:** 310-902-0431
**IMDB:** www.imdb.com/name/nm0001317

**Nikki Stanghetti**
**Title:** Co-Producer
**Phone:** 310-902-0431
**Email:** nikki@midnightsunproductions.com
**IMDB:** www.imdb.com/name/nm2325595

## MIKE LOBELL PRODUCTIONS

9477 Lloydcrest Drive
Beverly Hills, CA 90210

**Phone:** 323-822-2910
**Fax:** 310-205-2767

**Submission Policy:** Accepts query letter from unproduced, unrepresented writers
**Genre:** Action, Comedy, Drama, Romance
**Focus:** Feature Films
**Year Established:** 1973

**Mike Lobell**
**Title:** Producer
**Phone:** 323-822-2910
**IMDB:** www.imdb.com/name/nm0516465
**Assistant:** JanetChiarabaglio

## MILLAR/GOUGH INK

500 South Buena Vista Street
Animation Building 1E16
Burbank, CA 91521

**Phone:** 818-560-4260
**Fax:** 818-560-4216

**Submission Policy:** Accepts query letter from unproduced, unrepresented writers
**Genre:** Action, Drama, Family, Science Fiction, TV Drama
**Focus:** Feature Films, TV

**Alfred Gough**
**Title:** Principal
**Phone:** 818-560-4260
**IMDB:** www.imdb.com/name/nm0332184
**Assistant:** Mal Stares

**Miles Millar**
Title: Principal
Phone: 818-560-4260
IMDB: www.imdb.com/name/nm0587692
Assistant: Mal Stares

## MILLENNIUM FILMS

6423 Wilshire Boulevard
Los Angeles, CA 90048

Phone: 310-388-6900
Fax: 310-388-6901
Email: info@millenniumfilms.com
Website: www.millenniumfilms.com

Submission Policy: Accepts query letter from unproduced, unrepresented writers via email
Genre: Action, Comedy, Detective, Drama, Fantasy, Memoir & True Stories, Science Fiction, Thriller
Focus: Feature Films
Year Established: 1992

**Boaz Davidson**
Title: Head of Development and Creative Affairs
IMDB: www.imdb.com/name/nm0203246

**Avi Lerner**
Title: Co-Founder
IMDB: www.imdb.com/name/nm0503592

**Trevor Short**
Title: Co-Founder
IMDB: www.imdb.com/name/nm0795121

## MIMRAN SCHUR PICTURES

2400 Broadway, Suite 550
Santa Monica, CA 90404

Phone: 310-526-5410
Fax: 310-526-5405
Email: info@mimranschurpictures.com
Website: www.mimranschurpictures.com

Submission Policy: Accepts query letter from produced or represented writers
Genre: Drama
Focus: Feature Films
Year Established: 2009

**David Mimran**
Title: Co-Chairman
Phone: 310-526-5410
IMDB: www.imdb.com/name/nm3450764
Assistant: Caroline Haubold

**Lauren Pettit**
Title: Creative Executive
Phone: 310-526-5410
IMDB: www.imdb.com/name/nm2335692

**Jordan Schur**
Title: Co-Chairman/CEO
Phone: 310-526-5410
IMDB: www.imdb.com/name/nm2028525

## MIRADA

4235 Redwood Avenue
Los Angeles, CA 90066

Phone: 424-216-7470
Website: www.mirada.com

Submission Policy: Does not accept any unsolicited material
Genre: Animation, Drama, Fantasy, Myth
Focus: Feature Films, TV, Theater
Year Established: 2010

**Guillermo del Toro**
IMDB: www.imdb.com/name/nm0868219

**Javier Jimenez**
IMDB: www.imdb.com/name/nm3901643

**Guillermo Navarro**
IMDB: www.imdb.com/name/nm0622897

## MIRANDA ENTERTAINMENT

7337 Pacific View Drive
Los Angeles, CA 90068

Phone: 323-874-3600
Fax: 323-851-5350

Submission Policy: Does not accept any unsolicited material
Genre: Comedy, Horror, Thriller
Focus: Feature Films, TV

**Carsten Lorenz**
Title: Producer
Phone: 323-874-3600
Email: clorenz1@aol.com
IMDB: www.imdb.com/name/nm0520696

## MISHER FILMS

12233 Olympic Boulevard, Suite 354
Los Angeles, CA 90064

**Phone:** 310-405-7999
**Fax:** 310-405-7991
**Website:** www.misherfilms.com

**Submission Policy:** Does not accept any unsolicited material
**Genre:** Action, Crime, Drama
**Focus:** Feature Films, TV

**Kevin Misher**
**Title:** Producer/Owner
**Phone:** 310-405-7999
**Email:** kevin.misher@misherfilms.com
**IMDB:** http://pro.imdb.com/name/nm0592746/
**Assistant:** Sarah Ezrin

## MOCKINGBIRD PICTURES

Los Angeles, CA

**Email:** info@mockingbirdpictures.com
**Website:** www.mockinbirdpictures.com

**Submission Policy:** Accepts query letter from unproduced, unrepresented writers via email
**Genre:** Drama
**Focus:** Feature Films

**Bonnie Curtis**
**Title:** Principal
**IMDB:** www.imdb.com/name/nm0193268

**Julie Lynn**
**Title:** Principal
**IMDB:** www.imdb.com/name/nm0528724

**Kelly Thomas**
**Title:** Executive Producer
**IMDB:** www.imdb.com/name/nm1684437

## MOJO FILMS

500 South Buena Vista Street
Animation Building, Suite 1D 13
Burbank, CA 91521

**Phone:** 818-560-8370
**Fax:** 818-560-5045

**Submission Policy:** Accepts query letter from unproduced, unrepresented writers
**Focus:** Feature Films, TV
**Year Established:** 2007

**Mary-Beth Basile**
**Title:** Vice-President, Production & Development
**Phone:** 818-560-8370

**IMDB:** www.imdb.com/name/nm1039389
**Assistant:** Jay Ashenfelter

**Gary Fleder**
**Title:** President
**Phone:** 818-560-8370
**IMDB:** www.imdb.com/name/nm0001219
**Assistant:** Pamy Sue Anton

## MOMENTUM ENTERTAINMENT GROUP

8687 Melrose Avenue
8th Floor
Los Angeles, CA 90069

**Submission Policy:** Accepts query letter from unproduced, unrepresented writers via email
**Genre:** Action, Animation, Comedy, Crime, Detective, Drama, Family, Fantasy, Horror, Memoir & True Stories, Myth, Reality, Romance, Science Fiction, Sociocultural, Thriller, TV Drama, TV Sitcom
**Focus:** TV, Media (Commercials/Branding/Marketing)

**Nick Hamm**
**Title:** Head of Scripted Development
**Email:** nick.hamm@megww.com
**IMDB:** www.imdb.com/name/nm0358327

## MONSTERFOOT PRODUCTIONS

3450 Cahuenga Boulevard West
Loft 105
Los Angeles, CA 90068

**Phone:** 323-850-6116
**Fax:** 323-378-5232

**Submission Policy:** Accepts query letter from unproduced, unrepresented writers
**Focus:** Feature Films, TV, Reality Programming (Reality TV, Documentaries, Special Events, Sporting Events)

**Andrew Kimble**
**Title:** Creative Executive
**Phone:** 323-850-6116
**IMDB:** www.imdb.com/name/nm1130966

**Devon Schiff**
**Title:** Executive
**Phone:** 323-850-6116
**IMDB:** www.imdb.com/name/nm3825595

**Ahmet Zappa**
Title: CEO
Phone: 323-850-6116
IMDB: www.imdb.com/name/nm0953257

## MONTAGE ENTERTAINMENT

2600 Foothill Blvd
Ste 201
La Crescenta, CA 91214
USA

Phone: 1 818 248 0070
Fax: 1 818 248 0071
Email: david@montageentertainment.com
Website: www.montageentertainment.com

Submission Policy: Accepts query letter from
unproduced, unrepresented writers via email
Focus: Feature Films, TV

**Bill Ewart**
Title: Producer
Phone: 310-966-0222
Email: bill@montageentertainment.com
IMDB: www.imdb.com/name/nm0263867

**David Peters**
Title: Producer
Phone: 310-966-0222
Email: david@montageentertainment.com
IMDB: www.imdb.com/name/nm0007070

## MONTONE/YORN (UNNAMED YORN PRODUCTION COMPANY)

2000 Avenue of the Stars
3rd Floor North Tower
Los Angeles, CA 90067

Submission Policy: Accepts query letter from
unproduced, unrepresented writers
Genre: Action, Comedy, Family, Fantasy
Year Established: 2008

**Rick Yorn**
Title: Principal
IMDB: www.imdb.com/name/nm0948833

## MOONSTONE ENTERTAINMENT

PO Box 7400
Studio City, CA 91614

Phone: 818-985-3003
Fax: 818-985-3009

Email: submissions@moonstonefilms.com
Website: www.moonstonefilms.com

Submission Policy: Accepts query letter from
unproduced, unrepresented writers via email
Focus: Feature Films
Year Established: 1992

**Shahar Stroh**
Title: Director, Development & Acquisitions
Phone: 818-985-3003
IMDB: www.imdb.com/name/nm2325576

## MORGAN CREEK PRODUCTIONS

10351 Santa Monica Boulevard, Suite 200
Los Angeles, CA 90025

Phone: 310-432-4848
Fax: 310-432-4844

Submission Policy: Accepts query letter from
unproduced, unrepresented writers
Focus: Feature Films
Year Established: 1988

**Ryan Jones**
Title: Director of Development
Phone: 310-432-4848
IMDB: www.imdb.com/name/nm2325121

**Larry Katz**
Title: Senior Vice-President Development
Phone: 310-432-4848
IMDB: www.imdb.com/name/nm0441765

**Jordan Okun**
Title: Creative Executive
Phone: 310-432-4848
IMDB: www.imdb.com/name/nm1442312

## MORNINGSTAR ENTERTAINMENT

350 North Glenoaks Boulevard, Suite 300
Burbank, CA 91502

Phone: 818-559-7255
Fax: 818-559-7251

Submission Policy: Accepts query letter from
unproduced, unrepresented writers via email
Focus: TV, Reality Programming (Reality TV,
Documentaries, Special Events, Sporting Events)
Year Established: 1980

**Christian Robinson**
Title: Director, Development
Phone: 818-559-7255
IMDB: www.imdb.com/name/nm2384297

## MOSAIC/MOSAIC MEDIA GROUP

9200 West Sunset Boulevard
10th Floor
Los Angeles, CA 90069

Phone: 310-786-4900
Fax: 310-777-2185

Submission Policy: Accepts query letter from
unproduced, unrepresented writers
Genre: Action, Comedy, Family, Myth, TV Drama,
TV Sitcom
Focus: Feature Films, TV

**Mike Falbo**
Title: Vice-President Production & Development
Phone: 310-786-4900
Email: mfalbo@mosaicla.com
IMDB: www.imdb.com/name/nm3824648
Assistant: Mark Acomb

**David Householter**
Title: President, Production
Phone: 310-786-4900
Email: dhouseholter@mosaicla.com
IMDB: www.imdb.com/name/nm0396720
Assistant: Brendan Clougherty

**Jimmy Miller**
Title: CEO/Chairman/Producer
Phone: 310-786-4900
Email: jmiller@mosaicla.com
IMDB: www.imdb.com/name/nm0588612
Assistant: Alyx Carr

## MOSHAG PRODUCTIONS

c/o Mark Mower
1531 Wellesley Avenue
Los Angeles, CA 90025

Phone: 310-820-6760
Fax: 310-820-6960
Email: moshag@aol.com

Submission Policy: Accepts query letter from
unproduced, unrepresented writers via email
Focus: Feature Films, TV

**Mark Mower**
Title: Producer
Phone: 310-820-6760
IMDB: www.imdb.com/name/nm0610272

## MOXIE PICTURES

5890 West Jefferson Boulevard
Los Angeles, CA 90016

Phone: 310-857-1000
Fax: 310-857-1004
Website: http://www.moxiepictures.com/
IMDB: http://www.imdb.com/company/
co0119462/?ref_=fn_al_co_1

Submission Policy: Does not accept any unsolicited
material
Genre: Comedy, Documentary, Drama, Feature
Films, Reality, Romance, TV Drama, TV Sitcom
Focus: Feature Films, Television
Year Established: 2005

**David Casey**
Title: Director (Creative/TV)

**Katie Connell**
Title: Head of Production for New York
Phone: 212-807-6901

**Robert Fernandez**
Title: Chief Executive Officer
IMDB: http://www.imdb.com/name/
nm0273045/?ref_=fn_al_nm_3

**Dawn Laren**
Title: Managing Director

**Dan Levinson**
Title: President
IMDB: http://www.imdb.com/name/
nm1829495/?ref_=fn_al_nm_1

**Lizzie Schwartz**
Title: Vice President (Executive Producer)
IMDB: http://www.imdb.com/name/
nm2594272/?ref_=fn_al_nm_2

## MRB PRODUCTIONS

PO Box 311 N. Robertson Blvd., #513 Beverly
HIlls, ca 90211

Phone: 323-965-8881
Fax: 323-965-8882
Website: www.mrbproductions.com

**Submission Policy:** Does not accept any unsolicited material
**Genre:** Comedy, Documentary, Drama, Feature Films, Romance, Thriller, TV, TV Drama
**Focus:** Feature Films, TV

### Brenda Bank
**Title:** Producer
**Email:** brenda@mrbproductions.com
**IMDB:** www.imdb.com/name/nm1870773
**Assistant:** Erica Weiss

### Matthew Brady
**Title:** Executive Producer
**Email:** matthew@mrbproductions.com
**IMDB:** www.imdb.com/name/nm0103683

### Lori Huck
**Title:** Director of Development

### Yvette Lubinsky
**Title:** Executive

### Luke Watson
**Title:** Head of Production
**Email:** luke@mrbproductions.com
**IMDB:** www.imdb.com/name/nm2362830

## MR. MUDD

137 North Larchmont Boulevard, #113
Los Angeles, CA 9004

**Phone:** 323-932-5656
**Fax:** 323-932-5666

**Submission Policy:** Does not accept any unsolicited material
**Genre:** Comedy, Drama, Family, Romance
**Focus:** Feature Films
**Year Established:** 1998

### Lianne Halfon
**Title:** Producer
**IMDB:** www.imdb.com/name/nm0355147

### John Malkovich
**Title:** Producer/Director
**IMDB:** www.imdb.com/name/nm0000518

### Russell Smith
**Title:** Producer
**IMDB:** www.imdb.com/name/nm0809833

## MYRIAD PICTURES

3015 Main Street, Suite 400
Santa Monica, CA 90405

**Phone:** 310-279-4000
**Fax:** 310-279-4001
**Email:** info@myriadpictures.com
**Website:** www.myriadpictures.com
**IMDB:** www.imdb.com/company/co0033226

**Submission Policy:** Does not accept any unsolicited material
**Genre:** Comedy, Drama, Fantasy, Horror, Memoir & True Stories, Romance
**Focus:** Feature Films
**Year Established:** 1998

### Juliana Dacunha
**Title:** Office Assistant
**Email:** myriadasst@gmail.com

### Kirk D'Amico
**Title:** CEO
**IMDB:** www.imdb.com/name/nm0195136

### Ari Haas
**Title:** Director, Production & Acquisitions
**IMDB:** www.imdb.com/name/nm0351907

## NALA FILMS

2016 Broadway Place
Santa Monica, CA 90404

**Phone:** 310-264-2555
**Email:** info@nalafilms.com
**Website:** www.nalafilms.com

**Submission Policy:** Does not accept any unsolicited material
**Genre:** Drama, Thriller
**Focus:** Feature Films, TV

### Emilio Barroso
**Title:** CEO
**IMDB:** www.imdb.com/name/nm1950898

### Blair Richman
**Title:** Creative Executive
**IMDB:** www.imdb.com/name/nm3923771

### Rudy Scalese
**Title:** Vice-President of Development & Production
**IMDB:** www.imdb.com/name/nm0768800

## NANCY TENENBAUM FILMS

43 Lyons Plain Rd Weston, CT 06883

**Phone:** 203-221-6830
**Fax:** 203-221-6832
**Email:** ntfilms2@aol.com
**IMDB:** http://www.imdb.com/company/co0012648/?ref_=fn_al_co_1

**Submission Policy:** Accepts query letter from unproduced, unrepresented writers via email
**Genre:** Comedy, Drama
**Focus:** Feature Films
**Year Established:** 1996

**Meredith Hall**
**Title:** Director of Development

**Nancy Tenenbaum**
**Title:** President
**Assistant:** Lyndsy Celestino

## NBC PRODUCTIONS

3000 W Alameda Ave
Burbank, CA 91523-0001
USA

**Phone:** 818-840-4444
**Website:** http://www.nbcuni.com/
**IMDB:** http://www.imdb.com/company/co0065874/?ref_=fn_al_co_1

**Submission Policy:** Does not accept any unsolicited material
**Genre:** Action, Comedy, Crime, Documentary, Drama, Family, Fantasy, Feature Films, Horror, Memoir & True Stories, Romance, Science Fiction, Thriller, TV, TV Drama, TV Sitcom
**Focus:** Feature Films, Television
**Year Established:** 1947

## NBC STUDIOS

3000 W Alameda Ave
Burbank, CA 91523-0001
USA

**Phone:** 818-526-7000
**Website:** http://www.nbcuni.com/
**IMDB:** http://www.imdb.com/company/co0022762/?ref_=fn_al_co_1

**Submission Policy:** Does not accept any unsolicited material

**Genre:** Action, Comedy, Crime, Detective, Documentary, Drama, Feature Films, Memoir & True Stories, Thriller, TV, TV Drama, TV Sitcom
**Focus:** Feature Films, Television
**Year Established:** 1950

## NBCUNIVERSAL

30 Rockefeller Plaza
New York, NY 10112

**Phone:** 212-664-4444
**Website:** http://www.nbcumv.com/mediavillage/

**Genre:** Crime, Documentary, Drama, Feature Films, Period, Reality, Thriller, TV, TV Sitcom
**Focus:** Feature Films, Television
**Year Established:** 2009

**Dan Berkowitz**
**Title:** Manager of Product Development for Interactive Television

**Steve Burke**
**Title:** President
**IMDB:** http://www.imdb.com/name/nm4446434/?ref_=fn_al_nm_1

**Jon Dakss**
**Title:** Vice President of Product Development for Interactive Television

**Jessica Franks**
**Title:** Development Executive

**Pearlena Igbokwe**
**Title:** Executive Vice President of Drama Development
**IMDB:** http://www.imdb.com/name/nm2303684/?ref_=fn_al_nm_1

**Marci Klein**
**Title:** Executive Producer
**IMDB:** http://www.imdb.com/name/nm0458885/?ref_=fn_al_nm_1

**Josie Ventura**
**Title:** Vice President of Production

## NBC UNIVERSAL TELEVISION

100 Universal City Plaza Building 1320, Suite 2C
Universal City, CA 91608

**Phone:** 818-777-1000
**Fax:** 818-866-1430
**Website:** http://www.nbcuni.com/

**IMDB:** http://www.imdb.com/company/
co0129175/?ref_=fn_al_co_1

**Submission Policy:** Does not accept any unsolicited material
**Genre:** Action, Animation, Comedy, Crime, Detective, Documentary, Drama, Family, Fantasy, Feature Films, Horror, Reality, Science Fiction, Thriller, TV, TV Drama, TV Sitcom
**Focus:** Feature Films, Television
**Year Established:** 1971

### Bela Bajaria
**Title:** Executive Vice President
**IMDB:** http://www.imdb.com/name/
nm2704347/?ref_=fn_al_nm_1

### Jerry DiCanio
**Title:** Executive Vice President of Production Operations
**IMDB:** http://www.imdb.com/name/
nm3034292/?ref_=fn_al_nm_1

### Robert Greenblatt
**Title:** Chairman
**IMDB:** http://www.imdb.com/name/
nm0338612/?ref_=fn_al_nm_1

### Fernando J. Hernandez
**Title:** Senior Vice President of Alternative Development
**IMDB:** http://www.imdb.com/name/
nm0379943/?ref_=fn_al_nm_1

### Jennifer Nicholson-Salke
**Title:** President
**IMDB:** http://www.imdb.com/name/
nm2323622/?ref_=fn_al_nm_1

### Tracey Pakosta
**Title:** Senior Vice President of Comedy
**IMDB:** http://www.imdb.com/name/
nm2770837/?ref_=fn_al_nm_1

### Russell Rothberg
**Title:** Executive Vice President of Drama
**IMDB:** http://www.imdb.com/name/
nm1160205/?ref_=fn_al_nm_1

### Erin Underhill
**Title:** Senior Vice President of Drama
**IMDB:** http://www.imdb.com/name/
nm2492623/?ref_=fn_al_nm_1

### Andrew Weil
**Title:** Vice President of Comedy Development
**IMDB:** http://www.imdb.com/name/
nm0917944/?ref_=fn_al_nm_1

## NECROPIA ENTERTAINMENT

9171 Wilshire Boulevard, Suite 300
Beverly Hills, CA 9021

**Phone:** 323-865-0547

**Submission Policy:** Does not accept any unsolicited material
**Genre:** Action, Fantasy, Horror, Myth, Science Fiction
**Focus:** Feature Films

### Guillermo de Toro
**Title:** Director
**IMDB:** www.imdb.com/name/nm0868219

## NEO ART & LOGIC

5225 Wilshire Blvd Ste. 501
Los Angeles, CA 90036

**Phone:** 323-451-2040
**Email:** aaron@neoartandlogic.com
**Website:** http://www.neoartandlogic.com/
**IMDB:** http://www.imdb.com/company/
co0038165/?ref_=fn_al_co_1

**Submission Policy:** Accepts query letter from unproduced, unrepresented writers via email
**Genre:** Action, Animation, Comedy, Documentary, Drama, Family, Fantasy, Feature Films, Horror, Science Fiction, Thriller, TV
**Focus:** Feature Films, Television
**Year Established:** 2000

### Keith Border
**Title:** Principal
**IMDB:** http://www.imdb.com/name/
nm0096176/?ref_=fn_al_nm_1

### Mike Leahy
**Title:** Principal
**IMDB:** http://www.imdb.com/name/
nm0494999/?ref_=fn_al_nm_1

### Kirk Morri
**Title:** Executive
**IMDB:** http://www.imdb.com/name/
nm0606294/?ref_=fn_al_nm_1

**Aaron Ockman**
Title: Vice President of Production
IMDB: http://www.imdb.com/name/
nm1845744/?ref_=fn_al_nm_1

**Joel Soisson**
Title: Principal
IMDB: http://www.imdb.com/name/
nm0812373/?ref_=fn_al_nm_1

## NEW AMSTERDAM ENTERTAINMENT

1133 Ave. Of The Americas
Ste. 1621 New York, NY 10036

Phone: 212-922-1930
Fax: 212-922-0674
Email: mail@newamsterdamnyc.com
Website: http://www.newamsterdamnyc.com/
IMDB: http://www.imdb.com/company/
co0010962/?ref_=fn_al_co_1

Submission Policy: Does not accept any unsolicited
material
Genre: Action, Documentary, Drama, Fantasy,
Feature Films, Horror, Science Fiction, Thriller, TV,
TV Drama
Focus: Feature Films, Television
Year Established: 1996

**Katherine Kolbert**
Title: Vice President of Acquisitions
IMDB: http://www.imdb.com/name/
nm0463946/?ref_=fn_al_nm_1

**Michael Messina**
Title: Senior Vice President
IMDB: http://www.imdb.com/name/
nm0582175/?ref_=fn_al_nm_1

**Sarah Reiner**
Title: Executive Assistant
IMDB: http://www.imdb.com/name/
nm2200017/?ref_=fn_al_nm_1

**Richard Rubinstein**
Title: CEO
IMDB: http://www.imdb.com/name/
nm0748283/?ref_=fn_al_nm_1

## NEW ARTISTS ALLIANCE

16633 Ventura Boulevard, #1440
Encino, CA 91436

Phone: 1 818 784 8341
Email: info@newartistsalliance.com
Website: www.newartistsalliance.com

Submission Policy: Accepts query letter from
unproduced, unrepresented writers via email
Genre: Action, Drama, Horror, Thriller
Focus: Feature Films
Year Established: 2003

**Gabe Cowan**
Title: Founder/Producer
Email: gabe@naafilms.com
IMDB: www.imdb.com/name/nm1410462

**John Suits**
Title: Founder/Producer
Email: john@naafilms.com
IMDB: www.imdb.com/name/nm2986811

## NEW CRIME PRODUCTIONS

1041 North Formosa Avenue
Formosa Building, Room 219
West Hollywood, CA 90016

Phone: 323-850-2525
Email: newcrime@aol.com
Website: www.newcrime.com
IMDB: www.imdb.com/company/co0079035

Submission Policy: Accepts query letter from
unproduced, unrepresented writers via email
Genre: Comedy, Drama, Romance, Thriller
Focus: Feature Films

**John Cusack**
Title: Executive
IMDB: www.imdb.com/name/nm0000131

**Grace Loh**
Title: Executive
IMDB: www.imdb.com/name/nm0517808
Assistant: Judy Heinzen

## NEW LINE CINEMA

116 North Robertson Boulevard
Los Angeles, CA 90048

Phone: 310-854-5811
Fax: 310-854-1824
Website: http://www.warnerbros.com/
IMDB: http://www.imdb.com/company/
co0046718/?ref_=fn_al_co_1

**Submission Policy:** Does not accept any unsolicited material
**Genre:** Action, Comedy, Crime, Documentary, Drama, Family, Fantasy, Feature Films, Memoir & True Stories, Period, Romance, Science Fiction, Thriller, TV, TV Drama
**Focus:** Feature Films, Television
**Year Established:** 1967

**Richard Brener**
**Title:** President of Production
**IMDB:** http://www.imdb.com/name/nm0107196/?ref_=fn_al_nm_1
**Assistant:** Kristin Schmidt

**Sam Brown**
**Title:** Senior Vice President of Development
**IMDB:** http://www.imdb.com/name/nm1354041/?ref_=fn_al_nm_4
**Assistant:** Celia Khong

**Michael Disco**
**Title:** Senior Vice President of Development
**Assistant:** Celia Khong

**Toby Emmerich**
**Title:** President
**IMDB:** http://www.imdb.com/name/nm0256497/?ref_=fn_al_nm_1
**Assistant:** Joshua Mack

**Walter Hamada**
**Title:** Senior Vice President of Production
**IMDB:** http://www.imdb.com/name/nm1023578/?ref_=fn_al_nm_1
**Assistant:** Victoria Palmeri

**Andrea Johnston**
**Title:** Creative Executive

**Dave Neustadter**
**Title:** Production Executive
**IMDB:** http://www.imdb.com/name/nm2692520/?ref_=fn_al_nm_1
**Assistant:** Victoria Palmeri

## NEW REGENCY FILMS

10201 W Pico Blvd
Bldg 12
Los Angeles, CA 90035

**Phone:** 310-369-8300
**Fax:** 310-969-0470

**Email:** info@newregency.com
**Website:** www.newregency.com

**Genre:** Action, Comedy, Crime, Drama, Family, Romance, Science Fiction
**Focus:** Feature Films

**Justin Lam**
**Title:** Creative Executive
**IMDB:** www.imdb.com/name/nm3528759

**David Manpearl**
**Title:** Vice President of Production
**IMDB:** www.imdb.com/name/nm1818404

**Arnon Milchan**
**Title:** Chairman
**IMDB:** www.imdb.com/name/nm0586969

**Mimi Tseng**
**Title:** CFO
**IMDB:** www.imdb.com/name/nm2303729

## NEW SCHOOL MEDIA

9229 Sunset Boulevard, Suite 301
West Hollywood, CA 90069

**Phone:** 310-858-2989
**Fax:** 310-858 1841

**Submission Policy:** Accepts query letter from unproduced, unrepresented writers
**Focus:** Feature Films

**Brian Levy**
**Title:** Manager/CEO
**IMDB:** www.imdb.com/name/nm2546392

## NEW WAVE ENTERTAINMENT

2660 West Olive Avenue
Burbank, CA 91505

**Phone:** 818-295-5000
**Fax:** 818-295-5002
**Website:** www.nwe.com

**Submission Policy:** Does not accept any unsolicited material
**Genre:** Action, Animation, Comedy, Crime, Detective, Drama, Family, Fantasy, Horror, Memoir & True Stories, Myth, Reality, Romance, Science Fiction, Sociocultural, Thriller, TV Drama, TV Sitcom
**Focus:** Feature Films, TV, Post-Production (Editing, Special Effects), Reality Programming (Reality TV,

Documentaries, Special Events, Sporting Events),
Media (Commercials/Branding/Marketing)

**Paul Apel**
Title: CEO
Phone: 1 818 295 5000
IMDB: http://pro.imdb.com/name/nm1318269/

**Gregory Woertz**
Title: Executive Vice President
Phone: +1 818 295 5000
Email: gwoertz@nwe.com
IMDB: http://pro.imdb.com/name/nm0937343/

## NICK WECHSLER PRODUCTIONS

1437 7th Street, Suite 250
Santa Monica, CA 90401

Phone: 310-309-5759
Fax: 310-309-5716
Email: info@nwprods.com
Website: www.nwprods.com

Submission Policy: Does not accept any unsolicited
material
Genre: Action, Animation, Comedy, Crime, Drama,
Family, Fantasy, Horror, Science Fiction, Thriller,
TV Drama, TV Sitcom
Focus: Feature Films, TV
Year Established: 2005

**Felicity Aldridge**
Title: Creative Executive
Email: felicity@nwprods.com
IMDB: www.imdb.com/name/nm4504820

**Elizabeth Bradford**
Title: Director of Development
Email: lizzy@nwprods.com
IMDB: www.imdb.com/name/nm4504768

**Nick Wechsler**
Title: Producer/Chairman
Email: nick@nwprods.com
IMDB: www.imdb.com/name/nm0917059

## NIGHT & DAY PICTURES

5225 Wilshire Boulevard, Suite 524
Los Angeles, CA 90036

Phone: 323-930-2212
Email: info@nightanddaypictures.com
Website: www.nightanddaypictures.com
IMDB: www.imdb.com/company/co0253348

Submission Policy: Accepts query letter from
unproduced, unrepresented writers via email
Focus: Feature Films

**Rachel Berk**
Title: Creative Executive
IMDB: www.imdb.com/company/co0157684

**Michael Roiff**
Title: President
Email: michael@nightanddaypictures.com
IMDB: www.imdb.com/name/nm1988698

## NINJA'S RUNNIN' WILD PRODUCTIONS

7024 Melrose Ave, Suite 420
Los Angeles, CA 90038

Phone: 323-937-6100

Submission Policy: Accepts scripts from produced
or represented writers
Focus: Feature Films

**Jason Barrett**
Title: Producer
IMDB: www.imdb.com/name/nm2249074

**Zac Effron**
Title: Actor/Producer
IMDB: www.imdb.com/name/nm1374980

## NORTH BY NORTHWEST ENTERTAINMENT

903 W Broadway
Spokane, WA 99201

Phone: 509-324-2949
Fax: 509-324-2959
Email: moviesales@nxnw.net
Website: www.nxnw.net

Submission Policy: Does not accept any unsolicited
material
Genre: Thriller
Focus: Feature Film

**Rich Cowen**
Title: CEO
Phone: 509-324-2949
Email: rcowan@nxnw.net
IMDB: www.imdb.com/name/nm0184616

## NOVA PICTURES

6496 Ivarene Ave.
Los Angeles, CA 90068

**Phone:** 323-462-5502
**Fax:** 323-463-8903
**Email:** pbarnett@novapictures.com
**Website:** www.novapictures.com

**Submission Policy:** Does not accept any unsolicited material
**Focus:** Feature Film

### Peter Barnett
**Title:** Executive Producer
**IMDB:** www.imdb.com/name/nm0055963

## NU IMAGE FILMS

6423 Wilshire Blvd
Los Angeles, CA 90048

**Phone:** 310-388-6900
**Fax:** 310-388-6901
**Email:** info@millenniumfilms.com
**Website:** www.millenniumfilms.com

**Submission Policy:** Does not accept any unsolicited material
**Genre:** Action, Comedy, Drama, Science Fiction
**Focus:** Feature Film

### Christine Crow
**Title:** Director of Development
**Phone:** 310-388-6900
**IMDB:** www.imdb.com/name/nm4579268

### Boaz Davidson
**Title:** President of Production
**Phone:** 310-388-6900
**IMDB:** www.imdb.com/name/nm0203246

### Mark Gill
**Title:** President
**Phone:** 310-388-6900
**IMDB:** www.imdb.com/name/nm1247584

### Joan Mao
**Title:** Director of Development
**Phone:** 310-388-6900
**IMDB:** www.imdb.com/name/nm2668002

### John Thompson
**Title:** Head of Production
**Phone:** 310-388-6900
**IMDB:** www.imdb.com/name/nm0860315

## NUYORICAN PRODUCTIONS

1100 Glendon Ave, Suite 920
Los Angeles, CA 90024

**Phone:** 310-943-6600
**Fax:** 310-943-6609

**Submission Policy:** Does not accept any unsolicited material
**Genre:** Action, Comedy, Drama, Memoir & True Stories
**Focus:** Feature Films, TV, Reality Programming (Reality TV, Documentaries, Special Events, Sporting Events), Media (Commercials/Branding/Marketing)

### Simon Fields
**Title:** Producer - Vice-President of Development
**Email:** sfasst@jlopezent.com
**IMDB:** www.imdb.com/name/nm0276353

### Jennifer Lopez
**Title:** Founder-Entertainer-Producer
**IMDB:** www.imdb.com/name/nm0000182

### Brian Schornak
**Title:** Executive Film & TV
**Email:** bsasst@jlopezent.com
**IMDB:** www.imdb.com/name/nm1935985

## O2 FILMES

Rua Baumann, 930
Vila Leopoldina
São Paulo, SP 05318-000
Brazil

**Phone:** +55 1138 39 94 00
**Fax:** +55 11 38 32 48 11
**Email:** faleconosco@o2filmes.com
**Website:** www.o2filmes.com

**Submission Policy:** Does not accept any unsolicited material
**Genre:** Documentary, Drama
**Focus:** Feature Films

### Hank Levine
**Title:** President, Producer
**Phone:** +49-162-7040135
**Email:** hanklevine@mac.com
**IMDB:** www.imdb.com/name/nm0505810

## ODD LOT ENTERTAINMENT

9601 Jefferson Boulevard, Suite A
Culver City, CA 90232

**Phone:** 310-652-0999
**Fax:** 310-652-0718
**Email:** info@oddlotent.com
**Website:** www.oddlotent.com

**Submission Policy:** Does not accept any unsolicited material
**Genre:** Drama
**Focus:** Feature Films

**Linda McDonough**
**Title:** Exec Vice-President, Production and Development
**IMDB:** www.imdb.com/name/nm1261078

**Gigi Pritzker**
**Title:** CEO
**IMDB:** www.imdb.com/name/nm0698133

## OFFSPRING ENTERTAINMENT

8755 Colgate Avenue
Los Angeles, CA 90048

**Phone:** 310-247-0019
**Fax:** 310-550-6908

**Submission Policy:** Does not accept any unsolicited material
**Genre:** Comedy, Drama, Family
**Focus:** Feature Films

**Jennifer Gibgot**
**Title:** Executive
**IMDB:** www.imdb.com/name/nm0316774

**Adam Shankman**
**Title:** Executive
**IMDB:** www.imdb.com/name/nm0788202

## OLIVE BRIDGE ENTERTAINMENT

10202 West Washington Boulevard
Culver City, CA 90232

**Phone:** 310-244-1269
**Website:** http://www.olivebridge.com/
**IMDB:** http://www.imdb.com/company/co0219609/?ref_=fn_al_co_1

**Submission Policy:** Does not accept any unsolicited material

**Genre:** Action, Comedy, Feature Films, Period, Romance, TV, TV Drama, TV Sitcom
**Focus:** Feature Films, Television
**Year Established:** 2003

**Alicia Emmrich**
**Title:** Executive (Features)
**IMDB:** http://www.imdb.com/name/nm1445355/?ref_=fn_al_nm_1

**Will Gluck**
**Title:** Principal
**IMDB:** http://www.imdb.com/name/nm0323239/?ref_=fn_al_nm_1

**Jodi Hildebrand**
**Title:** Executive (Features)
**IMDB:** http://www.imdb.com/name/nm1637492/?ref_=fn_al_nm_1

**Richard Schwartz**
**Title:** Executive (Television)
**IMDB:** http://www.imdb.com/name/nm1108160/?ref_=fn_al_nm_2

## OLMOS PRODUCTIONS INC.

500 South Buena Vista Street
Old Animation Building, Suite 1G
Burbank, CA 91521

**Phone:** 818-560-8651
**Fax:** 818-560-8655
**Email:** olmosonline@yahoo.com

**Submission Policy:** Accepts query letter from unproduced, unrepresented writers via email
**Genre:** Comedy, Drama, Family
**Focus:** Feature Films, TV, Reality Programming (Reality TV, Documentaries, Special Events, Sporting Events), Media (Commercials/Branding/Marketing)
**Year Established:** 1980

**Edward Olmos**
**Title:** President
**IMDB:** www.imdb.com/name/nm0001579

## OLYMPUS PICTURES

2901 Ocean Park Boulevard, Suite 217
Santa Monica, CA 90405

**Phone:** 310-452-3335
**Fax:** 310-452-0108

**Email:** getinfo@olympuspics.com
**Website:** www.olympuspics.com

**Submission Policy:** Accepts query letter from unproduced, unrepresented writers via email
**Focus:** Feature Films
**Year Established:** 2007

**Mandy Beckner**
**Title:** Creative Executive
**Email:** rrdecter@olympuspics.com

**Leslie Urdang**
**Title:** President, Producer
**IMDB:** www.imdb.com/name/nm0881811

## OMBRA FILMS

12444 Ventura Boulevard, Suite 103
Studio City, CA 91604

**Phone:** 818-509-0552
**Email:** info@ombrafilms.com
**Website:** www.ombrafilms.com

**Submission Policy:** Accepts query letter from unproduced, unrepresented writers via email
**Genre:** Fantasy, Horror, Thriller
**Focus:** Feature Films, TV
**Year Established:** 2011

**Jaume Serra**
**Title:** Producer
**IMDB:** www.imdb.com/name/nm1429471

**Juan Sola**
**Title:** Producer
**IMDB:** www.imdb.com/name/nm4928159

## O.N.C.

11150 Santa Monica Boulevard, Suite 450
Los Angeles, CA 90025

**Phone:** 310-477-0670
**Fax:** 310-477-7710
**Website:** www.oncentertainment.com

**Submission Policy:** Does not accept any unsolicited material
**Genre:** Action, Comedy, Crime, Family, Romance, Thriller
**Focus:** Feature Films

**Michael Nathanson**
**Title:** Producer
**Email:** michaelnathanson@oncentertainment.com

**IMDB:** www.imdb.com/name/nm0622296
**Assistant:** Robyn Altman

## ONE RACE FILMS

9100 Wilshire Boulevard
East Tower, Suite 535
Beverly Hills, CA 90212

**Phone:** 310-401-6880
**Fax:** 310-401-6890
**Email:** info@oneracefilms.com
**Website:** www.oneracefilms.com

**Submission Policy:** Accepts query letter from unproduced, unrepresented writers via email
**Genre:** Action, Crime, Science Fiction, Thriller, TV Drama
**Focus:** Feature Films, TV
**Year Established:** 1995

**Vin Diesel**
**Title:** Actor/Writer/Prodcer
**IMDB:** www.imdb.com/name/nm0004874

**Thyrale Thai**
**Title:** Marketing and New Media
**Email:** thyrale@oneracefilms.com
**IMDB:** www.imdb.com/name/nm1394166

**Samantha Vincent**
**Title:** Producer/Partner
**Email:** samantha@oneracefilms.com
**IMDB:** www.imdb.com/name/nm2176972

## OOPS DOUGHNUTS PRODUCTIONS

500 South Buena Vista Street
Old Animation Building, Room 2F8
Burbank, CA 91521

**Phone:** 323-936-9811
**Fax:** 818 560 6185
**IMDB:** www.imdb.com/company/co0248742

**Submission Policy:** Accepts query letter from unproduced, unrepresented writers
**Genre:** Feature Films, Media (Commercials/Branding/Marketing), TV

**Andy Fickman**
**Title:** Director/Producer
**IMDB:** www.imdb.com/name/nm0275698
**Assistant:** Whitney Engstrom

**Betsy Sullenger**
Title: Producer
IMDB: www.imdb.com/name/nm0998095

## OPEN CITY FILMS

55 Liberty Street
New York, NY 10005
USA

Phone: 212-255-0500
Email: oc@opencityfilms.com
Website: www.opencityfilms.com

Submission Policy: Accepts query letter from
unproduced, unrepresented writers via email
Focus: Feature Films, Reality Programming (Reality
TV, Documentaries, Special Events, Sporting
Events)

**Jason Kilot**
Title: co-president, founder
IMDB: www.imdb.com/name/nm0459852

**Joana Vicente**
Title: Co-President, Founder

## OPEN ROAD FILMS

400 South Main Street
Suite 306
Los Angeles, CA 90013

Phone: 323-353-0551
Website: http://www.openroadfilms.net
IMDB: http://www.imdb.com/company/
co0178575/?ref_=fn_al_co_1

Submission Policy: Does not accept any unsolicited
material
Genre: Action, Crime, Documentary, Drama, TV
Drama
Focus: Feature Films, Shorts
Year Established: 2002

**Denis Henry Hennelly**
Title: Principal
IMDB: http://www.imdb.com/name/
nm0377203/?ref_=fn_al_nm_1

**Mary Pat Betel**
Title: Producer

**Casey Suchan**
Title: Principal
IMDB: http://www.imdb.com/name/
nm1093063/?ref_=fn_al_nm_1

## ORIGINAL FILM

11466 San Vicente Boulevard
Los Angeles, CA 90049

Phone: 310-575-6950
Fax: 310-575-6990

Submission Policy: Accepts query letter from
unproduced, unrepresented writers
Genre: Action, Comedy, Drama
Focus: Feature Films

**Toby Ascher**
Title: Producer
IMDB: www.imdb.com/name/nm4457111

**Vivian Cannon**
Title: Television Executive
IMDB: www.imdb.com/name/nm0134279
Assistant: Ashley Deaton

**Toby Jaffe**
Title: Producer
IMDB: www.imdb.com/name/nm0003993
Assistant: Hanna Ozer

**Ori Marmur**
Title: Production Executive
IMDB: www. imdb.com/name/nm1506459
Assistant: Miguel Raya

**Jeni Mulein**
Title: Creative Executive
IMDB: www.imdb.com/name/nm2630667

## ORIGINAL MEDIA

175 Varick Street
7th Floor
New York, NY 10014

Phone: 212-683-3086
Fax: 212-683-3162
Website: www.originalmedia.com

Submission Policy: Does not accept any unsolicited
material
Genre: Comedy, Drama, Family, Feature Films,
Romance, Thriller, TV, TV Drama, TV Sitcom
Focus: Feature Films, Television

**Charlie Corwen**
Title: Founder & CEO
IMDB: www.imdb.com/name/nm1231965

**Jessica Matthews**
Title: VP of Scripted Development

**Patrick Moses**
Title: VP of Current Series

**Colleen Ocean Hall**
Title: SVP of Unscripted Development
IMDB: www.imdb.com/name/nm5066841

**Michael Saffran**
Title: COO/EVP Production & Development

**Chelsey Throwbridge**
Title: VP of Post Productions & Operations
IMDB: www.imdb.com/name/nm2399791

## OSCILLOSCOPE LABORATORIES

511 Canal Street Suite 5E
New York City, NY 10013

Phone: 212-219-4029
Fax: 212-219-9538
Email: info@oscilloscope.net
Website: www.oscilloscope.net

Submission Policy: Does not accept any unsolicited material
Genre: Drama, Feature Films, Romance
Focus: Feature Films

**Dan Berger**
Title: Head of Productions & Acquisitions
IMDB: www.imdb.com/name/nm3088964

**Aaron Katz**
Title: Executive

**David Laub**
Title: Head of Distribution & Acquisitions
IMDB: www.imdb.com/name/nm3000864

**Amanda Lebow**
Title: Digital Sales
IMDB: www.imdb.com/name/nm4144904

**Tom Sladek**
Title: Head of Home Entertainment

## O'TAYE PRODUCTIONS

12001 Ventura Place
#340
Studio City, CA 91604
USA

Phone: 1 818 232 8580
Fax: 1 818 232 8108

Submission Policy: Accepts query letter from unproduced, unrepresented writers
Focus: TV

**Jennifer Bozell**
Title: Head of Development

**Taye Diggs**
Title: Executive/partner
IMDB: www.imdb.com/name/nm0004875

## OUTERBANKS ENTERTAINMENT

1149 North Gower Street, #101
Los Angeles, CA 90038

Phone: 1 310 858 8711
Fax: 1 310 858 6947

Submission Policy: Accepts query letter from unproduced, unrepresented writers via email
Focus: Feature Films, TV

**Kevin Williamson**
Title: President
Phone: 1 310 858 8711
Email: kevin@outerbanks-ent.com
IMDB: www.imdb.com/name/nm0932078

## OUT OF THE BLUE...ENTERTAINMENT

c/o Sony Pictures Entertainment
10202 West Washington Boulevard
Astaire Building, Suite 1200
Culver City, CA 90232-3195

Phone: 310-244-7811
Fax: 310-244-1539
Email: info@outoftheblueent.com
Website: www.outoftheblueent.com

Submission Policy: Accepts query letter from unproduced, unrepresented writers via email
Focus: Feature Films, TV

**Marta Camps**
Title: Creative Executive
IMDB: www.imdb.com/name/nm2585482

**Toby Conroy**
Title: Creative Executive
IMDB: www.imdb.com/name/nm1926762

**Sidney Ganis**
Title: Founder/Executive
IMDB: www.imdb.com/name/nm0304398

## OVERBROOK ENTERTAINMENT

450 North Roxbury Drive
4th Floor
Beverly Hills, CA 90210

Phone: 310-432-2400
Fax: 310-432-2401
Website: www.overbrookent.com

Submission Policy: Accepts query letter from
unproduced, unrepresented writers
Focus: Feature Films, TV
Year Established: 1998

**Gary Glushon**
Title: Film Executive
Phone: 310-432-2400
IMDB: www.imdb.com/name/nm2237223

**Will Smith**
Title: Producer/Partner, Actor
Phone: 310-432-2400
IMDB: www.imdb.com/name/nm0000226

## OVERNIGHT PRODUCTIONS

15 Mercer Street, Suite 4
New York, NY 10013

Phone: 212-625-0530

Submission Policy: Does not accept any unsolicited
material
Focus: Feature Films
Year Established: 2008

**Clara Kim**
Title: Head of Development and Production
Phone: 212-625-0530
IMDB: www.imdb.com/name/nm3247964

**Rick Schwartz**
Title: Chairman/CEO
Phone: 212-625-0530
IMDB: www.imdb.com/name/nm0777408

## OWN: OPRAH WINFREY NETWORK

5700 Wilshire Blvd
Ste 120
Los Angeles, CA 90036

Phone: 323-602-5500
Website: www.oprah.com/own

Submission Policy: Does not accept any unsolicited
material
Genre: Animation, Documentary, Family, Reality

**Oprah Winfrey**
Title: CEO
IMDB: www.imdb.com/name/nm0001856

## OZLA PICTURES, INC.

1800 Camino Palmero Street
Los Angeles, CA 90046

Phone: 323-876-0180
Fax: 323-876-0189
Email: ozla@ozla.com
Website: www.ozla.com

Submission Policy: Does not accept any unsolicited
material
Focus: Feature Films, TV
Year Established: 1992

**Erin Eggers**
Title: Development Vice-President
Phone: 323-876-0180
IMDB: www.imdb.com/name/nm0250929

**Taka Ichise**
Title: Producer
Phone: 323-876-0180
IMDB: www.imdb.com/name/nm0406772
Assistant: Chiaki Yanagimoto

## PACIFICA INTERNATIONAL FILM & TV CORPORATION

PO Box 8329
Northridge, CA 91237

Phone: 818-831-0360
Fax: 818-831-0352

Email: pacifica@pacifica.la
Website: www.pacifica.la

**Submission Policy:** Does not accept any unsolicited material
**Focus:** Distribution

**Christine Iso**
Title: Executive Producer
IMDB: www.imdb.com/name/nm1259606

## PACIFIC STANDARD

9720 Wilshire Blvd
4th Fl
Beverly Hills, CA 90212

Phone: 1 310 777 3119
Fax: 1 310 777 0150
IMDB: www.imdb.com/company/co0373561

**Submission Policy:** Does not accept any unsolicited material
**Focus:** Feature Films
**Year Established:** 2012

**Bruna Papandrea**
Title: Producer/Partner
IMDB: www.imdb.com/name/nm0660295

**Reese Witherspoon**
Title: Actor/Producer/Partner
IMDB: www.imdb.com/name/nm0000702

## PALERMO PRODUCTIONS

c/o Twentieth Century Fox
10201 West Pico Boulevard
Building 52, Room 103
Los Angeles, CA 90064

Phone: 310-369-1900

**Submission Policy:** Accepts query letter from unproduced, unrepresented writers
**Focus:** Feature Films, TV

**John Palermo**
Title: Producer
Phone: 310-369-1911
IMDB: www.imdb.com/name/nm0657561
Assistant: Mike Belyea

## PALMSTAR ENTERTAINMENT

14622 Ventura Blvd.
Suite 755
Sherman Oaks, CA 91403

Phone: 646-277-7356
Fax: 310-469-7855
Email: contact@palmstar.com
Website: www.palmstar.com

**Submission Policy:** Does not accept any unsolicited material
**Genre:** Action, Comedy, Drama, Family, Feature Films, Memoir & True Stories, Romance, Thriller
**Focus:** Feature Films
**Year Established:** 2004

**Courtney Andrialis**
Title: Producer

**Michael Bassick**
Title: Co-CEO

**Kevin Scott Frakes**
Title: CEO
IMDB: www.imdb.com/name/nm0289694

**Josh Monkarsh**
Title: Producer
IMDB: www.imdb.com/name/nm1586268

**Stephan Paternot**
Title: Chairman
IMDB: www.imdb.com/name/nm0665456

## PALOMAR PICTURES

PO Box 491986
Los Angeles, CA 90049

Phone: 310-440-3494
Email: ad@palomarpics.com

**Submission Policy:** Does not accept any unsolicited material
**Focus:** Feature Films, TV
**Year Established:** 1992

**Aditya Ezhuthachan**
Title: Head of Development
Phone: 310-440-3494
IMDB: www.imdb.com/name/nm2149074

**Joni Sighvatsson**
Title: CEO/Producer
Phone: 310-440-3494
IMDB: www.imdb.com/name/nm0797451

## PANAY FILMS

500 S Buena Vista
Old Animation Bldg, Rm 3c-6
Burbank, CA 91521

Phone: 818-560-4265

Submission Policy: Does not accept any unsolicited
material
Genre: Action, Comedy, Drama, Fantasy, Feature
Films
Focus: Feature Films

**Derrick Beyenka**
Title: Assistant

**Adam Blum**
Title: Vice President (Production)
IMDB: www.imdb.com/name/nm3597471

**Jared Iacino**
Title: Development Executive

**Andrew Panay**
Title: Principal
IMDB: www.imdb.com/name/nm0659123
Assistant: Lukas Stuart-Fry

## PANDEMONIUM

9777 Wilshire Boulevard, Suite 700
Beverly Hills, CA 90212

Phone: 310-550-9900
Fax: 310-550-9910

Submission Policy: Accepts query letter from
unproduced, unrepresented writers via email
Focus: Feature Films

**Bill Mechanic**
Title: President/CEO
Phone: 310-550-9900
IMDB: www.imdb.com/name/nm0575312
Assistant: David Freedman

**Suzanne Warren**
Title: Vice-President Production
Phone: 310-550-9900
IMDB: www.imdb.com/name/nm0913049

## PANTHER FILMS

1888 Century Park East
14th Floor
Los Angeles, CA 90067

Phone: 424-202-6630
Fax: 310-887-1001

Submission Policy: Does not accept any unsolicited
material
Focus: Feature Films

**Lindsay Culpepper**
Phone: 424-202-6630
IMDB: www.imdb.com/name/nm0258431

**Brad Epstein**
Title: Producer/Owner
Phone: 424-202-6630
IMDB: www.imdb.com/name/nm0258431

## PAPA JOE ENTERTAINMENT

14804 Greenleaf Street
Sherman Oaks, CA 91403

Phone: 818-788-7608
Fax: 818-788-7612
Email: info@papjoefilms.com
Website: www.papjoefilms.com

Submission Policy: Accepts query letter from
unproduced, unrepresented writers via email
Focus: Feature Films, TV

**Erin Alexander**
Title: Vice-President Development & Production
Phone: 818-788-7608
IMDB: www.imdb.com/name/nm0018408
Assistant: Amelia Garrison

**Joe Simpson**
Title: CEO
Phone: 818-788-7608
IMDB: www.imdb.com/name/nm1471425
Assistant: Heath Pliler

## PARADIGM STUDIO

2701 2nd Avenue North
Seattle, WA 98109

Phone: 206-282-2161
Fax: 206-283-6433
Email: info@paradigmstudio.com
Website: www.paradigmstudio.com

**Submission Policy:** Accepts query letter from unproduced, unrepresented writers via email
**Focus:** Feature Films, TV

### John Comerford
**Title:** President
**Phone:** 206-282-2161
**IMDB:** www.imdb.com/name/nm0173766

### B Dahlia
**Title:** Manager
**Phone:** 206-282-2161
**IMDB:** www.imdb.com/name/nm1148338

## PARADOX ENTERTAINMENT

8484 Wilshire Blvd
Ste 870
Beverly Hills, CA 90211

**Phone:** 323-655-1700
**Fax:** 323-655-1720
**Email:** info@paradox entertainment.com
**Website:** http://www.paradoxentertainment.com

**Submission Policy:** Does not accept any unsolicited material
**Genre:** Action, Comedy, Drama, Fantasy, Romance, Science Fiction
**Focus:** Feature Films

### Fredrik Malmberg
**Title:** CEO & President
**IMDB:** www.imdb.com/name/nm1573406

### Janet Sheppard
**Title:** CFO
**IMDB:** www.imdb.com/name/nm5128822

### Daniel Wagner
**Title:** President of Production
**IMDB:** www.imdb.com/name/nm1016628

## PARALLEL MEDIA

301 North Canon Dr, Suite 223
Beverly Hills, CA 90210

**Phone:** 310-858-3003
**Fax:** 310-858-3034
**Email:** info@parallelmediallc.com
**Website:** www.parallelmediafilms.com

**Submission Policy:** Does not accept any unsolicited material

**Focus:** Feature Films
**Year Established:** 2006

### Tim O'Hair
**Title:** Head of Production
**Phone:** 310-858-3003
**IMDB:** www.imdb.com/name/nm1943824

## PARAMOUNT FILM GROUP

5555 Melrose Avenue
Los Angeles, CA 90038

**Phone:** 323-956-5000
**Website:** www.paramount.com

**Submission Policy:** Does not accept any unsolicited material
**Focus:** Feature Films

### Ashley Brucks
**Title:** Vice-President Creative Affairs
**IMDB:** www.imdb.com/name/nm2087318

### Marc Evans
**Title:** President of Production
**IMDB:** www.imdb.com/name/nm0263010

### Allison Small
**Title:** Creative Executive
**IMDB:** www.imdb.com/name/nm1861333

## PARAMOUNT PICTURES

5555 Melrose Ave
Los Angeles, CA 90038

**Phone:** 323-956-5000
**Website:** www.paramount.com

**Submission Policy:** Does not accept any unsolicited material
**Genre:** Action, Comedy, Crime, Drama, Family, Horror, Romance, Science Fiction, Thriller
**Focus:** Feature Film

### Mark Badagliacca
**Title:** CFO
**IMDB:** www.imdb.com/name/nm3076670

### Marc Evans
**Title:** President/Production
**IMDB:** www.imdb.com/name/nm0263010

### Brad Grey
**Title:** CEO
**IMDB:** www.imdb.com/name/nm0340522

## PARIAH

9229 Sunset Blvd
Ste 208
West Hollywood, CA 90069
USA

**Phone:** 310-461-3460
**Fax:** 310-246-9622

**Submission Policy:** Does not accept any unsolicited material
**Focus:** Feature Films, TV

### Kathy Landsberg
**Title:** Vice-President Physical Production
**Phone:** 310-461-3460
**IMDB:** www.imdb.com/name/nm0485130
**Assistant:** Ali Gordon-Goldstein

### Lauren Pfeiffer
**Title:** Director of Development
**Phone:** 310-461-3460
**IMDB:** http://pro.imdb.com/name/nm3604387/

### Gavin Polone
**Title:** Owner
**Phone:** 310-461-3460
**IMDB:** www.imdb.com/name/nm0689780
**Assistant:** Stephen Iwanyk

## PARKER ENTERTAINMENT GROUP

8581 Santa Monica Boulevard #261
West Hollywood, CA 90069

**Phone:** 323-400-6622
**Fax:** 323-400-6655
**Email:** cparker@parkerentgroup.com
**Website:** www.parkerentgroup.com

**Submission Policy:** Accepts scripts from produced or represented writers
**Focus:** Feature Films
**Year Established:** 2008

### Gregory Parker
**Title:** CEO
**Phone:** 323-400-6622
**Email:** gparker@parkerentgroup.com
**IMDB:** imdb.com/name/nm2027023

### Christopher Parker
**Title:** President
**Email:** cparker@parkerentgroup.com
**IMDB:** www.imdb.com/name/nm2034521

## PARKES/MACDONALD PRODUCTIONS

1663 Euclid Street
Santa Monica, CA 90404

**Phone:** 310-581-5990
**Fax:** 310 581 5999

**Submission Policy:** Accepts query letter from unproduced, unrepresented writers
**Focus:** Feature Films, TV
**Year Established:** 2007

### Laurie MacDonald
**Title:** Producer
**Phone:** 310-581-5990
**IMDB:** www.imdb.com/name/nm0531827

### Walter Parkes
**Title:** Producer
**Phone:** 310-581-5990
**IMDB:** www.imdb.com/name/nm0662748

## PARKWAY PRODUCTIONS

7095 Hollywood Boulevard, Suite 1009
Hollywood, CA 90028

**Phone:** 323-874-6207
**Email:** parkwayprods@aol.com

**Submission Policy:** Accepts query letter from unproduced, unrepresented writers via email
**Focus:** Feature Films, TV

### Penny Marshall
**Title:** Director/Producer
**Phone:** 323-874-6207
**IMDB:** www.imdb.com/name/nm0001508

## PARTICIPANT MEDIA

331 Foothill Road
3rd Floor
Beverly Hills, CA 90210

**Phone:** 310-550-5100
**Fax:** 310-550-5106
**Email:** info@participantproductions.com
**Website:** www.participantmedia.com

**Submission Policy:** Does not accept any unsolicited material
**Focus:** Feature Films, TV, Reality Programming (Reality TV, Documentaries, Special Events, Sporting Events)
**Year Established:** 2004

**Erik Andreasen**
Title: Senior Director of Development, Narrative Films
Phone: 310-550-5100
IMDB: www.imdb.com/name/nm1849675

**Jonathan King**
Title: Executive Vice President of Production
Phone: 310-550-5100
IMDB: www.imdb.com/name/nm2622896

## PARTIZAN ENTERTAINMENT

1545 Wilcox Avenue Suite 200
Hollywood, CA 90028

Phone: 323-468-0123
Fax: 323-468-0129
Website: www.partizan.com
IMDB: Feature Films, Television

Submission Policy: Does not accept any unsolicited material
Genre: Action, Animation, Comedy, Crime, Drama, Fantasy, Feature Films, Horror, Romance, Science Fiction, Thriller, TV
Focus: Feature Films, Television
Year Established: 1991

**Li-Wei Chu**
Title: Head of Production & Development
Email: liwei.chu@partizan.us
Assistant: Jackson Sinder

**Melissa Ross**
Title: West Coast Sales Rep
Email: melissa.ross@partizan.us

**Sheila Stepanek**
Title: Executive Producer
Email: sstepanek@partizan.us
Assistant: Andrew Miller

**Lori Stonebraker**
Title: Head of Production
Email: lstonebraker@partizan.us

**Matt Tucker**
Title: Darkroom
Email: matt.tucker@partizan.com

## PATHE PICTURES

6 Ramillies Street
4th Floor
London W1F 7TY
United Kingdom

Phone: +44 207-462-4429
Fax: +44 207-631-3568
Email: reception.desk@pathe-uk.com
Website: www.pathe-uk.com

Submission Policy: Accepts query letter from unproduced, unrepresented writers via email
Focus: Feature Films, Reality Programming (Reality TV, Documentaries, Special Events, Sporting Events)

**Mike Runagall**
Title: Senior Vice-President International Sales
Phone: +44 207-462-4429
IMDB: www.imdb.com/name/nm2553445

## PATRIOT PICTURES

PO Box 46100
West Hollywood, CA 90046

Phone: 323-874-8850
Fax: 323-874-8851
Email: info@patriotpictures.com
Website: www.patriotpictures.com

Submission Policy: Accepts query letter from unproduced, unrepresented writers via email
Focus: Feature Films, TV, Reality Programming (Reality TV, Documentaries, Special Events, Sporting Events)

**Michael Mendelsohn**
Title: Chairman/CEO
Phone: 323-874-8850
IMDB: www.imdb.com/name/nm0578861

## PCH FILM

3380 Motor Ave
Los Angeles, CA 90034

Phone: 310-841-5817
Website: www.pchfilms.com

Submission Policy: Does not accept any unsolicited material
Genre: Comedy, Romance
Focus: Feature Film

**Jane Seymour**
Title: Producer
Phone: 310-841-5817
IMDB: www.imdb.com/name/nm0005412

**Kayla Thorton**
Title: Development Manager
Phone: 310-841-5817
Email: kayla@pchfilm.com
IMDB: www.imdb.com/name/nm4267414

## PEACE ARCH ENTERTAINMENT GROUP INC.

4640 Admiralty Way, Suite 710
Marina del Rey, CA 90292

Phone: 310-776-7200
Fax: 310-823-7147
Email: info@peacearch.com
Website: www.peacearch.com

Submission Policy: Does not accept any unsolicited material
Focus: Feature Films, TV
Year Established: 1986

**Sudhanshu Saria**
Title: Vice-President, Development
Phone: 310-776-7200
Email: ssaria@peacearch.com
IMDB: www.imdb.com/name/nm2738818

## PEACE BY PEACE PRODUCTIONS

c/o Michael Katcher/CAA
2000 Avenue of the Stars
Los Angeles, CA 90067

Phone: 323-552-1097
Email: peacebypeace1@mac.com

Submission Policy: Accepts query letter from unproduced, unrepresented writers via email
Focus: Feature Films, TV

**Alyssa Milano**
Title: Producer
Phone: 323-552-1097
IMDB: www.imdb.com/name/nm0000192
Assistant: Kelly Kall

## PEGGY RAJSKI PRODUCTIONS

918 Alandele Ave
Los Angeles, CA 90036
USA

Phone: 323 634 7020
Fax: 323 634 7021

Submission Policy: Does not accept any unsolicited material
Focus: Feature Films, Reality Programming (Reality TV, Documentaries, Special Events, Sporting Events)

**Peggy Rajski**
Title: Producer
Phone: 323 634 7020
Email: rajskip@aol.com
IMDB: www.imdb.com/name/nm0707475

## PERFECT STORM ENTERTAINMENT

1850 Industrial Street, Penthouse
Los Angeles, CA 90021

Phone: 323-546-8886
Email: info@theperfectstorment.com

Submission Policy: Does not accept any unsolicited material
Focus: Feature Films

**Justin Lin**
Title: Director
IMDB: www.imdb.com/name/nm0510912

**Troy Poon**
Title: President
IMDB: www.imdb.com/name/nm1359290

## PERMUT PRESENTATIONS

3535 Hayden Avenue
4th Floor
Culver City, CA 90232
USA

Phone: 310-838-0100
Fax: 310-838-0105
Email: info@permutpres.com

Submission Policy: Accepts query letter from unproduced, unrepresented writers
Focus: Feature Films, TV

**Chris Mangano**
Title: Development Executive
Phone: 310-248-2792
IMDB: www.imdb.com/name/nm2032016

**David Permut**
Title: Producer/President
Phone: 310-248-2792
IMDB: www.imdb.com/name/nm0674303

## PHOENIX PICTURES

10203 Santa Monica Boulevard, Suite 400
Los Angeles, CA 90067

Phone: 424-298-2788
Fax: 424-298-2588
Email: info@phoenixpictures.com
Website: www.phoenixpictures.com

Submission Policy: Accepts query letter from
unproduced, unrepresented writers via email
Focus: Feature Films, TV

**Edward McGurn**
Title: Vice-President Production
Phone: 424-298-2788
IMDB: www.imdb.com/name/nm0570342

**Douglas McKay**
Title: Vice-President Production
Phone: 424-298-2788
IMDB: www.imdb.com/name/nm1305822

**Ali Toukan**
Title: Creative Executive
Phone: 424-298-2788
IMDB: www.imdb.com/name/nm4371255

## PIERCE/WILLIAMS ENTERTAINMENT

1531 14th Street
Santa Monica, CA 90404

Phone: 310-656-9440
Fax: 310-656-9441
Website: www.piercewilliams.com

Genre: Drama, Horror, Thriller
Focus: Feature Film

**Mark Williams**
Title: Executive Producer
IMDB: www.imdb.com/name/nm0931251

## PILLER/SEGAN/SHEPHERD

7025 Santa Monica Boulevard
Hollywood, CA 90038

Phone: 323-817-1100
Fax: 323-817-1131

Submission Policy: Accepts query letter from
unproduced, unrepresented writers
Focus: Feature Films, TV
Year Established: 2010

**Shawn Piller**
Title: Producer/Principal
Phone: 323-817-1100
IMDB: www.imdb.com/name/nm0683525

**Lloyd Segan**
Title: Producer/Principal
Phone: 323-817-1100
IMDB: www.imdb.com/name/nm0781912

**Scott Shepherd**
Title: Producer/Principal
Phone: 323-817-1100
IMDB: www.imdb.com/name/nm0791863

## PINK SLIP PICTURES

1314 N. Coronado St.
Los Angeles, CA 90026
USA

Phone: 213-483-7100
Fax: 213-483-7200
Email: pinkslip@earthlink.net

Submission Policy: Does not accept any unsolicited
material
Focus: Feature Films, TV

**Karen Firestone**
Title: Producer
Phone: 949-228-2354
Email: karenfirestone@hotmail.com
IMDB: www.imdb.com/name/nm0278652

**Max Wong**
Title: Producer
Phone: 213-483-7100
IMDB: www.imdb.com/name/nm0939246

## PIPELINE ENTERTAINMENT

305 2nd Ave., Suite 302
New York, NY 10003

**Phone:** 212-372-7506
**Website:** www.pipeline-talent.com

**Submission Policy:** Accepts query letter from unproduced, unrepresented writers
**Genre:** Action, Comedy, Crime, Drama, Feature Films, Thriller, TV, TV Drama, TV Sitcom
**Focus:** Feature Films, Television

**Katherine Brislin**
**Title:** Executive Assistant
**Email:** Katherine@pipeline-talent.com

**Dan De Fillipo**
**Title:** Manager/Producer
**Email:** Dan@pipeline-talent.com
**IMDB:** www.imdb.com/name/nm2496568

**Virginia Donovan**
**Title:** Director of Film Financing
**Email:** Virginia@pipeline-talent.com
**IMDB:** www.imdb.com/name/nm3270342

**Dave Marken**
**Title:** Manager/Producer
**Email:** Dave@pipeline-talent.com
**IMDB:** www.mdb.com/name/nm2441741

**Patrick Wood**
**Title:** Manager/Producer
**Email:** Patrick@pipeline-talent.com
**IMDB:** www.imdb.com/name/nm3161377

### PIXAR

1200 Park Ave
Emeryville, CA 94608

**Phone:** 510-922-3000
**Fax:** 510-922-3151
**Email:** publicity@pixar.com
**Website:** www.pixar.com
**IMDB:** www.imdb.com/company/co0017902

**Submission Policy:** Does not accept any unsolicited material
**Genre:** Animation, Comedy, Family, Fantasy
**Focus:** Feature Film

**Ed Catmull**
**Title:** President
**IMDB:** www.imdb.com/name/nm0146216

**John Lasseter**
**Title:** Cheif Creative Officer
**IMDB:** www.imdb.com/name/nm0005124

**Jim Morris**
**Title:** Producer
**IMDB:** www.imdb.com/name/nm0606640

### PLAN B ENTERTAINMENT

9150 Wilshire Boulevard, Suite 350
Beverly Hills, CA 90210

**Phone:** 310-275-6135
**Fax:** 310-275-5234

**Submission Policy:** Does not accept any unsolicited material
**Genre:** Action, Animation, Drama, Fantasy, Myth
**Focus:** Feature Films, TV
**Year Established:** 2004

**Sarah Esberg**
**Title:** Creative Executive
**Phone:** 310-275-6135
**IMDB:** www.imdb.com/name/nm1209665

**Brad Pitt**
**Title:** Principal/Actor
**Phone:** 310-275-6135
**IMDB:** www.imdb.com/name/nm0000093

### PLATFORM ENTERTAINMENT

128 Sierra Street
El Segundo, CA 90425

**Phone:** 310-322-3737
**Fax:** 310-322-3729
**Website:** www.platformentertainment.com

**Submission Policy:** Accepts query letter from unproduced, unrepresented writers
**Focus:** Feature Films
**Year Established:** 1998

**Larry Gabriel**
**Title:** Producer
**Phone:** 310-322-3737
**IMDB:** www.imdb.com/name/nm0300181

**Daniel Levin**
**Title:** Producer
**Phone:** 310-322-3737
**IMDB:** www.imdb.com/name/nm0505575

**Scott Sorrentino**
**Title:** Producer
**Phone:** 310-322-3737
**IMDB:** www.imdb.com/name/nm1391744

## PLATINUM DUNES

631 Colorado Avenue
Santa Monica, CA 90401

**Phone:** 310-319-6565
**Fax:** 310-319-6570

**Submission Policy:** Does not accept any unsolicited material
**Focus:** Feature Films, TV
**Year Established:** 2001

### Michael Bay
**Title:** Partner
**Phone:** 310-319-6565
**IMDB:** www.imdb.com/name/nm0000881

### Sean Cummings
**Title:** Assistant
**Phone:** 310-319-6565
**IMDB:** www.imdb.com/name/nm3594167

## PLAYTONE PRODUCTIONS

PO Box 7340
Santa Monica, CA 90406

**Phone:** 310-394-5700
**Fax:** 310-394-4466
**Website:** www.playtone.com

**Submission Policy:** Accepts query letter from unproduced, unrepresented writers
**Focus:** Feature Films, TV
**Year Established:** 1996

### Tom Hanks
**Title:** Partner
**Phone:** 310-394-5700
**IMDB:** www.imdb.com/name/nm0000158

## PLUM PICTURES

New York City, New York

**Phone:** 212-529-5820
**IMDB:** www.imdb.com/company/co0113146

**Submission Policy:** Does not accept any unsolicited material
**Genre:** Comedy, Drama, Feature Films
**Focus:** Feature Films
**Year Established:** 2003

### Joy Goodwin
**Title:** Head of Development
**Email:** joy@pulmpic.com
**IMDB:** www.imdb.com/name/nm2205476

## POLSKY FILMS

9220 Sunset Blvd., Suite 309
West Hollywood, CA 90069

**Phone:** 310-271-4300
**Fax:** 310-271-4301
**Email:** info@polskyfilms.com
**Website:** www.polskyfilms.com

**Submission Policy:** Does not accept any unsolicited material
**Genre:** Crime, Documentary, Drama, Feature Films
**Focus:** Feature Films

### Gabe Polsky
**Title:** Producer
**IMDB:** www.imdb.com/name/nm2126907

### Alan Polsky
**Title:** Producer
**IMDB:** www.imdb.com/name/nm2611223

### Liam Satre-Meloy
**Title:** Executive
**IMDB:** www.imdb.com/name/nm3176310

## POLYMORPHIC PICTURES

4000 Warner Boulevard
Building 81, Suite 212
Burbank, CA 91522

**Phone:** 818-954-3822

**Submission Policy:** Does not accept any unsolicited material
**Focus:** Feature Films
**Year Established:** 2010

### Polly Johnsen
**Title:** Producer/Principal
**Phone:** 818-954-3822
**IMDB:** http://www.imdb.com/name/nm1882593/

## PORCHLIGHT FILMS

94 Oxford Street
Suite 31
Darlinghurst NSW 2010
Australia

Phone: 61-2-9326-9916
Fax: 61-2-9357-1479
Email: admin@porchlightfilms.com.au
Website: www.porchlightfilms.com.au

Genre: Comedy, Crime, Drama, Feature Films, Horror, Thriller, TV, TV Drama
Focus: Feature Films, Television
Year Established: 1996

**Vincent Sheehan**
Title: Principal
Email: vincent@porchlightfilms.com.au
IMDB: www.imdb.com/name/nm0790636

**Anita Sheehan**
Title: Principal
IMDB: www.mdb.com/name/nm1618460

**Liz Watts**
Title: Principal
IMDB: www.imdb.com/name/nm0915192

## PORTERGELLER ENTERTAINMENT

6352 De Longpre Avenue
Los Angeles, CA 90028

Phone: 323-822-4400
Fax: 323-822-7270
Email: info@portergeller.com
Website: www.portergeller.com

Submission Policy: Does not accept any unsolicited material
Focus: Feature Films, TV

**Aaron Geller**
Title: Producer
Phone: 323-822-4400
IMDB: www.imdb.com/name/nm1510467

**Darryl Porter**
Title: Producer
Phone: 323-822-4400
IMDB: www.imdb.com/name/nm0692080

**Michael Tyree**
Title: Producer
Phone: 323-822-4400
IMDB: www.imdb.com/name/nm2699784

## POW! ENTERTAINMENT

9440 Santa Monica Boulevard, Suite 620
Beverly Hills, CA 90210

Phone: 310-275-9933
Fax: 310-285-9955
Email: info@powentertainment.com
Website: www.powentertainment.com

Submission Policy: Accepts query letter from unproduced, unrepresented writers via email
Focus: Feature Films, TV
Year Established: 2001

**Ron Hawk**
Title: Chief Executive Assistant
Phone: 310-275-9933
IMDB: www.imdb.com/name/nm4078012

**Stan Lee**
Title: Chief Creative Offi cer
Phone: 310-275-9933
IMDB: www.imdb.com/name/nm0498278
Assistant: Mike Kelly

## POWER UP

419 North Larchmont Boulevard #283
Los Angeles, CA 90004

Phone: 323-463-3154
Fax: 323-467-6249
Email: info@powerupfilms.org
Website: www.powerupfilms.org

Submission Policy: Accepts query letter from unproduced, unrepresented writers via email
Focus: Feature Films, TV
Year Established: 2000

**Stacy Codikow**
Title: Producer/Writer
Phone: 323-463-3154
IMDB: www.imdb.com/name/nm0168499

**Lisa Thrasher**
Title: President, Film Production & Distribution
Phone: 323-463-3154
IMDB: www.imdb.com/name/nm1511212

## PRACTICAL PICTURES

2211 Corinth Avenue, Suite 303
Los Angeles, CA 90064

Phone: 310-405-7777
Fax: 310-405-7771

Submission Policy: Does not accept any unsolicited material

**Jason Koffeman**
Title: Creative Executive
IMDB: www.imdb.com/name/nm1788896

## PRANA STUDIOS

1145 North McCadden Place
Los Angeles, CA 90038

Phone: 323-645-6500
Fax: 323-645-6710
Email: info@pranastudios.com
Website: www.pranastudios.com

Genre: Action, Animation, Comedy, Drama,
Family, Fantasy, Feature Films
Focus: Feature Films

**Kristin Dornig**
Title: Co-Creative Director & CEO
IMDB: www.imdb.com/name/nm0233921

**Arish Fyzee**
Title: Creative Director
IMDB: www.imdb.com/name/nm0299564

**Samir Hoon**
Title: President

**Jason Lust**
Title: Executive VP of Feature Films & Content
Development

**Danielle Sterling**
Title: VP of Development
IMDB: www.imdb.com/name/nm1306678

## PREFERRED CONTENT

6363 Wilshire Boulevard, Suite 350
Los Angeles, CA 90048

Phone: 323-782-9193
Email: info@preferredcontent.net
Website: www.preferredcontent.net

Submission Policy: Does not accept any unsolicited
material
Genre: Action
Focus: Feature Films

**Ross Dinerstein**
Title: Partner/Producer
IMDB: www.imdb.com/name/nm1895871

**Kevin Iwashina**
Title: Partner/Producer
IMDB: www.imdb.com/name/nm2250990

**Trace Sheehan**
Title: Head of Development
IMDB: www.imdb.com/name/nm2618717

## PRETTY MATCHES PRODUCTIONS

1100 Avenue of the Americas
G26, Suite 32
New York, NY 10036

Phone: 212-512-5755
Fax: 212-512-5716
IMDB: www.imdb.com/company/co0173730

Submission Policy: Accepts query letter from
unproduced, unrepresented writers
Genre: Comedy, Romance
Focus: Feature Films, TV, Reality Programming
(Reality TV, Documentaries, Special Events,
Sporting Events)

**Alison Benson**
Title: Producer
IMDB: www.imdb.com/name/nm3929030
Assistant: Matt Nathanson

**Sarah Parker**
Title: President
IMDB: www.imdb.com/name/nm0000572

**Benjamin Stark**
Title: Director, Development

## PRETTY PICTURES

100 Universal City Plaza
Building 2352-A, 3rd Floor
Universal City, CA 91608

Phone: 818-733-0926
Fax: 818-866-0847

Submission Policy: Does not accept any unsolicited
material
Genre: Comedy, Drama, Memoir & True Stories,
Romance, Thriller, TV Drama
Focus: Feature Films, TV

**Gail Mutrux**
Title: Producer

**Tore Schmidt**
Title: Creative Executive

## PRINCIPATO-YOUNG ENTERTAINMENT

9465 Wilshire Boulevard, Suite 900
Beverly Hills, CA 90212

**Phone:** 310-274-4474
**Fax:** 310-274-4108

**Submission Policy:** Accepts query letter from
unproduced, unrepresented writers
**Genre:** Comedy, TV Sitcom
**Focus:** Feature Films, TV

**Peter Principato**
**Title:** President
**Phone:** 310-274-4130
**Assistant:** Max Suchov

**Susan Solomon**
**Title:** Manager
**Phone:** 310-274-4408

**Tucker Voorhees**
**Title:** Manager
**Phone:** 310-432-5992

## PROSPECT PARK

2049 Century Park East #2550
Century City, CA 90067

**Phone:** 310-746-4900
**Fax:** 310-746-4890
**IMDB:** www.imdb.com/company/co0276484

**Submission Policy:** Accepts query letter from
unproduced, unrepresented writers via email
**Genre:** Reality, TV Drama
**Focus:** Feature Films, TV, Reality Programming
(Reality TV, Documentaries, Special Events,
Sporting Events)

**Laurie Ferneau**
**Title:** Director, Development, TV
**IMDB:** www.imdb.com/name/nm1017980

**Paul Frank**
**Title:** Executive Producer/Head, TV
**IMDB:** www.imdb.com/name/nm1899773

**Jeff Kwatinetz**
**Title:** Executive Producer
**IMDB:** www.imdb.com/name/nm0477153

## PROTOZOA

104 North 7th Street
Brooklyn, NY 11211

**Phone:** 718-388-5280
**Fax:** 718-388-5425
**Website:** www.aronofsky.net

**Submission Policy:** Does not accept any unsolicited
material
**Genre:** Action, Fantasy, Horror, Science Fiction,
Thriller
**Focus:** Feature Films

**Darren Aronofsky**
**Title:** Director/Producer/Writer/CEO
**IMDB:** www.imdb.com/name/nm0004716

**Ali Mendes**
**Title:** Director Of Development
**Email:** ali@protozoa.com
**IMDB:** www.imdb.com/name/nm4070559

## PURE GRASS FILMS LTD.

1st Floor, 16 Manette Street
London, W1D 4AR

**Email:** info@puregrassfilms.com
**Website:** www.puregrassfilms.com

**Submission Policy:** Accepts query letter from
unproduced, unrepresented writers via email
**Genre:** Action, Drama, Horror, Memoir & True
Stories, Science Fiction, Thriller
**Focus:** Feature Films, Post-Production (Editing,
Special Effects)

**Ben Grass**
**Title:** CEO/Producer
**IMDB:** www.imdb.com/name/nm2447240

## QED INTERNATIONAL

1800 North Highland Ave, 5th Floor
Los Angeles, CA 90028

**Phone:** 323-785-7900
**Fax:** 323-785-7901
**Email:** info@qedintl.com
**Website:** www.qedintl.com

**Submission Policy:** Accepts scripts from
unproduced, unrepresented writers
**Genre:** Action, Comedy, Crime, Drama, Fantasy,
Horror, Myth, Romance, Thriller

**Focus:** Feature Films
**Year Established:** 2005

**Bill Block**
Title: Founder/CEO
IMDB: www.imdb.com/name/nm1088848

## QUADRANT PICTURES

9229 Sunset Boulevard, Suite 225
West Hollywood, CA 90069

**Phone:** 424-244-1860
**Email:** assistant@quadrantpictures.com
**Website:** www.quadrantpictures.com

**Submission Policy:** Accepts query letter from
unproduced, unrepresented writers via email
**Genre:** Action, Drama, Family, Horror, Science
Fiction, Thriller, TV Drama
**Focus:** Feature Films, TV
**Year Established:** 2011

**Doug Davison**
Title: President/Producer
IMDB: www.imdb.com/name/nm0205713

**John Schwartz**
Title: Producer
IMDB: www.imdb.com/name/nm1862748

## RABBITBANDINI PRODUCTIONS

3500 W Olive Ave
Ste 1470
Burbank, CA 91505

**Phone:** 818-953-7510
**Website:** www.rabbitbandinifilms.com

**Submission Policy:** Does not accept any unsolicited
material
**Genre:** Thriller
**Focus:** Feature Films

**James Franco**
Title: Executive Partner
IMDB: www.imdb.com/name/nm0290556

**Richie Hill**
Title: Producer
Email: richiehill44@gmail.com
IMDB: www.imdb.com/name/nm2002081

**Vince Jolivette**
Title: Executive Partner
Email: vince@rabbitbandini.com
IMDB: www.imdb.com/name/nm0006683

**Miles Levy**
Title: Executive Partner
Email: miles@jameslevymanagement.com
IMDB: www.imdb.com/name/nm0506553

## RADAR PICTURES

10900 Wilshire Boulevard, Suite 1400
Los Angeles, CA 90024

**Phone:** 310-208-8525
**Fax:** 310-208-1764
**Email:** info@radarpictures.com
**Website:** www.radarpictures.com
**IMDB:** www.imdb.com/company/co0023815

**Submission Policy:** Does not accept any unsolicited
material
**Genre:** Action, Drama
**Focus:** Feature Films

**Ted Field**
Title: Chairman
IMDB: www.imdb.com/name/nm0276059

**Thomas Van Dell**
Title: Partner/Producer
IMDB: www.imdb.com/name/nm0886033

## @RADICAL MEDIA

1630 12th Street
Santa Monica, CA 90404

435 Hudson Street, 6th Floor
New York, NY 10014

**Phone:** 310-664-4500/ 212-461-1500
**Fax:** 310-664-4600/ 212-462-1600
**Email:** info@radicalmedia.com
**Website:** www.radicalmedia.com
**IMDB:** www.imdb.com/company/co0029540

**Submission Policy:** Accepts query letter from
produced or represented writers

**Sidney Beaumont**
Title: NY - Executive Producer
Email: beaumont@radicalmedia.com

**Brent Eveleth**
Title: NY - Group Creative Director
Email: eveleth@radicalmedia.com

**Jon Kamen**
Title: NY - Chairman & CEO
Email: hammer@radicalmedia.com

**Adam Neuhaus**
Title: LA - Senior Director & Development
Email: neuhaus@radicalmedia.com

**Frank Scherma**
Title: LA - President
Email: bina@radicalmedia.com

**Cathy Shannon**
Title: NY - Executive Vice President
Email: shannon@radicalmedia.com

**Bob Stein**
Title: NY - Head of Production
Email: stein@radicalmedia.com

**Justin Wilkes**
Title: LA - President of Media & Entertainment
Email: wilkes@radicalmedia.com

## RAINBOW FILM COMPANY/RAINBOW RELEASING

1301 Montanta Avenue, Suite A
Santa Monica, CA 90403

Phone: 310-271-0202
Fax: 310-271-2753
Email: therainbowfilmco@aol.com

Submission Policy: Accepts query letter from unproduced, unrepresented writers via email
Genre: Comedy, Drama, Memoir & True Stories, Romance
Focus: Feature Films

**Lauren Beck**
Title: Development

**Henry Jaglom**
Title: President

**Sharon Kohn**
Title: Vice-President, Distribution

## RAINMAKER ENTERTAINMENT

200-2025 West Broadway
Vancouver, BC
Canada
V6J 1Z6

Phone: 604-714-2600
Fax: 604-714-2641
Website: www.rainmaker.com
IMDB: www.imdb.com/company/co0298750

Submission Policy: Does not accept any unsolicited material
Genre: Animation, Family, Fantasy
Focus: Feature Films, TV

**Kimberly Dennison**
Title: Director of Development

**Kylie Ellis**
Title: Director of Production

**Craig Graham**
Title: Executive Chairman & CEO

**Michael Hefferon**
Title: President

## RAINMAKER FILMS INC.

4212 San Felipe St 399
Houston, TX 77027

Phone: 832-287-9372
Email: rainmaker.inc@gmail.com

Submission Policy: Accepts query letter from unproduced, unrepresented writers via email
Genre: Science Fiction
Focus: Feature Films

**Grant Gurthie**
Title: President - Executive Producer
IMDB: www.imdb.com/name/nm0349262

## RAINSTORM ENTERTAINMENT, INC.

345 North Maple Dr, Suite 105
Beverly Hills, CA 90210

Phone: 818-269-3300
Fax: 310-496-0223
Email: info@rainstormentertainment.com
Website: www.rainstormentertainment.com

Submission Policy: Accepts query letter from unproduced, unrepresented writers via email

**Focus:** Feature Films, TV, Reality Programming
(Reality TV, Documentaries, Special Events,
Sporting Events)

**Alec Rossel**
**Title:** Development Executive
**Phone:** 818-269-3300
**IMDB:** www.imdb.com/name/nm1952377

## RALPH WINTER PRODUCTIONS

10201 West Pico Boulevard Building 6 suite 1
Los Angeles, CA 90035

**Phone:** 310-369-4723
**Fax:** 310-969-0727

**Submission Policy:** Does not accept any unsolicited
material
**Genre:** Action, Comedy
**Focus:** Feature Films

**Ralph Winter**
**Title:** Founder/Producer
**IMDB:** www.imdb.com/name/nm0003515

**Susana Zepeda**
**Title:** President
**Email:** susana.zepeda@fox.com
**IMDB:** www.imdb.com/name/nm0954978

## RANDOM HOUSE FILMS

1745 Broadway
New York, NY 10019

**Phone:** 212-782-9000
**Website:** www.randomhouse.com

**Submission Policy:** Accepts query letter from
unproduced, unrepresented writers
**Focus:** Feature Films
**Year Established:** 2007

**Valerie Cates**
**Title:** Executive Story Editor
**Phone:** 212-782-9000
**IMDB:** www.imdb.com/name/nm1161200

**Brady Emerson**
**Title:** Story Editor
**Phone:** 212-782-9000
**IMDB:** www.imdb.com/name/nm3031708

**Christina Malach**
**Title:** Story Editor
**Phone:** 212-782-9000
**IMDB:** www.imdb.com/name/nm409)138

## RAT ENTERTAINMENT

100 Universal City Plz
Bungalow 5196
Universal City, CA 91608

**Phone:** 818-733-4603
**Fax:** 818-733-4612

**Submission Policy:** Accepts query letter from
unproduced, unrepresented writers
**Focus:** Feature Films, TV, Reality Prcgramming
(Reality TV, Documentaries, Special Events,
Sporting Events)

**Agustine Calderon**
**Title:** Creative Executive

**John Cheng**
**Title:** Head of Feature Development
**Phone:** 818-733-4603
**IMDB:** www.imdb.com/name/nm176738

**Brett Ratner**
**Title:** Director/Producer/Chairman
**Phone:** 818-733-4603
**IMDB:** www.imdb.com/name/nm071 840
**Assistant:** Anita S. Chang

**Jay Stern**
**Title:** President
**IMDB:** www.imdb.com/name/nm082''731

## RCR MEDIA GROUP

1169 Loma Linda Drive,
Beverly Hills, CA 90210

**Phone:** 310-273-3888
**Fax:** 310-273-2888
**Email:** info@rcrmg.com
**Website:** www.rcrmediagroup.com

**Submission Policy:** Does not accept a ly unsolicited
material
**Genre:** Action, Comedy, Crime, Drama, Feature
Films, Horror, Romance, Science Ficti)n, Thriller
**Focus:** Feature Films

**Rui Costa Reis**
Title: Chairman
IMDB: www.imdb.com/name/nm3926066

**Ricardo Costa Reis**
Title: Producer/Creative Executive
IMDB: www.imdb.com/name/nm4579160

**Eliad Josephson**
Title: CEO
IMDB: www.imdb.com/name/nm4035615

## RCR PICTURES

8840 Wilshire Boulevard
Beverly Hills, CA 90211

Phone: 310-358-3234
Fax: 310-358-3109

Submission Policy: Accepts query letter from
unproduced, unrepresented writers
Genre: Crime, Drama, Romance, Science Fiction
Focus: Feature Films

**Robin Schorr**
Title: Producer
IMDB: www.imdb.com/name/nm0774908

## RECORDED PICTURE COMPANY

24 Hanway Street
London W1T 1UH
United Kingdom

Phone: +44 20-7636-2251
Fax: +44 20-7636-2261
Email: rpc@recordedpicture.com
Website: www.recordedpicture.com

Submission Policy: Accepts scripts from produced
or represented writers
Focus: Feature Films

**Alainee Kent**
Title: Senior Development Executive
Phone: +44 20 7636 2251
IMDB: www.imdb.com/name/nm1599134

**Jeremy Thomas**
Title: Producer/Chairman
Phone: +44 20 7636 2251
IMDB: www.imdb.com/name/nm0859016
Assistant: Karin Padgham

**Peter Watson**
Title: Managing Director
Phone: +44 20 7636 2251
IMDB: www.imdb.com/name/nm0914838

## RED CROWN PRODUCTIONS

630 5th Ave, Suite 2505
New York, NY 10111

Phone: 212-355-9200
Fax: 212-719-7029
Email: info@redcrownproductions.com
Website: www.redcrownproductions.com

Submission Policy: Does not accept any unsolicited
material
Genre: Comedy, Drama
Focus: Feature Films
Year Established: 2010

**Daniel Crown**
Title: Founder/Producer
Phone: 212-355-9200
Email: dcrown@crownnyc.com
IMDB: www.imdb.com/name/nm3259054

**Alish Erman**
Title: Creative Executive
Email: alish@redcrownproductions.com
IMDB: www.imdb.com/name/nm2289542

**Riva Marker**
Title: Head of Production & Development
Email: riva@redcrownproductions.com
IMDB: www.imdb.com/name/nm1889450

## RED GIANT MEDIA

535 5th Avenue, 5th Floor
New York, NY 10017

Phone: 212-989-7200
Fax: 212-937-3505
Email: info@redgiantmedia.com
Website: www.redgiantmedia.com

Submission Policy: Does not accept any unsolicited
material
Genre: Science Fiction
Focus: Feature Films
Year Established: 2008

**Kevin Fox**
Title: Executive Producer/Writer

**Isen Robbins**
Title: Producer

**Aimee Schoof**
Title: Producer

## RED GRANITE PICTURES

9255 Sunset Boulevard, Suite 710
Los Angeles, CA 90069

Phone: 310-703-5800
Fax: 310-246-3849
IMDB: www.imdb.com/company/co0325207

Submission Policy: Does not accept any unsolicited
material
Genre: Drama
Focus: Feature Films

**Riza Aziz**
Title: CEO
IMDB: www.imdb.com/name/nm4265383

**Joe Gatta**
Title: President of Production
IMDB: www.imdb.com/name/nm2211910

## RED HEN PRODUCTIONS

3607 W Magnolia
Ste. L
Burbank, CA 91505

Phone: 818-563-3600
Fax: 818-787-6637
Website: www.redhenprods.com

Submission Policy: Accepts query letter from
unproduced, unrepresented writers
Genre: Drama, Thriller

**Stuart Gordon**
Title: Director/Writer/Producer
Phone: 818-563-3600
IMDB: www.imdb.com/name/nm0002340

## RED HOUR FILMS

629 North La Brea Avenue
Los Angeles, CA 90036

Phone: 323-602-5000
Fax: 323-602 5001
Website: www.redhourfilms.com

Submission Policy: Does not accept any unsolicited
material
Genre: Action, Comedy, Family, Fantasy, Science
Fiction
Focus: Feature Films, TV

**Robin Mabrito**
Title: Story Editor
Email: robin@redhourfilms.com
IMDB: www.imdb.com/name/nm3142663

**Ben Stiller**
Title: Writer/Director/Producer
IMDB: www.imdb.com/name/nm0001774

**Conor Welch**
Title: Director of Development
Email: conor@redhourfilms.com
IMDB: www.imdb.com/name/nm3137428

## RED OM FILMS, INC.

3000 Olympic Boulevard
Building 3, Suite 2330
Santa Monica, CA 90404

Phone: 310-594-3467

Submission Policy: Does not accept any unsolicited
material
Genre: Action, Comedy, Drama, Family
Focus: Feature Films, TV

**Lisa Gillian**
Title: Producer
IMDB: www.imdb.com/name/nm0731359

**Julia Roberts**
Title: Actress/Producer
IMDB: www.imdb.com/name/nm0000210

**Philip Rose**
Title: Producer
IMDB: www.imdb.com/name/nm0741615

## RED PLANET PICTURES

13 Doolittle Mill
Froghall Road
Ampthill, Bedfordshire MK45 2ND
UK

Phone: +44 (0)1525 408 970
Fax: +44 (0)1525 408 971
Email: info@redplanetpictures.co.uk
Website: www.redplanetpictures.co.uk

**Submission Policy:** Does not accept any unsolicited material
**Genre:** Crime, Drama, TV Drama
**Focus:** TV

### Simon Winstone
**Title:** Director of Development
**Email:** simonwinstone@redplanetpictures.co.uk
**IMDB:** www.imdb.com/name/nm0935654

## RED WAGON ENTERTAINMENT

10202 West Washington Boulevard
Hepburn Building West
Culver City, CA 90232-3195

**Phone:** 310-244-4466
**Fax:** 310-244-1480

**Submission Policy:** Does not accept any unsolicited material
**Genre:** Animation, Drama, Fantasy, Horror
**Focus:** Feature Films, TV

### Lucy Fisher
**Title:** Producer
**Phone:** 310 244 4466
**IMDB:** www.imdb.com/name/nm0279651

### Rachel Shane
**Title:** Executive Vice-President
**Phone:** 310 244 4466
**IMDB:** www.imdb.com/name/nm1247594

### Douglas Wick
**Title:** Producer
**Phone:** 310 244 4466
**IMDB:** www.imdb.com/name/nm0926824

## REGENCY ENTERPRISES

10201 West Pico Boulevard
Building 12
Los Angeles, CA 90035

**Phone:** 310-369-8300
**Fax:** 310-969-0470
**Email:** info@newregency.com
**Website:** www.newregency.com
**IMDB:** www.imdb.com/company/co0021592

**Submission Policy:** Accepts query letter from unproduced, unrepresented writers via email
**Focus:** Feature Films

### Ryan Horrigan
**Title:** Director of Development
**IMDB:** www.imdb.com/name/nm1673839

### Michelle Kroes
**Title:** Director, Feature & Literary Development
**IMDB:** www.imdb.com/name/nm3129676

## REGENT ENTERTAINMENT

10940 Wilshire Boulevard, Suite 1600
Los Angeles, CA 90024

**Phone:** 310-806-4290
**Fax:** 310 806 6351
**Email:** info@regententertainment.com
**Website:** www.regententertainment.com
**IMDB:** www.imdb.com/company/co0045895

**Submission Policy:** Accepts query letter from unproduced, unrepresented writers via email
**Genre:** Action, Drama, Horror, Science Fiction
**Focus:** Feature Films, TV

### David Millbern
**Title:** Director of Development
**Phone:** 310-806-4290
**IMDB:** www.imdb.com/name/nm0587778

### Roxana Vatan
**IMDB:** www.imdb.com/name/nm2985872

## REHAB ENTERTAINMENT

1416 North La Brea Avenue
Hollywood, CA 90028

**Phone:** 323-645-6444
**Fax:** 323-645-6445
**Email:** info@rehabent.com
**Website:** www.rehabent.com

**Submission Policy:** Accepts query letter from unproduced, unrepresented writers via email
**Focus:** Feature Films

### Brett Coker
**Title:** Production Executive

### John Hyde
**Title:** President

## REINER/GREISMAN

335 North Maple Drive, Suite 350
Beverly Hills, CA 90210

**Phone:** 310-285-2300
**Fax:** 310-285-2345

**Submission Policy:** Accepts query letter from unproduced, unrepresented writers
**Genre:** Comedy, Drama
**Focus:** Feature Films

**Alan Greisman**
**Title:** Producer
**Phone:** 310-205-2766

**Pam Jones**
**Title:** Assistant to Rob Reiner
**Phone:** 310-285-2352

**Rob Reiner**
**Title:** Director/Producer
**Phone:** 310-285-2328
**IMDB:** www.imdb.com/name/nm0001661
**Assistant:** Pam Jones

## RELATIVITY MEDIA, LLC

9242 Beverly Boulevard, Suite 300
Beverly Hills, CA 90210

**Phone:** 310-724-7700
**Fax:** 310-724-7701

**Submission Policy:** Accepts query letter from produced or represented writers
**Focus:** Feature Films, TV, Reality Programming (Reality TV, Documentaries, Special Events, Sporting Events), Media (Commercials/Branding/ Marketing)

**Jonathan Karsh**
**Title:** Sr. Vice-President, Creative Affairs

**Julie Link**
**Title:** Sr. Vice-President, Development

## RELEVANT ENTERTAINMENT GROUP

10323 Santa Monica Blvd
Ste 101
Los Angeles, CA 90025

**Phone:** 310-277-0853

**Genre:** Comedy, Feature Films
**Focus:** Feature Films, TV

## REMEMBER DREAMING, LLC

8252 1/2 Santa Monica Boulevard, Suite B
West Hollywood, CA 90046

**Phone:** 323-654-3333

**Submission Policy:** Accepts query letter from unproduced, unrepresented writers
**Focus:** Feature Films, Reality Programming (Reality TV, Documentaries, Special Events, Sporting Events)

**Courtney Brin**
**Title:** Director, Production & Development
**Email:** courtney@freefall-films.com

**Stan Spry**
**Title:** President

## RENAISSANCE PICTURES

315 South Beverly Drive, Suite 216
Beverly Hills, CA 90210

**Phone:** 310-785-3900
**Fax:** 310-785-9176

**Submission Policy:** Accepts query letter from unproduced, unrepresented writers
**Genre:** Action, Drama, Fantasy, Horror
**Focus:** Feature Films, TV

**Sam Raimi**
**Title:** Director/Executive Producer

**J.R. Young**
**Title:** Producer, Creative Executive

## RENART FILMS

135 Grand St.
3rd Floor
New York, NY 10013

**Phone:** 212-274-8224
**Fax:** 212-274-8229
**Email:** info@renartfilms.com
**Website:** www.renartfilms.com

**Submission Policy:** Accepts query letter from produced or represented writers
**Genre:** Comedy, Drama, Feature Films, Romance
**Focus:** Feature Films

**Julie Christeas**
**Title:** EVP of Development & Production
**Email:** julie@renartfilms.com
**IMDB:** www.imdb.com/name/nm2184127

**Caroline Dillon**
**Title:** Creative Director
**Email:** caroline@renartfilms.com
**IMDB:** www.imdb.com/name/nm0226974

**Tim Duff**
**Title:** President
**Email:** tim@renartfilms.com
**IMDB:** www.imdb.com/name/nm2178779

**TJ Federico**
**Title:** EVP of Production
**Email:** tj@renartfilms.com

**Dan Schechter**
**Title:** EVP of Development
**Email:** dan@renartfilms.com

## RENEE MISSEL PRODUCTIONS

2376 Adrian Street, Suite A
Newbury Park, CA 91320

**Phone:** 310-463-0638
**Fax:** 805-669-4511
**Email:** fi lmtao@aol.com

**Submission Policy:** Accepts query letter from unproduced, unrepresented writers via email
**Focus:** Feature Films
**Year Established:** 1983

**Renee Missel**
**Title:** Producer

**Bridget Stone**
**Title:** Story Editor

## RENEE VALENTE PRODUCTIONS

13547 Ventura Boulevard, #195
Sherman Oaks, CA 91423

**Phone:** 310-472-5342
**Email:** valenteprod@aol.com

**Submission Policy:** Accepts query letter from unproduced, unrepresented writers via email
**Focus:** Feature Films, TV

**Renee Valente**
**Title:** Executive Producer

## RENEGADE ANIMATION, INC.

111 East Broadway, Suite 208
Glendale, CA 91205

**Phone:** 818-551-2351
**Fax:** 818-551-2350
**Email:** contactus@renegadeanimation.com
**Website:** www.renegadeanimation.com

**Submission Policy:** Accepts query letter from unproduced, unrepresented writers via email
**Focus:** TV

**Ashley Postlewaite**
**Title:** Vice-President/Executive Producer

**Darrell Van Citters**
**Title:** President/Direct

## RENFIELD PRODUCTIONS

c/o Th e Lot
1041 North Formosa Avenue
Writer's Building, Suite 321
West Hollywood, CA 90046

**Phone:** 323-850-3905
**Fax:** 323-850-3907
**Email:** development@renfieldproductions.com
**Website:** www.renfieldproductions.com

**Submission Policy:** Accepts query letter from unproduced, unrepresented writers via email
**Genre:** Action, Animation, Comedy, Drama, Family, Horror
**Focus:** TV, Reality Programming (Reality TV, Documentaries, Special Events, Sporting Events)

**Mark Alan**
**Title:** Development Executive
**Phone:** 323-850-3905
**IMDB:** www.imdb.com/name/nm1591345

**Joe Dante**
**Title:** Director/Producer
**Phone:** 323-850-3905
**IMDB:** http://www.imdb.com/name/nm0001102/

**T.L. Kittle**
**Title:** Director, Development
**Phone:** 323-850-3905
**IMDB:** www.imdb.com/name/nm1473622

## REVEILLE, LLC/SHINE INTERNATIONAL

1741 Ivar Avenue
Los Angeles, CA 90028

**Phone:** 323-790-8000
**Fax:** 323-790-8399

**Submission Policy:** Does not accept any unsolicited material
**Focus:** TV, Reality Programming (Reality TV, Documentaries, Special Events, Sporting Events)

**Carolyn Bernstein**
Title: Executive Vice-President, Scripted TV
IMDB: www.imdb.com/name/nm3009190

**Todd Cohen**
Title: Vice-President, Domestic Scripted TV

**Rob Cohen**
Title: Vice-President Creative Affairs

## REVELATIONS ENTERTAINMENT

1221 Second Street
4th Floor
Santa Monica, CA 90401

**Phone:** 310-394-3131
**Fax:** 310-394-3133
**Email:** info@revelationsent.com
**Website:** www.revelationsent.com

**Submission Policy:** Does not accept any unsolicited material
**Genre:** Action, Detective, Drama, Family
**Focus:** Feature Films, TV

**Morgan Freeman**
Title: President/Actor/Producer
Phone: 310-394-3131
IMDB: www.imdb.com/name/nm0000151

**Lori McCreary**
Title: CEO/Producer
Phone: 310-394-3131
IMDB: www.imdb.com/name/nm0566975

**Tracy Mercer**
Title: Vice-President, Development
Phone: 310-394-3131
IMDB: www.imdb.com/name/nm0580312

## REVOLUTION FILMS

9-A Dallington St
London EC1V 0BQ
UK

**Phone:** +44-20-7566-0700
**Email:** email@revolution-films.com
**Website:** www.revolution-films.com
**IMDB:** www.mdb.com/company/co0103733

**Submission Policy:** Does not accept any unsolicited material
**Genre:** Action, Comedy, Drama, Feature Films, Memoir & True Stories, Period, Thriller
**Focus:** Feature Films

**Andrew Eaton**
Title: Producer
IMDB: www.imdb.com/name/nm0247787

**Michael Winterbottom**
Title: Producer
IMDB: www.imdb.com/name/nm0935863

## RHINO FILMS

10501 Wilshire Boulevard, Suite 814
Los Angeles, CA 90024

**Phone:** 310-441-6557
**Fax:** 310-441-6584
**Email:** contact@rhinofilms.com
**Website:** www.rhinofilms.com

**Submission Policy:** Accepts query letter from unproduced, unrepresented writers via email
**Focus:** Feature Films

**Stephen Nemeth**
Title: CEO
Email: stephennemeth@rhinofi lms.com
IMDB: www.imdb.com/name/nm0625932

**Betsy Stahl**
Email: betsystahl@rhinofi lms.com
IMDB: www.imdb.com/name/nm0821439

## RHOMBUS MEDIA

99 Spadina Ave
Ste 600
Toronto, ON M5V 3P8
Canada

**Phone:** 416-971-7856
**Fax:** 416-971-9647

**Email:** info@rhombusmedia.com
**Website:** www.rhombusmedia.com

**Submission Policy:** Does not accept any unsolicited material
**Genre:** Action, Comedy, Crime, Horror, Science Fiction, Thriller
**Focus:** Feature Films

**Fraser Ash**
**Title:** Assosiate Producer
**IMDB:** www.imdb.com/name/nm4350218

**Kevin Krikst**
**Title:** Assosiate Producer
**IMDB:** www.imdb.com/name/nm2844322

**Larry Weistein**
**Title:** Co-Founder
**IMDB:** www.imdb.com/name/nm0918452

## RHYTHM & HUES

2100 E Grand Ave
El Segundo, CA 90245

**Phone:** 310-448-7500
**Fax:** 310-448-7600
**Email:** webmaster@rhythm.com
**Website:** www.rhythm.com

**Submission Policy:** Does not accept any unsolicited material
**Genre:** Action, Comedy, Crime, Drama, Family, Fantasy, Romance, Science Fiction
**Focus:** Feature Film

**Lee Burger**
**Title:** President
**IMDB:** www.imdb.com/name/nm0074260

**Venecia Duran**
**Title:** Director of Development
**IMDB:** www.imdb.com/name/nm1330358

**Heather Jennings**
**Title:** Production
**IMDB:** www.imdb.com/name/nm0997142

**Pauline Ts'o**
**Title:** Vice President of Development
**IMDB:** www.imdb.com/name/nm1173396

## RICE & BEANS PRODUCTIONS

30 North Raymond, Suite 605
Pasadena, CA 91103

**Phone:** 626-792-9171
**Fax:** 626-792-9171
**Email:** vin88@pacbell.net

**Submission Policy:** Accepts query letter from unproduced, unrepresented writers via email
**Genre:** Comedy, TV Drama, TV Sitcom
**Focus:** Feature Films, TV

**Vince Cheung**
**Title:** Writer/Producer
**IMDB:** www.imdb.com/name/nm0156588

**Ben Montanio**
**Title:** Writer/Producer
**IMDB:** www.imdb.com/name/nm0598996

## RICHE PRODUCTIONS

9336 West Washington Boulevard
Above Stage 3 West, Room 305
Culver City, CA 90232

**Phone:** 310-202-4850

**Submission Policy:** Accepts query letter from unproduced, unrepresented writers
**Genre:** Action, Family
**Focus:** Feature Films, TV

**Alan Riche**
**Title:** Partner
**Assistant:** Adrienne Novelly

**Peter Riche**
**Title:** Partner

## RIVE GAUCHE TELEVISION

15442 Ventura Blvd.
Ste. 101
Sherman Oaks, CA 91403

**Phone:** 818-784-9912
**Fax:** 818-784-9916
**Website:** www.rgitv.com

**Genre:** Documentary
**Focus:** Feature Film

**Jon Kramer**
**Title:** CEO
**IMDB:** www.imdb.com/name/nm2883855

**Mark Rafalowski**
**Title:** President of Production
**IMDB:** www.imdb.com/name/nm2883793

## RIVER ROAD ENTERTAINMENT

2000 Avenue of the Stars, Suite 620-N
Los Angeles, CA 90067

**Phone:** 213-253-4610
**Fax:** 310-843-9551
**Website:** www.riverroadentertainment.com

**Submission Policy:** Does not accept any unsolicited material
**Genre:** Comedy, Drama, Memoir & True Stories
**Focus:** Feature Films, Reality Programming (Reality TV, Documentaries, Special Events, Sporting Events)

**Sarah Hammer**
**Title:** Head, Creative Affairs
**IMDB:** www.imdb.com/name/nm3741550

## ROADSIDE ATTRACTIONS

7920 Sunset Blvd
Suite 402
Los Angeles, CA 90046

**Phone:** 323-882-8490
**Fax:** 323-882-8493
**Email:** info@roadsideattractions.com
**Website:** www.roadsideattractions.com

**Submission Policy:** Accepts query letter from produced or represented writers
**Genre:** Comedy, Drama, Feature Films, Horror, Thriller
**Focus:** Feature Films

**Gail Blumenthal**
**Title:** SVP of Distribution
**IMDB:** www.imdb.com/name/nm0089812

**Howard Cohen**
**Title:** Co-President
**IMDB:** www.imdb.com/name/nm1383518

**Eric d'Arbeloff**
**Title:** Co-President
**IMDB:** www.imdb.com/name/nm0195396

**Vita Lusty**
**Title:** Office Manager

## ROBERT CORT PRODUCTIONS

1041 North Formosa Avenue
Administration Building, Suite 196
West Hollywood, CA 90046

**Phone:** 323-850-2644
**Fax:** 323-850-2634

**Submission Policy:** Accepts query letter from unproduced, unrepresented writers
**Genre:** Comedy, Drama
**Focus:** Feature Films, TV

**Robert Cort**
**Title:** Producer
**IMDB:** www.imdb.com/name/nm0181202
**Assistant:** Maritza Berta

**Eric Hetzel**
**Title:** Vice-President, Production
**IMDB:** www.imdb.com/name/nm0381796

## ROBERT GREENWALD PRODUCTIONS

10510 Culver Boulevard
Culver City, CA 90232-3400

**Phone:** 310-204-0404
**Fax:** 310-204-0174
**Email:** info@rgpinc.com
**Website:** www.rgpinc.com

**Submission Policy:** Does not accept any unsolicited material
**Genre:** Comedy, Drama, Memoir & True Stories
**Focus:** Feature Films, TV

**Robert Greenwald**
**Title:** Producer/Director
**IMDB:** www.imdb.com/name/nm0339254

**Philip Kleinbart**
**Title:** Producer/Executive Vice-President
**IMDB:** www.imdb.com/name/nm0459036

## ROBERT LAWRENCE PRODUCTIONS

1810 14th St
Ste 102
Santa Monica, CA 90404

**Phone:** 1 310 399 2762

**Submission Policy:** Accepts query letter from unproduced, unrepresented writers
**Genre:** Action, Comedy, Drama
**Focus:** Feature Films

**Robert Lawrence**
**Title:** President
**IMDB:** www.imdb.com/name/nm0492994

## ROBERTS/DAVID FILMS, INC.

100 Universal City Plaza
Bldg. 1320
Universal City, CA 91608

**Phone:** 818-733-2143
**Fax:** 818-733-1551

**Submission Policy:** Does not accept any unsolicited material
**Genre:** Comedy
**Focus:** Feature Films, TV, Reality Programming (Reality TV, Documentaries, Special Events, Sporting Events)

**Lorena David**
**Title:** Partner
**Email:** lorena@robertsdavid.com

**Mark Roberts**
**Title:** Partner
**Email:** mark@robertsdavid.com

## ROBERT SIMONDS COMPANY

10202 Washington Boulevard
Stage 6, 7th Floor
Culver City, CA 90232

**Phone:** 310-244-5222
**Fax:** 310-244-0348
**Website:** www.rscfilms.com

**Submission Policy:** Does not accept any unsolicited material
**Genre:** Action, Comedy, Family, Thriller
**Focus:** Feature Films
**Year Established:** 2012

**Robert Simonds**
**Title:** CEO
**Email:** rasst@rscfilms.com
**IMDB:** www.imdb.com/name/nm0800465
**Assistant:** Jennifer Jiang

## ROCKLIN/FAUST

10390 Santa Monica Boulevard, Suite 200
Los Angeles, CA 90025

**Phone:** 310-789-3066
**Fax:** 310-789-3060

**Submission Policy:** Does not accept any unsolicited material
**Genre:** Animation, Comedy, Drama

**Focus:** Feature Films, TV, Reality Programming (Reality TV, Documentaries, Special Events, Sporting Events)

**Blye Faust**
**Title:** Producer
**IMDB:** www.imdb.com/name/nm1421308

## ROOM 101, INC.

9677 Charleville Blvd.
Beverly Hills 90212

**Phone:** 310 271 1130

**Submission Policy:** Accepts query letter from unproduced, unrepresented writers
**Genre:** Crime, Drama, Horror
**Focus:** Feature Films, TV

**Steven Schneider**
**Title:** Producer
**IMDB:** www.imdb.com/name/nm2124081

## ROOM 9 ENTERTAINMENT

9229 Sunset Boulevard, Suite 505
West Hollywood, CA 90069

**Phone:** 310-651-2001
**Fax:** 310-651-2010
**Email:** info@room9entertainment.com
**Website:** www.room9entertainment.com

**Submission Policy:** Does not accept any unsolicited material
**Genre:** Drama, Memoir & True Stories
**Focus:** Feature Films, TV

**Daniel Brunt**
**Title:** Partner, Co-President
**IMDB:** www.imdb.com/name/nm1616292

**Michael Newman**
**Title:** Partner, Co-President
**IMDB:** www.imdb.com/name/nm1616293

**David Sacks**
**Title:** CEO
**IMDB:** www.imdb.com/name/nm1616294

## ROSA ENTERTAINMENT

7288 Sunset Boulevard, Suite 208
Los Angeles, CA 90046

**Phone:** 310-470-3506
**Fax:** 310-470-3509
**Email:** info@rosaentertainment.com
**Website:** www.rosaentertainment.com

**Submission Policy:** Does not accept any unsolicited material
**Genre:** Comedy, Drama
**Focus:** Feature Films, TV

**Sidney Sherman**
Title: Producer
Email: sidney@rosaentertainment.com
IMDB: www.imdb.com/name/nm0792587

## ROSEROCK FILMS

4000 Warner Boulevard
Building 81
Burbank, CA 91522

**Phone:** 818-954-7528

**Submission Policy:** Does not accept any unsolicited material
**Focus:** Feature Films

**Hunt Lowry**
Title: Producer
IMDB: www.imdb.com/name/nm0523324

**Patricia Reed**
Title: Director of Development
Phone: 818-954-7673
IMDB: www.imdb.com/name/nm0715623

## ROTH FILMS

2900 West Olympic Boulevard
Santa Monica, CA 90404

**Phone:** 310-255-7000

**Submission Policy:** Accepts query letter from unproduced, unrepresented writers
**Focus:** Feature Films

**Palak Patel**
Title: President, Production
IMDB: www.imdb.com/name/nm2026983

**Joe Roth**
Title: Producer
IMDB: www.imdb.com/name/nm0005387

## ROUGH HOUSE

1722 Whitley Avenue
Hollywood, CA 90028

**Phone:** 323-469-3161

**Submission Policy:** Accepts scripts from produced or represented writers
**Genre:** Drama, Romance
**Focus:** Feature Films

**David Green**
Title: Director/Writer/Producer
IMDB: www.imdb.com/name/nm0337773

## ROUTE ONE FILMS

1041 North Formosa Avenue
Santa Monica East #200
West Hollywood, CA 90046

**Phone:** 323-850-3855
**Fax:** 323-850-3866
**Website:** www.routeonefilms.com

**Submission Policy:** Does not accept any unsolicited material
**Focus:** Feature Films

**Chip Diggins**
Title: Founder/Partner/Producer
IMDB: www.imdb.com/name/nm0226505

**Russell Levine**
Title: Founder/Partner/Producer
IMDB: www.imdb.com/name/nm4149902

**Jay Stern**
Title: Founder/Partner/Producer
IMDB: www.imdb.com/name/nm0827731

## RUBICON ENTERTAINMENT

3406 Tareco Dr.
Los Angeles, CA 90068

**Phone:** 323-850-9200
**Fax:** 323-378-5584
**Email:** submissions@rubiconentertainment.com
**Website:** www.rubiconentertainment.com

**Submission Policy:** Accepts query letter from unproduced, unrepresented writers via email
**Genre:** Comedy, Drama, Feature Films
**Focus:** Feature Films

## RUNAWAY PRODUCTIONS

7336 Santa Monica Blvd.
Ste 751
West Hollywood, CA 90046

**Phone:** 310-801-0885
**Email:** lindapalmer@runawayproductions.tv
**Website:** www.runawayproductions.tv

**Genre:** Comedy, Feature Films, TV
**Focus:** Feature Films, TV

**Linda Palmer**
**Title:** Producer, Writer
**IMDB:** www.imdb.com/namc/nm1881313

**Todd Wade**
**Title:** Producer, Director
**IMDB:** www.imdb.com/name/nm0905520

## RYAN MURPHY PRODUCTIONS

5555 Melrose Avenue Modular Building, First Floor
Los Angeles, CA 90038

**Phone:** 323-956-2408
**Fax:** 323-862-2235
**IMDB:** http://www.imdb.com/company/co0156994/?ref_=fn_al_co_1

**Submission Policy:** Does not accept any unsolicited material
**Genre:** Comedy, Documentary, Drama, Feature Films, Horror, Memoir & True Stories, Science Fiction, Thriller, TV Drama
**Focus:** Feature Films, Television
**Year Established:** 2008

**Dante Di Loreto**
**Title:** President
**IMDB:** http://www.imdb.com/name/nm0223994/?ref_=fn_al_nm_1

**Ryan Murphy**
**Title:** Principal
**IMDB:** http://www.imdb.com/name/nm0614682/?ref_=fn_al_nm_1

## SACRED DOGS ENTERTAINMENT LLC

311 North Robertson Blvd.
Ste. 249
Beverly Hills, CA 90211

**Phone:** 323-656-6900
**Email:** victory@sacreddogs.com
**Website:** www.sacreddogs.com

**Genre:** Documentary, Feature Films
**Focus:** Feature Films

**Arden Brotman**
**Phone:** 323-656-6900
**IMDB:** www.imdb.com/name/nm2231224

**Victory Tischler-Blue**
**Title:** Owner
**Phone:** 323-656-6900
**IMDB:** www.imdb.com/name/nm0089548

## SAFRAN COMPANY

8748 Holloway Drive
West Hollywood, CA 90069

**Phone:** 310-278-1450

**Submission Policy:** Does not accept any unsolicited material
**Genre:** Comedy, Family
**Focus:** Feature Films, TV
**Year Established:** 2006

**Tom Drumm**
**Title:** Manager
**IMDB:** www.imdb.com/name/nm1619641

**Peter Safran**
**Title:** Manager/Producer
**IMDB:** www.imdb.com/name/nm0755911

## SALTIRE ENTERTAINMENT

6352 De Longpre Avenue
Los Angeles, CA 90028

**IMDB:** www.imdb.com/company/co0104114

**Submission Policy:** Does not accept any unsolicited material
**Genre:** Drama, Myth, Science Fiction
**Focus:** Feature Films

**Stuart Pollok**
**Title:** Producer
**IMDB:** www.imdb.com/name/nm0689415

## SALTY FEATURES

682 Avenue of the Americas, Suite 3
New York, NY 10010

Phone: 212-924-1601
Fax: 212-924-2306
Email: info@saltyfeatures.com
Website: www.saltyfeatures.com

**Submission Policy:** Accepts query letter from unproduced, unrepresented writers via email
**Focus:** Feature Films, Reality Programming (Reality TV, Documentaries, Special Events, Sporting Events)

### Eva Kolodner
Title: Co-Founder, Producer
IMDB: www.imdb.com/name/nm0464286

### Yael Melamede
Title: Producer
IMDB: www.imdb.com/name/nm0577336

## SALVATORE/ORNSTON PRODUCTIONS

5650 Camellia Ave
North Hollywood, CA 91601

Phone: 310-466-8980
Fax: 818-752-9321

**Submission Policy:** Accepts query letter from produced or represented writers
**Genre:** Action, Animation, Comedy, Crime, Drama, Feature Films, Romance, Thriller
**Focus:** Feature Films

### David E. Ornston
Title: Executive
IMDB: www.imdb.com/name/nm0650361

### Richard Salvatore
Title: Executive
IMDB: www.imdb.com/name/nm0759363

## SAMUELSON PRODUCTIONS LIMITED

10401 Wyton Drive
Los Angeles, CA 90024-2527

Phone: 310-208-1000
Fax: 323-315-5188
Email: info@samuelson.la
Website: www.samuelson.la

**Submission Policy:** Does not accept any unsolicited material
**Genre:** Action, Comedy, Drama
**Focus:** Feature Films, TV

### Renato Celani
IMDB: www.imdb.com/name/nm1954607

### Saryl Hirsch
Title: Controller
IMDB: www.imdb.com/name/nm1950244

### Josie Law
IMDB: www.imdb.com/name/nm1656468

### Peter Samuelson
Title: Owner
IMDB: www.imdb.com/name/nm0006873
Assistant: Brian Casey

### Marc Samuelson
IMDB: www.imdb.com/name/nm0760555

## SANDER/MOSES PRODUCTIONS, INC.

c/o Disney
500 South Buena Vista Street
Animation Building 1 E 13
Burbank, CA 91521-1657

Phone: 818-560-4500
Fax: 818-860-6284
Email: info@sandermoses.com
Website: www.sandermoses.com

**Submission Policy:** Accepts query letter from unproduced, unrepresented writers via email
**Genre:** Drama, Memoir & True Stories
**Focus:** Feature Films, TV, Reality Programming (Reality TV, Documentaries, Special Events, Sporting Events), Media (Commercials/Branding/Marketing)

### Kim Moses
Title: Executive Producer/Writer/Director
IMDB: www.imdb.com/name/nm0608593

### Ian Sander
Title: Executive Producer/Writer/Director
IMDB: www.imdb.com/name/nm0761401

## SANITSKY COMPANY

9200 Sunset Blvd.
Los Angeles, CA 90069

Phone: 310-274-0120
Fax: 310-274-1455

**Submission Policy:** Does not accept any unsolicited material

**Genre:** TV, TV Drama
**Focus:** Television, Television Movies

**Larry Sanitsky**
**Title:** President
**IMDB:** www.imdb.com/name/nm0762792

## SCARLET FIRE ENTERTAINMENT

561 28th Ave
Venice, CA 90291

**Phone:** 310-302-1001
**Fax:** 310-302-1002

**Submission Policy:** Does not accept any unsolicited material
**Genre:** Comedy, TV Sitcom
**Focus:** Feature Films, TV

**Allen Loeb**
**Title:** Producer
**Phone:** 310-302-1001
**IMDB:** www.imdb.com/name/nm1615610

**Steven Pearl**
**Title:** Producer
**Phone:** 310-302-1001
**IMDB:** www.imdb.com/name/nm0669093

## SCORE PRODUCTIONS INC.

2401 Main St.
Santa Monica, CA 90405

**Phone:** 604-868-7377
**Email:** score@scoreproductions.com
**Website:** www.scoreproductions.com

**Submission Policy:** Accepts query letter from produced or represented writers
**Genre:** Detective, Fantasy, Science Fiction, TV, TV Drama
**Focus:** Feature Films, TV

## SCOTT FREE PRODUCTIONS

634 North La Peer Drive
Los Angeles, CA 90069

**Phone:** 310-659-1577
**Fax:** 310-659-1377

**Submission Policy:** Does not accept any unsolicited material
**Genre:** Action, Animation, Crime, Detective, Drama, Memoir & True Stories, Thriller, TV Drama

**Focus:** Feature Films, TV, Reality Programming (Reality TV, Documentaries, Special Events, Sporting Events)

**Maresa Pullman**
**Title:** Director, Film Development

**Ridley Scott**
**Title:** Co-Chairman
**IMDB:** www.imdb.com/name/nm0000631
**Assistant:** Nancy Ryan

**David Zucker**
**Title:** President, TV
**IMDB:** www.imdb.com/name/nm0001878
**Assistant:** Mark Pfeffer

## SCOTT RUDIN PRODUCTIONS

120 West 45th Street
10th Floor
New York, NY 10036

**Phone:** 212-704-4600

**Submission Policy:** Accepts query letter from unproduced, unrepresented writers
**Focus:** Feature Films
**Year Established:** 1993

**Eli Bush**
**Title:** Executive
**Phone:** 212-704-4600
**Email:** eli@scottrudinprod.com
**IMDB:** www.imdb.com/name/nm4791912

**Julie Oh**
**Title:** Executive
**Phone:** 212-704-4600
**IMDB:** www.imdb.com/name/nm4791935

**Scott Rudin**
**Title:** Producer
**Phone:** 212-704-4600
**IMDB:** www.imdb.com/name/nm0748784

## SCOTT SANDERS PRODUCTIONS

500 South Buena Vista Drive
Animation Building 3C-1
Burbank, CA 91521

**Phone:** 818-560-6350
**Fax:** 818-560-3541
**Website:** www.scottsandersproductions.com

**Submission Policy:** Accepts query letter from unproduced, unrepresented writers
**Focus:** Feature Films, TV

**Bryan Kalfus**
**Title:** Creative Executive, Film
**IMDB:** www.imdb.com/name/nm0435729

**Scott Sanders**
**Title:** President, CEO
**IMDB:** www.imdb.com/name/nm0761712
**Assistant:** Jaime Quiroz

## SCREEN DOOR ENTERTAINMENT

15223 Burbank Blvd.
Sherman Oaks, CA 91411

**Phone:** 818-781-5600
**Fax:** 818-781-5601
**Email:** info@sdetv.com
**Website:** www.sdetv.com

**Submission Policy:** Accepts query letter from unproduced, unrepresented writers
**Genre:** Reality, TV
**Focus:** TV, Reality TV Programming
**Year Established:** 2001

**M. Alessandra Ascoli**
**Title:** Director of Development & Programming
**Email:** generalinfo@sdetv.com
**IMDB:** www.imdb.com/name/nm0038529/

**Joel Rizor**
**Title:** President
**IMDB:** www.imdb.com/name/nm1381432

**Dave Shikiar**
**Title:** Co-Executive Producer

## SCREEN GEMS

10202 West Washington Boulevard
Culver City, CA 90232

**Phone:** 310-244-4000
**Fax:** 310-244-2037
**IMDB:** http://www.imdb.com/company/co0010568/

**Submission Policy:** Does not accept any unsolicited material
**Genre:** Action, Comedy, Documentary, Drama, Fantasy, Feature Films, Horror, Reality, Romance, Science Fiction, Thriller, TV, TV Drama

**Focus:** Feature Films, Television, Shorts
**Year Established:** 1926

**Clint Culpepper**
**Title:** President
**IMDB:** http://www.imdb.com/name/nm0191695/?ref_=fn_al_nm_1

**Glenn Gainor**
**Title:** Head of Physical Production/ Senior Vice President
**IMDB:** http://www.imdb.com/name/nm0004636/?ref_=fn_al_nm_1

**Pamela Kunath**
**Title:** Executive Vice President (General Manager)
**IMDB:** http://www.imdb.com/name/nm2242666/?ref_=fn_al_nm_1

**James Lopez**
**Title:** Senior Vice President of Production
**IMDB:** http://www.imdb.com/name/nm5144603/?ref_=fn_al_nm_2

**Eric Paquette**
**Title:** Senior Vice President of Development
**IMDB:** http://www.imdb.com/name/nm1789841/?ref_=fn_al_nm_1

**Loren Schwartz**
**Title:** Executive Vice President (Marketing)
**IMDB:** http://www.imdb.com/name/nm2817219/?ref_=fn_al_nm_1

**Carol Smithson**
**Title:** Vice President of Business

**Scott Strauss**
**Title:** Executive Vice President of Production
**IMDB:** http://www.imdb.com/name/nm0833873/?ref_=fn_al_nm_1

## SE8 GROUP

9560 Cedarbrook Drive
Beverly Hills, CA 90210

**Phone:** 310-285-6090
**Fax:** 310-285-6097

**Submission Policy:** Accepts query letter from unproduced, unrepresented writers
**Genre:** Drama, Thriller
**Focus:** Feature Films

**Gary Oldman**
Title: Actor/Producer
IMDB: www.imdb.com/name/nm0000198

**Douglas Urbanski**
Title: Producer
IMDB: www.imdb.com/name/nm0881703

## SECOND AND 10TH INC.

51 MacDougal Street, Suite 383
New York, NY 10012

Phone: 347-882-4493

Submission Policy: Does not accept any unsolicited material
Genre: Drama
Focus: Feature Films

**Anne Carey**
Title: Producer
IMDB: www.imdb.com/name/nm0136904

**Shani Geva**
Title: Creative Executive
IMDB: www.imdb.com/name/nm2802616

## SEE FILM INC./LAGO FILM GMBH

6399 Wilshire Boulevard, Suite 1002
Los Angeles, CA 90048

Phone: 310-653-7826
Email: lago@lagofilm.com
Website: www.lagofilm.com

Submission Policy: Does not accept any unsolicited material
Genre: Comedy, Drama, Horror
Focus: Feature Films

**Luane Gauer**
Title: Project Manager

**Marco Mehlitz**
Title: Producer

## SEISMIC PICTURES

8899 Beverly Boulevard, Suite 810
Los Angeles, CA 90048

Phone: 213-245-1180
Email: info@seismicpictures.com
Website: www.seismicpictures.com

Submission Policy: Does not accept any unsolicited material
Genre: Comedy, Drama, Memoir & True Stories
Focus: Feature Films, Reality Programming (Reality TV, Documentaries, Special Events, Sporting Events)

**Robert Schwartz**
Title: Producer/President
IMDB: www.imdb.com/name/nm0777412

## SENART FILMS

555 West 25th Street, 4th Floor
New York, NY 10001

Phone: 212-406-9610
Fax: 212-406-9581
Email: info@senartfilms.com
Website: www.senartfilms.com

Submission Policy: Does not accept any unsolicited material
Genre: Drama, Memoir & True Stories
Focus: Feature Films, Reality Programming (Reality TV, Documentaries, Special Events, Sporting Events)

**Robert May**
Title: Producer
IMDB: www.imdb.com/name/nm1254338

## SERAPHIM FILMS

c/o Sheryl Petersen/APA
405 South Beverly Drive
Beverly Hills, CA 90212

Phone: 310-888-4200 or 310-246-0050
Email: assistant@seraphimfilms.com
Website: www.seraphimfilms.com

Submission Policy: Accepts query letter from unproduced, unrepresented writers via email
Genre: Animation, Drama, Fantasy, Horror
Focus: Feature Films

**Clive Barker**
Title: President

**Joe Daley**
Title: Executive Vice-President, Produ

**Anthony DiBlasi**
Title: Writer/Director

## SERENDIPITY POINT FILMS

9 Price Street
Toronto, ON M4W 1Z1
Canada

**Phone:** 416-960-0300
**Fax:** 416-960-8656
**Website:** www.serendipitypoint.com

**Submission Policy:** Does not accept any unsolicited material
**Genre:** Action, Comedy, Drama, Thriller
**Focus:** Feature Films, TV

**Robert Lantos**
**Title:** Producer
**Assistant:** Cherri Campbell

**Wendy Saffer**
**Title:** Head, Publicity & Marketing

## SERENDIPITY PRODUCTIONS, INC.

15260 Ventura Boulevard, Suite 1040
Sherman Oaks, CA 91403

**Phone:** 818-789-3035
**Fax:** 818-235-0150

**Submission Policy:** Does not accept any unsolicited material
**Genre:** Drama, Horror, Memoir & True Stories
**Focus:** Feature Films, TV

**Daniel Heffner**
**Title:** Producer/Principal
**Email:** danheffner@earthlink.net
**IMDB:** www.imdb.com/name/nm0004527

**Ketura Kestin**
**Email:** keturak@gmail.com
**IMDB:** www.imdb.com/name/nm3109585

## SEVEN ARTS PICTURES

8439 Sunset Boulevard 4th Floor
Los Angeles, CA 90069

**Phone:** 323-372-3080
**Fax:** 323-372-3088
**Email:** info@7artspictures.com
**Website:** www.7artspictures.com

**Submission Policy:** Does not accept any unsolicited material

**Genre:** Comedy, Drama, Science Fiction, Thriller
**Focus:** Feature Films

**Peter Hoffman**
**Title:** CEO
**IMDB:** www.imdb.com/name/nm0389056
**Assistant:** Linda Silverthorn

**Susan Hoffman**
**Title:** Producer
**IMDB:** www.imdb.com/name/nm1624597

## SHADOWCATCHER ENTERTAINMENT

4701 SW Admiral Way
Box 32
Seattle, WA 98116

**Phone:** 206-328-6266
**Fax:** 206-447-1462
**Email:** kate@shadowcatcherent.com
**Website:** www.shadowcatcherent.com

**Submission Policy:** Accepts query letter from unproduced, unrepresented writers via email
**Genre:** Animation, Comedy, Drama, Memoir & True Stories, TV Sitcom
**Focus:** Feature Films, TV, Reality Programming (Reality TV, Documentaries, Special Events, Sporting Events), Th eater

**Tom Gorai**
**Title:** Producer

**Robin Gurland**
**Title:** Producer

**David Skinner**
**Title:** Executive Producer
**Assistant:** Kate Wickstrom

## SHAFTESBURY FILMS

CANADA:
163 Queen Street East Suite 100
Toronto, ON, Canada, M5A 1S1

LOS ANGELES:
4370 Tujunga Avenue Suite 300
Studio City, CA 91604

**Phone:** Canada: 416-363-1411/ LA: 818-505-3361
**Fax:** Canada: 416-363-1428
**Website:** www.shaftesbury.ca

**Submission Policy:** Does not accept any unsolicited material

**Genre:** Action, Animation, Comedy, Drama, Family, Feature Films, Romance, Thriller, TV, TV Drama
**Focus:** Feature Films, TV
**Year Established:** 1987

**Suzanne French**
Title: Vice President, Children's & Family
Email: sfrench@shaftesbury.ca
IMDB: www.imdb.com/name/nm0294220/

**Adam Haight**
Title: Senior Vice President, Scripted Content
Email: ahaight@shaftesbury.ca

**Christina Jennings**
Title: Chairman & CEO
Email: cjennings@shaftesbury.ca
IMDB: www.imdb.com/name/nm0421126/

**Julie Lacey**
Title: Vice President, Creative Affairs
Email: jlacey@shaftesbury.ca
IMDB: www.imdb.com/name/nm0479936

**Jan Peter Meyboon**
Title: Senior Vice President, Production
Email: pmeyboom@shaftesbury.ca
IMDB: www.imdb.com/name/nm0582978/

## SHAUN CASSIDY PRODUCTIONS

500 South Buena Vista Street
Old Animation Building
Burbank, CA 91521-1844

Phone: 818-560-6320

Submission Policy: Accepts query letter from unproduced, unrepresented writers
Genre: TV Drama, TV Sitcom
Focus: TV

**Shaun Cassidy**
Title: Producer/Writer
Assistant: Dan Williams

## SHEEP NOIR FILMS

438 West 17th Avenue
Vancouver, BC V5Y 2A2

Fax: 604-762-8933
Email: info@sheepnoir.com
Website: www.sheepnoir.com

Submission Policy: Does not accept any unsolicited material
Genre: Drama
Focus: Feature Films, TV

**Nathaniel Geary**
Title: Writer/Director
IMDB: www.imdb.com/name/nm0311303

**Wendy Hyman**
Title: Producer
IMDB: www.imdb.com/name/nm0405207

**Marc Stephenson**
Title: Producer
Phone: 604-762-8933
Email: marc@sheepnoir.com

## SHOE MONEY PRODUCTIONS

10202 West Washington Boulevard
Poitier Building, Suite 3100
Culver City, CA 90232

Phone: 310-244-6188
Email: shoemoneyproductions@mac.com

Submission Policy: Accepts query letter from unproduced, unrepresented writers via email
Genre: Drama, TV Drama
Focus: Feature Films, TV

**Thomas Schlamme**
Title: Executive Producer/Director
IMDB: www.imdb.com/name/nm0772095

## SHONDALAND

4151 Prospect Ave
4th Fl
Los Angeles, CA 90027

Phone: 323-671-4650

Submission Policy: Does not accept any unsolicited material
Genre: TV Drama, TV Sitcom
Focus: Feature Films, TV

**Betsy Beers**
Title: Producer

**Rachel Eggebeen**
Title: Development Executive

**Shonda Rhimes**
Title: Writer/Producer

## SHORELINE ENTERTAINMENT, INC.

1875 Century Park East, Suite 600
Los Angeles, CA 90067

**Phone:** 310-551-2060
**Fax:** 310-201-0729
**Email:** info@shorelineentertainment.com
**Website:** www.shorelineentertainment.com

**Submission Policy:** Does not accept any unsolicited material
**Genre:** Drama, Horror, Science Fiction, Thriller
**Focus:** Feature Films, Reality Programming (Reality TV, Documentaries, Special Events, Sporting Events)

**Sam Eigen**
**Title:** Executive Vice-President
**Assistant:** Erin Schroeder

**Brandon Paine**
**Title:** Director, Acquisitions

**Morris Ruskin**
**Title:** CEO/Producer
**Assistant:** Timothy Tahir

## SHOWTIME NETWORKS

10880 Wilshire Blvd
Ste 1600
Los Angeles, CA 90024

**Phone:** 310-234-5200
**Website:** www.sho.com

**Submission Policy:** Does not accept any unsolicited material
**Genre:** Action, Animation, Comedy, Crime, Detective, Drama, Family, Fantasy, Feature Films, Horror, Memoir & True Stories, Myth, Romance, Science Fiction, Thriller, TV, TV Drama
**Focus:** TV, Feature Film

**Matthew Blank**
**Title:** Chairman, CEO
**IMDB:** www.imdb.com/name/nm2303194

**Joan Boorstein**
**Title:** Vice President of Creative Affairs
**IMDB:** www.imdb.com/name/nm1140886

**Tim Delaney**
**Title:** Production Operations
**IMDB:** www.imdb.com/name/nm2303906

**Christina Spade**
**Title:** CFO
**IMDB:** www.imdb.com/name/nm5268270

## SID & MARTY KROFFT PICTURES CORP.

4024 Radford Avenue
Building 5, Suite 102
Studio City, CA 91604

**Phone:** 818-655-5314
**Fax:** 818-655-8235
**Email:** smkroft@aol.com

**Submission Policy:** Accepts query letter from unproduced, unrepresented writers via email
**Genre:** Animation, Family, TV Sitcom
**Focus:** Feature Films, TV

**Sid Krofft**
**Title:** Executive Vice-President
**Assistant:** Bill Tracy

**Marty Krofft**
**Title:** President
**Email:** marty@krofft pictures.com
**Assistant:** Christine Bedolla

## SIDNEY KIMMEL ENTERTAINMENT

9460 Wilshire Boulevard., Suite 500
Beverly Hills, CA 90212

**Phone:** 310-777-8818
**Fax:** 310-777-8892
**Email:** reception@skefilms.com
**Website:** www.skefilms.com

**Submission Policy:** Does not accept any unsolicited material
**Genre:** Comedy, Crime, Drama, Feature Films, Romance
**Focus:** Feature Films
**Year Established:** 2004

**Matt Berenson**
**Title:** President
**IMDB:** www.imdb.com/name/nm0073554

**Sidney Kimmel**
**Title:** CEO/Chairman
**IMDB:** www.imdb.com/name/nm0454004

**Mark Mikutowicz**
**Title:** Vice President (Production)
**IMDB:** www.imdb.com/name/nm2963870

**Jim Tauber**
Title: COO/President
IMDB: www.imdb.com/name/nm0851433

## SIERRA/AFFINITY

9378 Wilshire Blvd.
Suite 210
Beverly Hills, CA 90212

Phone: 424-253-1060
Fax: 424-653-1977
Email: info@sierra-affinity.com
Website: www.sierra-affinity.com

Submission Policy: Does not accept any unsolicited material
Genre: Action, Comedy, Crime, Detective, Drama, Fantasy, Feature Films, Horror, Romance, Science Fiction, Thriller
Focus: Feature Films

**Alexandru Celea**
Title: Executive Assistant
IMDB: www.imdb.com/name/nm5088556

**Jen Gorton**
Title: Creative Executive
IMDB: www.imdb.com/name/nm4224815

**Ben Kuller**
Title: Executive Assistant

**Kelly McCormick**
Title: SVP of Production & Development
IMDB: www.imdb.com/name/nm0566555

**Nicholas Meyer**
Title: CEO
IMDB: www.imdb.com/name/nm0583293
Assistant: Pip Ngo

**Hillary Taylor**
Title: Assitant
Email: hillary@sierra-affinity.com
IMDB: www.imdb.com/name/nm4751305

## SIGNATURE PICTURES

8285 West Sunset Boulevard, Suite 7
West Hollywood, CA 90046

Phone: 323-848-9005
Fax: 323-848-9305
Email: james@signaturepictures.com
Website: www.signaturepictures.com

Submission Policy: Does not accept any unsolicited material
Genre: Action, Drama, Memoir & True Stories, Romance, Thriller
Focus: Feature Films

**Illana Diamant**
Title: Producer

**Moshe Diamant**
Title: Producer

**James Portolese**
Title: Production Executive

## SIKELIA PRODUCTIONS

110 West 57th Street
5th Floor
New York, NY 10019

Phone: 212-906-8800
Fax: 212-906-8891

Submission Policy: Does not accept any unsolicited material
Genre: Action, Crime, Drama, Feature Films, Romance, Thriller
Focus: Feature Films

**Margaret Bodde**
Title: Producer

**Lisa Frechette**
Title: Assistant

**Emma Koskoff**
Title: President of Production
IMDB: www.imdb.com/name/nm0863374

**Martin Scorsese**
Title: Director/Producer
IMDB: www.imdb.com/name/nm0000217

## SILLY ROBIN PRODUCTIONS

30 Slope Drive
Short Hills, NJ 07078

Phone: 310-487-8234
Fax: 973-376-7639
Email: ribz99@aol.com
Website: http://www.alanzweibel.com

Submission Policy: Accepts query letter from unproduced, unrepresented writers via email

**Genre:** Drama, TV Drama, TV Sitcom
**Focus:** Feature Films, TV, Th eater

**John Robertson**
**Title:** Director of Development

**Alan Zweibel**
**Title:** Writer/Producer/Director

## SILVER DREAM PRODUCTIONS

3452 East Foothill Boulevard, Suite 620
Pasadena, CA 91107

**Phone:** 626-799-3880
**Fax:** 626-799-5363
**Email:** luoyan@silverdreamprods.com
**Website:** www.silverdreamprods.com

**Submission Policy:** Accepts query letter from unproduced, unrepresented writers via email
**Genre:** Drama, Myth
**Focus:** Feature Films

**Luo Yan**
**Title:** Actress/Producer
**Assistant:** Diana Chin

## SILVER NITRATE

12268 Ventura Boulevard
Studio City, CA 91604

**Phone:** 818-762-9559
**Fax:** 818-762-9177

**Submission Policy:** Does not accept any unsolicited material
**Genre:** Animation, Comedy, Drama, Science Fiction
**Focus:** Feature Films

**Ash Shah**
**Title:** Producer
**Email:** ash@silvernitrate.net

## SILVER PICTURES

4000 Warner Boulevard
Building 90
Burbank, CA 91522

**Phone:** 818-954-4490
**Fax:** 818-954-3237

**Submission Policy:** Accepts query letter from unproduced, unrepresented writers
**Genre:** Action, Animation, Drama, Family, Science

Fiction, Thriller
**Focus:** Feature Films, TV, Reality Programming (Reality TV, Documentaries, Special Events, Sporting Events)

**Alex Heineman**
**Title:** Sr. Vice-President, Production

**Sarah Meyer**
**Title:** Director of Development

**Joel Silver**
**Title:** Chairman

## SILVERS/KOSTER PRODUCTIONS, LLC

353 South Reeves Drive, Penthouse
Beverly Hills, CA 90212

**Phone:** 310-551-5245
**Fax:** 310-284-5797
**Email:** skfi lmco@aol.com
**Website:** www.silvers-koster.com

**Submission Policy:** Accepts query letter from unproduced, unrepresented writers via email
**Focus:** Feature Films, TV, Reality Programming (Reality TV, Documentaries, Special Events, Sporting Events), Media (Commercials/Branding/ Marketing)

**Karen Corcoran**
**Title:** Vice-President, Development

**Iren Koster**
**Title:** President

**Tracey Silvers**
**Title:** Chairman

## SIMON SAYS ENTERTAINMENT

12 Desbrosses Street
New York, NY 10013

**Phone:** 917-797-9704
**Email:** info@simonsaysentertainment.net
**Website:** www.simonsaysentertainment.net

**Submission Policy:** Accepts scripts from unproduced, unrepresented writers
**Genre:** Crime, Drama, Feature Films, Romance
**Focus:** Feature Films

**Nora Duffy**
**Title:** COO

**Ron Simons**
Title: Principal
IMDB: www.imdb.com/name/nm1839399

**April Yvette Thompson**
Title: Producing Associate
IMDB: www.imdb.com/name/nm1690743

## SIMON WEST PRODUCTIONS

3450 Cahuenga Boulevard West
Building 510
Los Angeles, CA 90068

Phone: 323-845-0821
Fax: 323-845-4582
Email: submissions@simonwestproductions.com
Website: www.simonwestproductions.com

Submission Policy: Accepts query letter from
unproduced, unrepresented writers
Genre: Action, Drama, Science Fiction
Focus: Feature Films, TV

**Jib Polhemus**
Title: President, Production

**Simon West**
Title: Director/Producer

## SIMSIE FILMS LLC/MEDIA SAVANT

2934 1/2 Beverly Glen Circle
Suite 264
Los Angeles, CA 90077

Email: simsiefilms@mac.com

Submission Policy: Accepts query letter from
unproduced, unrepresented writers
Genre: Comedy, Drama, Feature Films
Focus: Feature Films

**Gwen Field**
Title: Partner
IMDB: www.imdb.com/name/nm0275947

## SINGE CELL PICTURES

PO Box 69691
West Hollywood, CA 90069
USA

Phone: 310-360-7600
Fax: 310-360-7011

Submission Policy: Accepts query letter from
unproduced, unrepresented writers
Genre: Comedy, Drama
Focus: Feature Films, TV

**Sandy Stern**
Title: Producer

**Michael Stipe**
Title: Producer

## SINOVOI ENTERTAINMENT

1317 North San Fernando Boulevard, Suite 395
Burbank, CA 91504

Phone: 818-562-6404
Fax: 818-567-0104
Email: maxwell@sinovoientertainment.com
Website: www.sinovoientertainment.com

Submission Policy: Accepts query letter from
unproduced, unrepresented writers via email
Genre: Comedy, Drama, Horror
Focus: Feature Films

**Kimberly Estrada**
Title: Vice President of Development

**Maxwell Sinovoi**
Title: Producer

## SKETCH FILMS

Submission Policy: Does not accept any unsolicited
material
Genre: Action, Fantasy, Horror, Myth, Science
Fiction
Focus: Feature Films

**David Bernardi**
Title: President
Email: d.bernardi@sbcglobal.net
IMDB: www.imdb.com/name/nm2050171

**Len Wiseman**
Title: Producer/Director/Writer
IMDB: www.imdb.com/name/nm0936482

## SKYDANCE PRODUCTIONS

5555 Melrose Avenue
Dean Martin Building
Hollywood, CA 90038

Phone: 323-956-9900
Fax: 323-956-9901

**Email:** info@skydance.com
**Website:** www.skydance.com

**Submission Policy:** Accepts scripts from produced or represented writers
**Genre:** Action, Comedy, Drama, Family, Fantasy, Myth, Science Fiction, Thriller
**Focus:** Feature Films, TV

**Michelle Beress**
**Title:** Office Manager
**IMDB:** www.imdb.com/name/nm2234266

**David Ellison**
**Title:** President
**IMDB:** www.imdb.com/name/nm1911103
**Assistant:** Bill Bost

**Dana Goldberg**
**Title:** President of Production
**IMDB:** www.imdb.com/name/nm1602154
**Assistant:** Matt Grimm

**Shannon Gregory**
**Title:** Creative Executive
**IMDB:** www.imdb.com/name/nm4087474
**Assistant:** Kyle Hebenstreit

**Matthew Milam**
**Title:** Vice-President Production
**IMDB:** www.imdb.com/name/nm1297784
**Assistant:** Kyle Hebenstreit

## SKYLARK ENTERTAINMENT, INC.

12405 Venice Boulevard, Suite 237
Los Angeles, CA 90066

**Phone:** 310-390-2659
**Website:** www.skylark.net

**Submission Policy:** Does not accept any unsolicited material
**Genre:** Comedy, Drama, Memoir & True Stories
**Focus:** Feature Films, TV

**Jacobus Rose**
**Title:** President/Producer

## SKY NETWORKS

9220 Sunset Boulevard, Suite 230
West Hollywood, CA 90069

**Phone:** 310-860-2740
**Fax:** 310-860-2471
**Website:** www.sky.com

**Submission Policy:** Accepts query letter from unproduced, unrepresented writers
**Genre:** Action, Science Fiction
**Focus:** TV

**Rebecca Siegal**
**Title:** Sr. Vice-President

## SMART ENTERTAINMENT

9595 Wilshire Boulevard, Suite 900
Beverly Hills, CA 90212

**Phone:** 310-205-6090
**Fax:** 310-205-6093
**Email:** assistant@smartentertainment.com
**Website:** www.smartentertainment.com

**Submission Policy:** Accepts query letter from unproduced, unrepresented writers via email
**Genre:** Comedy, Horror, Thriller, TV Sitcom
**Focus:** Feature Films, TV, Reality Programming (Reality TV, Documentaries, Special Events, Sporting Events)

**John Jacobs**
**Title:** President
**Email:** john@smartentertainment.com

**Zac Unterman**
**Title:** VP,Director, Development
**Email:** zac@smartentertainment.com

## SMASH MEDIA, INC.

1208 Georgina Avenue
Santa Monica, CA 90402

**Phone:** 310-395-0058
**Fax:** 310-395-8850
**Email:** info@smashmediafilms.com
**Website:** www.smashmediafilms.com

**Submission Policy:** Accepts query letter from unproduced, unrepresented writers via email
**Genre:** Comedy, Drama, Science Fiction, TV Drama
**Focus:** Feature Films, TV

**Shelley Hack**
**Title:** Vice-President, Development
**Email:** shelley.hack@smashmediafi lms.com

**Harry Winer**
**Title:** President
**Email:** harry.winer@smashmediafi lms.com

**Susan Winer**
Title: Vice-President, Business Affairs
Email: susan.winer@smashmediafi lms.com

## SMOKEHOUSE PICTURES

12001 Ventura Pl., Suite 200
Studio City, CA 91604

Phone: 818-432-0330
Fax: 818-432-0337
IMDB: www.imdb.com/company/co0184096

Submission Policy: Does not accept any unsolicited material
Genre: Comedy, Drama, Thriller
Focus: Feature Films

**George Clooney**
Title: Partner
IMDB: www.imdb.com/name/nm0000123

**Grant Heslov**
Title: Partner
IMDB: www.imdb.com/name/nm0381416
Assistant: Tara Oslin

**Katie Murphy**
Title: Creative Executive
IMDB: www.imdb.com/name/nm3682023

## SNEAK PREVIEW ENTERTAINMENT

6705 Sunset Boulevard
2nd Floor
Hollywood, CA 90028

Phone: 323-962-0295
Fax: 323-962-0372
Email: indiefilm@sneakpreviewentertain.com
Website: www.sneakpreviewentertain.com

Submission Policy: Accepts query letter from unproduced, unrepresented writers via email
Focus: Feature Films
Year Established: 1991

**Chris Hazzard**
Title: Director of Development
Phone: 323-962-0295
Email: ch@sneakpe.com
IMDB: www.imdb.com/name/nm3302502

**Steven Wolfe**
Title: Chairman/CEO/Producer
Phone: 323-962-0295

Email: sjwolfe@sneakpreviewentertain.com
IMDB: www.imdb.com/name/nm0938145

## SOBINI FILMS

10203 Santa Monica Boulevard
Los Angeles, CA 90067

Phone: 310-432-6900
Fax: 310-432-6939
Website: www.sobini.com
IMDB: www.imdb.com/company/co0086773

Submission Policy: Does not accept any unsolicited material
Genre: Comedy, Drama, Family, Thriller
Focus: Feature Films

**Mark Amin**
Title: Producer/Chairman
IMDB: www.imdb.com/name/nm0024909

**David Higgin**
Title: President/Producer
IMDB: www.imdb.com/name/nm0383371

**Cami Winikoff**
Title: President
IMDB: www.imdb.com/name/nm0935121

## SOCIAL CAPITAL FILMS

1617 Broadway, Suite A
Santa Monica, CA 90404

Phone: 310-401-6100
Fax: 310-401-6289
Email: info@socialcapitalfilms.com
Website: www.socialcapitalfilms.com

Submission Policy: Does not accept any unsolicited material
Genre: Comedy, Drama, Family, Horror, Science Fiction, Thriller
Focus: Feature Films, TV, Reality Programming (Reality TV, Documentaries, Special Events, Sporting Events)

**Andy Schefter**
Title: Head of Production

**Martin Shore**
Title: Chairman/Producer

## SOGNO PRODUCTIONS

PO Box 55476
Portland, OR 97238

**Phone:** 561-676-4696
**Email:** angaelica@gmail.com
**Website:** www.ANGAELICA.com

**Submission Policy:** Accepts scripts from
unproduced, unrepresented writers
**Genre:** Action, Comedy, Documentary, Drama,
Fantasy, Feature Films, Romance, Thriller

### Breven Angaelica Warren
**Title:** Producer
**IMDB:** www.imdb.com/name/nm1938686

### Braman Ariana Warren
**Title:** Executive
**Email:** sognoproductions@gmail.com
**IMDB:** www.imdb.com/name/nm2736980

## SOLIPSIST FILMS

465 N Crescent Heights Blvd
Los Angeles, CA 90048

**Phone:** 323 272 3122
**Fax:** 323 375 1649
**Email:** info@solipsistfilms.com
**Website:** www.solipsistfilms.com

**Submission Policy:** Accepts query letter from
unproduced, unrepresented writers via email
**Genre:** Detective, Drama, Fantasy, Memoir & True
Stories, Thriller
**Focus:** Feature Films, Reality Programming (Reality
TV, Documentaries, Special Events, Sporting
Events)

### Stephen L'Heureux
**Title:** Managing Director

## S PICTURES, INC.

4420 Hayvenhurst Ave
Encino, CA 91436

**Phone:** 1 818 995 1585
**Fax:** 1 818 995 1677
**Email:** info@spictures.tv
**Website:** www.spictures.tv

**Submission Policy:** Does not accept any unsolicited
material
**Genre:** Comedy, Memoir & True Stories, Science

Fiction
**Focus:** Feature Films, TV, Reality Programming
(Reality TV, Documentaries, Special Events,
Sporting Events)

### Chuck Simon
**Title:** President/Producer
**Phone:** 818-995-1585
**Email:** chuck@Spictures.TV
**IMDB:** www.imdb.com/name/nm1247168

## SPITFIRE PICTURES

9100 Wilshire Blvd
Beverly Hills, CA 90212

**Phone:** 310-300-9000
**Fax:** 310-300-9001
**Website:** www.spitfirepictures.com

**Submission Policy:** Does not accept any unsolicited
material
**Genre:** Documentary, Drama, Feature Films,
Romance, Thriller
**Focus:** Feature Films
**Year Established:** 2003

### Anna Bocchi
**Title:** Creative Executive
**IMDB:** www.imdb.com/name/nm3070564

### Guy East
**Title:** Principal
**IMDB:** www.imdb.com/name/nm0247524

### Ben Holden
**Title:** Creative Executive
**IMDB:** www.imdb.com/name/nm1592118

### Nigel Sinclair
**Title:** Principal
**IMDB:** www.imdb.com/name/nm0801691

## SPYGLASS ENTERTAINMENT

245 North Beverly Drive
Beverly Hills, CA 90024

**Phone:** 310-443-5800
**Fax:** 310-443-5912
**Website:** www.spyglassentertainment.com

**Submission Policy:** Does not accept any unsolicited
material
**Genre:** Action, Comedy, Drama, Family, Horror,

Memoir & True Stories, Thriller
**Focus:** Feature Films

**Gary Barber**
**Title:** Co-Chairman/Founder

**Rebekah Rudd**
**Title:** Executive Vice-President, Post Production

## STAGE 6 FILMS

10202 West Washington Boulevard
Culver City, CA 90232

**Phone:** 310-244-4000
**Fax:** 310-244-2626
**Website:**
http://www.sonypicturesworldwideacquisitions.com/
**IMDB:** http://www.imdb.com/company/
co0222021/?ref_=fn_al_co_1

**Submission Policy:** Does not accept any unsolicited material
**Genre:** Action, Animation, Comedy, Crime, Documentary, Drama, Family, Feature Films, Horror, Period, Romance, Science Fiction, Thriller
**Focus:** Feature Films
**Year Established:** 2007

## ST. AMOS PRODUCTIONS

3480 Barham Boulevard
Los Angeles, CA 90068

**Phone:** 323-850-9872
**Email:** st.amosproductions@earthlink.net

**Submission Policy:** Accepts query letter from unproduced, unrepresented writers via email
**Genre:** Comedy, Memoir & True Stories, TV Drama, TV Sitcom
**Focus:** Feature Films, TV, Reality Programming (Reality TV, Documentaries, Special Events, Sporting Events)

**Marc Alexander**
**Title:** Producer/Writer/Development

**John Stamos**
**Title:** Producer/Actor

## STARRY NIGHT ENTERTAINMENT

1414 Avenue of the Americas, 12th Floor
New York, NY 10019

**Phone:** 212-717-2750
**Fax:** 212-794-6150
**Email:** info@starrynightentertainment.com
**Website:** www.starrynightentertainment.com
**IMDB:** http://www.imdb.com/company/
co0183209/?ref_=fn_al_co_1

**Submission Policy:** Accepts query letter from unproduced, unrepresented writers via email
**Genre:** Comedy, Drama
**Focus:** Feature Films, TV, Reality Programming (Reality TV, Documentaries, Special Events, Sporting Events), Media (Commercials/Branding/Marketing), Th eater

**Neika Masoori**
**Title:** Development Executive
**Email:** nyasst@starrynightentertainment.com

**Ryan Meekins**
**Title:** Creative Executive (LA)

**Craig Saavedra**
**Title:** Partner (LA)
**Email:** cs@starrynightentertainment.com

**Michael Shulman**
**Title:** Partner (NY)
**Email:** ms@starrynightentertainment.com

## STATE STREET PICTURES

8075 West 3rd Street, Suite 306
Los Angeles, CA 90048

**Phone:** 323-556-2240
**Fax:** 323-556-2242
**Website:** www.statestreetpictures.com
**IMDB:** www.imdb.com/company/
co0068765/?ref_=fn_al_co_1

**Submission Policy:** Does not accept any unsolicited material
**Genre:** Comedy, Drama
**Focus:** Feature Films, TV

**Stacy Glassgold**
**Title:** Creative Executive

**Robert Teitel**
**Title:** Producer
**Assistant:** Michael Flavin

**George Tillman**
**Title:** Director
**Assistant:** Jason Veley

## STEAMROLLER PRODUCTIONS, INC.

100 Universal City Plaza #7151
Universal City, CA 91608

**Phone:** 818-733-4622
**Fax:** 818-733-4608
**Email:** steamrollerprod@aol.com

**Submission Policy:** Accepts query letter from
unproduced, unrepresented writers via email
**Genre:** Action, Crime, Detective, Thriller
**Focus:** Feature Films, TV, Reality Programming
(Reality TV, Documentaries, Special Events,
Sporting Events)

**Binh Dang**
**Title:** Production Executive

**Steven Seagal**
**Title:** CEO/Director/Writer/Producer/Actor
**Assistant:** Tracy Irvine

## STEFANIE EPSTEIN PRODUCTIONS

427 North Canon Drive, Suite 214
Beverly Hills, CA 90210

**Phone:** 310-385-0300
**Fax:** 310-385-0302
**Email:** billseprods@aol.com
**IMDB:** www.imdb.com/company/co0171458/

**Submission Policy:** Accepts query letter from
unproduced, unrepresented writers via email
**Genre:** Comedy, Drama, TV Drama
**Focus:** Feature Films, TV

**Stefanie Epstein**
**Title:** Producer

**Bill Gienapp**
**Title:** Creative Executive

## STEVEN BOCHCO PRODUCTIONS

3000 Olympic Boulevard, Suite 1310
Santa Monica, CA 90404

**Phone:** 310-566-6900
**Email:** yr@bochcomedia.com
**IMDB:** www.imdb.com/company/
co0085628/?ref_=fn_al_co_1

**Submission Policy:** Accepts query letter from
unproduced, unrepresented writers

**Genre:** Crime, Detective, Drama
**Focus:** TV

**Steven Bochco**
**Title:** Chairman/CEO

**Dayna Kalins**
**Title:** President

**Yemaya Royce**
**Title:** Director of Media Relations

**Craig Shenkler**
**Title:** CFO/Vice-President, Finance

## STOKELY CHAFFIN PRODUCTIONS

1456 Sunset Plaza Drive
Los Angeles, CA 90069

**Phone:** 310-657-4559

**Submission Policy:** Accepts query letter from
unproduced, unrepresented writers via email
**Genre:** Action, Comedy, Horror, Memoir & True
Stories, Thriller
**Focus:** Feature Films, TV

**Stokely Chaffin**
**Title:** Producer

**David Reed**
**Title:** Development Assistant

## STONEBROOK ENTERTAINMENT

10061 Riverside Drive, Suite 813
Toluca Lake, CA 91602

**Phone:** 818-766-8797

**Submission Policy:** Accepts query letter from
unproduced, unrepresented writers via email
**Focus:** Feature Films, TV

**Danny Roth**
**Title:** Producer
**Email:** danny@stonebrookent.com

## STONE & COMPANY ENTERTAINMENT

c/o Hollywood Center Studios
1040 North Las Palmas Avenue, Building 1
Los Angeles, CA 90038

**Phone:** 323-960-2599
**Fax:** 323-960-2437
**Email:** info@stonetv.com

**Website:** www.stonetv.com/home.html
**IMDB:** www.imdb.com/company/
co0173288/?ref_=fn_al_co_1

**Submission Policy:** Accepts query letter from unproduced, unrepresented writers via email
**Genre:** Reality
**Focus:** Reality Programming (Reality TV, Documentaries, Special Events, Sporting Events)

**Ben Parrish**
**Title:** Development Producer

**Scott Stone**
**Title:** Principal

**David Weintraub**
**Title:** Vice-President, Series Development

## STONE VILLAGE PICTURES

9200 W Sunset Blvd
Ste 520
West Hollywood, CA 90069

**Phone:** 310-402-5171
**Fax:** 310-402-5172
**Website:** www.stonevillagepictures.com

**Submission Policy:** Does not accept any unsolicited material
**Genre:** Drama, Romance, Thriller
**Focus:** Feature Film

**Dylan Russell**
**Title:** Vice President of Production
**IMDB:** www.imdb.com/name/nm1928375

**Scott Steindorff**
**Title:** Executive Producer
**IMDB:** www.imdb.com/name/nm1127589

## STOREFRONT PICTURES

1112 Montana Avenue
Santa Monica, CA 90403

**Phone:** 310-459-4235
**Email:** betty@storefrontpics.com
**Website:** www.storefrontpics.com

**Submission Policy:** Accepts query letter from unproduced, unrepresented writers via email
**Genre:** Comedy, Drama, Family, Fantasy, Romance
**Focus:** Feature Films

**Susan Cartsonis**
**Title:** Producer
**Assistant:** Betty Davolo

**Roz Weisberg**
**Title:** Vice-President/Producer

## STORY AND FILM

2934 1/2 Beverly Glen Circle, Suite 195
Los Angeles, CA 90077

**Phone:** 310-480-8833
**IMDB:** www.imdb.com/company/
co0120778/?ref_=fn_al_co_1

**Submission Policy:** Accepts query letter from unproduced, unrepresented writers via email

## STORYLINE ENTERTAINMENT

8335 Sunset Boulevard, Suite 207
West Hollywood, CA 90069

**Phone:** 323-337-9045
**Fax:** 323-210-7263
**Email:** info@storyline-entertainment.com
**Website:** www.storyline-entertainment.com
**IMDB:** www.imdb.com/company/
co0091980/?ref_=fn_al_co_1

**Submission Policy:** Does not accept any unsolicited material
**Genre:** Comedy, Drama, Memoir & True Stories, Reality, Romance
**Focus:** Feature Films, TV, Th eater

**Neil Meron**
**Title:** Executive Producer
**Phone:** 323-337-9046
**Email:** neil@storyline-entertainment.com

**Mark Nicholson**
**Title:** Head, Development
**Phone:** 323-337-9047
**Email:** mark@storyline-entertainment.com

**Craig Zadan**
**Title:** Executive Producer
**Phone:** 323-337-9045
**Email:** craig@storyline-entertainment.com

## STRAIGHT UP FILMS

185 Franklin St., 2nd Floor
New York, NY 10013

**Phone:** 212-243-7837
**Email:** assistant@straightupfilms.com
**Website:** www.straightupfilms.com

**Submission Policy:** Accepts query letter from unproduced, unrepresented writers via email
**Genre:** Comedy, Crime, Drama, Feature Films, TV
**Focus:** Feature Films, TV

### Regency Boies
**Title:** Muse/Producer
**IMDB:** www.imdb.com/name/nm3151361

### Casey A. Carroll
**Title:** Creative Executive
**IMDB:** www.imdb.com/name/nm3554230

### Kate Cohen
**Title:** Co-CEO/Producer
**IMDB:** imdb.com/name/nm3154628

### Marisa Polvino
**Title:** Co-CEO/Producer
**IMDB:** imdb.com/name/nm0689909

## STRIKE ENTERTAINMENT

3000 West Olympic Boulevard
Building 5, Suite 1250
Santa Monica, CA 90404

**Phone:** 310-315-0550
**Fax:** 310-315-0560

**Submission Policy:** Accepts query letter from unproduced, unrepresented writers via email
**Genre:** Action, Comedy, Drama, Horror, Science Fiction, Thriller
**Focus:** Feature Films
**Year Established:** 2002

### Marc Abraham
**Title:** Producer
**Assistant:** Jamie Zakowski

### Tom Bliss
**Title:** Producer
**Assistant:** Mark Barclay

### Kristel Laiblin
**Assistant:** Nhu Tran

### Eric Newman
**Title:** Producer
**Assistant:** Jesse Rose Moore

## STUDIO CANAL

9250 Wilshire Boulevard, Suite 210
Beverly Hills, CA 90212

**Phone:** 310-247-0994

**Submission Policy:** Does not accept any unsolicited material
**Genre:** Comedy, Crime, Drama, Fantasy, Horror, Memoir & True Stories, Romance, Thriller
**Focus:** Feature Films, Reality Programming (Reality TV, Documentaries, Special Events, Sporting Events)

### Ron Halpern
**Title:** Executive Vice-President, Int'l Production & Special Projects

## SUBMARINE ENTERTAINMENT

525 Broadway
Ste 601
New York, NY 10012

**Phone:** 212-625-1410
**Fax:** 212-625-9931
**Email:** info@submarine.com
**Website:** www.submarine.com

**Submission Policy:** Accepts query letter from produced or represented writers
**Genre:** Documentary, Drama, Feature Films
**Focus:** Feature Films

### Dan Braun
**Title:** Co-Founder
**Email:** dan@submarine.com
**IMDB:** www.imdb.com/name/nm2250854

### Josh Braun
**Title:** Co-Founder
**Email:** josh@submarine.com
**IMDB:** www.imdb.com/name/nm2248562

### David Koh
**Title:** Executive

## SUCH MUCH FILMS

Santa Monica, CA 90405

**Email:** info@suchmuchfilms.com
**Website:** www.suchmuchfilms.com

**Submission Policy:** Accepts query letter from unproduced, unrepresented writers via email

Genre: Documentary, Drama
Focus: Feature Film

**Judi Levine**
Title: Executive
IMDB: www.imdb.com/name/nm0505861

**Ben Lewin**
IMDB: www.imdb.com/name/nm0506802

## SUMMIT ENTERTAINMENT

1630 Stewart St
Ste 120
Santa Monica, CA 90404

Phone: 310-309-8400
Fax: 310-828-4132
Website: www.summit-ent.com
IMDB: www.imdb.com/company/co0046206

Submission Policy: Does not accept any unsolicited material
Genre: Action, Comedy, Crime, Drama, Fantasy, Feature Films, Romance, Science Fiction, Thriller
Focus: Feature Films

**Gillian Bohrer**
Title: Vice President of Production
Phone: 310-309-8400
IMDB: www.imdb.com/name/nm2023551

**Rob Friedman**
Title: CEO
Phone: 310-309-8400
IMDB: www.imdb.com/name/nm2263981

**Merideth Milton**
Title: Senior Vice President of Production
Phone: 310-309-8400
IMDB: www.imdb.com/name/nm0590693

**Patrick Wachsberger**
Title: President
Phone: 310-309-8400
IMDB: www.imdb.com/name/nm0905163

## SUNDIAL PICTURES

511 Sixth Ave., Suite 375
New York, NY 10011

Email: info@sundialpicturesllc.com
Website: www.sundial-pictures.com

Submission Policy: Does not accept any unsolicited material

Genre: Comedy, Documentary, Drama, Feature Films, Thriller
Focus: Feature Films

**Joey Carey**
Title: Partner
IMDB: www.imdb.com/name/nm2909903

**Stefan Norwicki**
Title: President
IMDB: www.imdb.com/name/nm3378356

**Benjamin Weber**
Title: EVP Development
IMDB: www.imdb.com/name/nm3373548

## SUNLIGHT PRODUCTIONS

854-A Fifth Street
Santa Monica, CA 90403

Phone: 310-899-1522
Email: contactus@sunlightproductions.com
Website: www.mikebinder.net
IMDB: www.imdb.com/company/co0028319/?ref_=fn_al_co_1

Submission Policy: Does not accept any unsolicited material
Genre: Comedy, Drama, Memoir & True Stories
Focus: Feature Films, TV

**Mike Binder**
Title: Writer/Director/Actor

**Rachel Zimmerman**
Title: Producer
Email: Rachel@sunlightproductions.com

## SUNSWEPT ENTERTAINMENT

10201 West Pico Boulevard
Building 45
Los Angeles, CA 90064

Phone: 310-369-0878
Fax: 310-969-0726
IMDB: www.imdb.com/company/co0226011/

Submission Policy: Does not accept any unsolicited material
Genre: Animation, Comedy, Family, Fantasy, Romance
Focus: Feature Films
Year Established: 2004

**Emmy Castlen**
Title: Story Editor

**Caroline MacVicar**
Title: Assistant

**Karen Rosenfelt**
Title: President/Producer
Assistant: Caroline MacVicar

## SUNTAUR ENTERTAINMENT

1581 North Crescent Heights Boulevard
Los Angeles, CA 90046

Phone: 323-656-3800
Email: info@suntaurent.com
Website: www.suntaurent.com
IMDB: www.imdb.com/company/
co0183461/?ref_=fn_al_co_1

Submission Policy: Does not accept any unsolicited material
Genre: Comedy, Drama
Focus: Feature Films, TV

**Paul Aaron**
Title: President/CEO
Assistant: Matt Blessing

**Zac Sanford**
Title: Vice-President, Development
Assistant: Adam Morris

## SUPERFINGER ENTERTAINMENT

c/o Chris Hart/UTA
9560 Wilshire Boulevard
Beverly Hills, CA 90212

Phone: 310-385-6715
IMDB: www.imdb.com/company/co0181284/

Submission Policy: Accepts query letter from unproduced, unrepresented writers via email
Genre: Animation, Comedy, Reality
Focus: Feature Films, TV, Reality Programming (Reality TV, Documentaries, Special Events, Sporting Events)

**Dane Cook**
Title: President/Actor/Comedian

## SWEET 180

141 West 28th Street #300
NYC, NY 10001

Phone: 212-541-4443
Fax: 212-563-9655
Website: www.sweet180.com

Submission Policy: Does not accept any unsolicited material
Genre: Comedy, Drama, Memoir & True Stories, Reality, Romance
Focus: Feature Films, TV

**Catherine Clausi**
Title: Office Manager/Executive Assistant
Assistant: Lindsay Carlson

**Lillian LaSalle**
Title: Prseident/Manager/Producer
Email: lillian@sweet180.com

**Rachel Maran**
Title: Assistant
Email: assistant@sweet180.com

**Nina Schreiber**
Title: Manager
Email: nina@sweet180.com

## TAGGART PRODUCTIONS

9000 W Sunset Blvd
Suite 1020
West Hollywood, CA 90069

Phone: 424-249-3350
Fax: 424-249-3972
Website: www.taggart-productions.com

Submission Policy: Does not accept any unsolicited material
Genre: Action, Comedy, Crime, Drama, Feature Films, Thriller
Focus: Feature Films

**Jason Michael Berman**
Title: Producer
Email: jberman@taggart-productions.com
IMDB: www.imdb.com/name/nm4132650

**Rob Nardelli**
Title: Producer
IMDB: www.imdb.com/name/nm4360108

**Michael Nardelli**
Title: President & CEO
IMDB: www.imdb.com/name/nm1660148

**Lindsey Reiman**
Title: Assistant
Email: lindsey@taggart-productions.com
IMDB: www.imdb.com/name/nm4701862

## TAGLINE PICTURES

9250 Wilshire Boulevard
Ground Floor
Beverly Hills, CA 90212

Phone: 310-595-1515
Fax: 310-595-1505
Email: info@taglinela.com
Website: www.taglinela.com

Submission Policy: Does not accept any unsolicited
material
Genre: TV Drama, TV Sitcom
Focus: TV

**Chris Henze**
Title: Partner/Owner

**Kelly Kulchak**
Title: President
Assistant: Tim Goessling

**William Mercer**
Title: Partner/Owner

**J.B. Roberts**
Title: Partner/Owner

**Ron West**
Title: Parnter/Owner

## TAMARA ASSEYEV PRODUCTIONS

1187 Coast Village Rd.
Suite 134
Santa Barbara, CA 93108

Phone: 323-656-4731
Fax: 323-656-2211
Email: tamaraprod@aol.com

Submission Policy: Accepts query letter from
unproduced, unrepresented writers
Genre: TV, TV Drama
Focus: TV

**Tamara Asseyev**
Title: Producer
Assistant: Constance Mead

## TAPESTRY FILMS, INC.

9328 Civic Center Drive, 2nd Floor
Beverly Hills, CA 90210

Phone: 310-275-1191
Fax: 310-275-1266

Submission Policy: Does not accept any unsolicited
material
Genre: Action, Comedy, Family, Romance, Thriller
Focus: Feature Films

**Peter Abrams**
Title: Producer/Partner
IMDB: www.imdb.com/name/nm0009222

**Kat Blasband Page**
Title: VP Development
IMDB: www.imdb.com/name/nm2321097/

**Robert Levy**
Title: Producer/Partner
IMDB: www.imdb.com/name/nm0506597

**Michael Schreiber**
Title: President
IMDB: www.imdb.com/name/nm2325100

## TAURUS ENTERTAINMENT COMPANY

5555 Melrose Avenue
Marx Brothers Building, Suite 103/104
Hollywood, CA 90038

Phone: 818-935-5157
Fax: 323-686-5379
Email: taurusentco@yahoo.com
Website: www.taurusec.com

Submission Policy: Accepts query letter from
unproduced, unrepresented writers via email
Genre: Action, Animation, Drama, Family
Focus: Feature Films, TV
Year Established: 1991

**James Dudelson**
Title: President/CEO
Email: jgdudelson@yahoo.com
IMDB: www.imdb.com/name/nm0240054

**Robert Dudelson**
Title: President/COO
Email: rfdudelson@mac.com
IMDB: www.imdb.com/name/nm0240055

## T&C PICTURES

3122 Santa Monica Boulevard #200
Santa Monica, CA 90404

**Phone:** 310-828-1340
**Fax:** 310-828-1581
**Email:** info@tandcpictures.com

**Submission Policy:** Accepts query letter from
unproduced, unrepresented writers
**Genre:** Action, Comedy, Drama, Family, Memoir &
True Stories, Thriller, TV Drama
**Focus:** Feature Films, TV

**Bill Borden**
**Title:** Producer
**Email:** christine@tandcpictures.com
**IMDB:** www.imdb.com/name/nm0096115

**Arata Matsushima**
**Title:** President/Producer
**Phone:** 310-828-7801
**IMDB:** www.imdb.com/name/nm2606503

**Barry Rosenbush**
**Title:** Producer
**IMDB:** www.imdb.com/name/nm0742492

## TEAM DOWNEY

1311 Abbot Kinney
Venice, CA 90291

**Phone:** 310-450-5100

**Submission Policy:** Does not accept any unsolicited
material
**Genre:** Action, Comedy, Drama, Feature Films
**Focus:** Feature Films
**Year Established:** 2010

**Susan Downey**
**Title:** Producer
**IMDB:** www.imdb.com/name/nm1206265

**Robert Downey**
**Title:** Producer
**IMDB:** www.imdb.com/name/nm0000375

**David Gambino**
**Title:** President of Production
**IMDB:** www.imdb.com/name/nm1312724

## TEAM G

1839 Blake Avenue #5 Los Angeles, CA 90039

**Phone:** 213-915-8106
**Fax:** 323-843-9210
**Email:** info@teamgproductions.com
**Website:** www.teamgproductions.com

**Genre:** Comedy, Drama, Feature Films, Science
Fiction
**Focus:** Feature Films

**Trey Hock**
**Title:** Producer/Partner
**IMDB:** www.imdb.com/name/nm2465366

**Jett Steiger**
**Title:** Producer/Partner
**IMDB:** www.imdb.com/name/nm2532520

## TEAM TODD

2900 West Olympic Boulevard
Santa Monica, CA 91404

**Phone:** 310-255-7265
**Fax:** 310-255-7222

**Submission Policy:** Accepts scripts from produced
or represented writers
**Genre:** Animation, Drama, Family, Myth, Romance
**Focus:** Feature Films

**Julianna Hays**
**Title:** Creative Executive
**IMDB:** www.imdb.com/name/nm3057670

**Suzanne Todd**
**Title:** Producer
**IMDB:** www.imdb.com/name/nm0865297

## TEMPLE HILL PRODUCTIONS

9255 Sunset Boulevard, Suite 801
Los Angeles, CA 90069

**Phone:** 310-270-4383
**Fax:** 310-270-4395
**Website:** www.templehillent.com

**Submission Policy:** Does not accept any unsolicited
material
**Genre:** Comedy, Drama, Family, Fantasy, Thriller,
TV, TV Drama
**Focus:** Feature Films, TV
**Year Established:** 2006

**Marty Bowen**
**Title:** Partner
**IMDB:** www.imdb.com/name/nm2125212

**Wyck Godfrey**
Title: Partner
IMDB: www.imdb.com/name/nm0324041

**Isaac Klausner**
Title: Director of Development
IMDB: www.imdb.com/name/
nm2327099/?ref_=fn_al_nm_1

**Adam C. Londy**
Title: Director of Development
IMDB: www.imdb.com/name/nm2173131

**Tracy Nyberg**
Title: Senior Vice President
IMDB: www.imdb.com/name/
nm2427937/?ref_=fn_al_nm_1

## TERRA FIRMA FILMS

468 North Camden Drive, Suite 365T
Beverly Hills, CA 90210

Phone: 310-480-5676
Fax: 310-862-4717
Email: info@terrafirmafilms.com
Website: www.terrafirmafilms.com

Submission Policy: Accepts query letter from
unproduced, unrepresented writers via email
Genre: Action, Comedy, Drama, Family, Romance
Focus: Feature Films
Year Established: 2003

**Adam Herz**
Title: Writer/Producer
Phone: 310-860-7480
Email: info@terrafi rmafi lms.com
IMDB: www.imdb.com/name/nm0381221

**Gregory Lessans**
Title: Co-President
IMDB: www.imdb.com/name/nm0504298

**Gregory Lessans**
Title: Co-President
IMDB: www.imdb.com/name/nm0504298/

**Josh Shader**
Title: Co-President
IMDB: www.imdb.com/name/nm1003558

## THE AMERICAN FILM COMPANY

c/o Business Affairs, Inc.
2415 Main Street, 2nd Floor
Santa Monica, CA 90405

Phone: 310-392-0777
Email: info@americanfilmco.com
Website: www.theamericanfilmcompany.com

Submission Policy: Accepts query letter from
unproduced, unrepresented writers via email
Genre: Drama, Feature Films, Memoir & True
Stories, Period, Thriller
Focus: Feature Films
Year Established: 2008

**Brian Falk**
Title: President
Email: bfalk@americanfi lmco.com
IMDB: www.imdb.com/name/nm1803137

**Kurt Graver**
Title: Manager of Development
Email: kgraver@americanfilmco.com
IMDB: www.imdb.com/name/nm4621255

**Alfred Levitt**
Title: COO
IMDB: www.imdb.com/name/nm4662708/

## THE ASYLUM

72 E Palm Ave
Burbank, CA 91502

Phone: 323-850-1214
Fax: 818-260-9811
Email: theasylum@theasylum.cc
Website: www.theasylum.cc

Submission Policy: Does not accept any unsolicited
material
Genre: Action, Fantasy, Horror, Science Fiction,
Thriller
Focus: Feature Film

**Joseph Lawson**
Title: Supervisor
IMDB: www.imdb.com/name/nm1037472

**Mark Quod**
Title: Post Production Supervisor
IMDB: www.imdb.com/name/nm0704517

**Micho Rutare**
Title: Director of Development
IMDB: www.imdb.com/name/nm3026436

## THE AV CLUB

2629 Main Street #211
Santa Monica, CA 90405

Phone: (310) 396-1165

Submission Policy: Does not accept any unsolicited
material
Genre: Comedy, Drama, Memoir & True Stories,
Romance, Science Fiction
Focus: Feature Films

**Amy Robertson**
Title: Film and TV Producer
IMDB: www.imdb.com/name/nm1516144

## THE BADHAM COMPANY

16830 Ventura Boulevard, Suite 300
Encino, CA, 91436

Phone: 818-990-9495
Fax: 818-981-9163
Email: development@badhamcompany.com
Website: www.badhamcompany.com

Submission Policy: Accepts scripts from produced
or represented writers
Genre: Drama, Family, Feature Films, Memoir &
True Stories, TV, TV Drama
Focus: Feature Films, TV

**John Badham**
Title: Director/Producer
IMDB: www.imdb.com/name/nm0000824

## THE BEDFORD FALLS COMPANY

409 Santa Monica Blvd
Penthouse
Santa Monica, CA 90401-2388

Phone: 310-394-5022
Fax: 310-394-2512

Submission Policy: Does not accept any unsolicited
material
Genre: Action, Drama
Focus: Feature Films

**Troy Putney**
Title: Creative Executive
IMDB: www.imdb.com/name/nm1586726

## THE BUREAU

18 Phipp Street
2nd Floor
London - EC2A 4NU
United-Kingdom

Phone: +44-0-207-033-0555
Email: mail@thebureau.co.uk
Website: www.thebureau.co.uk

Submission Policy: Does not accept any unsolicited
material
Genre: Comedy, Documentary, Drama, Feature
Films, Romance, Thriller
Focus: Feature Films
Year Established: 2000

**Valentina Brazzini**
Title: Development

**Matthew de Braconier**
Title: Producer/Development

**Bertrand Faivre**
Title: Producer
IMDB: www. imdb.com/name/nm0265724

**Soledad Gatti-Pascual**
Title: Founder & Manager
IMDB: www.imdb.com/name/nm0309806

**Tristan Golighter**
Title: Producer

## THE COLLETON COMPANY

20 Fifth Avenue, Suite 13F
New York, NY 10011

Phone: 212-673-0916
Fax: 212-673-1172

Submission Policy: Accepts scripts from produced
or represented writers
Genre: Crime, Detective, Drama, Feature Films,
Memoir & True Stories, Thriller, TV, TV Drama
Focus: Feature Films, TV

**Sara Colleton**
IMDB: www.imdb.com/name/nm0171780

## THE DONNERS' COMPANY

9465 Wilshire Blvd
Ste 420
Beverly Hills, CA 90212

**Phone:** 310-777-4600
**Fax:** 310-777-4610
**Website:** www.donnerscompany.com

**Submission Policy:** Does not accept any unsolicited material
**Genre:** Action Fantasy, Science Fiction
**Focus:** Feature Films

**Richard Donner**
Title: Producer
IMDB: www.imdb.com/name/nm0001149

## THE GOLD COMPANY

499 North Canon Drive, Suite 306
Beverly Hills, CA 90210

**Phone:** 310-270-4653

**Submission Policy:** Accepts query letter from unproduced, unrepresented writers
**Genre:** Comedy
**Focus:** Feature Films

**Eric Gold**
Title: Chairman/Producer
IMDB: www.imdb.com/name/nm0324970

**Jessica Green**
Title: VP Production
IMDB: www.imdb.com/name/nm2783652/?ref_=fn_al_nm_2

**Caryn Weingarten**
Title: Manager
IMDB: www.imdb.com/name/nm1086864/

## THE GOLDSTEIN COMPANY

1644 Courtney Avenue
Los Angeles, CA 90046

**Phone:** 310-659-9511
**Website:** www.garywgoldstein.com

**Submission Policy:** Accepts query letter from unproduced, unrepresented writers via email
**Genre:** Action, Comedy, Memoir & True Stories, Romance, Thriller
**Focus:** Feature Films, Reality Programming (Reality

TV, Documentaries, Special Events, Sporting Events), Media (Commercials/Branding/Marketing)

**Gary Goldstein**
Title: Producer
Email: gary@garywgoldstein.com
IMDB: www.imdb.com/name/nm0326214

**Sandra Tomita**
Title: Associate Producer
IMDB: www.imdb.com/name/nm0866739/?ref_=fn_al_nm_1

**Catherine Wachter**
Title: Development Associate

## THE GOODMAN COMPANY

8491 Sunset Boulevard, Suite 329
Los Angeles, CA 90069

**Phone:** 323-655-0719
**Email:** ilyssagoodman@sbcglobal.net

**Submission Policy:** Accepts query letter from unproduced, unrepresented writers
**Genre:** Comedy, Family, TV Drama, TV Sitcom
**Focus:** Feature Films, TV, Reality Programming (Reality TV, Documentaries, Special Events, Sporting Events)

**Ilyssa Goodman**
Title: President/Producer
IMDB: www.imdb.com/name/nm1058415

## THE GOTHAM GROUP

9255 Sunset Boulevard, Suite 515
Los Angeles, CA 90069

**Phone:** 310-285-0001
**Fax:** 310-285-0077
**Website:** www.gotham-group.com

**Submission Policy:** Does not accept any unsolicited material
**Genre:** Action, Animation, Comedy, Drama, Family, Fantasy, Science Fiction, TV Drama, TV Sitcom
**Focus:** Feature Films, TV, Reality Programming (Reality TV, Documentaries, Special Events, Sporting Events), Media (Commercials/Branding/Marketing)

**Ellen Goldsmith-Vein**
Title: CEO/Founder
Email: egv@gotham-group.com
IMDB: www.imdb.com/name/nm1650412/

**Julie Kane-Ritsch**
Title: Manager/Producer
Email: jkr@gotham-group.com
IMDB: www.imdb.com/name/nm1415970

**Peter McHugh**
Title: Manager/Producer
Email: peter@gotham-group.com

## THE GREENBERG GROUP

2029 South Westgate Avenue
Los Angeles, CA 90025

Email: info@greenberggroup.com
Website: www.greenberggroup.com

Submission Policy: Accepts query letter from
unproduced, unrepresented writers via email
Genre: Action, Thriller
Focus: Feature Films, TV, Reality Programming
(Reality TV, Documentaries, Special Events,
Sporting Events), Media (Commercials/Branding/
Marketing)

**Randy Greenberg**
Title: CEO, Executive Producer
Email: randy@greenberggroup.com
IMDB: www.imdb.com/name/nm2985843

## THE GROUP ENTERTAINMENT

115 West 29th Street #1102
New York, NY 10001

Phone: 212-868-5233
Fax: 212-504-3082
Email: info@thegroupentertainment.com
Website: www.thegroupentertainment.com

Submission Policy: Does not accept any unsolicited
material
Genre: Action, Comedy, Drama, Feature Films,
Romance
Focus: Feature Films, TV, Reality Programming
(Reality TV, Documentaries, Special Events,
Sporting Events)

**Rebecca Atwood**
Title: Creative Executive
Email: rebecca@thegroupentertainment.com

**Gil Holland**
Title: Partner/Producer
IMDB: www.imdb.com/name/nm0390693

**Kyle Luker**
Title: Partner
Email: kyle@thegroupentertainment.com

**Jill McGrath**
Title: Partner
Email: jill@thegroupentertainment.com

## THE HALCYON COMPANY

8455 Beverly Boulevard
Penthouse Suite
Los Angeles, CA 90048

Phone: 323-650-0222
Email: info@thehalcyoncompany.com
Website: www.thehalcyoncompany.com

Submission Policy: Does not accept any unsolicited
material
Genre: Action, Science Fiction, Thriller
Focus: Feature Films
Year Established: 2006

**Derek Anderson**
Title: Co-CEO
IMDB: www.imdb.com/name/nm2203770/

**Victor Kubicek**
Title: Co-CEO
IMDB: www.imdb.com/name/nm2127497/

**James Middleton**
Title: Creative Development and Production
IMDB: www.imdb.com/name/nm2194360

## THE HAL LIEBERMAN COMPANY

8522 National Boulevard, Suite 108
Culver City, CA 90232

Phone: 310-202-1929
Fax: 323-850-5132

Submission Policy: Accepts query letter from
unproduced, unrepresented writers via email
Genre: Drama, Family, Fantasy, Feature Films,
Horror, Thriller
Focus: Feature Films

**Hal Lieberman**
Title: Producer
IMDB: www.imdb.com/name/nm0509386

**Dan Scheinkman**
Title: Vice President

**THE HATCHERY**

2950 North Hollywood Way
3rd Floor
Burbank, CA 91505

Phone: 818-748-4507
Fax: 818-748-4615/Attn: Dan Angel
Email: dangel@thehatcheryllc.com
Website: www.thehatcheryllc.com

Submission Policy: Does not accept any unsolicited material
Genre: Comedy, Family, Horror, Science Fiction
Focus: Feature Films, TV

**Dan Angel**
Title: CCO/Executive Producer
Email: dangel@thehatcheryllc.com
IMDB: www.imdb.com/name/nm0029445

**THE HECHT COMPANY**

3607 West Magnolia, Suite L
Burbank, CA 91505

Phone: 310-989-3467
Email: hechtco@aol.com

Submission Policy: Accepts query letter from unproduced, unrepresented writers via email
Genre: Drama, Thriller
Focus: Feature Films, TV, Reality Programming (Reality TV, Documentaries, Special Events, Sporting Events)

**Duffy Hecht**
Title: Producer
IMDB: www.imdb.com/name/nm0372953

**THE JIM HENSON COMPANY**

1416 North La Brea Avenue
Hollywood, CA 90028

Phone: 323-802-1500
Fax: 323-802-1825
Email: info@henson.com
Website: www.henson.com

Submission Policy: Does not accept any unsolicited material
Genre: Animation, Comedy, Family, Fantasy,
Science Fiction, TV Sitcom
Focus: Feature Films, TV, Post-Production (Editing, Special Effects), Reality Programming (Reality TV, Documentaries, Special Events, Sporting Events), Media (Commercials/Branding/Marketing), Th eater
Year Established: 1958

**Brian Henson**
Title: Chairman

**Blanca Lista**
Title: Director of Development

**Jason Lust**
Title: Sr. Vice-President, Feature Films

**Halle Stanford**
Title: Executive Vice-President, Children's TV

**Halle Stanford-Grossman**
Title: EVP Children's Television

**THE LITTLEFIELD COMPANY**

500 South Buena Vista Street Animation Building, Suite 3D-2
Burbank, CA 91521

Phone: 818-560-2280
Fax: 818-560-3775

Submission Policy: Does not accept any unsolicited material
Genre: TV, TV Drama
Focus: TV

**Andrew Bourne**
Title: Senior Vice President of Development
Phone: 818-560-2280
IMDB: www.imdb.com/name/nm2044331
Assistant: Janelle Young

**Warren Littlefield**
Title: Principal
Phone: 818-560-2280
IMDB: www.imdb.com/name/nm0514716
Assistant: Patricia Mann

**Jill Young**
Title: Development Executive

**THE MARK GORDON COMPANY**

12200 West Olympic Boulevard, Suite 250
Los Angeles, CA 90064

**Phone:** 310-943-6401
**Fax:** 310-943-6402

**Submission Policy:** Does not accept any unsolicited material
**Genre:** Action, Drama, TV Drama
**Focus:** Feature Films, TV

**Mark Gordon**
**Title:** Principal/Producer
**IMDB:** www.imdb.com/name/nm0330428
**Assistant:** Lindsey Martin

**Shara Senderoff**
**Title:** Vice-President New Media & Director, Film Development
**IMDB:** www.imdb.com/name/nm2994844

**Bryan Zuriff**
**Title:** Executive Vice-President, Film
**IMDB:** www.imdb.com/name/nm3050339
**Assistant:** Ivey Harden

## THE MAZUR/KAPLAN COMPANY

3204 Pearl Street
Santa Monica, CA 90405

**Phone:** 310-450-5838
**Email:** info@mazurkaplan.com
**Website:** www.mazurkaplan.com

**Submission Policy:** Does not accept any unsolicited material
**Genre:** Comedy, Family, Fantasy, Romance, Thriller
**Focus:** Feature Films, TV, Reality Programming (Reality TV, Documentaries, Special Events, Sporting Events)
**Year Established:** 2009

**Kimi Armstrong Stein**
**Title:** Vice-President of Development
**Email:** kimi@mazurkaplan.com
**IMDB:** www.imdb.com/name/nm2148964

**Sarah Carbiener**
**Title:** Creative Executive
**Email:** sarah@mazurkaplan.com
**IMDB:** www.imdb.com/name/nm3745774

**Mitchell Kaplan**
**Title:** Producer
**IMDB:** www.imdb.com/name/nm3125086/

**Paula Mazur**
**Title:** Producer
**Phone:** 310-450-5838
**IMDB:** www.imdb.com/name/nm0563394

## THE MONTECITO PICTURE COMPANY

9465 Wilshire Boulevard, Suite 920
Beverly Hills, CA 90212

**Phone:** 310-247-9880
**Fax:** 310-247-9498
**Website:** www.montecitopicturecompany.com

**Submission Policy:** Accepts query letter from unproduced, unrepresented writers
**Genre:** Action, Comedy, Drama, Family, Feature Films, Memoir & True Stories, Period, Thriller
**Focus:** Feature Films, TV
**Year Established:** 2000

**Joe Medjuck**
**Title:** Partner
**IMDB:** www.imdb.com/name/nm0575817/

**Alex Plapinger**
**Title:** Vice-President of Development
**Phone:** 310-247-9880
**IMDB:** www.imdb.com/name/nm3292687

**Tom Pollock**
**Title:** Partner
**IMDB:** www.imdb.com/name/nm0689696/
**Assistant:** Krystee Morgan

**Ivan Reitman**
**Title:** Partner
**IMDB:** www.imdb.com/name/nm0718645
**Assistant:** Eric Reich

## THE PITT GROUP

9465 Wilshire Boulevard, Suite 420
Beverly Hills, CA 90212

**Phone:** 310-246-4800
**Fax:** 310-275-9258

**Submission Policy:** Accepts query letter from unproduced, unrepresented writers
**Genre:** Animation, Comedy, Crime, Detective, Drama, Feature Films, Romance
**Focus:** Feature Films, TV
**Year Established:** 2000

**Jeremy Conrady**
Title: Creative Executive
Email: jconrady@pittgroup.com
IMDB: www.imdb.com/name/nm262042

**Lou Pitt**
Title: President
Email: lpitt@pittgroup.com
IMDB: www.imdb.com/name/nm2229316

## THE RADMIN COMPANY

9201 Wilshire Boulevard, Suite 102
Beverly Hills, CA 90210

Phone: 310-274-9515
Fax: 310-274-0739
Email: queries@radmincompany.com
Website: www.radmincompany.com

Submission Policy: Accepts query letter from
unproduced, unrepresented writers via email
Genre: Comedy, Drama, Romance
Focus: Feature Films
Year Established: 1993

**Libby Allen**
Title: Creative Executive

**Linne Radmin**
Title: Producer

**Isabel Shanahan**
Title: Creative Executive
Email: isabel@radmincompany.com

## THE SHEPHARD/ROBIN COMPANY

c/o Raleigh Studios
5300 Melrose Avenue, Suite 225E
Los Angeles, CA 90038

Phone: 323-871-4412
Fax: 323-871-4418

Submission Policy: Does not accept any unsolicited
material
Genre: TV Drama
Focus: TV

**Michael Robin**
Title: Executive Producer/Owner

**Greer Shephard**
Title: Executive Producer/Owner

## THE STEVE TISCH COMPANY

10202 West Washington Boulevard
Astaire Building, 3rd Floor
Culver City, CA 90232

Phone: 310-244-6612
Fax: 310-204-2713

Submission Policy: Accepts query letter from
unproduced, unrepresented writers
Genre: Action, Comedy, Drama, Thriller
Focus: Feature Films

**Lacy Boughn**
Title: Director, Development
Phone: 310-244-6620
Email: lacy_boughn@spe.sony.com

**Steve Tisch**
Title: Chairman

## THE TANNENBAUM COMPANY

c/o CBS Studios
4024 Radford Avenue, Bungalow 16
Studio City, CA 91604

Phone: 818-655-7181
Fax: 818-655-7193

Submission Policy: Does not accept any unsolicited
material
Genre: Comedy, Drama, Reality, TV Sitcom
Focus: Feature Films, TV, Reality Programming
(Reality TV, Documentaries, Special Events,
Sporting Events)

**Kim Haswell-Tannenbaum**
Title: Producer

**Nicholas Pietryga**
Title: Assistant

**Eric Tannenbaum**
Title: Producer

**Amanda Tomasetti**
Title: Assistant

**Jason Wang**
Title: Creative Affairs

## THE WALT DISNEY COMPANY

500 South Buena Vista Street
Burbank, CA 91521

Phone: 818-560-1000
Fax: 818-560-2500
Website: www.disney.com

**Submission Policy:** Does not accept any unsolicited material
**Genre:** Action, Animation, Comedy, Drama, Family, Fantasy, Memoir & True Stories, Myth, TV Drama, TV Sitcom
**Year Established:** 1923

**Rita Ferro**
Title: Executive Vice President

**Mary Ann Hughes**
Title: Vice President
IMDB: www.imdb.com/name/nm3134377/

**Robert Iger**
Title: Chairman of the Board, CEO
Email: bob.iger@disney.com
IMDB: www.imdb.com/name/nm2250609

## THE WEINSTEIN COMPANY

New York Branch:
375 Greenwich Street, Lobby A
New York, NY 10013-2376

Los Angeles Branch:
9100 Wilshire Boulevard, Suite 700W
Beverly Hills, CA 90212

Phone: NY:212-941-3800/LA: 424-204-4800
Fax: NY:212-941-3949
Email: info@weinsteinco.com
Website: www.weinsteinco.com

**Submission Policy:** Does not accept any unsolicited material
**Genre:** Action, Animation, Comedy, Drama, Family, Memoir & True Stories, Myth, Romance, Thriller, TV Drama, TV Sitcom
**Focus:** Feature Films, TV
**Year Established:** 2005

**Collin Creighton**
Title: Vice President (Production & Development)

**Barbara Schneeweiss**
Title: Vice President (Development & Production for TV & Film)

**Harvey Weinstein**
Title: Co-Chairman
Assistant: Brendon Boyea

**Bob Weinstein**
Title: Co-Chairman

## THE WOLPER ORGANIZATION

4000 Warner Blvd.
Bldg. 14, Ste. 200
Burbank, CA 91504

Phone: 818-954-1421
Fax: 818-954-1593
Website: www.wolperorg.com

**Submission Policy:** Does not accept any unsolicited material
**Genre:** Crime, Detective, Feature Films, TV, TV Drama
**Focus:** Feature Films, TV
**Year Established:** 1987

**Sam Alexander**
Title: Director of Development
Email: Sam.Alexander@wbtvprod.com
IMDB: www.imdb.com/name/nm3303012

**Kevin Nicklaus**
Title: Vice-President Development
IMDB: www.imdb.com/name/nm2102454

**David L. Wolper**
Title: President/Executive Producer
IMDB: www.imdb.com/name/nm0938678/

**Mark Wolper**
Title: President/Executive Producer
IMDB: www.imdb.com/name/nm0938679

## THE ZANUCK COMPANY

16 Beverly Park
Beverly Hills, CA 90210

Phone: 310-274-0261
Fax: 310-273-9217

**Submission Policy:** Does not accept any unsolicited material
**Genre:** Action, Comedy, Crime, Drama, Family, Fantasy, Feature Films, Period, Romance, Thriller
**Focus:** Feature Films, TV
**Year Established:** 1988

**Brenda Berrisford**
Title: Assistant

**Lili Fini Zanuck**
Title: Producer/Director
Phone: 310-274-0209
IMDB: www.imdb.com/name/nm0005572
Assistant: Aubrie Artiano

**Harrison Zanuck**
Title: Producer
Phone: 310-274-5929

**Richard Zanuck**
Title: Producer
Phone: 310-274-0261
IMDB: www.imdb.com/name/nm0005573

## THOUSAND WORDS

110 South Fairfax Avenue, Suite 370
Los Angeles, CA 90036

Phone: 323-936-4700
Fax: 323-936-4701
Email: info@thousand-words.com
Website: www.thousand-words.com

Submission Policy: Accepts query letter from
unproduced, unrepresented writers via email
Genre: Animation, Drama, Feature Films, Thriller
Focus: Feature Films
Year Established: 2000

**Jesse Johnston**
Title: Director of Development

**Jonah Smith**
Title: Co-President
Phone: 323-936-4700
Email: info@thousand-words.com
IMDB: www.imdb.com/name/nm0808819

**Michael Van Vliet**
Title: Creative Executive
Phone: 323-936-4700
Email: info@thousand-words.com
IMDB: www.imdb.com/name/nm2702900

**Palmer West**
Title: Founder, Co-President
Phone: 323-936-4700
Email: info@thousand-words.com
IMDB: www.imdb.com/name/nm0922279

## THREE STRANGE ANGELS, INC.

9050 West Washington Boulevard
Culver City, CA 90232

Phone: 310-840-8213
Submission Policy: Does not accept any unsolicited
material
Genre: Action, Comedy, Fantasy, Feature Films
Focus: Feature Films

**Lindsay Doran**
Title: President, Producer
Phone: 310-840-8213
IMDB: www.imdb.com/name/nm0233386
Assistant: Natasha Khrolenko

## THUNDER ROAD PICTURES

1411 5th Street Suite 400
Santa Monica, CA 90401

Phone: 310-573-8885

Submission Policy: Does not accept any unsolicited
material
Genre: Action, Crime, Detective, Drama, Feature
Films, Memoir & True Stories, Thriller
Focus: Feature Films, TV
Year Established: 2003

**Kerri L. Anderson**
Title: Executive - Director of Television
IMDB: www.imdb.com/name/nm2563841/

**Basil Iwanyk**
Title: Owner
IMDB: www.imdb.com/name/nm0412588

**Kent Kubena**
Title: Sr. Vice-President, Development &
Production/Producer
IMDB: www.imdb.com/name/nm0473423
Assistant: Noah Winter

**Peter Lawson**
Title: President
IMDB: www.imdb.com/name/nm4498662/
Assistant: Taylor Zea

**Erica Lee**
Title: Vice President- Development
IMDB: www.imdb.com/name/nm3102707
Assistant: Noah Winter

## TIG PRODUCTIONS

4450 Lakeside Dr
Ste 225
Burbank, CA 91505

Phone: 818-260-8707

**Submission Policy:** Does not accept any unsolicited material
**Genre:** Drama, Romance
**Focus:** Feature Films

**Kevin Costner**
**Title:** Executive Partner
**IMDB:** www.imdb.com/name/nm0000126

## TIM BURTON PRODUCTIONS

8033 Sunset Boulevard, Suite 7500
West Hollywood, CA 90046

**Phone:** 310-300-1670
**Fax:** 310-300-1671
**Website:** www.timburton.com

**Submission Policy:** Does not accept any unsolicited material
**Genre:** Action, Family, Fantasy
**Focus:** Feature Films
**Year Established:** 1989

**Tim Burton**
**Title:** Director/Producer
**Phone:** 310-300-1670
**Email:** kory.edwrds@timburton.com
**IMDB:** www.imdb.com/name/nm0000318
**Assistant:** Kory Edwards

**Derek Frey**
**Title:** Executive/Producer
**Email:** derek@lazerfilm.com
**IMDB:** www.imdb.com/name/nm0294553/

## TOM WELLING PRODUCTIONS

4000 Warner Boulevard
Building 146, Room 201
Burbank, CA 91522

**Phone:** 818-954-4012

**Submission Policy:** Does not accept any unsolicited material
**Genre:** TV, TV Drama
**Focus:** TV
**Year Established:** 2010

**Stephanie Levine**
**Title:** President
**Phone:** 818-954-4012

**Amy Suh**
**Title:** Director of Development
**Phone:** 818-954-4012

**Tom Welling**
**Title:** Principal
**Phone:** 818-954-4012
**IMDB:** www.imdb.com/name/nm0919991

## TOOL OF NORTH AMERICA

LA Branch:
2210 Broadway
Santa Monica, CA 90404

NY Branch:
50 West. 17th Street, 4th Floor, New York, NY 10011

**Phone:** LA:310-453-9244/NY: 212-924-1100
**Fax:** 310-453-4185/NY:212-924-1156
**Website:** www.toolofna.com

**Submission Policy:** Accepts query letter from unproduced, unrepresented writers via email
**Genre:** Drama, Horror, Thriller
**Focus:** Feature Films, TV, Reality Programming (Reality TV, Documentaries, Special Events, Sporting Events), Media (Commercials/Branding/Marketing)

**Dustin Callif**
**Email:** dustin@toolofna.com
**IMDB:** www.imdb.com/name/nm2956668

**Oliver Fuselier**
**Title:** Executive Producer
**Email:** oliver@toolofna.com
**IMDB:** www.imdb.com/name/nm0299336

**Rio Dylan Hernandez**
**Title:** Head of Feature Film and TV Development

**Brian Latt**
**Title:** Managing Director
**Email:** brian@toolofna.com
**IMDB:** www.imdb.com/name/nm0490373

## TORNELL PRODUCTIONS

80 Varick Street, Suite 10C
New York, NY 10013

**Phone:** 212-625-2530
**Fax:** 212-625-2532

**Submission Policy:** Accepts query letter from unproduced, unrepresented writers
**Focus:** Feature Films

**Lisa Tornell**
**Title:** Producer
**Phone:** 212-625-2530
**IMDB:** www.imdb.com/name/nm0868178

## TOWER OF BABBLE ENTERTAINMENT

854 North Spaulding Avenue
Los Angeles, CA 90046

**Phone:** 323-230-6128
**Fax:** 323-822-0312
**Email:** info@towerofb .com
**Website:** www.towerofb .com

**Submission Policy:** Accepts query letter from unproduced, unrepresented writers via email
**Genre:** Comedy, Feature Films, Romance
**Focus:** Feature Films, TV

**Beau Bauman**
**Title:** Writer/Producer
**Phone:** 323-230-6128
**Email:** info@towerofb .com
**IMDB:** www.imdb.com/name/nm0062149

**Jeff Wadlow**
**Title:** Writer/Director
**Phone:** 323-230-6128
**Email:** info@towerofb .com
**IMDB:** www.imdb.com/name/nm0905592

## TRANCAS INTERNATIONAL FILMS

2021 Pontius Ave
2nd Fl
Los Angeles, CA 90025

**Phone:** 310-477-6569
**Fax:** 310-477-7126
**Email:** info@trancasfilms.com
**Website:** www.trancasfilms.com

**Submission Policy:** Does not accept any unsolicited material
**Genre:** Action, Comedy, Drama, Feature Films, Horror, Thriller
**Focus:** Feature Films, TV

**Malek Akkad**
**Title:** Chairman & CEO
**IMDB:** www.imdb.com/name/nm0015443

**Thomas Fleming**
**Title:** Assistant Director Digital & New Media

**Louis Nader**
**Title:** Vice President of Production & Development
**IMDB:** www.imdb.com/name/nm0618868

## TRIBECA PRODUCTIONS

375 Greenwich Street, 8th Floor
New York, NY 10013

**Phone:** 212-941-2400
**Fax:** 212-941-3939
**Email:** info@tribecafilm.com
**Website:** www.tribecafilm.com

**Submission Policy:** Does not accept any unsolicited material
**Genre:** Action, Comedy, Crime, Drama, Fantasy, Feature Films, Memoir & True Stories, Period, Romance, Thriller
**Focus:** Feature Films, TV
**Year Established:** 1989

**Robert De Niro**
**Title:** Partner
**Phone:** 212-941-2400
**IMDB:** www.imdb.com/name/nm0000134

**Jane Rosenthal**
**Title:** Partner
**Assistant:** Gigi Graff

**Berry Welsh**
**Title:** Director of Development
**Phone:** 212-941-2400
**IMDB:** www.imdb.com/name/nm2654730

## TRICOAST STUDIOS

11124 West Washington Boulevard
Culver City, CA 90232

**Phone:** 310-458-7707
**Fax:** 310-204-2450
**Email:** tricoast@tricoast.com
**Website:** www.tricoast.com

**Submission Policy:** Does not accept any unsolicited material
**Focus:** Feature Films, TV

**Tory Weisz**
Title: Vice-President Development, Producer
Phone: 310-458-7707
IMDB: www.imdb.com/name/nm3258419

## TRICOR ENTERTAINMENT

1613 Chelsea Road
San Marino, CA 91108

Phone: 626-282-5184
Fax: 626-282-5185
Email: ExecutiveOffices@TricorEntertainment.com
Website: www.TricorEntertainment.com

Submission Policy: Does not accept any unsolicited material
Focus: Feature Films

**Craig Darian**
Title: Co-Chairman/CEO
Phone: 626-282-5184
IMDB: www.imdb.com/name/nm1545768

## TRILOGY ENTERTAINMENT GROUP

627 South Plymouth Boulevard The Studio
Los Angeles, CA 90005

Phone: 310-656-9733
Fax: 310-424-5816
Website: www.trilogyent.com

Submission Policy: Does not accept any unsolicited material
Genre: Action, Comedy, Fantasy, Feature Films, Romance, Thriller
Focus: Feature Films, TV

**Alex Daltas**
Title: President, Production
Email: adaltas@trilogyent.com
IMDB: www.imdb.com/name/nm0198226

**Nevin Densham**
Title: Creative Executive/Head, Development
Email: bfl am@trilogyent.com
IMDB: www.imdb.com/name/nm0219719

**Pen Densham**
Title: Partner
Phone: 310-656-9733
IMDB: www.imdb.com/name/nm0219720

**Howard Han**
Title: Consultant

**John Watson**
Title: Partner
IMDB: www.imdb.com/name/nm2302370/

## TROIKA PICTURES

2019 South Westgate Avenue
2nd Floor
Los Angeles, CA 90025

Phone: 310-696-2859
Email: troikapics@gmail.com
Website: www.troikapictures.com

Submission Policy: Does not accept any unsolicited material
Genre: Action, Crime, Fantasy, Feature Films, Romance, Thriller
Focus: Feature Films

**Bradley Gallo**
Title: Head of Production & Development
Phone: 310-696-2859
IMDB: www.imdb.com/name/nm0303010

**Michael Helfant**
Title: Co-CEO
Phone: 310-696-2859
IMDB: www.imdb.com/name/nm0375033

**Robert Stein**
Title: Co-CEO
Phone: 310-696-2859
IMDB: www.imdb.com/name/nm3355501

## TROMA ENTERTAINMENT

36-40 11th St
Long Island City, NY 11106

Phone: 718-391-0110
Fax: 718-391-0255
Email: troma1@gmail.com
Website: www.troma.com

Submission Policy: Accepts scripts from unproduced, unrepresented writers
Genre: Action, Drama, Fantasy, Feature Films, Horror, Science Fiction, Sociocultural, Thriller
Focus: Feature Films

**Michael Herz**
Title: Vice President
IMDB: www.imdb.com/name/nm0381230

**Lloyd Kaufman**
Title: President
Email: lloyd@troma.com
IMDB: www.imdb.com/name/nm0442207

## TURTLEBACK PRODUCTIONS, INC.

11736 Gwynne Lane
Los Angeles, CA, CA 90077

Phone: 310-440-8587
Fax: 310-440-8903

Submission Policy: Accepts query letter from
unproduced, unrepresented writers
Genre: Crime, Fantasy, Feature Films, Thriller, TV,
TV Drama
Focus: Feature Films, TV
Year Established: 1988

**Howard Meltzer**
Title: President/Executive Producer
Phone: 310-440-8587
IMDB: www.imdb.com/name/nm0578430

## TV LAND

1515 Broadway 38th Floor
New York, NY 10036

Phone: 212-258-7500
Email: info@tvland.com
Website: www.tvland.com

Submission Policy: Accepts query letter from
unproduced, unrepresented writers via email
Genre: TV, TV Drama, TV Sitcom
Focus: TV
Year Established: 1996

**Miranda Acevedo**
Title: Executive Assistant

**Bradley Gardner**
Title: Vice President (Development & Original
Programming)

**Scott Gregory**
Title: Vice President (Programming)

**Larry Jones**
Title: President
Phone: 212-846-6000
Email: larry.jones@tvland.com
IMDB: www.imdb.com/name/nm1511130

**Rose Catherine Pinkney**
Title: Vice President (Development & Original
Programming)
IMDB: www.imdb.com/name/nm0684384/

## TV ONE LLC

1010 Wayne Avenue
Silver Spring, MD 20910

Phone: 301-755-0400
Website: www.tvoneonline.com

Submission Policy: Accepts query letter from
produced or represented writers
Genre: TV, TV Drama, TV Sitcom
Focus: TV
Year Established: 2004

**Toni Judkins**
Title: Senior Vice President (Original Programming)

**Alfred Liggins**
Title: Chairman
Phone: 301-755-0400
Email: aliggins@tv-one.tv
IMDB: www.imdb.com/name/nm3447190

**Jubba Seyyid**
Title: Director (Programming & Production)

## TV REPAIR

857 Castaic Place
Pacific Palisades, CA 90272

Phone: 310-459-3671
Fax: 310-459-4251
Email: davidjlatt@earthlink.net

Submission Policy: Accepts query letter from
unproduced, unrepresented writers via email
Focus: TV

**David Latt**
Title: Producer/Writer
Phone: 310-459-3671
Email: davidjlatt@earthlink.net
IMDB: www.imdb.com/name/nm0490374

## TWENTIETH CENTURY FOX FILM

10201 West Pico Boulevard
Los Angeles, CA 90035

Phone: 310-369-1000
Fax: 310-203-1558

**Email:** foxmovies@fox.com
**Website:** www.fox.com

**Submission Policy:** Does not accept any unsolicited material
**Genre:** Action, Comedy, Crime, Detective, Drama, Family, Fantasy, Horror, Memoir & True Stories, Myth, Romance, Thriller
**Focus:** Feature Films, TV
**Year Established:** 1935

**Kimberly Cooper**
**Title:** Executive Vice President (Feature Productions)

**Ted Dodd**
**Title:** Senior Vice President (Creative Affairs)

**Steve Freedman**
**Title:** Vice President (Feature Production)

**David A Starke**
**Title:** Senior Vice President (Production)

**Emma Watts**
**Title:** President (Production)

## TWENTIETH CENTURY FOX TELEVISION

10201 West Pico Boulevard
Building 103, Room 5286
Los Angeles, CA 90035

**Phone:** 310-369-1000
**Fax:** 310-369-8726
**Email:** info@fox.com
**Website:** www.fox.com

**Submission Policy:** Does not accept any unsolicited material
**Genre:** TV Drama, TV Sitcom
**Year Established:** 1949

**Mark Ambrose**
**Title:** Director (Drama Development)

**Jennifer Carreras**
**Title:** Director (Comedy Development)

**Jonathan Davis**
**Title:** Executive Vice President (Comedy Development & Animation)

**Dana Honor**
**Title:** Senior Vice President (Comedy Development)

**Lisa Katz**
**Title:** Senior Vice President (Drama Development)

**Gary Newman**
**Title:** Chairman
**Email:** gary.newman@fox.com
**IMDB:** www.imdb.com/name/nm3050096

**Dana Walden**
**Title:** Chairman

## TWENTIETH TELEVISION

2121 Avenue of the Stars
17th Floor
Los Angeles, CA 90067

**Phone:** 310-369-1000
**Email:** info@fox.com
**Website:** www.fox.com

**Submission Policy:** Does not accept any unsolicited material
**Genre:** TV Drama, TV Sitcom
**Year Established:** 1992

**Roger Ailes**
**Title:** Chairman

**Stephen Brown**
**Title:** EVP Programming and Development

**Greg Meidel**
**Title:** President, Twentieth Television
**IMDB:** www.imdb.com/name/nm2518163

**Deborah Norton**
**Title:** VP, Programming

## TWINSTAR ENTERTAINMENT

4041 MacArthur Boulevard, Suite 475
Newport Beach, CA 92660

**Phone:** 949-474-8600
**Email:** info@twinstarentertainment.com
**Website:** www.twinstarentertainment.com

**Submission Policy:** Accepts scripts from unproduced, unrepresented writers
**Genre:** Animation, Comedy, Family, TV Drama, TV Sitcom
**Year Established:** 2003

**Russell Werdin**
**Title:** CEO
**Phone:** 949-474-8600
**Email:** info@twinstarentertainment.com
**IMDB:** www.imdb.com/name/nm2232609

## TWISTED PICTURES

901 N Highland Ave
Los Angeles, CA 90038

**Phone:** 323-850-3232
**Fax:** 323-850-0521

**Submission Policy:** Accepts query letter from
unproduced, unrepresented writers
**Genre:** Crime, Feature Films, Horror, Thriller, TV
**Focus:** Feature Films, Television

**Mark Burg**
**Title:** Principal
**IMDB:** www.imdb.com/name/nm0121117
**Assistant:** James Cole

**Oren Koules**
**Title:** Executive
**IMDB:** www.imdb.com/name/nm0467977
**Assistant:** James Cole

**Carl Mazzocone**
**Title:** Executive
**IMDB:** www.imdb.com/name/nm0563604

**Michael J. Menchel**
**Title:** President

## TWO TON FILMS

375 Greenwich Street
New York, NY 10013

**Phone:** 212-941-3863
**Email:** info@twotonfilms.com
**Website:** www.twotonfilms.com

**Submission Policy:** Accepts query letter from
unproduced, unrepresented writers via email
**Genre:** Action, Drama, Family, TV Drama, TV
Sitcom
**Focus:** Feature Films

**Clay Pecorin**
**Title:** Partner/Producer
**Phone:** 212-941-3863
**Email:** info@twotonfilms.com
**IMDB:** www.imdb.com/name/nm2668976

**Justin Zackham**
**Title:** Partner/Producer/Writer
**Phone:** 212-941-3863
**Email:** info@twotonfilms.com
**IMDB:** www.imdb.com/name/nm0951698

## UFLAND PRODUCTIONS

963 Moraga Drive
Los Angeles, CA 90049

**Phone:** 310-476-4520
**Fax:** 310-476-4891
**Email:** ufland.productions@verizon.net

**Submission Policy:** Does not accept any unsolicited
material
**Genre:** Drama, Romance, TV Drama, TV Sitcom
**Focus:** Feature Films, TV
**Year Established:** 1972

**Mary Jane Ufland**
**Title:** Producer
**IMDB:** www.imdb.com/name/nm0880040/

**Harry Ufland**
**Title:** Principal/Producer
**Phone:** 310-437-0805
**IMDB:** www.imdb.com/name/nm0880036

## UNDERGROUND FILMS

447 South Highland Avenue
Los Angeles, CA 90036

**Phone:** 323-930-2588
**Fax:** 323-930-2334
**Email:** submissions@undergroundfilms.net
**Website:** www.undergroundfilms.net

**Submission Policy:** Accepts scripts from
unproduced, unrepresented writers via email
**Genre:** Action, Animation, Comedy, Drama,
Family, Fantasy, Horror, Memoir & True Stories,
Myth, Romance, Thriller, TV Drama, TV Sitcom
**Year Established:** 2003

**Austin Bedell**
**Title:** Producer
**Phone:** 323-930-2588
**Email:** austin@undergroundfilms.net

**Chris Dennis**
**Title:** Producer/Principal
**Phone:** 323-930-2588
**Email:** chris@undergroundfilms.net

**Trevor Engelson**
**Title:** Principal/Producer
**Phone:** 323-930-2569
**Email:** trevor@undergroundfilms.net
**IMDB:** www.imdb.com/name/nm0257333

**Josh McGuire Turner**
Title: Producer
Phone: 323-930-2435
Email: josh@undergroundfilms.net

**Noah Rothman**
Title: Producer
Phone: 323-930-2588
Email: noah@undergroundfilms.net

**Evan Silverberg**
Title: Producer
Phone: 323-930-2588
Email: evan@undergroundfilms.net

## UNIFIED PICTURES

19773 Bahama Street
Northridge, CA 91324

Phone: 818-576-1006
Fax: 818-534-3347
Email: info@unifiedpictures.com
Website: www.unifiedpictures.com

Submission Policy: Accepts query letter from unproduced, unrepresented writers
Genre: Action, Comedy, Crime, Detective, Drama, Horror, Thriller
Focus: Feature Films
Year Established: 2004

**Shaun Clapham**
Title: Creative Executive
Email: sclapham@unifi edpictures.com
IMDB: www.imdb.com/name/nm4111097

**Steve Goldstein**
Title: President/Business Development
IMDB: www.imdb.com/name/nm2179640/

**Keith Kjarval**
Title: Founder/Producer
IMDB: www.imdb.com/name/nm1761309

**Kurt Rauer**
Title: Founder/Producer
IMDB: www.imdb.com/name/nm0970009

**Paul Michael Ruffman**
Title: Vice President/Business Development

## UNION ENTERTAINMENT

9255 Sunset Boulevard, Suite 528
West Hollywood, CA 90069

Phone: 310-274-7040
Fax: 310-274-1065
Email: info@unionent.com
Website: www.unionent.com
IMDB: www.imdb.com/company/co0183888

Submission Policy: Does not accept any unsolicited material
Genre: Animation
Focus: Video Games
Year Established: 2006

**Howard Bliss**
Title: Business Affairs
Email: howard@unionent.com
IMDB: www.imdb.com/name/nm2973051

**Richard Leibowitz**
Title: President
Phone: 310-274-7040
Email: rich@unionent.com
IMDB: www.imdb.com/name/nm2325318
Assistant: Sarah Logie

## UNIQUE FEATURES

888 7th Avenue, 16th Floor
New York, NY 10106

Phone: 212-649-4980
Fax: 212-649-4999
IMDB: www.imdb.com/company/co0242085

Submission Policy: Does not accept any unsolicited material
Focus: Feature Films, TV
Year Established: 2008

**Mark Kaufman**
Title: Head, East Coast Production & Development
Phone: 212-649-4855
IMDB: www.imdb.com/name/nm0442212

**Michael Lynne**
Title: Executive - West Coast Branch
Phone: 310-492-8009
IMDB: www.imdb.com/name/nm1088153

**Dylan Sellers**
Title: Head, West Coast Production & Development
Phone: 310-492-8009
IMDB: www.imdb.com/name/nm0783346

## UNIQUE FEATURES

116 North Robertson Boulevard, Suite 909
Los Angeles, CA 90048

**Phone:** 310-492-8009
**Fax:** 310-492-8022
**IMDB:** www.imdb.com/company/co0242085

**Submission Policy:** Does not accept any unsolicited material
**Focus:** Feature Films, TV
**Year Established:** 2008

**Mark Kaufman**
**Title:** Head, East Coast Production & Development
**Phone:** 212-649-4855
**IMDB:** www.imdb.com/name/nm0442212

**Michael Lynne**
**Title:** Executive - West Coast Branch
**Phone:** 310-492-8009
**IMDB:** www.imdb.com/name/nm1088153

**Dylan Sellers**
**Title:** Head, West Coast Production & Development
**Phone:** 310-492-8009
**IMDB:** www.imdb.com/name/nm0783346

## UNISON FILMS

790 Madison Ave
Suite 306
New York, NY 10065

**Phone:** 212-226-1200
**Fax:** 646-349-1738
**Email:** info@unisonfilms.com
**Website:** www.unisonfilms.com

**Genre:** Comedy, Drama, Feature Films, Romance
**Focus:** Feature Films
**Year Established:** 2004

**Ryan Brooks**
**Title:** Executive Producer

**Cliff Curtis**
**Title:** Producer

**Cassandra Kulukundis**
**Title:** Partner
**IMDB:** www.imdb.com/name/nm0474697

**Emanuel Michael**
**Title:** Partner
**IMDB:** www.imdb.com/name/nm1639578

## UNITED ARTISTS

245 North Beverly Drive
Beverly Hills, CA 90210

**Phone:** 310-449-3000
**Fax:** 310-586-8358
**Website:** www.unitedartists.com
**IMDB:** www.imdb.com/company/co0026841

**Submission Policy:** Does not accept any unsolicited material
**Genre:** Action, Crime, Drama, TV Drama
**Focus:** Feature Films, TV
**Year Established:** 1919

**Tom Cruise**
**Title:** Producer
**Phone:** 310-449-3000
**IMDB:** www.imdb.com/name/nm0000129

**Don Granger**
**Title:** President, Production
**Phone:** 310-449-3000
**IMDB:** www.imdb.com/name/nm1447370

**Elliot Kleinberg**
**Title:** COO
**Phone:** 310-449-3000
**IMDB:** www.imdb.com/name/nm2552087

## UNIVERSAL CABLE PRODUCTIONS

100 Universal City Plaza
Building 1440, 14th Floor
Universal City, CA 91608

**Phone:** 818-840-4444
**Website:** www.nbcumv.com
**IMDB:** www.imdb.com/company/co0242101

**Submission Policy:** Accepts query letter from unproduced, unrepresented writers
**Genre:** TV Drama, TV Sitcom
**Year Established:** 1997

**Bonnie Hammer**
**Title:** Chairman, NBCUniversal Cable Entertainment
**Phone:** 818-840-4444
**IMDB:** www.imdb.com/name/nm1045499

## UNIVERSAL STUDIOS

100 Universal City Plaza
Universal City, CA 91608

**Phone:** 818-840-4444
**Website:** http://www.universalstudios.com/
**IMDB:** http://www.imdb.com/company/
co0000534/?ref_=fn_al_co_1

**Submission Policy:** Accepts query letter from
unproduced, unrepresented writers
**Genre:** Action, Animation, Comedy, Crime,
Detective, Drama, Family, Fantasy, Horror, Memoir
& True Stories, Myth, Romance, Science Fiction,
Thriller, TV Drama, TV Sitcom
**Focus:** Feature Films, Television
**Year Established:** 1912

**Ron Meyer**
**Title:** President & COO, Universal Studios &
NBCUniversal
**Phone:** 818-840-4444
**IMDB:** www.imdb.com/name/nm0005228

## UNIVERSAL TELEVISION (FORMERLY UNIVERSAL MEDIA STUDIOS)

100 Universal City Plaza
Building 1360, 3rd Floor
Universal City, CA 91608

**Phone:** 818-777-1000
**Website:** www.universalstudios.com
**IMDB:** www.imdb.com/company/co0096447

**Submission Policy:** Accepts query letter from
unproduced, unrepresented writers
**Genre:** Action, Animation, Comedy, Crime,
Detective, Drama, Family, Fantasy, Memoir & True
Stories, Myth, Romance, Science Fiction, Thriller,
TV Drama, TV Sitcom

**Bela Bajaria**
**Title:** Executive Vice-President, Universal
Television
**IMDB:** www.imdb.com/name/nm0338612

## UNSTOPPABLE

c/o Independent Talent Agency
76 Oxford Street
London W1D 1BS
United Kingdom

**Email:** info@unstoppableentertainmentuk.com
**Website:** www.unstoppableentertainmentuk.com

**Submission Policy:** Accepts scripts from
unproduced, unrepresented writers

**Genre:** Action, Comedy, Crime, Drama, Romance,
Science Fiction, Thriller
**Focus:** Feature Films
**Year Established:** 2007

**Noel Clarke**
**Title:** Actor/Writer/Producer
**Email:** noel@unstoppableentertainmentuk.com

## UNTITLED ENTERTAINMENT

350 South Beverly Drive, Suite 200
Beverly Hills, CA 90212

**Phone:** 310-601-2100
**Fax:** 310-601-2344
**IMDB:** www.imdb.com/company/co0034249

**Submission Policy:** Accepts query letter from
unproduced, unrepresented writers
**Genre:** Drama, Fantasy, Memoir & True Stories,
Myth, Romance, TV Drama, TV Sitcom

**Jason Weinberg**
**Title:** Partner
**Phone:** 310-601-2100
**IMDB:** www.imdb.com/name/nm4156256

## UPPITV

c/o CBS Studios
4024 Radford Avenue, Bungalow 9
Studio City, CA 91604

**Phone:** 818-655-5000

**Submission Policy:** Does not accept any unsolicited
material
**Genre:** TV Drama, TV Sitcom

**Samuel Jackson**
**Title:** Principal
**Phone:** 818-655-5000
**IMDB:** www.imdb.com/name/nm0000168

## USA NETWORK

30 Rockefeller Plaza
21st Floor
New York, NY 10112

**Phone:** 212-664-4444
**Fax:** 212-703-8582
**IMDB:** www.imdb.com/company/co0014957

**Submission Policy:** Accepts query letter from
unproduced, unrepresented writers via email

**Genre:** TV Drama, TV Sitcom
**Year Established:** 1971

**Sally Whitehill**
**Title:** Director Of Development
**Phone:** 212-644-4444

## VALHALLA MOTION PICTURES

3201 Cahuenga Boulevard W
Los Angeles, CA 90068-1301

**Phone:** 323-850-3030
**Fax:** 323-850-3038
**Email:** vmp@valhallapix.com
**Website:** www.valhallapix.com

**Submission Policy:** Does not accept any unsolicited material
**Genre:** Action, Drama, Fantasy, Horror, Thriller
**Focus:** Feature Films, TV

**Kris Henigman**
**Title:** Director of Development
**Email:** vmp@valhallapix.com
**IMDB:** www.imdb.com/name/nm1898339

**Gale Hurd**
**Title:** CEO/Producer
**Phone:** 323-850-3030
**Email:** gah@valhallapix.com
**IMDB:** www.imdb.com/name/nm0005036

## VANDERKLOOT FILM & TELEVISION

750 Ralph McGill Boulevard N.E.
Atlanta, GA 30312

**Phone:** 404-221-0236
**Fax:** 404-221-1057
**Email:** bv@vanderkloot.com
**Website:** www.vanderkloot.com

**Submission Policy:** Does not accept any unsolicited material
**Genre:** Action, Family, Memoir & True Stories, TV Drama, TV Sitcom
**Year Established:** 1976

**Erin Grass**
**Title:** Director of Marketing
**Email:** erin@magiclantern.com
**IMDB:** www.imdb.com/name/nm3084570

**William VanDerKloot**
**Title:** President/Producer/Director
**Phone:** 404-221-0236
**Email:** william@vanderkloot.com
**IMDB:** www.imdb.com/name/nm0886281

## VANGUARD FILMS/VANGUARD ANIMATION

8703 West Olympic Boulevard
Los Angeles, CA 90035

**Phone:** 310-888-8020
**Fax:** 310-362-8685
**Email:** contact@vanguardanimation.com
**Website:** www.vanguardanimation.com

**Submission Policy:** Does not accept any unsolicited material
**Genre:** Animation
**Focus:** Feature Films
**Year Established:** 2004

**Robert Moreland**
**Title:** President Production & Development
**Phone:** 310-888-8020
**IMDB:** www.imdb.com/name/nm0603668

**John Williams**
**Title:** Chairman & CEO
**Phone:** 310-888-8020
**IMDB:** www.imdb.com/name/nm0930964

## VANGUARD PRODUCTIONS

12111 Beatrice Street
Culver City, CA 90230

**Phone:** 310-306-4910
**Fax:** 310-306-1978
**Email:** info@vanguardproductions.biz
**Website:** www.vanguardproductions.biz

**Submission Policy:** Accepts query letter from unproduced, unrepresented writers via email
**Genre:** Action, Family, Memoir & True Stories, TV Drama, TV Sitcom
**Year Established:** 1986

**Terence O'Keefe**
**Title:** Founder/Writer/Producer/Director
**Phone:** 310-306-4910
**Email:** terry@vanguardproductions.biz
**IMDB:** www.imdb.com/name/nm0641496

## VANQUISH MOTION PICTURES

10 Universal City Plaza
NBC/Universal Building, 20th Floor
Universal City, CA 91608

**Phone:** 818-753-2319
**Email:** submissions@vanquishmotionpictures.com
**Website:** www.vanquishmotionpictures.com

**Submission Policy:** Accepts query letter from
unproduced, unrepresented writers via email
**Focus:** Feature Films, TV
**Year Established:** 2009

### Neetu Sharma
**Title:** Creative Executive
**Phone:** 818-753-2319
**Email:** ns@vanquishmotionpictures.com
**IMDB:** www.imdb.com/name/nm3434485

### Ryan Williams
**Title:** Creative Executive
**Phone:** 818-753-2319
**Email:** rs@vanquishmotionpictures.com
**IMDB:** www.imdb.com/name/nm4426713

## VARSITY PICTURES

1040 North Las Palmas Avenue
Building 2, First Floor
Los Angeles, CA 90038

**Phone:** 310-601-1960
**Fax:** 310-601-1961

**Submission Policy:** Accepts query letter from
unproduced, unrepresented writers
**Focus:** Feature Films, TV
**Year Established:** 2007

### Meghann Collins
**Title:** Film Development
**Phone:** 310-601-1960
**IMDB:** www.imdb.com/name/nm1937533

### Carter Hansen
**Title:** Creative Executive
**Phone:** 310-601-1960
**IMDB:** www.imdb.com/name/nm3255715

### Shauna Phelan
**Title:** Television Development
**Phone:** 310-601-1960
**IMDB:** www.imdb.com/name/nm1016912

## VELOCITY PICTURES

4132 Woodcliff Road
Sherman Oaks, CA 91403

**Phone:** 310-804-8554
**Fax:** 310-496-1329

**Submission Policy:** Accepts query letter from
unproduced, unrepresented writers
**Genre:** Action, Drama, Memoir & True Stories,
Romance, Thriller
**Year Established:** 2006

### Patrick Gallagher
**Title:** Co-Founder
**Phone:** 310-804-8554
**Email:** pfgla@aol.com
**IMDB:** www.imdb.com/name/nm1725050

### Ryan Johnson
**Title:** Co-Founder
**Phone:** 310-804-8554
**Email:** ryanj@prettydangerousfilms.com
**IMDB:** www.imdb.com/name/nm1010198

## VERISIMILITUDE

225 West 13th St
New York, NY 10011

**Phone:** 212-989-1038
**Fax:** 212-989-1943
**Email:** info@verisimilitude.com
**Website:** www.verisimilitude.com

**Submission Policy:** Accepts query letter from
produced or represented writers
**Genre:** Comedy, Drama, Feature Films, Romance,
Thriller
**Focus:** Feature Films

### Tyler Brodie
**Title:** Partner
**IMDB:** www.mdb.com/name/nm0110921

### Hunter Gray
**Title:** Partner
**IMDB:** www.imdb.com/name/nm0336683

### Alex Orlovsky
**Title:** Partner
**IMDB:** www.imdb.com/name/nm0650164

### Phaedon Papadopoulos
**Title:** Creative Executive
**IMDB:** www.imdb.com/name/nm3011396

## VERITE FILMS

15 Beaufort Rd
Toronto, ON M4E 1M6
Canada

**Phone:** 416 693 8245
**Fax:** 416 693 8252
**Email:** verite@veritefilms.ca
**Website:** www.veritefilms.ca

**Submission Policy:** Accepts query letter from unproduced, unrepresented writers
**Genre:** Comedy, Drama, Family, TV Drama, TV Sitcom
**Year Established:** 2004

### Virginia Thompson
**Title:** Partner/President/Executive Producer
**Phone:** 306-585-1737
**Email:** virginia@veritefilms.ca
**IMDB:** www.imdb.com/name/nm1395111

## VERTEBRA FILMS

1608 Vine Street, Suite 503
Hollywood, CA 90028

**Phone:** 323-461-0021
**Fax:** 323-461-0031
**Website:** www.vertebrafilms.com

**Submission Policy:** Accepts query letter from unproduced, unrepresented writers
**Genre:** Horror, Thriller
**Focus:** Feature Films
**Year Established:** 2010

### Mac Cappucino
**IMDB:** www.imdb.com/name/nm2225247

## VERTIGO FILMS

The Big Room Studios 77 Fortess Road
London, United Kingdom,
NW5 1AG

**Phone:** +44-0-20-7428-7555
**Fax:** +44-0-20-7485-9713
**Email:** mail@vertigofilms.com
**Website:** www.vertigofilms.com

**Submission Policy:** Does not accept any unsolicited material
**Genre:** Action, Comedy, Crime, Drama, Fantasy, Feature Films, Horror, Romance, Science Fiction,

Thriller
**Focus:** Feature Films
**Year Established:** 2002

### Nick Love
**Title:** Principal
**IMDB:** www.imdb.com/name/nm0522393

### Allan Niblo
**Title:** Producer
**IMDB:** www.imdb.com/name/nm0629242

### Rupert Preston
**Title:** Producer
**IMDB:** www.imdb.com/name/nm0696486

### James Richardson
**Title:** Producer
**IMDB:** www.imdb.com/name/nm0724597

### Jim Spencer
**Title:** Producer
**IMDB:** www.imdb.com/name/nm2005794

## VH1

2600 Colorado Ave
Santa Monica, CA 90404

**Phone:** 310 752 8000
**Email:** info@vh1.com
**Website:** www.vh1.com

**Submission Policy:** Accepts query letter from unproduced, unrepresented writers
**Genre:** Comedy, Drama, Memoir & True Stories, Romance, TV Drama, TV Sitcom
**Year Established:** 1986

### Van Toffler
**Title:** President, MTVN Music, LOGO & Film
**Phone:** 212-846-8000
**Email:** van.toffler@vh1.com
**IMDB:** www.imdb.com/name/nm0865508

## VIACOM INC.

1515 Broadway
New York, NY 10036

**Phone:** 212-258-6000
**Website:** www.viacom.com

**Submission Policy:** Does not accept any unsolicited material
**Genre:** Comedy, Drama, Memoir & True Stories,

TV Drama, TV Sitcom
**Year Established:** 1971

**Philippe Dauman**
**Title:** President & CEO
**Phone:** 212-258-6000
**Email:** philippe.dauman@viacom.com
**IMDB:** www.imdb.com/name/nm2449184

## VILLAGE ROADSHOW PICTURES

100 North Crescent Drive, Suite 323
Beverly Hills, CA 90210

**Phone:** 310-385-4300
**Fax:** 310-385-4301
**Website:** http://www.vreg.com/films

**Submission Policy:** Does not accept any unsolicited material
**Focus:** Feature Films
**Year Established:** 1998

**Bruce Berman**
**Title:** Chairman/CEO
**Phone:** 310-385-4300
**IMDB:** www.imdb.com/name/nm0075732
**Assistant:** Suzy Figueroa

**Matt Skiena**
**Title:** Vice President of Production
**Phone:** 310-385-4300
**Email:** mskiena@vrpe.com
**IMDB:** www.imdb.com/name/nm3466832

## VINCENT NEWMAN ENTERTAINMENT

8840 Wilshire Boulevard
3rd Floor
Los Angeles, CA 90211

**Phone:** 310-358-3050
**Fax:** 310-358-3289
**Email:** general@liveheart-vne.com

**Submission Policy:** Accepts query letter from unproduced, unrepresented writers via email
**Genre:** Action, Drama, Fantasy, Myth, Thriller, TV Drama, TV Sitcom
**Year Established:** 2011

**Vincent Newman**
**Title:** Principal
**Phone:** 310-358-3050
**Email:** vincent@liveheart-vne.com

**IMDB:** www.imdb.com/name/nm0628304
**Assistant:** John Funk

## VIN DI BONA PRODUCTIONS

12233 West Olympic Boulevard, Suite 170
Los Angeles, CA 90064

**Phone:** 310-571-1875
**Website:** www.vdbp.com

**Submission Policy:** Accepts query letter from unproduced, unrepresented writers
**Genre:** Comedy, TV Sitcom
**Year Established:** 1987

**Vin DiBona**
**Title:** Chairman
**IMDB:** www.imdb.com/name/nm0223688

**Cara Di Bona**
**Title:** Vice President (Creative Affairs)
**IMDB:** www.imdb.com/name/nm0223685/

**Joanne Moore**
**Title:** President

## VIRGIN PRODUCED

315 South Beverly Drive, Suite 506
Beverly Hills, CA 90212

**Phone:** 310-941-7300
**Email:** media@virginproduced.com
**Website:** www.virginproduced.com

**Submission Policy:** Does not accept any unsolicited material
**Genre:** Action, Animation, Drama, Fantasy, Thriller, TV Drama, TV Sitcom
**Year Established:** 2010

**Rebecca Farrell**
**Title:** Director of Operations
**IMDB:** www.imdb.com/name/nm2761874

**Jason Felts**
**Title:** CEO
**Phone:** 310-941-7300
**Email:** jfelts@virginproduced.com
**IMDB:** www.imdb.com/name/nm1479777

## VOLTAGE PRODUCTIONS

662 North Crescent Heights Boulevard
Los Angeles, CA 90048

Phone: 323-606-7630
Fax: 323-315-7115
Email: sales@voltagepictures.com
Website: www.voltagepictures.com

Submission Policy: Accepts scripts from produced or represented writers
Genre: Action, Animation, Drama, Fantasy, Memoir & True Stories, Romance, Science Fiction
Focus: Feature Films
Year Established: 2011

**Nicolas Chartier**
Email: nicolas@voltagepictures.com
IMDB: www.imdb.com/name/nm1291566

**Craig Flores**
Title: President/Partner Voltage Productions
IMDB: www.imdb.com/name/nm1997836
Assistant: Edmond Guidry

**Zev Foreman**
Title: Head of Development
IMDB: www.imdb.com/name/nm2303301

## VON ZERNECK SERTNER FILMS

c/o HCVT
11444 West Olympic Boulevard
11th Floor
Los Angeles, CA 90064

Phone: 310-652-3020
Email: vzs@vzsfilms.com
Website: www.vzsfilms.com
IMDB: www.imdb.com/company/co0094479

Submission Policy: Does not accept any unsolicited material
Genre: Crime, Detective, Drama, Memoir & True Stories, Thriller
Year Established: 1987

**Robert M. Srtner**
Title: Partner
IMDB: www.imdb.com/name/nm0785750

**Frank Von Zerneck**
Title: Partner
Phone: 310-652-3020
Email: vonzerneck@gmail.com
IMDB: www.imdb.com/name/nm0903273

## VOX3 FILMS

315 Bleecker Street #111
New York, NY 10014

Phone: 212-741-0406
Fax: 212-741-0424
Email: contact@vox3films.com
Website: www.vox3films.com
IMDB: www.imdb.com/company/co0146502

Submission Policy: Does not accept any unsolicited material
Genre: Drama, Romance, Thriller, TV Drama
Year Established: 2004

**Andrew Fierberg**
Title: Partner/Founder/Producer
Phone: 212-741-0406
Email: andrew.fi erberg@vox3fi lms.com
IMDB: www.imdb.com/name/nm0276404

**Christina Lurie**
Title: Partner
IMDB: www.imdb.com/name/nm1417371

**Steven Shainberg**
Title: Partner
IMDB: www.imdb.com/name/nm078760

## VULCAN PRODUCTIONS

505 Fifth Ave. S., Suite 900
Seattle WA 98104

Phone: 206-342-2277
Email: production@vulcan.com
Website: www.vulcan.com
IMDB: www.imdb.com/company/co0042766

Submission Policy: Accepts query letter from unproduced, unrepresented writers via email
Genre: Action, Memoir & True Stories, Thriller
Year Established: 1983

**Jody Allen**
Title: President
Phone: 206-342-2277
Email: jody@vulcan.com
IMDB: www.imdb.com/name/nm0666580

## WALDEN MEDIA

1888 Century Park East
14th Floor
Los Angeles, CA 90067

**Phone:** 310-887-1000
**Fax:** 310-887-1001
**Email:** info@walden.com
**Website:** www.walden.com
**IMDB:** www.imdb.com/company/co0073388

**Submission Policy:** Accepts query letter from unproduced, unrepresented writers via email
**Focus:** Feature Films
**Year Established:** 2001

**Amanda Palmer**
**Title:** Sr. Vice-President, Development & Production
**Phone:** 310-887-1000
**IMDB:** www.imdb.com/name/nm2198853

**Eric Tovell**
**Title:** Creative Executive
**Email:** etovell@walden.com
**Assistant:** Carol Tang ctang@walden.com

**Evan Turner**
**Title:** Sr. Vice-President, Development & Production
**Phone:** 310-887-1000
**IMDB:** www.imdb.com/name/nm1602263

## WALKER/FITZGIBBON TV & FILM PRODUCTION

2399 Mt. Olympus
Los Angeles, CA 90046

**Phone:** 323-469-6800
**Fax:** 323-878-0600
**Website:** www.walkerfitzgibbon.com
**IMDB:** www.imdb.com/company/co0171571

**Submission Policy:** Accepts query letter from unproduced, unrepresented writers via email
**Genre:** Animation, Comedy, Drama, Memoir & True Stories, TV Drama
**Year Established:** 1996

**Mo Fitzgibbon**
**Title:** Principal, Executive Producer/Director
**Phone:** 323-469-6800
**Email:** mo@walkerfitzgibbon.com
**IMDB:** www.imdb.com/name/nm0280422

**Robert W. Walker**
**Title:** Writer/Director (Executive)
**IMDB:** www.imdb.com/name/nm0908166

## WALT BECKER PRODUCTIONS

8530 Wilshire Blvd.
Suite 550
Beverly Hills, CA 90212
USA

**Phone:** 323-871-8400
**Fax:** 323-871-2540
**IMDB:** www.imdb.com/company/co0236068

**Submission Policy:** Does not accept any unsolicited material
**Focus:** TV

**Walt Becker**
**Title:** Director/Producer
**IMDB:** www.imdb.com/name/nm0065608

**Kelly Hayes**
**Title:** Director of Development
**IMDB:** www.imdb.com/name/nm0971886

## WARNER BROS. ANIMATION

411 North Hollywood Way
Burbank, CA 91505

**Phone:** 818-977-8700
**Email:** info@warnerbros.com
**Website:** www.warnerbros.com
**IMDB:** http://www.imdb.com/company/co0072876/?ref_=fn_al_co_1

**Submission Policy:** Does not accept any unsolicited material
**Genre:** Animation
**Focus:** Television
**Year Established:** 1930

**Sam Register**
**Title:** Executive Vice-President, Creative
**Email:** sam.register@warnerbros.com
**IMDB:** www.imdb.com/name/nm1882146

## WARNER BROS. ENTERTAINMENT INC.

4000 Warner Boulevard
Burbank, CA 91522-0001

**Phone:** 818-954-6000
**Website:** www.warnerbros.com

**Submission Policy:** Does not accept any unsolicited material
**Genre:** Action, Animation, Comedy, Crime, Detective, Drama, Family, Fantasy, Memoir & True

Stories, Myth, Romance, Science Fiction, Thriller, TV Drama, TV Sitcom
**Year Established:** 1923

**Barry Meyer**
Title: Chairman/CEO
Email: barry.meyer@warnerbros.com
IMDB: www.imdb.com/name/nm0583028

## WARNER BROS. HOME ENTERTAINMENT GROUP

4000 Warner Boulevard
Burbank, CA 91522-0001

Phone: 818-954-6000
Email: info@warnerbros.com
Website: www.warnerbros.com
IMDB: http://www.imdb.com/company/co0200179/?ref_=fn_al_co_1

**Submission Policy:** Does not accept any unsolicited material
**Genre:** Action, Animation, Comedy, Crime, Drama, Family, Fantasy, Horror, Memoir & True Stories, Myth, Romance, Science Fiction, Thriller, TV
**Focus:** Feature Films, Television, Shorts
**Year Established:** 2005

**Kevin Tsujihara**
Title: President
Email: kevin.tsujihara@warnerbros.com
IMDB: www.imdb.com/name/nm2493597

## WARNER BROS. PICTURES

4000 Warner Boulevard
Burbank, CA 91522-0001

Phone: 818-954-6000
Email: info@warnerbros.com
Website: www.warnerbros.com
IMDB: http://www.imdb.com/company/co0026840/?ref_=fn_al_co_1

**Submission Policy:** Does not accept any unsolicited material
**Genre:** Action, Animation, Comedy, Crime, Detective, Drama, Family, Fantasy, Memoir & True Stories, Myth, Romance, Thriller
**Focus:** Feature Films
**Year Established:** 1923

**Racheline Benveniste**
Title: Creative Executive
IMDB: http://www.imdb.com/name/nm3367909/?ref_=fn_al_nm_1
Assistant: Matthew Crespy

**Andrew Fischel**
Title: Creative Executive (Production Group)
Assistant: Stephanie Rosenthal

**Lynn Harris**
Title: Executive Vice President of Production
IMDB: http://www.imdb.com/name/nm0365036/?ref_=fn_al_nm_2
Assistant: Alexandra Amin

**Jeff Robinov**
Title: President
Email: jeff.robinov@warnerbros.com
IMDB: www.imdb.com/name/nm0732268
Assistant: Carrie Frymer

**Greg Silverman**
Title: President of Production
IMDB: http://www.imdb.com/name/nm0798909/?ref_=fn_al_nm_1
Assistant: Cate Adams

## WARNER BROS. TELEVISION GROUP

4000 Warner Boulevard
Burbank, CA 91522-0001

Phone: 818-954-6000
Email: info@warnerbros.com
Website: www.warnerbros.com
IMDB: http://www.imdb.com/company/co0253255/?ref_=fn_al_co_1

**Submission Policy:** Does not accept any unsolicited material
**Genre:** Action, Animation, Comedy, Drama, Family, Fantasy, Memoir & True Stories, Myth, Romance, Thriller, TV Sitcom
**Focus:** Feature Films, Television
**Year Established:** 2005

**Bruce Rosenblum**
Title: President
Email: bruce.rosenblum@warnerbros.com
IMDB: www.imdb.com/name/nm2686463

## WARNER HORIZON TELEVISION

4000 Warner Boulevard
Burbank, CA 91522-0001

**Phone:** 818-954-6000
**Email:** info@warnerbros.com
**Website:** www.warnerbros.com
**IMDB:** www.mdb.com/company/co0183230

**Submission Policy:** Does not accept any unsolicited material
**Genre:** Action, Animation, Comedy, Drama, Family, Fantasy, Memoir & True Stories, Myth, Romance, TV Drama, TV Sitcom
**Year Established:** 1999

### Peter Roth
**Title:** President
**Phone:** 818-954-6000
**Email:** peter.roth@warnerbros.com
**IMDB:** www.imdb.com/name/nm2325137

## WARNER SISTERS PRODUCTIONS

PO Box 50104
Santa Barbara, CA 93150

**Phone:** 818-766-6952
**Email:** info@warnersisters.com
**Website:** www.warnersisters.com
**IMDB:** http://www.imdb.com/company/co0121034/?ref_=fn_al_co_2

**Submission Policy:** Does not accept any unsolicited material
**Genre:** Memoir & True Stories
**Focus:** Feature Films, Television
**Year Established:** 2003

### Cass Warner
**Title:** CEO/President
**IMDB:** www.imdb.com/name/nm2064300

## WARP FILMS

Spectrum House 32-34 Gordon House Road
London, United Kingdom, NW5 1LP

**Phone:** (011) 442072848350
**Fax:** 011) 442072848360
**Email:** info@warpfilms.co.uk
**Website:** http://warp.net/films/
**IMDB:** http://www.imdb.com/company/co0251927/?ref_=fn_co_co_4

**Submission Policy:** Accepts query letter from unproduced, unrepresented writers via email
**Genre:** Action, Comedy, Documentary, Drama, Feature Films, Horror, Memoir & True Stories, Romance
**Focus:** Feature Films
**Year Established:** 2004

### Peter Carlton
**Title:** Head of Warp Films Europe
**IMDB:** http://www.imdb.com/name/nm1275058/?ref_=fn_al_nm_1

### Mark Herbert
**Title:** Principal
**IMDB:** http://www.imdb.com/name/nm0378591/?ref_=fn_al_nm_1

## WARP X

Electric Works
Digital Campus
Sheffield S1 2BJ
UK

**Phone:** +44-114-286-6280
**Fax:** +44-114-286-6283
**Email:** info@warpx.co.uk
**Website:** http://www.warpx.co.uk
**IMDB:** http://www.imdb.com/company/co0202028/?ref_=fn_al_co_1

**Submission Policy:** Does not accept any unsolicited material
**Genre:** Comedy, Crime, Documentary, Drama, Horror, Thriller
**Focus:** Feature Films
**Year Established:** 2008

### Mary Burke
**Title:** Producer
**IMDB:** http://www.imdb.com/name/nm1537339/?ref_=fn_al_nm_1

### Robin Gutch
**Title:** Managing Director
**IMDB:** http://www.imdb.com/name/nm0349168/?ref_=fn_al_nm_1

### Mark Herbert
**Title:** Producer
**IMDB:** http://www.imdb.com/name/nm0378591/?ref_=fn_al_nm_1

**Barry Ryan**
Title: Head of Production
IMDB: http://www.imdb.com/name/
nm1419213/?ref_=fn_al_nm_1

## WARREN MILLER ENTERTAINMENT

5720 Flatiron Parkway
Boulder CO 80301

Phone: 303-253-6300
Fax: 303-253-6380
Email: info@warrenmillertv.com
Website: www.warrenmillertv.com
IMDB: http://www.imdb.com/company/
co0040142/?ref_=fn_al_co_1

Submission Policy: Accepts query letter from
unproduced, unrepresented writers
Genre: Action, Memoir & True Stories, Reality
Focus: Feature Films, Television
Year Established: 1952

**Warren Miller**
Title: Chief Executive Officer

**Jeffrey Moore**
Title: Sr. Executive Producer
Email: jeffm@warrenmiller.com
IMDB: www.imdb.com/name/nm2545455

**Ginger Sheehy**
Title: Manager of Development
IMDB: http://www.imdb.com/name/
nm1200078/?ref_=fn_al_nm_1

**Ginger Sheehy**
Title: Manager of Development
IMDB: www.imdb.com/name/nm1200078

## WARRIOR POETS

76 Mercer Street Fourth Floor
New York, NY 10012

Phone: 212-219-7617
Fax: 212-219-2920
Email: em@warrior-poets.com
Website: www.warrior-poets.com
IMDB: http://www.imdb.com/company/
co0169151/?ref_=fn_al_co_1

Submission Policy: Does not accept any unsolicited
material
Genre: Drama, Memoir & True Stories

Focus: Feature Films, Television
Year Established: 2005

**Jeremy Chilnick**
Title: Partner (Head of Production and
Development)
IMDB: http://www.imdb.com/name/
nm2505733/?ref_=fn_al_nm_1
Assistant: Marjon Javadi

**Ethan Goldman**
Title: Executive Vice President of Development
IMDB: http://www.imdb.com/name/
nm1134121/?ref_=fn_al_nm_1

**Morgan Spurlock**
Title: President/Producer
IMDB: www.imdb.com/name/nm1041597
Assistant: Emmanuel Moran

## WAYANS BROTHERS ENTERTAINMENT

8730 West Sunset Boulevard, Suite 290
Los Angeles, CA 90069-2247

Phone: 323-930-6720
Fax: 424-202-3520
Email: thawkins@wayansbros.com
IMDB: http://www.imdb.com/company/
co0001823/?ref_=fn_co_co_1

Submission Policy: Does not accept any unsolicited
material
Genre: Comedy, Crime, Family, Horror, TV Sitcom
Year Established: 1980

**Rick Alvarez**
Title: Principal
IMDB: http://www.imdb.com/name/
nm0023315/?ref_=fn_al_nm_1

**Mike Tiddes**
Title: Creative Executive

**Marlon Wayans**
Title: Principal
IMDB: http://www.imdb.com/name/
nm0005541/?ref_=fn_al_nm_1
Assistant: Shane Miller

**Keenan Wayans**
Title: Principal
IMDB: www.imdb.com/name/nm0005540

**Shawn Wayans**
Title: Principal
IMDB: http://www.imdb.com/name/
nm0915465/?ref_=fn_al_nm_1

**WAYFARE ENTERTAINMENT VENTURES LLC**

435 West 19th Street
4th Floor
New York, NY 10011

Phone: 212-989-2200
Email: info@wayfareentertainment.com
Website: www.wayfareentertainment.com
IMDB: http://www.imdb.com/company/
co0239158/?ref_=fn_al_co_1

Submission Policy: Does not accept any unsolicited material
Genre: Action, Comedy, Drama, Family, Fantasy, Memoir & True Stories, Myth, Romance, Science Fiction, Thriller
Focus: Feature Films
Year Established: 2008

**Ben Browning**
Title: Co-Founder & CEO
Email: info@wayfareentertainment.com
IMDB: www.imdb.com/name/nm1878845

**Michael Maher**
Title: Co-Founder
IMDB: http://www.imdb.com/name/
nm3052130/?ref_=fn_al_nm_1

**Sarah Shepard**
Title: Vice President (Development)
IMDB: http://www.imdb.com/name/
nm2416896/?ref_=fn_al_nm_1

**Jeremy Kipp Walker**
Title: Head (Production)
IMDB: http://www.imdb.com/name/
nm0907844/?ref_=fn_al_nm_1

**WEED ROAD PICTURES**

4000 Warner Boulevard
Building 81, Suite 115
Burbank, CA 91522

Phone: 818-954-3771
Fax: 818-954-3061

IMDB: http://www.imdb.com/company/
co0093488/?ref_=fn_al_co_1

Submission Policy: Does not accept any unsolicited material
Genre: Action, Animation, Drama, Family, Fantasy, Horror, Memoir & True Stories, Science Fiction, Thriller
Focus: Feature Films, Television
Year Established: 2004

**Nicki Cortese**
Title: Vice President (Film and Television)
IMDB: http://www.imdb.com/name/
nm2492480/?ref_=fn_al_nm_1
Assistant: Mike Pence

**Akiva Goldsman**
Title: President/Producer
IMDB: www.imdb.com/name/nm0326040
Assistant: Bonnie Balmos

**WEINSTOCK PRODUCTIONS**

316 North Rossmore Avenue
Los Angeles, CA 90004

Phone: 323-791-1500
IMDB: http://www.imdb.com/company/
co0032259/?ref_=fn_al_co_1

Submission Policy: Accepts query letter from unproduced, unrepresented writers
Genre: Comedy, Crime, Drama, Family, Thriller
Focus: Feature Films

**Charles Weinstock**
Title: Producer
IMDB: www.imdb.com/name/nm091848

**WEINTRAUB/KUHN PRODUCTIONS**

1351 Third Street Promenade, Suite 206
Santa Monica, CA 90401

Phone: 310-458-3300
Fax: 310-458-3302
Email: fred@fredweintraub.com
Website: www.fredweintraub.com
IMDB: http://www.imdb.com/company/
co0031680/?ref_=fn_al_co_1

Submission Policy: Does not accept any unsolicited material
Genre: Action, Comedy, Drama, Family, Fantasy, Memoir & True Stories, Myth, Romance, Science

Fiction, Thriller, TV Drama
**Focus:** Feature Films, Television
**Year Established:** 1976

### Tom Kuhn
**Title:** Producer
**IMDB:** http://www.imdb.com/name/nm0474166/?ref_=fn_al_nm_1

### Maxwell Meltzer
**Title:** Business Affairs
**IMDB:** http://www.imdb.com/name/nm0578443/?ref_=fn_al_nm_1

### Fred Weintraub
**Title:** President
**Email:** fred@fredweintraub.com
**IMDB:** www.imdb.com/name/nm0918518

### Jackie Weintraub
**Title:** Vice President Of Development
**IMDB:** http://www.imdb.com/name/nm0918520/?ref_=fn_al_nm_1

## WELLER/GROSSMAN PRODUCTIONS

5200 Lankershim Boulevard
5th Floor
North Hollywood, CA 91601

**Phone:** 818-755-4800
**Email:** contact@wellergrossman.com
**Website:** www.wellergrossman.com
**IMDB:** http://www.imdb.com/company/co0102774/?ref_=fn_al_co_1

**Submission Policy:** Accepts scripts from produced or represented writers
**Genre:** Reality, TV Drama, TV Sitcom
**Focus:** Television
**Year Established:** 1993

### Gary Grossman
**Title:** Partner
**IMDB:** http://www.imdb.com/name/nm0343646/?ref_=fn_al_nm_1

### Debbie Supnik
**Title:** Director Of Development
**IMDB:** http://www.imdb.com/name/nm0839489/?ref_=fn_al_nm_1

### Robb Weller
**Title:** Partner/Executive Producer
**Email:** contact@wellergrossman.com
**IMDB:** www.imdb.com/name/nm0919888

## WENDY FINERMAN PRODUCTIONS

144 South Beverly Drive, #304
Beverly Hills, CA 90212

**Phone:** 310-694-8088
**Fax:** 310-694-8088
**Email:** info@wendyfinermanproductions.com
**Website:** www.wendyfinermanproductions.com
**IMDB:** http://www.imdb.com/company/co0004317/?ref_=fn_al_co_1

**Submission Policy:** Accepts query letter from unproduced, unrepresented writers via email
**Genre:** Comedy, Drama, Family, Fantasy, Period, Romance
**Focus:** Feature Films, Television

### Wendy Finerman
**Title:** Producer
**Email:** wfinerman@wendyfinermanproductions.com
**IMDB:** www.imdb.com/name/nm0277704

### Lisa Zupan
**Title:** Vice-President
**Email:** lzupan@wendyfinermanproductions.com
**IMDB:** www.imdb.com/name/nm0958702

## WESSLER ENTERTAINMNET

11661 San Vicente Blvd., Suite 609
Los Angeles, CA 90049

**Submission Policy:** Accepts query letter from unproduced, unrepresented writers
**Genre:** Comedy, Family, Feature Films
**Focus:** Feature Films

### Charles B. Wessler
**Title:** President
**IMDB:** www.imdb.com/name/nm0921853

## WE TV NETWORK

11 Penn Plaza
19th Floor
New York, NY 10001

**Phone:** 212-324-8500
**Fax:** 212-324-8595
**Email:** contactwe@wetv.com
**Website:** http://www.wetv.com
**IMDB:** http://www.imdb.com/company/co0340786/?ref_=fn_al_co_1

**Submission Policy:** Does not accept any unsolicited material
**Genre:** Family, Reality, TV Sitcom
**Focus:** Television
**Year Established:** 1997

**Laurence Gellert**
**Title:** SVP, Original Production and Development
**IMDB:** http://www.imdb.com/name/nm1557598/?ref_=fn_al_nm_1

## WHITEWATER FILMS

11264 La Grange Avenue
Los Angeles, CA 90025

**Phone:** 310-575-5800
**Fax:** 310-575-5802
**Email:** info@whitewaterfilms.com
**Website:** www.whitewaterfilms.com
**IMDB:** http://www.imdb.com/company/co0109361/?ref_=fn_al_co_1

**Submission Policy:** Does not accept any unsolicited material
**Genre:** Comedy, Crime, Drama, Memoir & True Stories, Romance, Thriller
**Focus:** Feature Films
**Year Established:** 2008

**Trent Brion**
**Title:** Producer

**Bert Kern**
**Title:** Producer
**IMDB:** www.imdb.com/name/nm2817387

**Nick Morton**
**Title:** Producer
**IMDB:** www.imdb.com/name/nm1134288

**Rick Rosenthal**
**Title:** President/Producer
**IMDB:** www.imdb.com/name/nm0742819

## WHYADUCK PRODUCTIONS INC.

4804 Laurel Canyon Boulevard
PMB 502
North Hollywood, CA 91607-3765

**Phone:** (818) 980-5355
**Email:** info@duckprods.com
**Website:** www.duckprods.com
**IMDB:** http://www.imdb.com/company/co0034143/?ref_=fn_al_co_1

**Submission Policy:** Does not accept any unsolicited material
**Genre:** Comedy, Drama, Memoir & True Stories, Romance, Science Fiction, TV Drama, TV Sitcom
**Focus:** Feature Films, Television
**Year Established:** 1981

**Robert Weide**
**Title:** Principal
**Email:** rbw@duckprods.com
**IMDB:** www.imdb.com/name/nm0004332

## WIDEAWAKE INC.

Los Angeles
8752 Rangely Avenue
Los Angeles, CA 90048

**Phone:** 310-652-9200
**IMDB:** http://www.imdb.com/company/co0145942/?ref_=fn_al_co_1

**Submission Policy:** Does not accept any unsolicited material
**Genre:** Action, Comedy, Family, Romance
**Focus:** Feature Films, Television
**Year Established:** 2004

**Jake Detharidge**
**Title:** Creative Executive
**IMDB:** http://www.imdb.com/name/nm4681516/?ref_=fn_al_nm_1

**Luke Greenfield**
**Title:** Writer/Director/Producer
**IMDB:** www.imdb.com/name/nm0339004

## WIGRAM PRODUCTIONS

4000 Warner Boulevard
Building 81, Room 215
Burbank, CA 91522

**Phone:** 818-954-2412
**Fax:** 818-954-6538
**IMDB:** http://www.imdb.com/company/co0204562/?ref_=fn_al_co_1

**Submission Policy:** Accepts query letter from unproduced, unrepresented writers
**Genre:** Action, Comedy, Crime, Fantasy, Science Fiction, Thriller
**Focus:** Feature Films
**Year Established:** 2006

**Peter Eskelsen**
Title: Vice-President
Email: peter.eskelsen@wbconsultant.com
IMDB: www.imdb.com/name/nm2367411

**Lionel Wigram**
Title: Principal/Producer
IMDB: www.imdb.com/name/nm0927880
Assistant: Jeff Ludwig
jeff.ludwig@wbconsultant.com

## WILD AT HEART FILMS

868 West Knoll Drive, Suite 9
West Hollywood, CA 90069

Phone: 310-855-1538
Fax: 310-855-0177
Email: wildheartfilms@aol.com
Website: www.wildatheartfilms.us
IMDB: http://www.imdb.com/company/co0096528/?ref_=fn_al_co_1

Submission Policy: Does not accept any unsolicited material
Genre: Animation, Comedy, Drama, Family, Memoir & True Stories, Myth, Romance
Year Established: 2000

**James Egan**
Title: CEO/Writer/Producer
Email: jamesegan@wildatheartfilms.us
IMDB: www.imdb.com/name/nm0250680

**Boris Geiger**
Title: Business Affairs
IMDB: http://www.imdb.com/name/nm1788313/?ref_=fn_al_nm_1

**Jewell Sparks**
Title: Head of Development/Producer
IMDB: http://www.imdb.com/name/nm3876152/?ref_=fn_al_nm_1

## WILDBRAIN ENTERTAINMENT INC.

15000 Ventura Boulevard
3rd Floor
Sherman Oaks, CA 91403

Phone: 818-290-7080
Email: info@wildbrain.com
Website: www.wildbrain.com
IMDB: http://www.imdb.com/company/co0077172/?ref_=fn_al_co_1

Submission Policy: Accepts query letter from produced or represented writers
Genre: Animation, Comedy, Family, Fantasy, TV Sitcom
Focus: Feature Films, Television, Shorts
Year Established: 1994

**Bob Higgins**
Title: Head of Creative
IMDB: http://www.imdb.com/name/nm0383338/?ref_=fn_al_nm_1

**Michael Polis**
Title: President
Email: mpolis@wildbrain.com
IMDB: www.imdb.com/name/nm1277040

**Lisa Ullmann**
Title: Vice President of Development
IMDB: http://www.imdb.com/name/nm0880520/?ref_=fn_al_nm_1

## WILDWOOD ENTERPRISES, INC.

725 Arizona Avenue, Suite 306
Santa Monica, CA 90401

Phone: 310-451-8050
IMDB: http://www.imdb.com/company/co0034515/?ref_=fn_al_co_1

Submission Policy: Does not accept any unsolicited material
Genre: Comedy, Crime, Drama, Fantasy, Memoir & True Stories, Romance, Thriller
Focus: Feature Films, Television, Shorts

**Bill Holderman**
Title: Development Executive
IMDB: www.imdb.com/name/nm2250139

**Robert Redford**
Title: Owner
IMDB: www.imdb.com/name/nm0000602

## WIND DANCER FILMS

315 South Beverly Drive, Suite 502
Beverly Hills, CA 90212

Phone: 310-601-2720
Fax: 310-601-2725
Website: www.winddancer.com
IMDB: http://www.imdb.com/company/co0028602/?ref_=fn_al_co_1

**Submission Policy:** Does not accept any unsolicited material
**Genre:** Comedy, Crime, Drama, Fantasy, Romance, TV Drama, TV Sitcom
**Focus:** Feature Films, Television
**Year Established:** 1989

### David McFadzean
**Title:** Principal
**IMDB:** www.imdb.com/name/nm05687
**Assistant:** David Caruso

### Judd Payne
**IMDB:** http://www.imdb.com/name/nm1450928/?ref_=fn_al_nm_1

### Catherine Redfearn
**Title:** Creative Executive
**Email:** Catherine_Redfearn@winddancer.com
**IMDB:** www.imdb.com/name/nm1976144

### Matt Williams
**Title:** Principal
**IMDB:** www.imdb.com/name/nm0931285
**Assistant:** Jake Perron

## WINGNUT FILMS LTD.

PO Box 15 208
Miramar
Wellington 6003
New Zealand

**Phone:** +64-4-388-9939
**Fax:** +64-4-388-9449
**Email:** reception@wingnutfilms.co.nz
**Website:** www.wingnutfilms.co.nz
**IMDB:** http://www.imdb.com/company/co0046203/?ref_=fn_al_co_1

**Submission Policy:** Does not accept any unsolicited material
**Genre:** Animation, Comedy, Crime, Family, Fantasy, Horror, Memoir & True Stories, Romance, Science Fiction, Thriller
**Focus:** Feature Films, Television

### Carolynne Cunningham
**Title:** Producer
**IMDB:** www.imdb.com/name/nm0192254

### Peter Jackson
**Title:** Director/Producer
**IMDB:** www.imdb.com/name/nm0001392

## WINKLER FILMS

190 North Canon Drive Suite 500 Penthouse
Beverly Hills, CA 90210

**Phone:** 310-858-5780
**Fax:** 310-858-5799
**Email:** winklerfilms@sbcglobal.net
**Website:** http://www.winklerfilms.com/
**IMDB:** http://www.imdb.com/company/co0049390/?ref_=fn_al_co_1

**Submission Policy:** Accepts query letter from unproduced, unrepresented writers
**Genre:** Action, Crime, Drama, Feature Films, Romance, TV
**Focus:** Feature Films, Television

### Jill Cutler
**Title:** President
**IMDB:** http://www.imdb.com/name/nm1384594/?ref_=fn_al_nm_1

### Charles Winkler
**Title:** Director/Producer
**Phone:** 310-858-5780
**IMDB:** www.imdb.com/name/nm0935203
**Assistant:** Jose Ruisanchez

### David Winkler
**Title:** Producer
**Phone:** 310-858-5780
**IMDB:** www.imdb.com/name/nm0935210

### Irwin Winkler
**Title:** CEO
**Phone:** 310-858-5780
**IMDB:** www.imdb.com/name/nm0005563
**Assistant:** Selina Gomeau

## WINSOME PRODUCTIONS

PO Box 2071
Santa Monica, CA 90406

**Phone:** 310-656-3300
**Email:** info@winsomeprods.com
**Website:** www.winsomeprods.com
**IMDB:** http://www.imdb.com/company/co0129854/?ref_=fn_al_co_1

**Submission Policy:** Does not accept any unsolicited material
**Genre:** Action, Comedy, Drama, Memoir & True Stories, TV Drama

**Focus:** Feature Films, Television
**Year Established:** 1989

**A.D. Oppenheim**
**Title:** Producer/Writer/Director
**Email:** info@winsomeprods.com
**IMDB:** www.imdb.com/name/nm0649148

**Daniel Oppenheim**
**Title:** VP
**IMDB:** http://www.imdb.com/name/
nm0649151/?ref_=fn_al_nm_1

## WITT-THOMAS PRODUCTIONS

11901 Santa Monica Boulevard, Suite 596
Los Angeles, CA 90025

**Phone:** 310-472-6004
**Fax:** 310-476-5015
**Email:** pwittproductions@aol.com
**IMDB:** http://www.imdb.com/company/
co0083928/?ref_=fn_al_co_1

**Submission Policy:** Does not accept any unsolicited material
**Genre:** Action, Comedy, Crime, Drama, Period, Romance
**Focus:** Feature Films
**Year Established:** 2010

**Tony Thomas**
**Title:** Partner
**IMDB:** www.imdb.com/name/nm0859597
**Assistant:** Marlene Fuentes

**Paul Witt**
**Title:** Partner
**Email:** pwittproductions@aol.com
**IMDB:** www.imdb.com/name/nm0432625
**Assistant:** Ellen Benjamin

## WOLF FILMS, INC.

100 Universal City Plaza #2252
Universal City, CA 91608-1085

**Phone:** 818-777-6969
**Fax:** 818-866-1446
**IMDB:** http://www.imdb.com/company/
co0019598/?ref_=fn_al_co_1

**Submission Policy:** Does not accept any unsolicited material
**Genre:** Drama, Memoir & True Stories, TV, TV

Drama
**Focus:** Feature Films, Television, Shorts

**Tony Ganz**
**Title:** Feature Development
**IMDB:** www.imdb.com/name/nm0304673

**Danielle Gelber**
**Title:** Executive Producer
**IMDB:** www.imdb.com/name/nm1891764

**Dick Wolf**
**Title:** CEO
**IMDB:** http://www.imdb.com/name/
nm0937725/?ref_=fn_al_nm_1

## WOLFMILL ENTERTAINMENT

9027 Larke Ellen Circle
Los Angeles, CA 90035

**Phone:** 310-559-1622
**Fax:** 310-559-1623
**Email:** info@wolfmill.com
**Website:** www.wolfmill.com
**IMDB:** http://www.imdb.com/company/
co0184078/?ref_=fn_al_co_1

**Submission Policy:** Accepts query letter from unproduced, unrepresented writers via email
**Genre:** Animation
**Focus:** Feature Films, TV
**Year Established:** 1997

**Craig Miller**
**Title:** Partner
**Email:** craig@wolfmill.com
**IMDB:** www.imdb.com/name/nm0003653

**Marv Wolfman**
**Title:** Partner
**Email:** marv@wolfmill.com
**IMDB:** www.imdb.com/name/nm0938379

## WOLFRAM PRODUCTIONS

2104 Pisani Place
Venice, CA 90291

**Phone:** 323-253-8185
**Website:** www.wolfromproductions.com

**Submission Policy:** Accepts query letter from unproduced, unrepresented writers via email
**Genre:** Family, Romance
**Focus:** Feature Films

**Dawn Wolfrom**
Title: Producer
Email: dawnwolfrom@wolfromproductions.com
IMDB: www.imdb.com/name/nm0938402

## WONDERLAND SOUND AND VISION

8739 Sunset Boulevard
West Hollywood, CA 90069

Phone: 310-659-4451
Fax: 310-659-4451
Website:
http://www.wonderlandsoundandvision.com/
IMDB: http://www.imdb.com/company/
co0080859/?ref_=fn_al_co_1

Submission Policy: Does not accept any unsolicited material
Genre: Action, Comedy, Crime, Drama, Horror, Memoir & True Stories, Romance, Science Fiction, TV Drama
Focus: Feature Films, Television
Year Established: 2000

**Steven Bello**
Title: Creative Executive
IMDB: www.imdb.com/name/nm2086605

**Peter Johnson**
Title: President of Production (Television)
IMDB: http://www.imdb.com/name/
nm1928296/?ref_=fn_al_nm_1

**Mary Viola**
Title: President of Production (Features)
IMDB: www.imdb.com/name/nm0899193

## WONDERPHIL PRODUCTIONS

4712 Admiralty Way #324
Marina del Rey, CA. 90292

Phone: 310-482-1324
Website: www.wonderphil.biz

Submission Policy: Accepts scripts from unproduced, unrepresented writers
Genre: Action, Drama, Fantasy, Feature Films, Horror, Science Fiction, Thriller
Focus: Feature Films

**Phil Gorn**
Title: CEO
Email: phil@wonderphil.biz

**Sanders Robinson**
Title: President
Phone: 925-525-7583
Email: sandman@wonderphil.biz

## WORKING TITLE FILMS

9720 Wilshire Boulevard
4th Floor
Beverly Hills, CA 90212

Phone: 310-777-3100
Fax: 310-777-5243
Website: www.workingtitlefilms.com
IMDB: http://www.imdb.com/company/
co0057311/?ref_=fn_al_co_1

Submission Policy: Does not accept any unsolicited material
Genre: Action, Comedy, Crime, Drama, Family, Fantasy, Feature Films, Memoir & True Stories, Romance, Science Fiction, Thriller, TV, TV Drama, TV Sitcom
Focus: Feature Films, Television, Shorts
Year Established: 1983

**Liza Chasin**
Title: President, Production (US)
Email: liza.chasin@workingtitlefilms.com
IMDB: www.imdb.com/name/nm0153877
Assistant: Johanna Byer

**Amelia Granger**
Title: Literary Acquisitions Executive (United Kingdom)
Phone: +44 20 7307 3000
IMDB: www.imdb.com/name/nm0335028

**Michelle Wright**
Title: Head (Production)
IMDB: http://www.imdb.com/name/
nm0942657/?ref_=fn_al_nm_1

## WORLD FILM SERVICES, INC

150 East 58th Street
29th Floor
New York, NY 10155

Phone: 212-632-3456
Fax: 212-632-3457
IMDB: http://www.imdb.com/company/co0184077/

Submission Policy: Accepts query letter from unproduced, unrepresented writers

**Genre:** Action, Comedy, Crime, Drama, Family, Fantasy, Horror, Memoir & True Stories, Romance, Science Fiction, Thriller
**Focus:** Feature Films, TV

**Dahlia Heyman**
Title: Creative Executive
IMDB: www.imdb.com/name/nm3101094

**John Heyman**
Title: CEO
IMDB: www.imdb.com/name/nm0382274

**Pamela Osowski**
Title: Creative Executive
IMDB: http://www.imdb.com/name/nm1948494/?ref_=fn_al_nm_1

## WORLD OF WONDER PRODUCTIONS

6650 Hollywood Boulevard, Suite 400
Hollywood, CA 90028

Phone: 323-603-6300
Fax: 323-603-6301
Email: support@worldofwonder.net
Website: www.worldofwonder.net
IMDB: http://www.imdb.com/company/co0093416/

**Submission Policy:** Does not accept any unsolicited material
**Genre:** Action, Comedy, Crime, Family, Memoir & True Stories, Period, Reality, TV Drama, TV Sitcom
**Focus:** Feature Films, Television
**Year Established:** 1990

**Fenton Bailey**
Title: Executive Producer/Co-Director
IMDB: www.imdb.com/name/nm0047259

**Tom Campbell**
Title: Head (Development)
IMDB: http://www.imdb.com/name/nm1737859/?ref_=fn_al_nm_3

**Chris Skura**
Title: Head (Production)
IMDB: http://www.imdb.com/name/nm1048940/?ref_=fn_al_nm_1

## WORLDVIEW ENTERTAINMENT

1384 Broadway
25th Floor
New York, NY 10018

Phone: 212-431-3090
Fax: 212-431-0390
Email: info@worldviewent.com
Website: www.worldviewent.com

**Submission Policy:** Does not accept any unsolicited material
**Genre:** Action, Comedy, Documentary, Drama, Feature Films, Romance
**Focus:** Feature Films
**Year Established:** 2007

**Amanda Bowers**
Title: Vice President/Production
IMDB: www.imdb.com/name/nm4112873

**Maria Cestone**
Title: Co-Founder
IMDB: www.imdb.com/name/nm2906036

**Sarah Johnson Redlich**
Title: Partner
IMDB: www.imdb.com/name/nm3164071

**Christopher Woodrow**
Title: Chairman/CEO
IMDB: www.imdb.com/name/nm2002108

## WORLDWIDE BIGGIES

545 West 45th Street
5th Floor
New York, NY 10036

Phone: 646-442-1700
Fax: 646-557-0019
Email: info@wwbiggies.com
Website: www.wwbiggies.com
IMDB: http://www.imdb.com/company/co0173152/?ref_=fn_al_co_1

**Submission Policy:** Does not accept any unsolicited material
**Genre:** Action, Animation, Comedy, Family, Fantasy, Memoir & True Stories, Reality, TV Drama, TV Sitcom
**Focus:** Feature Films, Television
**Year Established:** 2007

**Albie Hecht**
Title: CEO
IMDB: www.imdb.com/name/nm0372935

**Kari Kim**
Title: VP Development
IMDB: http://www.imdb.com/name/
nm2004613/?ref_=fn_al_nm_1

**Scott Webb**
Title: Chief Creative Officer
IMDB: http://www.imdb.com/name/
nm1274591/?ref_=fn_al_nm_2

## WORLDWIDE PANTS INC.

1697 Broadway
New York, NY 10019

Phone: 212-975-5300
Fax: 212-975-4780
IMDB: http://www.imdb.com/company/
co0066959/?ref_=fn_al_co_1

Submission Policy: Does not accept any unsolicited material
Genre: Action, Animation, Comedy, Drama, Memoir & True Stories, Romance, TV Drama, TV Sitcom
Focus: Feature Films, Television

**Rob Burnett**
Title: President/CEO
IMDB: www.imdb.com/name/nm0122427

**Tom Keaney**
Title: Executive
IMDB: http://www.imdb.com/name/
nm3174758/?ref_=fn_al_nm_1

**David Letterman**
Title: Principal
IMDB: http://www.imdb.com/name/nm0001468/

## WWE STUDIOS

12424 Wilshire Boulevard, Suite 1400
Los Angeles, CA 90025

Phone: 310-481-9370
Fax: (310) 481-9369
Email: talent.marketing@wwe.com
Website: www.wwe.com
IMDB: http://www.imdb.com/company/
co0242604/?ref_=fn_al_co_1

Submission Policy: Does not accept any unsolicited material
Genre: Action, Comedy, Crime, Detective, Drama, Family, Horror, Memoir & True Stories, Science

Fiction, Thriller, TV
Focus: Feature Films
Year Established: 2002

**Richard Lowell**
Title: Director (Senior Director of Development)
IMDB: http://www.imdb.com/name/
nm1144067/?ref_=fn_al_nm_1
Assistant: Cherie Harris
Cherie.harris@wwecorp.com

**Michael Luisi**
Title: President
IMDB: http://www.imdb.com/name/
nm0525405/?ref_=fn_al_nm_1

## X FILME CREATIVE POOL

Kurfuerstenstrasse 57
10785 Berlin
Germany

Phone: 49-30-230-833-11
Fax: 49-30-230-833-22
Email: x-filme@x-filme.de
Website: www.x-filme.de
IMDB: http://www.imdb.com/company/
co0055954/?ref_=fn_al_co_1

Submission Policy: Does not accept any unsolicited material
Genre: Action, Comedy, Drama, Family, Romance
Year Established: 1994

**Stefan Arndt**
Title: Founder/Managing Partner/Producer
Email: stefan.arndt@x-filme.de
IMDB: www.imdb.com/name/nm0036155

**Wolfgang Becker**
Title: Partner (Co-Founder)
IMDB: http://www.imdb.com/name/
nm0065615/?ref_=fn_al_nm_1

**Dani Levy**
Title: Partner (Co-Founder)
IMDB: http://www.imdb.com/name/
nm0506374/?ref_=fn_al_nm_1

## XINGU FILMS LTD.

12 Cleveland Row
St. James
London SW1A 1DH
United Kingdom

**Phone:** 44-20-7451-0600
**Fax:** 44-20-7451-0601
**Email:** mail@xingufilms.com
**Website:** www.xingufilms.com

**Submission Policy:** Does not accept any unsolicited material
**Genre:** Action, Animation, Comedy, Crime, Detective, Drama, Family, Fantasy, Horror, Memoir & True Stories, Myth, Romance, Science Fiction, Thriller, TV Drama, TV Sitcom
**Year Established:** 1993

**Alex Francis**
**Title:** Producer
**IMDB:** http://www.imdb.com/name/nm2123360/?ref_=fn_al_nm_3

**Kate Henderson**
**Title:** Executive (Script Development)

**Trudie Styler**
**Title:** Chairman/Producer/Director
**Email:** trudie@xingufilms.com
**IMDB:** www.imdb.com/name/nm0836548

**Anita Sumner**
**Title:** CEO and Co-Producer
**IMDB:** http://www.imdb.com/name/nm0838856/?ref_=fn_al_nm_1

## XIX ENTERTAINMENT

9000 West Sunset Boulevard, Penthouse
West Hollywood, CA 90069

**Phone:** 310-746-1919
**Fax:** 310-746-1920
**Email:** info@xixentertainment.com
**Website:** www.xixentertainment.com

**Submission Policy:** Does not accept any unsolicited material
**Genre:** Drama, Memoir & True Stories, Period, Reality, Romance, Thriller
**Focus:** Feature Films, Television
**Year Established:** 2010

**Robert Dodds**
**Title:** CEO
**Email:** robert.dodds@xixentertainment.com
**IMDB:** www.imdb.com/name/nm2142323

## XYZ FILMS

4223 Glencoe Ave, Suite B119
Marina del Rey, CA 90292

**Phone:** 310-956-1550
**Fax:** 310-827-7690
**Email:** team@xyzfilms.com
**Website:** www.xyzfilms.com
**IMDB:** http://www.imdb.com/company/co0244345/?ref_=fn_al_co_1

**Submission Policy:** Does not accept any unsolicited material
**Genre:** Action, Comedy, Crime, Drama, Horror, Memoir & True Stories, Science Fiction, Thriller
**Focus:** Feature Films

**Nate Bolotin**
**Title:** Partner
**Email:** nate@xyzfilms.com
**IMDB:** www.imdb.com/name/nm1924867

**Todd Brown**
**Title:** Partner
**Email:** info@xyzfilms.com
**IMDB:** www.imdb.com/name/nm1458075

**Kyle Franke**
**Title:** Head of Development
**Phone:** 310-359-9099
**Email:** kyle@xyzfilms.com
**IMDB:** www.imdb.com/name/nm3733941

## YAHOO!

2400 Broadway
1st Floor
Santa Monica, CA 90404

**Phone:** 310-907-2700
**Fax:** 310-907-2701
**Website:** http://www.yahoo.com/
**IMDB:** http://www.imdb.com/company/co0054481/?ref_=fn_co_co_1

**Submission Policy:** Accepts query letter from unproduced, unrepresented writers
**Genre:** Comedy, Family, Media (Commercials/Branding/Marketing), Memoir & True Stories, Reality, TV
**Focus:** Television, Shorts
**Year Established:** 1995

**Ryan Clifford**
**Title:** Senior Manager (Creative Services)

**David Filo**
Title: Founder

**Jacqueline Reses**
Title: Executive VP (People and Development)

## YARI FILM GROUP

10850 Wilshire Boulevard
6th Floor
Los Angeles, CA 90024

**Phone:** 310-689-1450
**Fax:** 310-234-8975
**Email:** info@yarifilmgroup.com
**Website:** www.yarifilmgroup.com
**IMDB:** http://www.imdb.com/company/
co0136740/?ref_=fn_al_co_1

**Submission Policy:** Does not accept any unsolicited material
**Genre:** Action, Animation, Comedy, Crime, Drama, Family, Romance, Thriller, TV Drama
**Focus:** Feature Films, Television

**Ethen Adams**
Title: Director Of Development
IMDB: http://www.imdb.com/name/
nm2319337/?ref_=fn_al_nm_1

**David Clark**
Title: VP (Television)
IMDB: http://www.imdb.com/name/
nm1354046/?ref_=fn_al_nm_2

**Bob Yari**
Title: President & CEO
Email: byari@yarifilmgroup.com
IMDB: www.imdb.com/name/nm0946441
Assistant: Julie Milstead

## YORK SQUARE PRODUCTIONS

17328 Ventura Boulevard, Suite 370
Encino, CA 91316

**Phone:** 818-789-7372
**Email:** assistant@yorksquareproductions.com
**Website:** www.yorksquareproductions.com

**Submission Policy:** Accepts query letter from unproduced, unrepresented writers via email
**Genre:** Comedy, Drama
**Focus:** Feature Films

**Jonathan Mostow**
Title: Executive
IMDB: www.imdb.com/name/nm0609236
Assistant: Emily Somers

## YORKTOWN PRODUCTIONS

18 Gloucester Lane
4th Floor
Toronto ON M4Y 1L5
Canada

**Phone:** 416-923-2787
**Fax:** 416-923-8580
**IMDB:** http://www.imdb.com/company/co0184088/

**Submission Policy:** Does not accept any unsolicited material
**Genre:** Action, Comedy, Drama, Family, Fantasy, Romance, Science Fiction
**Focus:** Feature Films, Short, Television
**Year Established:** 1986

**Norman Jewison**
Title: Founder
Phone: 416-923-2787
IMDB: www.imdb.com/name/nm0422484

**Michael Jewison**
Title: Producer
IMDB: http://www.imdb.com/name/
nm0422483/?ref_=fn_al_nm_1

## YOUR FACE GOES HERE ENTERTAINMENT

1041 N Formosa Ave
Santa Monica Bldg W, #7
West Hollywood, CA 90046

**Phone:** 323-850-2433

**Submission Policy:** Does not accept any unsolicited material
**Genre:** Drama, Fantasy, Horror, Romance, Science Fiction, Thriller, TV, TV Drama
**Focus:** TV

**Alan Ball**
Title: Head Producer
Phone: 323-850-2433
IMDB: www.imdb.com/name/nm0050332

## ZACHARY FEUER FILMS

9348 Civic Center Drive, 3rd Floor
Beverly Hills, CA 90210

**Phone:** 310-729-2110
**Fax:** 310-820-7535

**Submission Policy:** Accepts query letter from unproduced, unrepresented writers
**Genre:** Action, Drama, Thriller, TV Drama, TV Sitcom

**Zachary Feuer**
**Title:** Producer
**Phone:** 310-729-2110
**IMDB:** www.imdb.com/name/nm0275400

## ZAK PENN'S COMPANY

6240 West Third Street, Suite 421
Los Angeles, CA 90036

**Phone:** (323) 939-1700
**Fax:** (323) 930-2339
**IMDB:** http://www.imdb.com/company/
co0185423/?ref_=fn_al_co_1

**Submission Policy:** Does not accept any unsolicited material
**Genre:** Comedy, Family, Fantasy, Memoir & True Stories, Science Fiction, Thriller, TV Sitcom
**Focus:** Feature Films

**Morgan Gross**
**Title:** Editorial Guru
**IMDB:** www.imdb.com/name/nm2092616

**Zak Penn**
**Title:** Writer/Producer/Director
**IMDB:** www.imdb.com/name/nm0672015
**Assistant:** Hannah Rosner

## ZANUCK INDEPENDENT

1951 North Beverly Drive
Beverly Hills, CA 90210

**Phone:** (310) 274-7586
**Fax:** (310) 273-9217
**IMDB:** http://www.imdb.com/company/
co0279611/?ref_=fn_al_co_1

**Submission Policy:** Accepts query letter from unproduced, unrepresented writers
**Genre:** Action, Comedy, Drama, Thriller
**Focus:** Feature Films

**Dean Zanuck**
**Title:** Producer
**IMDB:** www.imdb.com/name/nm0953124

## ZEMECKIS/NEMEROFF FILMS

264 South La Cienega Boulevard, Suite 238
Beverly Hills, CA 90211

**Phone:** (310) 736-6586
**Email:** info@enfantsterriblesmovie.com
**Website:** http://www.enfantsterriblesmovie.com
**IMDB:** http://www.imdb.com/company/
co0141237/?ref_=fn_al_co_1

**Submission Policy:** Does not accept any unsolicited material
**Genre:** Comedy, Drama
**Focus:** Feature Films

**Terry Nemeroff**
**Title:** Writer/Director/Producer
**IMDB:** www.imdb.com/name/nm0625892

**Leslie Zemeckis**
**Title:** Producer
**IMDB:** www.imdb.com/name/nm0366667

## ZENTROPA ENTERTAINMENT

Filmbyen 22
Hvidovre, Denmark, 2650

**Phone:** +45-36-86-87-88
**Fax:** +45-36-86-87-89
**Email:** receptionen@filmbyen.dk
**Website:** http://www.zentropa.dk
**IMDB:** http://www.imdb.com/company/co0136662/

**Submission Policy:** Accepts scripts from unproduced, unrepresented writers
**Genre:** Action, Comedy, Crime, Drama, Family, Fantasy, Horror, Memoir & True Stories, Romance, Science Fiction, Thriller
**Focus:** Feature Films
**Year Established:** 1992

**Peter Aalbaek Jensen**
**Title:** Managing Director (Co-Founder)
**IMDB:** http://www.imdb.com/name/
nm0421639/?ref_=fn_al_nm_1

**Ib Tardini**
**Title:** Producer
**Email:** ib.tardini@filmbyen.com
**IMDB:** http://www.imdb.com/name/
nm0850385/?ref_=fn_al_nm_1

**Lars von Trier**
**Title:** Managing Director (Co-Founder)
**IMDB:** http://www.imdb.com/name/
nm0001885/?ref_=fn_al_nm_1

## ZEPHYR FILMS

33 Percy Street
London W1T 2DF

**Phone:** +44 207-255-3555
**Fax:** +44 207-255-3777
**Email:** info@zephyrfilms.co.uk
**Website:** www.zephyrfilms.co.uk

**Submission Policy:** Accepts query letter from
unproduced, unrepresented writers via email
**Genre:** Action, Animation, Comedy, Crime, Drama,
Family, Fantasy, Horror, Romance, Thriller, TV
**Focus:** Feature Films, Television

**Luke Carey**
**Title:** Assistant Producer
**IMDB:** www.imdb.com/name/nm2294645

**Chris Curling**
**Title:** Producer
**IMDB:** www.imdb.com/name/nm0192770

**Phil Robertson**
**Title:** Producer
**IMDB:** www.imdb.com/name/nm0731990

## ZETA ENTERTAINMENT

3422 Rowena Avenue
Los Angeles, CA 90027

**Phone:** (310) 595-0494
**IMDB:** http://www.imdb.com/company/
co0037026/?ref_=fn_al_co_1

**Submission Policy:** Does not accept any unsolicited
material
**Genre:** Action, Comedy, Crime, Drama, Family,
Fantasy, Horror, Thriller, TV
**Focus:** Feature Films

**Lisa Jan Savy**
**Title:** Creative Executive
**IMDB:** http://www.imdb.com/name/
nm2957586/?ref_=fn_al_nm_1

**Zane Levitt**
**Title:** President
**Email:** zanewlevitt@gmail.com
**IMDB:** www.imdb.com/name/nm0506254

## ZIEGER PRODUCTIONS

**Phone:** 310-476-1679
**Fax:** 310-476-7928
**IMDB:** www. imdb.com/company/co0114742

**Submission Policy:** Accepts query letter from
unproduced, unrepresented writers

**Michele Zieger**
**Title:** Producer
**IMDB:** www.imdb.com/name/nm1024135

## ZING PRODUCTIONS, INC.

220 South Van Ness Avenue
Hollywood, CA 90004

**Phone:** (323) 466-9464
**Website:** www.zinghollywood.com

**Submission Policy:** Does not accept any unsolicited
material
**Genre:** Animation, Comedy, Drama, Family,
Fantasy, Reality, Romance, TV Drama
**Focus:** Feature Films, Television, Shorts

**Laura Black**
**Title:** Director Creative of Affairs
**Email:** laura@zinghollywood.com
**IMDB:** www.imdb.com/name/nm4549208

**Rob Loos**
**Title:** President
**IMDB:** www.imdb.com/name/nm0519763

## ZODIAK USA

520 Broadway Suite 500
Santa Monica, CA 90401

**Phone:** (310) 460-4490
**Fax:** (310) 460-4494
**Email:** contact@zodiakusa.com
**Website:** www.zodiakusa.com
**IMDB:** http://www.imdb.com/company/co0314564/

**Submission Policy:** Accepts query letter from
unproduced, unrepresented writers via email
**Genre:** Animation, Comedy, Memoir & True

Stories, Reality, Romance
**Focus:** Television

**Timothy Sullivan**
**Title:** Senior VP (Development)
**Phone:** (212) 488-1699
**IMDB:** http://www.imdb.com/name/
nm2432438/?ref_=fn_al_nm_4

**Natalka Znak**
**Title:** CEO
**IMDB:** http://www.imdb.com/name/
nm1273500/?ref_=fn_al_nm_1

## ZUCKER PRODUCTIONS

2401 Mandeville Canyon Road
Los Angeles, CA 90049

**Phone:** 310-656-9202
**Fax:** 310-656-9220
**IMDB:** http://www.imdb.com/company/co0110404/

**Submission Policy:** Accepts query letter from
unproduced, unrepresented writers
**Genre:** Comedy, Drama, Fantasy, Romance,
Thriller, TV Sitcom
**Year Established:** 1972

**Farrell Ingle**
**Title:** Creative Executive
**IMDB:** www.imdb.com/name/nm3377346

**Jerry Zucker**
**Title:** Producer
**IMDB:** www.imdb.com/name/nm0958387

**Janet Zucker**
**Title:** Producer
**IMDB:** www.imdb.com/name/nm0958384

# Index by Company Name

# Index of Company Websites

# Index by Contact Name

# Index by Submission Policy

## Accepts query letter from unproduced, unrepresented writers via email

## Accepts scripts from produced or represented writers

## Accepts scripts from unproduced, unrepresented writers

BALLYHOO, INC., 51
BBC FILMS, 53
BOGNER ENTERTAINMENT, 60
CAMELOT ENTERTAINMENT GROUP, 66
DOBRE FILMS, 91
FRESH & SMOKED, 115
KATALYST FILMS, 147
MAD HATTER ENTERTAINMENT, 158
QED INTERNATIONAL, 196
SIMON SAYS ENTERTAINMENT, 219
SOGNO PRODUCTIONS, 223
TROMA ENTERTAINMENT, 243
TWINSTAR ENTERTAINMENT, 245
UNSTOPPABLE, 249
WONDERPHIL PRODUCTIONS, 265
ZENTROPA ENTERTAINMENT, 270

## Accepts scripts from unproduced, unrepresented writers via email

HYDE PARK ENTERTAINMENT, 135
MASIMEDIA, 162
UNDERGROUND FILMS, 246

## Does not accept any unsolicited material

19 ENTERTAINMENT, LTD, 25
21 LAPS ENTERTAINMENT, 25
2S FILMS, 26
360 PICTURES, 27
40 ACRES & A MULE FILMWORKS, INC., 27
44 BLUE PRODUCTIONS, INC., 28
495 PRODUCTIONS, 28
4TH ROW FILMS, 28
7ATE9 ENTERTAINMENT, 30
8:38 PRODUCTIONS, 30
AARDMAN ANIMATIONS, 31
ABANDON PICTURES, INC., 31
ABC STUDIOS, 32
ACTUAL REALITY PICTURES, 33
ADELSTEIN PRODUCTIONS, 33
AD HOMINEM ENTERPRISES, 33
ADULT SWIM, 34
A&E NETWORK, 34
AFTER DARK FILMS, 34
AGGREGATE FILMS, 35

ALAN BARNETTE PRODUCTIONS, 36
ALAN DAVID MANAGEMENT, 36
ALAN SACKS PRODUCTIONS, 36
ALCHEMY ENTERTAINMENT, 36
ALCON ENTERTAINMENT, LLC, 37
A-LINE PICTURES, 38
ALLENTOWN PRODUCTIONS, 38
ALLIANCE FILMS, 39
ALOE ENTERTAINMENT, 39
AL ROKER PRODUCTIONS, 39
ALTA LOMA ENTERTAINMENT, 39
ALTURAS FILMS, 40
A-MARK ENTERTAINMENT, 40
AMBASSADOR ENTERTAINMENT, 40
AMBER ENTERTAINMENT, 40
AMBLIN ENTERTAINMENT, 41
ANNAPURNA PICTURES, 43
ANTIDOTE FILMS, 44
APATOW PRODUCTIONS, 45
APPIAN WAY, 45
ARTFIRE FILMS, 47
ATLAS ENTERTAINMENT (PRODUCTION BRANCH OF MOSAIC), 48
AUTOMATIK ENTERTAINMENT, 49
BAD ROBOT, 50
BALDWIN ENTERTAINMENT GROUP, LTD., 50
BALTIMORE PICTURES, 51
BARNSTORM PICTURES LLC, 52
BAY FILMS, 52
BAZELEVS PRODUCTION, 53
BEACON PICTURES, 53
BEFORE THE DOOR PICTURES, 54
BELISARIUS PRODUCTIONS, 55
BENDERSPINK, 56
BERK LANE ENTERTAINMENT, 56
BERMANBRAUN, 56
BET NETWORKS, 57
BIG TALK PRODUCTIONS, 57
BLIND WINK PRODUCTIONS, 59
BLONDIE GIRL PRODUCTIONS, 59
BLUEGRASS FILMS, 59
BLUEPRINT PICTURES, 60
BLUE SKY STUDIOS, 60
BOKU FILMS, 61
BOLD FILMS, 61
BORDERLINE FILMS, 61
BOSS MEDIA, 62
BRANDED FILMS, 62